THE
AGATHA
CHRISTIE
COMPANION

Delacorte Books by Dennis Sanders

The First of Everything

THE
AGATHA
CHRISTIE
COMPANION

DENNIS SANDERS
&
LEN LOVALLO

The Complete Guide to
Agatha Christie's Life and Work

DELACORTE PRESS / NEW YORK

Published by
Delacorte Press
1 Dag Hammarskjold Plaza
New York, N.Y. 10017

Grateful acknowledgment is made for permission to reprint the following copyrighted material:

Excerpts from the *New Yorker*. © 1955, 1959, 1965, 1966, 1967–1982. Reprinted by permission.

Excerpts from the *New York Herald Tribune*. © I. H. T. Corporation. Reprinted by permission.

Excerpts from the *New York Times*. © 1922, 1923, 1926, 1929, 1930, 1932, 1933, 1934, 1935, 1936, 1937, 1939, 1940, 1941, 1942, 1944, 1945, 1946, 1947, 1949, 1950, 1951, 1952, 1953, 1954, 1955, 1956, 1957, 1958, 1959, 1960, 1962, 1963, 1964, 1965, 1966, 1967, 1970, 1974, 1975, 1976, 1978, 1980, 1981, 1982 by The New York Times Company. Reprinted by permission.

Excerpts from the *Times* (London) and the *Times Literary Supplement* reprinted by permission of Times Newspapers Limited.

Excerpt from *The Lost Pleasures of the Great Trains* by Martin Page. Reprinted by permission of the publisher, George Weidenfeld & Nicolson Ltd.

Excerpts reprinted by permission of Dodd, Mead & Company, Inc. from AN AUTOBIOGRAPHY by Agatha Christie. Copyright © 1977 by Agatha Christie Ltd.

Excerpts reprinted by permission of Dodd, Mead & Company, Inc. from MALLOWAN'S MEMOIRS by Max Mallowan. Copyright © 1977 by Max Mallowan.

Excerpt from "Harlequin's Song" from POEMS and excerpts from APPOINTMENT WITH DEATH by Agatha Christie are reprinted by permission of the publisher, Dodd, Mead & Company, Inc.

Manufactured in the United States of America

First printing

Designed by Judith Neuman

Library of Congress Cataloging in Publication Data

Sanders, Dennis, 1949–
   The Agatha Christie companion.

   Bibliography.
   Includes index.
   1. Christie, Agatha, 1890–1976. 2. Christie, Agatha, 1890–1976—Plots. 3. Authors, English—20th century—Biography. I. Lovallo, Len. II. Title.
PR6005.H66Z85   1984   823'912
ISBN 0-385-29285-6
Library of Congress Catalog Card Number: 83-5167

For
Ted Caldwell and Ken Harkins
And
To the memory of
James R. F. Guy

For
Jed Conwell and Kurt Hochman
and
To the memory of
Janice H. McCoy

I regard my work as of no importance—
I've simply been out to entertain.

—AGATHA CHRISTIE

ACKNOWLEDGMENTS

Our thanks to those who have helped bring this four-year labor of love to completion. First, to our editors: Sandi Gelles-Cole, who believed in the project from the beginning, and Paul McCarthy, who spent long and patient hours in attending to the details of the editing of a very long and complex manuscript. A special debt is owed to Susan Petito and Carolyn Parqueth, for many days of typing and retyping portions of the manuscript; thanks also to Paul Sheren for typing some rather dull lists. Gerry Geddes of The Bookstore was good enough to let us use his research library, and Otto Penzler of Mysterious Bookshop kindly let us see his large collection of Christie first editions. Our appreciation to the New York Public Library, to Jonathan Dodd of Dodd, Mead, and to Richard Hunte for their help. Thanks also to Sandra Ruch of Mobil Showcase and to Jane Foster of Thames Television for giving us information on Christie television adaptations. Finally, love and gratitude to Polo and Kitty Karlisle, who exhibited a patience and understanding of the problems of frantic authors that is only to be found in canine and feline companions.

Contents

Contents

Miscellaneous Christie Books

PART TWO: CHRISTIE ON STAGE, FILM, AND TELEVISION

Plays

Contents

Films

Television

THE CHRISTIE LISTS

BIOGRAPHICAL SKETCH

Agatha Mary Clarissa Miller Christie Mallowan was born September 15, 1890, at Ashfield, her family's home in the seaside resort of Torquay, Devon. She was the youngest child of Frederick Alvah Miller, a wealthy American expatriate, and his English wife, Clarissa "Clara" Boechmer. The main influences in Agatha's affluent late-Victorian upbringing, aside from her parents, were her nursemaid, her older sister and brother, Margaret "Madge" and Louis "Monty" Miller, and her grandmothers. Agatha was educated at home by her mother and father.

Alvah Miller died in 1901, leaving his family in much reduced financial circumstances. During Agatha's adolescence, her mother periodically rented Ashfield at a profit to make ends meet while she and her daughter traveled economically abroad.

Agatha attended finishing school in Paris beginning in 1906, where she showed particular talent as a singer and pianist. She considered a musical career, but eventually decided that her shyness in public would be an insurmountable barrier to a concert career.

In 1913 Agatha met Archibald Christie, a young army officer, and they were married December 24, 1914. The couple were separated for most of the war, and Agatha continued to live at Ashfield while she volunteered as a nurse and pharmaceutical dispenser at local hospitals. After the war Archie Christie went into business in London, while Agatha remained at home with their daughter, Rosalind, born in 1919.

Christie's first mystery novel, *The Mysterious Affair at Styles,* which had been written circa 1916, was published in 1920. She published one or more books a year almost every year for the next fifty-five years.

In 1926 the death of her mother coupled with severe marital problems led to a nervous breakdown, which climaxed with

Agatha's much-publicized disappearance for ten days in December of that year. The Christies were divorced in April 1928.

In 1930, while on a journey to the Middle East, Christie met Max Mallowan, an archaeologist fourteen years her junior, and the couple were married in Scotland in September 1930.

During the 1930s, the Mallowans divided their time between several homes in England and archaeological expeditions in the Middle East. During World War II, Max Mallowan served as an intelligence liaison officer in North Africa, while Agatha remained in London and worked once again as a volunteer at a dispensary.

Early in the war Christie's daughter, Rosalind, married Hubert Prichard, an army major, who was later killed in service in France. Christie's only grandchild, Mathew, was born in 1943. Rosalind Prichard was later remarried, to Anthony Hicks.

After the war, the Mallowans resumed their trips to the Middle East, which continued for almost a decade. During the early 1950s, Christie's second career, as a playwright, reached its peak, with the production of *The Mousetrap* and *Witness for the Prosecution* in London in 1952 and 1953. *The Mousetrap* would become the world's longest-running play.

In 1960, in recognition of his work as scholar and archaeologist, Max Mallowan was made Commander of the British Empire, and in 1968 he was knighted. Christie was made Commander of the British Empire in 1956 and Dame of the British Empire in 1971.

After a leg injury in 1971, Christie's health began to deteriorate, and both the quality and frequency of her books declined. Her last formal public appearance was in 1974 at the opening of the film *Murder on the Orient Express,* which was attended by Queen Elizabeth and members of the royal family.

Christie died at her home at Wallingford, Berkshire, on January 12, 1976, and was buried in a private ceremony at St. Mary's Churchyard, Cholsey, Berkshire.

At the time of her death, her books had sold an estimated total of 400 million copies worldwide.

INTRODUCTION

Agatha Christie is one of the most famous and successful authors of all time. Her ninety-five books have sold more than 500 million copies since 1920, when her first novel *The Mysterious Affair at Styles* was published; she has been translated into more languages than Shakespeare and is second only to the Bible in the number of tongues in which she can be read. The twenty Christie works that have appeared on the stage include *The Mousetrap,* the world's longest-running play, which has been running continuously in London's West End since opening night November 25, 1952. The twenty-two film versions of Christie works include such big-budget, all-star productions as *Death on the Nile* and *The Mirror Crack'd,* which have increased the Christie audience by millions of people, and swollen the Christie coffers by millions of dollars; *Murder on the Orient Express* was for many years the biggest money-making film in British history.

Considering the immensity of the Christie phenomenon, there has been surprisingly little written about her life and works. There are several reasons for this. First, Agatha Christie was an extremely, almost obsessively private woman. At the height of her fame she rarely gave interviews, and then only to carefully selected journalists. Her public appearances were mainly restricted to banquets and receptions given by her publishers and producers in honor of some milestone in her career—she was not the kind of author who signs her latest volume at bookstores, or who makes the rounds of television talk shows. The details of her private life were and still are jealously guarded by Christie's family. Her personal papers and manuscripts are not available for public scrutiny, and what information is available to the general public tends to be very controlled, screened material of a "public-relations" nature. As a result, there are only four biographical sources of any consequence: Christie's own autobiography, which contains much important information, but which leaves out a good deal as well, and

Come, Tell Me How You Live, her brief reminiscences of travels in the Middle East. Gwen Robyns's biography, *The Mystery of Agatha Christie,* is seriously hampered as a biographical source because of the author's lack of access to Christie's personal records. Finally, *Mallowan's Memoirs,* by Christie's second husband, Max, has several chapters on Agatha's life and work, though for the most part it overlaps Christie's autobiography. In addition to these limited biographical resources, a writer on Christie must rely on a handful of critical and reference books of varied scope and value, all but one published in the last decade. Other sources are magazine interviews with Christie, and secondhand information passed along through articles and interviews with people who knew Christie. Perhaps the most important sources of all are Christie's books themselves, which all in all reveal more about this complex, immensely talented woman than any strictly biographical source.

The Agatha Christie Companion is intended to be a companion to the reader in the truest sense of the word, of interest to the neophyte Christie reader as well as to the seasoned veteran. It is both a work biography and a reference book. In the background sections on each of Christie's books, plays, films, and television adaptations, the reader will get a comprehensive look at how Christie's works relate to her life, and vice versa. For example, we explain how many of the books came into being, and what real-life events and experiences and people were transformed by Christie's superb imagination and craft into the plots and characters of her books. We also discuss in detail how the books fit into the author's life: where and when they were written, and what was happening in her personal life at the time. Included, too, are Christie's own opinions on her works (which she expressed only infrequently), and excerpts from major reviews of each book, which appeared at the time of publication. The reader will even find explanations, where possible, of the identity of recipients of book dedications. Along the way, the book will offer explanations and answers to thousands of questions and points of interest about Christie and her works. For example, it will explain why Arthur Bantry is alive and well in *Sleeping Murder* in 1976, when he was dead and buried in 1962 in *The Mirror Crack'd from Side to Side.* The *Companion* will also reveal such things as why Christie liked the film version of *Murder on the Orient Express,* and why she disliked Margaret Rutherford's screen portrayal of Jane Marple equally as much, even though she dedicated a book to Rutherford.

In addition to this background and biographical information, there are plot summaries for all novels and short stories, which will help whet the new reader's appetite for Christies yet unread, and which will aid the longtime fan in recalling that title he can't quite remember from a few years back. There are also alphabetical lists of the major characters in each novel, and information on the first editions of each book.

The *Companion* also includes comprehensive listings on Christie stage plays, films, and television adaptations, including dates, reviews, producers and casts, where available.

The book concludes with a series of lists designed to give the reader easy access to the book and to Christie's works—lists such as all short story titles, with the volumes they appear in, titles of Ariadne Oliver and Superintendent Battle books, and a chronology of Christie's life.

In short, we have attempted to make *The Agatha Christie Companion* as complete, informed, and entertaining a reader's guide as possible—a companion in that unforgettable never-never land of chintz and country houses, manipulation and murder and incomparable puzzles that is the world of Agatha Christie.

HOW TO USE
THE AGATHA CHRISTIE COMPANION

All of Agatha Christie's works are listed and discussed in the *Companion,* grouped in two major sections. Part One covers the mystery and miscellaneous titles and Part Two, the plays (both original and adaptations by others), the film and television adaptations based on her works.

Within the categories we have listed works chronologically according to publication date (or opening night, or studio release, in case of plays and films). We have assigned a number to each title in its chronological order, to make cross-referencing easier and to give the reader a clearer idea of what place a book occupies in Christie's long career (so that *Murder on the Orient Express* is readily identifiable as her nineteenth detective book, or *Postern of Fate* her eightieth).

Titles are oftentimes confusing with Christie, as American publishers from 1930 to the 1960s often published North American editions under different titles; a few volumes have had three titles over the years. To simplify things as much as possible, we use the original English title first, and refer to this title in discussing the book. At the beginning of each listing, and in the table of contents, we list the American title second. (The reader will find a complete alphabetical list of English and American titles in the appendices.) A few American editions have appeared briefly under still other titles (*Hercule Poirot's Christmas,* for example, which, though best known in this country as *Murder for Christmas,* also appeared for a time as *A Holiday for Murder*). To avoid a surplus of titles, we have listed in the main part of the book only the well-known American titles.

PART ONE: THE CHRISTIE BOOKS

"The Mystery Novels and Short Stories," the first section of Part One, is of course the heart of *The Agatha Christie Companion.*

Under the listing for each title, the reader will find the background —the "story behind the book": how Christie came to write the book, what was happening in her private life at the time the book was written, what real-life events or people inspired plots or characters in the mysteries. In addition, the backgrounds contain Christie's own opinions of her books (though she expressed them in only a few cases) and what critics thought about the books at the time they were published—which provides an interesting and often surprising barometer of Christie's superlatively successful career.

Whenever possible we have attempted to identify the fictional locations in the books as thinly disguised places that Christie knew in her own life.

Many editions, especially American paperbacks, omit dedications; we have included them even though in some cases a dedication appears only in early British hardcover editions. We have also attempted where possible to identify the dedicatees.

In our discussions of the detective novels we have tried to keep our personal evaluations of the merits as much in the background as possible—not that they haven't come out here and there. But the most avid Christie fan will read anything with her name on it, no questions asked, while the reader who doesn't fall under her spell will probably never fall under her spell, whether he's reading *Five Little Pigs* (one of her best) or *Passenger to Frankfurt* (one of her worst). Christie is an uneven writer, however, and the reader who picks up the occasional Christie off the book rack runs the risk of being introduced to one of her weakest books which, with their colorful, skillfully designed paperback covers, are indistinguishable at sight from her masterpieces. So when we *have* ventured an opinion as to a book's merits or faults, we have done so only when one or more critics or other writers on Christie have echoed our opinion.

On the point of critical evaluation, the reader who has only newly discovered the joys of Agatha Christie should be warned: though Christie's long list of works is a treasure trove of reading pleasure, there are some paste jewels and fool's gold thrown in. Some of the titles are simply not up to her usual standard. A few of us have read every Christie, and enjoyed or appreciated them to one degree or another, and there will always be those of us who will want to read them all, several times, for better or worse. But the vast majority of Christie readers will get to only twenty or thirty titles in their lifetimes, and a bit of judicious picking and choosing can be of help. There are some Christie titles that are "not to be missed."

Here is a sampler of the best:

The Murder of Roger Ackroyd, the book that made Christie famous, mainly because of the sensational and controversial solution to the mystery. Some critics complained that she broke the rules, though most agreed she fooled us while playing fair.

Murder on the Orient Express, another high on the list of must-read titles. Its setting, characters, and plotting are all top drawer, though hard-core critics may balk at the improbability of the premise. If one is not prepared to believe impossible things before breakfast, one should not read Christie.

The ABC Murders, another brilliantly plotted deception, revolving around railroad timetables, letter games, and diversionary murders.

Cards on the Table, the best of Christie's closed-room murders, masterfully worked out with only four possible suspects, bridge enthusiasts may have an edge on guessing the solution.

Ten Little Niggers, one of Christie's most popular works, and the best of her nursery-rhyme books, a classic murder puzzle in which everyone is a victim.

Five Little Pigs, the first and best of Christie's murder-in-retrospect novels, noted for richness of writing and depth of characterization.

A Murder Is Announced, perhaps most memorable of the village murder novels, thanks to its cast of delightfully eccentric characters and the details of life in a postwar English village.

The "Plots" which follow the backgrounds are brief synopses of the books. These give the settings, the characters, and the events leading to murder . . . not giving away any secrets, of course. They are designed to help the new reader pick an as-yet-unread Christie which looks appealing; for the more advanced Christie reader, they will help with that tendency we all have to forget that we have read certain of her books. (How often have many of us gotten thirty pages into a Christie, only to exclaim, "I've read this one!")

Following the "Plots" are alphabetical lists of the "Principal Characters." Christie was one of the great creators of names in English fiction, and reading a list of her characters can be not only amusing but revealing about the general ambience of the book in which they appear. One of the recurrent cocktail-party Christie conversations includes the line, "Wasn't so-and-so in that book?"

American readers should also note that the lists of characters with one-line descriptions that sometimes appear at the fronts of books ("MAUDE WILLIAMS—Belligerently blond, and perhaps not quite a lady . . .") are not original, and were added by the publishers.

"First Editions" included with each book listing, gives the publisher in England and America, date of publication, length, and price.

There are three major publishers involved in Christie's career: the Bodley Head/John Lane, which published her first six books in England; William Collins, which published the balance of Christie after she left John Lane; and Dodd, Mead, her American publisher. Readers should note that special editions often appear under other imprints after the first British or American editions, so it is not unheard of to see an old Christie hardcover with the imprint Collier or Triangle. And the Collins and Dodd, Mead imprints vary as well: many volumes appear as Collins Crime Club books, or as Dodd, Mead Red Badge Detective books.

We have included the prices of first hardcover editions, which reveal on the one hand how stable prices were between 1920 and 1940, when the price of a Christie held firm at 7s. 6d.; on the other hand, the escalation of hardcover prices between World War II and today reveals in part how Christie's mighty fortune from little shillings grew.

Whenever possible we have taken publishing information directly from British and American first editions; however, it was not possible to locate first editions in all cases.

Miscellaneous Christie Books

The miscellaneous books discussed in the second section of Part One include the six romantic novels that Christie wrote under the pseudonym Mary Westmacott, and the miscellaneous titles, such as her book of poems, her reminiscences about the Middle East, and her autobiography. They are of interest to Christie readers primarily because of the information they shed on the life of this most reticent author. They are discussed briefly so the reader will be more familiar with Christie's nondetective writings.

PART TWO: CHRISTIE ON STAGE, FILM, AND TELEVISION

Christie's stage career was as notably successful as her publishing career. The twenty-one plays, both originals and adaptations by Christie, and adaptations of her works by other playwrights, are listed in chronological order of writing. Information is given on how the plays came into being, and when they were first produced in England and America, with lists of original casts and producers.

The twenty-two films based on Christie works are listed in order of release, with lists of casts and producers and directors, and brief discussions of grosses, reviews, and other background information on each film. Similar information is given for the television adaptations.

PART ONE

The Christie Books

MYSTERY NOVELS AND SHORT STORIES

The eighty-four novels and short story collections of Agatha Christie are among the most widely read books in the world. Among them, they tally an astonishing 500 million copies in print, and there is no sign of their popularity abating. These works fall roughly into two categories—pure detection novels, and adventure thrillers—with a number of hybrids and cross-breedings between the two types. Within these categories Christie explores almost every possible permutation and nuance; she is a master of variation on a theme.

Within her five-decade output, there are a few bad books, a few mediocre ones, very many good ones, and more than a handful of masterpieces. Though she was not the most stylish or intellectual of mystery writers, Christie's works, from the bad to the brilliant, have a charm, an appeal, a masterly cleverness and ingenuity that are unsurpassed, as reading and rereading the books themselves so clearly shows.

THE MYSTERIOUS AFFAIR AT STYLES (1920)

One winter afternoon in 1910, when Agatha Miller was twenty years old, she lay in her bed at Ashfield, the family home in Torquay, Devon, recovering from a bout of influenza. As the famous author recalled in her autobiography many years later, the boredom of convalescence had led her to dealing herself bridge hands to pass the hours.

Agatha's mother, Clara, stopped in to see how her daughter was doing, and, noticing the patient's boredom, made a suggestion.

"Why don't you write a story?"

When Agatha protested that she didn't think she could, her mother replied, "Why not? You don't know that you can't, because you've never tried."

Mother Miller disappeared, then promptly returned with a writing exercise book. Agatha put aside her deck of cards, and by the following evening had finished her first story, *The House of Beauty.* Half a century later, on rereading the still unpublished story, Christie thought it was not a bad effort on the whole, though "amateurishly written . . . and showing the influence of all that I had read the week before," which she said "had obviously" been D. H. Lawrence.

No matter what the relative merits of this little story, it launched a superlative career. On that rainy winter day at Ashfield, Christie showed the stuff that was going to make her famous: once she began writing, she finished what she started (a sign of true professionalism), and once she finished one thing, she went on to another.

In no time at all, she had written other stories, and gone on to a romantic novel. From Christie's own description, *Snow Upon the Desert* was a rather awkward mishmash of overplotting and overwriting. She admits that the book somehow wound up with two distinct plots and sets of characters and she'd found herself "occasionally forcing them to mix with each other in a way which they did not seem to wish to do."

Agatha's mother suggested that her daughter send some of her writings to Eden Phillpotts. Phillpotts (1862–1960), the novelist and poet famous for books like *Children of the Mist* and *Sons of the Morning,* which celebrated rural Devonshire life, was the first professional to read Agatha's work. Phillpotts recognized the talent in his young fellow Devonian, and he gave her not only encouragement, but some very sound and perceptive advice.

"You have a great feeling for dialogue," he wrote in his letter to Christie. "You should stick to gay, natural dialogue. Try and cut all moralizations out of your novels; you are much too fond of them"—as would be evidenced in Christie's last books—"and nothing is more boring to read. Try and leave your characters *alone,* so that they can speak for *themselves,* instead of always rushing in to tell them what they ought to say, or to explain to the reader what they mean by what they are saying. That is for the reader to judge for himself."

This last advice Christie took to heart. Part of the brilliance of her best detective puzzles arises from letting the reader reach his own conclusions, usually incorrect ones, based on what characters have said.

Phillpotts also put Agatha in touch with the London literary agents Hughes Massie, Ltd., who were to handle her books starting in 1926, and who continue to represent her literary estate today. Hughes Massie, "a large, swarthy man" of whom Agatha was terrified, turned down *Snow Upon the Desert* as unplaceable, but encouraged Miss Miller to write another book.

By her own account, she didn't rise to the task immediately, but settled into writing a few more short stories and poems, which she likened to the hobbies of embroidery and china painting. However, there was still the professional writer taking shape: her literary "pastimes" were duly posted to various magazines, in spite of the fact that they were usually returned.*

Two major events were to distract from, yet influence, her ca-

---

* Christie was vague about exactly what she wrote during this period; some of the occult short stories that appear in later collections are among her early works.

reer: the outbreak of war in 1914, and her marriage on Christmas
Eve of the same year to the handsome, charming young officer
Archibald Christie. Archie was soon in France with the Flying
Corps, and the young Mrs. Christie, like so many Englishwomen
her age, stayed at home in Torquay doing war volunteer work.

Agatha worked with the V.A.D.s—Volunteer Aid Detachment—
and did her share of rolling bandages and emptying bedpans. Later
she worked in the hospital dispensary, and it was here, working
with curare and arsenic and digitalis, that she got her in-depth
knowledge of chemicals and poisons that was to stand her in such
good stead during the sixty years of writing that lay ahead of her.

Not only did the war teach Agatha a great deal about the chem-
istry of death, but she found herself with a great deal of time on
her hands as well, both at home and during slack periods at the
dispensary.

Agatha's attention turned again to writing, and to a challenge
that her sister, Madge, had made before the war.

In order to chart Christie's career, which began in earnest during the war, it is necessary to backtrack a bit, to her childhood
years, which were marked by an intense love of books.

She loved to read as a young child, despite her mother's opinion
that children should not read until they were eight years old, "better for the eyes and also for the brain." However, young Agatha
had her own ideas, and to the surprise and "distress" of her
mother, she was able to make sense of words before she was five.
Christie noted in her autobiography that her first book was *The
Angel of Love,* which she read "quite successfully to myself."

Christie would request books as presents for birthdays and
Christmas. Her earliest reading included fairy tales, animal stories
by Andrew Lang, and children's stories by Mrs. Molesworth.
Christie recalled that by the time she was eight years old "[she]
was allowed to read as much as [she] pleased, and took every opportunity to do so."

When Christie's father died in 1901, she was eleven years old.
She and her mother grew closer, and Mrs. Miller began to read
aloud to her, starting with the works of Sir Walter Scott, then
graduating to Charles Dickens, for whom Christie developed a
"passion." Their first Dickens was *Nicholas Nickleby,* and Chris-

tie's favorite was *Bleak House*. Among the other books that filled the Christie household were works by Jane Austen and William Makepeace Thackeray, and John Milton's *Paradise Lost,* which led Christie to comment, "of course I didn't understand it but I loved its sonorous tones."

The Prisoner of Zenda by Anthony Hope was Christie's introduction to romantic novels. She also liked to read Alexandre Dumas, and the novels of May Sinclair. Agatha and her sister Madge both loved detective stories, especially those by Sir Arthur Conan Doyle. It was Madge, five years Agatha's elder, who introduced her to Sherlock Holmes, when Agatha was eight. They both became what Agatha described as "connoisseurs of the detective story," and steeped themselves in *Arsène Lupin,* the novels of Wilkie Collins, and other popular mysteries of the day. It was after reading Gaston Le Roux's *The Mystery of the Yellow Room,* the father of all classic locked-room mysteries, at its height of popularity in 1908, that Agatha proclaimed that she would like to try her hand at a detective novel, to which Madge replied (the story has come down in various versions), "I'll bet you can't," or "I'll bet you can't write one in which the reader can't guess the murderer."

Though the seed of mystery writing was already planted in Agatha's head, it wasn't until 1916 that it germinated. By her own account, it was while working in the dispensary that she began to mull over the specifics of her first detective story.

She chose poison as the method (a logical enough choice), and the family as the setting (again, a wise choice for the possibilities it allows for setting up motives and suspicion in a closely contained situation).

Then she turned her attention to her detective.

"A Belgian came into my head. It was as simple as that," Christie said of Poirot in her autobiography, admitting that the formation of the second most famous detective in literature was something of a mystery even to her. To be sure, there were the logical considerations: he couldn't be too much like Holmes; he had to have a curious but logical mind to enable him to probe the mystery; and he had to have a personality which stood out and apart from the characters who were at the core of the puzzle.

Christie students for decades have pointed out the similarities

between Christie's creation and that of French author Marie Bel-
loc Lowndes (1868–1947). Mrs. Lowndes, who wrote mysteries
in the florid late-Victorian style, created Hercules Popeau, a detective retired from the Paris Sûreté. Colin Watson, in his essay in
Agatha Christie, First Lady of Crime (1977), describes Popeau as
"self-opinionated, bossy . . . pushing in style . . . a late Victorian creation. . . . Every inch a foreigner, certainly, but [unlike
Poirot] neither comical nor endearing."

Watson points out that the two detectives were appearing side
by side at the booksellers' in anthologies published in the 1930s,
and Lowndes authored one story, *A Labour of Hercules,* in 1936,
eleven years before Christie's collection, *The Labours of Hercules*
(#47, 1947). However, in spite of similarity of name and background, Watson reminds us that Poirot and Popeau are very
different detectives and that "Hercule Poirot worked, and Hercules Popeau did not." This is due in no small part to the "endearing" qualities of Christie's character, and to her ability to employ him so well as a catalyst in her plots.

Christie was well read in detective fiction, by her own account,
and it is unlikely that she was unaware of Popeau when she
created Poirot. However, there is no comment on record about
Mrs. Lowndes's character, or his influence on Poirot. For her part,
Mrs. Lowndes was equally circumspect.

What is remarkable is that, given these few "logical" considerations, the inexperienced twenty-five-year-old writer created a
masterful, fully realized, and eminently serviceable detective (as
the decades were to show). Like Athena, who sprang fully formed
from the brow of Zeus, Poirot sprang from the mind of young
Agatha Christie with every little gray cell in working order, along
with his looks, his mannerisms, his peculiar figures of speech.
Hastings describes his friend Poirot during their second case,
Murder on the Links (#3, 1923), as "an extraordinary little man!
Height, five feet four inches, egg-shaped head carried a little to
one side, eyes that shone green when he was excited, stiff military
moustache, air of dignity immense! He was neat and dandified in
appearance. . . . 'Order' and 'Method' were his gods. He had a
certain disdain for tangible evidence, . . ." Poirot would often
remark to his friend "with great satisfaction 'The true work, it is

done from *within. The little gray* cells*—remember always the little gray cells, *mon ami!*'" Over the years a detail was added here or there (the striped trousers came later, along with his passion for *moderne* decor), but Hercule himself never "as you say, suffered the changes."

Agatha began writing her first mystery at home in 1916, drafting a chapter in longhand, then retyping it. She soon succumbed to all the problems of writers in midproject: absentmindedness, irritability, carelessness.

Mrs. Miller, who seems to have had a genius for making timely suggestions, proposed that Agatha take the time off from the dispensary and hole up somewhere quiet, like Dartmoor, to finish the book.

Agatha booked herself into the "large, dreary" Moorland Hotel, where she wrote in the mornings, longhand ("till my hand ached"), ignored the guests at lunch, lest they distract her, then walked alone on the bleak moors in the afternoon, "talking" scenes of the book to herself.

She would then return to the hotel, have dinner, and fall asleep until the routine began again the next morning.

The Mysterious Affair at Styles was finished by the end of the holiday, though Christie subjected it to another round of rewriting ("mostly the overcomplicated middle"), before bundling the newly typed manuscript off to the publishers Hodder and Stoughton.

They were the first of six houses to reject it.

The Bodley Head was the seventh to receive *The Mysterious Affair,* and the book languished in the publisher's office for more than eighteen months before Agatha received a letter asking her to come to London to meet with John Lane, the head of Bodley, to discuss the book.

Even though Agatha had previously met with agent Hughes Massie, she had not signed on with them, and her negotiations were directly with John Lane. She was offered a contract, which

---

* The spelling appears variously as *grey* and *gray* from book to book and even at times from edition to edition; *gray* is the most common spelling, and we have adopted it for consistency, though the reader should be prepared for some *grey* cells.

she readily accepted with little or no attention paid to the provisions (a mistake she was *not* to repeat in the future). What she got, in exchange for seeing *Styles* in print, was a contract that paid no advance and no royalties until after 2,500 copies had been sold, with a provision that her next five novels would be offered to the Bodley Head at only slightly higher royalties than had been offered on *Styles*.

At Lane's suggestion, Christie rewrote the last chapter of the book, which originally had been a courtroom scene. Christie later admitted in her autobiography that she had made the scene up out of her head, and that it bore little resemblance to actual courtroom procedure. In the future, she asked an expert—legal, medical, archaeological, whatever—when she didn't have all her facts straight.

The Mysterious Affair at Styles finally appeared in February 1921 (it was copyrighted in 1920). Christie was dissuaded by her publisher from using a nom de plume such as Martin West or Mostyn Grey, and the name that was to be famous one day was launched into the public world.

Reviewers liked the book, and it is interesting to note that they picked out several qualities that were to run through all of Christie's work.

The *Times Literary Supplement* (London) in the first review of Christie's long career wrote that "the only fault in this brilliant story is that it is almost too ingenious. Styles is a country house in Essex and the mysterious affair is the death of its mistress by poison. There is an extraordinary assortment of persons in the house and the neighborhood, and suspicion is tossed about from one to another among them in the most baffling way. But the problem does not baffle little M. Poirot, a retired Belgian detective, who is one of the queer characters brought together at Styles, and after many singular twists and turns he lays his hand on the guilty persons. They are superhumanly clever, but he is cleverer still. In spite of its intricacy the story is very clearly and brightly told. There is a good deal of human interest in it apart from the crime, and it has a very happy ending. It is said to be the author's first book, and the result of a bet about the possibility of writing a detective story in which the reader would not be able to spot the criminal. Every reader must admit that the bet was won" (2/3/21).

"All in all a pleasant book for an evening by the grate fire," said Beatrice Blackman in *New York World*. "Mrs. Christie does not take her mystery with too deadly seriousness, delicately spoofs the amateur detective instinct through one who blunders, and manages to convey enough of character to make her puppets suggest people" (1/16/27).*

Literary Review said, "The reader is ingeniously confused, by means of a kegful of red herrings and a narrative of Watsonian stupidity, but two important pieces of knowledge are withheld to the very end when the detective—her engaging Poirot—makes his explanation" (1/22/27).

Christie's own favorite review of *Styles* (as she relates in her autobiography) came not from the *Times Literary Supplement* (London) but from *Pharmaceutical Journal,* which praised "this detective story for dealing with poisons in a knowledgeable way, and not with the nonsense about untraceable substances that so often happens. Miss Agatha Christie knows her job."

The book sold well—2,000 of the 2,500 copies printed, but because of the contract with John Lane, Agatha didn't collect any royalties. Her only income from the book was her half of a magazine serial sale—about £25 (or $100 at the exchange rate of the time). A modest beginning for an author who, at the end of her career, would be paid $1 million for the American paperback rights to a single book, *Sleeping Murder* (#83, 1976).

PLOT:
John Hastings, on a month's sick leave after convalescing from war injuries, is invited by his friend John Cavendish to stay at Styles Court, the Cavendish country estate near the village of Styles St. Mary in Essex.

On arriving at the estate, Hastings finds a good deal of tension among members of the household. Emily Inglethorp, stepmother to John and his brother, Lawrence, has had control of the vast family fortune since her husband's death years before. The Cavendish sons, John, a son of leisure, and Lawrence, an aspiring

---

* We have not been able to find any American reviews prior to 1927.

poet, are both dependent on their stepmother for their incomes, and are admittedly spendthrifts. The former Emily Cavendish has recently married Alfred Inglethorp, a man of dubious appearance and background, and twenty years her junior.

Other inhabitants of Styles are: Mary, John Cavendish's beautiful wife; Evelyn Howard, Mrs. Inglethorp's factotum; Dr. Bauerstein, a friend of Mary's (and coincidentally an expert in poisons); and Cynthia Murdoch, a young orphan taken in by Mrs. Inglethorp (and coincidentally working in a hospital medical dispensary).

While touring Styles St. Mary in the company of his host, Hastings bumps into his old friend Hercule Poirot, the five-foot-four Belgian who was "in his time one of the most celebrated members of the Belgian police." Poirot is now one of a group of Belgian refugees living in the village.

Late that night the Styles household is suddenly awakened by noises from Mrs. Inglethorp's room. She "seems to be having some kind of fit." After breaking open the locked door, they find Mrs. Inglethorp in the grip of terrible convulsions. The woman calls out her husband's name, then dies.

The family doctor blames Mrs. Inglethorp's heart, but Dr. Bauerstein recognizes the severity of the convulsions as being artificially produced.

Hastings immediately thinks of his famous Belgian detective friend, and within hours Poirot is launched full scale into his investigation of the mysterious affair.

Principal Characters: Dr. Bauerstein, John Cavendish, Lawrence Cavendish, Mary Cavendish, Mr. Denby, Captain Hastings, Sir Ernest Heavyweather, Evelyn Howard, Alfred Inglethorp, Emily Agnes Inglethorp, Chief Inspector James Japp, Manning, Cynthia Murdoch, Hercule Poirot, Mrs. Raikes, Howard Raikes.

First Editions: **British**: John Lane, London & New York, copyright 1920, released February 1921. 296 pp., 7s. 6d. **American**: John Lane, London & New York, copyright 1920, released February 1921. 296 pp., $2.00.

Adaptation: None.

❖ 2 ❖

THE SECRET ADVERSARY (1922)

According to her autobiography, Christie's second book was written to help defray the costs of maintaining the family home, Ashfield. She still did not consider herself a professional author. Her writing was a hobby, and the Christies were financially comfortable enough not to have any pressing need for the money. It was husband Archie Christie who suggested that, even though her first book had only made her twenty-five pounds, a second might bring in more money, an idea that Agatha "didn't think was likely."

She was persuaded to write *something,* but the question of exactly *what* eluded her, until one day in a tea shop she overheard a couple at a neighboring table discussing one Jane Fish. *"That* I thought would make a good beginning to a story—a name overheard at a tea shop—an unusual name, so that whoever heard it remembered it. A name like Jane Fish—or perhaps Jane Finn would be even better. I settled for Jane Finn."

The Secret Adversary marks the first appearance of Christie's detective couple, Tommy and Tuppence Beresford. The Beresfords—or rather Tuppence Cowley and Tommy Beresford, who would one day become Mr. and Mrs.—were not unlike thousands of British youth after World War I: out of money, out of jobs, and ready to plunge headlong into the Roaring Twenties.

The Beresfords were also not unlike a romanticized version of the Christies as well. Tuppence worked in the V.A.D.s (Volunteer Aid Detachment) during the war, as did Agatha, and Tommy Beresford had been in the Flying Corps, as had Archibald Christie. The Christies, however, were not nearly in the same financial straits as Tommy and Tuppence and most discharged officers and soldiers in Britain in the late teens and early twenties.

In her recollections, the author makes it quite clear that she considered *Secret Adversary* a book of "espionage: this would be a spy book, a thriller, not a detective story. . . . It was fun on the whole, and much easier to write than a detective story, as thrillers always are."

Publisher John Lane did not like the book very much, and in fact wavered as to whether he would publish it at all. Once published, the book did well enough to be serialized in the *Weekly Times* and netted Christie fifty pounds to put toward expenses at her home at Ashfield. Yet the book's moderate success was "not encouraging enough to make me think I had as yet adopted anything so grand as a profession."

The reviews were generally positive, though recognizing the light weight of the book. The *Times Literary Supplement* (London) said, "Tuppence and Tommy, although given much to 'old bean' and 'old thing,' are refreshingly original as criminal investigators, and the identity of the arch criminal . . . is cleverly concealed to the end" (1/26/22).

The *Spectator,* on the other hand, thought "Miss Christie has not quite succeeded in maintaining the level of her first novel. Though the mystery of the story is extremely involved, the experienced reader will have no difficulty in determining who is the real criminal long before any of the characters have the slightest inkling of the truth" (2/18/22).

"This is as jaunty in tone as a book for college girls," said *Literary Review* (8/12/22), while the *New York Times* complained that "many of the situations are a bit moth-eaten from frequent usage by other writers, but at that Miss Christie manages to invest them with a new sense of individuality that renders them rather absorbing" (1/11/22).

Tommy and Tuppence were to be with Christie to the very last novel she wrote, *Postern of Fate* (#80, 1973), though their adventures appeared at widely scattered intervals. And they are unique among the author's detectives in that they (unlike Poirot and Marple) are on a timetable that resembles the aging of mere mortals—a fact that may simply be a function of their having been created as young characters. Yet, in spite of becoming grandparents, they still remain very much adventurers, given to "old bean" and "old girl" enthusiasms. Christie may have retained her fondness for Tommy and Tuppence because they were such an idealized, untroubled couple—the former volunteer nurse and the army veteran who, unlike Archie Christie and Agatha Miller, lived happily ever after.

The dedication, appropriate for a story in which two ordinary people are caught up in danger and intrigue, is "to all those who lead monotonous lives, in the hope that they may experience at second hand the delights and dangers of adventure."

PLOT:

Tuppence Cowley and Tommy Beresford, two childhood friends, run across one another on Dover Street in London just after the Great War. Over tea at Lyons', they catch up on their lives since their last meeting at the military hospital where Tuppence was doing ward work and Tommy convalescing from wounds. Like many young Britishers after the war, they are both flat broke and out of a job.

After running down a list of possible means of employment, the high-spirited pair decide to be unorthodox and hire themselves out as adventurers. Their ad in the *Times* is to read, "Two young adventurers for hire. Willing to do anything, go anywhere. Pay must be good. No unreasonable offer refused."

Outside Lyons', Tuppence is approached by a well-dressed but suspicious-looking man who has overheard her conversation with Tommy, and he offers her her first assignment, to be discussed in a meeting at his office the following day. At his office, Mr. Whittington offers Tuppence the generous sum of £100 and expenses for traveling to Paris and posing as an American girl for three months.

During their discussion of this intriguing proposal, Whittington asks Tuppence her name. Stuck for an alias, Tuppence offhandedly uses a name that Tommy mentioned over tea the day before, a name he had overheard in a conversation between two men on the street: Jane Finn. Tuppence uses the name in all innocence, but Whittington's reaction makes her realize she has stumbled onto real intrigue of some sort: Whittington tells her to spill what she *really* knows, to "own up" to her part in things. He even offers her hush money.

Astonished by finding what looks to be real adventure on her first outing as "Young Adventurers, Limited," Tuppence manages to bluff her way into a bribe from Whittington.

The next day, Whittington and his office have evaporated into thin air, but Tommy and Tuppence find that more people than Whittington are interested in Jane Finn. The young pair soon find themselves involved in international intrigue, and a good deal of danger.

Principal Characters: Albert Batt, Tommy Beresford, Mr. Brown, A. Carter, Tuppence Cowley, Sir James Peel Edgerton, Jane Finn, Julius P. Hersheimmer, Boris Ivanovitch, Kramenin, Marguerite Vandemeyer, Edward Whittington.

First Editions: **British**: John Lane, London & New York, January 1922. 312 pp., 7s. 6d. **American**: Dodd, Mead & Co., New York, 1922. 330 pp., $1.75.

Adaptation: *The Secret Adversary* was the source for the first screen adaptation of a Christie work. The film, made in Germany, was titled *Die Abenteuer G.m.b.H.* (*Adventure Inc.*). It was released in 1928.

MURDER ON THE LINKS (1923)

With *Murder on the Links* Christie returned to Hercule Poirot and the pure detective story. Since Poirot was such a success in *Styles* it was suggested to Christie that she "continue to employ him." As was to be the case with a number of her later books such as *Murder on the Orient Express* (#19, 1934) and *The Mirror Crack'd* (#68, 1962), the germ of *Links* came from an actual headline story: a group of masked bandits entered a house, tied up the members of the family, killed the head of the household, then departed with the family valuables. This violent robbery gained notoriety in the press of the time when facts came to light indicating that the robbery-murder might have been staged—with the complicity of one of the people in the household.

"*Murder on the Links* was slightly less in the Sherlock Holmes tradition and was influenced, I think, by *The Mystery of the Yellow Room*," Christie said. "It had rather that high-flown, fanciful type of writing." The author also thought that *Murder on the Links* was "a moderately good example of its kind—though rather melodramatic." Her publishers were pleased with the book as well, though they found themselves in confrontation with their author over the jacket design—a confrontation that was to recur many times over the next half century.

"Apart from being in ugly colours, it was badly drawn, and represented, as far as I could make out, a man in pyjamas on a golf links, dying of an epileptic fit. Since the man who had been murdered had been fully dressed and stabbed with a dagger, I objected."

By now, Christie was beginning to look out for her best interests, and learning to get her way with publishers.

"There was a good deal of bad feeling over this, but I was really furious, and it was agreed that in future I should see the jacket first and approve of it."

Literary Review said, "The plot is really clever; its suspense is well kept up and the solution is fair enough. What more need one ask of a detective yarn?" (4/14/23). In the same vein, the *New York Times* wrote, "A remarkably good detective story which can be warmly recommended to those who like that kind of fiction" (3/25/23).

Golf was to assume an ironic importance in Christie's life within a few years of her landing one of her murder victims on the green. At the time *Links* was written, the Christies were a promising young couple. Archie's business career was going nicely, and Agatha's writing had taken a turn for the professional and profitable. Their daughter, Rosalind, born in 1919, was nearing school age in a home that promised the comforts and stimulations of two bright, successful young parents.

During this period, Christie described herself as "happily married," and part of that happy marriage was husband and wife playing golf together. On weekends, they traveled from their flat in Addison Mansions, London, to the golf links at East Croydon. Agatha said she had "never been much of a golfer," while Archie, who had a little more experience than she, "became keenly appreciative of the game."

It was Archie's keenness on golf that moved Agatha to dedicate her third novel "To my husband." However, Archie's enthusiasm was eventually to cause domestic problems. "After a while, we seemed to go *every* weekend to East Croydon: Little by little I was becoming that well-known figure a golf widow. . . . I did not really mind, but . . . in the end that choice of recreation was to make a big difference in our lives" (see *The Big Four, #8,* 1927 and *The Mystery of the Blue Train, #9,* 1928).

By the time of Christie's divorce from Archie in 1928, her lack of interest in golf had soured into distaste, and she stopped playing altogether. In a 1928 letter to Michael Morton, the writer who adapted *The Murder of Roger Ackroyd* (#7, 1926) for the stage, and a former golfing companion of the Christies, Agatha wrote, "I hope golf goes well. I haven't played since . . ."

PLOT:

Captain Hastings is returning from Paris to London, where he now shares a flat with his friend Hercule Poirot. On the near-deserted Calais coach, Hastings encounters a modern young woman, a flapper, who smokes, sports a scarlet mouth, and employs four-letter words. Though not at all approving of the "new" woman, Hastings is charmed by the young traveling companion, who turns out to be an actress/acrobat. Hastings learns that her sister and coperformer has disappeared, and he tells her of his friendship with the eminent detective.

When Hastings gets back to his flat, Poirot shows him a letter asking for help in handling an unspecified matter. The letter urges Poirot to come to Calais at once, for the prospective client's life is in danger. Poirot and Hastings recognize the name, Renauld, as that of a South American millionaire.

On arriving at the Renauld estate in Merlinville, between Boulogne and Calais, Hastings and Poirot find the police in attendance. Renauld has been murdered. Poirot's reputation gains him access to the estate and to the police investigation. The millionaire was found stabbed in the back, lying in a freshly dug open grave on the golf course that adjoins his property. His wife had been bound and gagged in her room by two intruders, who abducted and killed her husband. With Hastings in tow, Poirot launches full-force into the investigation, and it isn't long before Hastings gets his wish to see the young woman from the train once again.

Principal Characters: Joseph Aarons, Francoise Arrichet, Monsieur Lucien Bex, Madame Daubreuil, Marthe Daubreuil, Bella Duveen, Monsieur Giraud, Captain Hastings, Dulcie Duveen Hastings, Hercule Poirot, Jack Renauld, Madame Renauld, Paul T. Renauld, Gabriel Stonor.

First Editions: British: John Lane, London, May 1923. 319 pp., 7s. 6d. **American**: Dodd, Mead & Co., New York, 1923. 298 pp., $1.75.

Adaptation: None.

◈ 4 ◈

POIROT INVESTIGATES (1924)

It was Bruce Ingram, editor of the *Sketch,* who suggested to the young Christie that Poirot, whom Ingram had read and liked in *The Mysterious Affair at Styles* (#1, 1920), would do well in a series of short stories. Ingram agreed to publish a series in his magazine, and Christie's string of more than one hundred short stories began in the *Sketch* issue of March 7, 1923.

Ingram asked for a series of twelve stories. Christie produced eight, then an additional four "rather more hastily than I wanted." The *Sketch* also commissioned illustrator W. Smithson Broadhead to do a "portrait" of Poirot for their publication; the author found Broadhead's conception of the Belgian "not unlike my idea of him, though . . . a little smarter and more aristocratic." The illustration remained a favorite among the hundreds of Poirot book-jacket portraits that were to appear over the years, and when John Lane published the collection of twelve stories in 1924, Christie insisted that the *Sketch* illustration be used for the book's cover.

According to biographer Gwen Robyns, several titles were considered for the collection of stories in book form before the final choice. The original title of the collection was to be *The Curious Disappearance of the Opalsen Pearls,* which then became *The Jewel Robbery at the Metropolitan,* which Christie decided was a better title. *The Gray Cells of Monsieur Poirot* and *Poirot Investigates* were the publisher's suggestions for the title. Christie finally chose *Poirot Investigates.*

It was with *Poirot Investigates* that Christie began to realize not only that her writing future lay with the detective story, but that it lay—at that time—with Poirot and Captain Hastings.

"It had escaped my notice that not only was I now tied to the detective story, I was also tied to two people: Hercule Poirot and Captain Hastings.

"I quite enjoyed Captain Hastings," the author recalled in her memoirs, though later (in *Dumb Witness,* #29, 1937), she was only too relieved to pack him off to oblivion in Argentina. "He was a stereotyped creation, but he and Poirot represented my idea of a detective team. I was still writing in the Sherlock Holmes tradition . . . eccentric detective, stooge assistant, with a Lestrade-type Scotland Yard detective, Inspector Japp. . . . Now I saw what a terrible mistake I had made in starting with Hercule Poirot so *old*—I ought to have abandoned him after the first three or four books, and begun again with someone much younger."

The *Times Literary Supplement* (London) said, "The story is quite original. Moreover, if Captain Hastings, who tells the story, is a little like Watson, always anxious to display his cleverness and always getting snubbed, every detective has had a foil since the days of Lecoq. In fact, Poirot is a thoroughly pleasant and entertaining person, an admirable companion for a railway journey" (4/3/24).

Literary Review thought, "Poirot's gorgeous self-conceit gives a dash of humor to this capital collection of mystery stories. They are ingeniously constructed, and told with an engaging lightness of style" (1/18/25). The *New York Tribune* wrote, "In all good faith I cannot say that Agatha Christie's stories are good. Certainly they are badly written. And one finds it hard to forgive an author a hero who reminds the reader of nothing so much as the individual portrayed in the advertising of a certain well-known perfume company" (1/7/25).

PLOTS:

"The Adventure of 'The Western Star' "

Miss Mary Marvell, famous film star, calls on Poirot when she receives three threatening letters, warning her that her famous diamond, the Western Star, "which is the left eye of the god must return whence it came."

"The Tragedy at Marsdon Manor"

The North Union Insurance Company calls on Hercule Poirot to investigate the death of Mr. Maltravers of Marsdon Manor. Though Maltravers was found dead in a field on the property, apparently of a cerebral hemorrhage, the fact that he was known to be near bankruptcy, and had only a few weeks before taken out a huge life insurance policy, causes them to be suspicious.

"The Adventure of the Cheap Flat"

Poirot and Hastings lease an expensive flat in a posh apartment building when the detective becomes suspicious of why Hastings's acquaintances, the Robinsons, were able to rent a flat in the same building for a ridiculously low rent.

"The Mystery of Hunter's Lodge"

An ailing Poirot sends Hastings down to Roger Havering's hunting lodge in Derbyshire to investigate the murder of Havering's wealthy uncle, Mr. Harrison Pace. Poirot insists that Inspector Japp and Hastings keep him informed of the investigation by wire, but the two men on the scene finger the wrong murderer while Poirot, of course, gets it right, even long distance.

"The Million-Dollar Bond Robbery"

Charming Esmee Farquhar asks Poirot to act on behalf of her fiancé, Philip Ridgeway, whose banking career is threatened because of suspected, but unprovable, carelessness in the matter of Liberty Bonds that were stolen while in his possession on board the *Olympia* out of New York. The question is how the bonds, in a locked briefcase in a locked trunk, to which Philip had the only key, could have been taken out before arrival in England.

"The Adventure of the Egyptian Tomb"

Archaeologist Sir John Willard dies of a heart attack soon after opening a pharaoh's tomb, causing the press to dredge up "cursed tomb" stories. But when his co-excavator John Bleibner dies a fortnight later of blood poisoning, followed shortly by his nephew's suicide, Lady Willard contacts Poirot and asks him to investigate "the Curse of Men-her-Ra."

"The Jewel Robbery at the Grand Metropolitan"

The wealthy Opalsens meet Poirot at a posh Brighton resort. Mrs. Opalsen insists on going upstairs to fetch her valuable pearls to show the detective, only to find them missing. Suspicion falls on the French maids, especially when the pearls are found under one of their mattresses.

"The Kidnapped Prime Minister"

During the last days of World War I, the prime minister is shot at and kidnapped by enemy agents. The government hushes up the affair—it's the eve of a crucial conference—but calls in Poirot to uncover his whereabouts before the meeting.

"The Disappearance of Mr. Davenheim"

When a wealthy banker named Davenheim leaves his estate to post a letter and never returns, Poirot challenges Inspector Japp to a duel: his gray cells versus the inspector's more conventional sleuthing. Poirot even claims he can solve the disappearance within a week—without leaving his flat.

"The Adventure of the Italian Nobleman"

Poirot and Hastings are being visited by their acquaintance and neighbor, Dr. Hawker, when the doctor's housekeeper bursts in: the phone has rung, and one of the doctor's patients, Count Foscatini, has gasped to her that "They've killed me." The three men rush to the count's flat in Regent's Court, to find the count bludgeoned to death with a marble statue, and the remains of a three-person meal still set at the table.

"The Case of the Missing Will"

Violet Marsh, a young careerwoman, asks Poirot's help in finding the will of her late uncle, who, not approving of "independent" women, gave his ward only a one-year trust on his death, as a "test of her wits." Violet suspects the "test" is to discover where in his house his second and final will is hidden, leaving the entire estate to her free and clear.

"The Veiled Lady"

Lady Millicent Vaughn calls on Poirot for help in saving her forthcoming marriage to the Duke of Southshire. It seems an unscrupulous character named Lavington has gotten hold of a letter Miss Vaughn wrote to a soldier she loved, killed in the war. Her duke-to-be doesn't know of the affair, and, jealous bloke that he is, he would probably call the whole thing off if he found out.

"The Lost Mine"

Poirot tells Hastings how he came to own 14,000 shares in Burma Mines, Ltd., by virtue of exercising his little gray cells. A mining company was interested in finding the ore deposits in an abandoned flooded mine in Burma. An old Chinese family had the only record of the location of the mine. Wu-Ling, the head of the family, is invited to London to negotiate the sale of the document. However, Wu-Ling disappears and his body is found floating in the Thames River. Poirot is called in on the case to find the missing documents.

"The Chocolate Box"

Poirot tells Hastings of one case from years before, in Belgium, when he "made the complete ass" of himself in investigating the death of M. Paul Déroulard, a French deputy. Poirot is presented with two major clues, a bottle of Trinitrin tablets and a box of chocolates. He fails to notice the significance of the blue lid on the pink candy box.

First Editions: British: John Lane, London, March 1924. 298 pp., 7s. 6d. **American:** Dodd, Mead & Co., New York, 1925. 282 pp., $2.00.

Adaptation: None.

THE MAN IN THE BROWN SUIT (1924)

Sir Eustace Pedler, the bluff, gregarious owner of the country estate Mill House in *The Man in the Brown Suit* is a rare instance in Christie's work of a character that is clearly based on a personal friend of the author. The real-life model for Pedler was Major Ernest R. Belcher, who was in Christie's words, "a man with terrific powers of bluff . . . how much of Belcher's stories was invented and how much was true, we never knew."

Belcher's powers of bluff landed him in a series of cushy jobs, which he himself admitted he was little qualified to hold: comptroller of potatoes during World War I (he knew next to nothing about agriculture), then headmaster of a New Zealand school (a job he was offered because of his bluff about expertise in Education Management, and which he was soon highly paid to vacate). In 1922 Belcher landed what was possibly the cushiest job of all: director of the British Empire Mission. His task was to travel around the world, with stopovers in major countries of the British Empire, paying goodwill visits to local dignitaries, and organizing the countries' participation in the upcoming British Empire Exhibition of 1924.

Belcher had known Archibald Christie since Archie's days at Clifton School, where Belcher had been a master, and he had kept up with the young former officer after the war and his marriage to Agatha. Well aware of his own lack of executive ability, Major Belcher convinced Archie to leave the security of his £500 a year job in London to travel around the world as Belcher's business manager. The ten-month tour would include South Africa, Australia, New Zealand, Hawaii, and Canada. Agatha was welcome to come along, so long as she could pay her expenses out of the £1,000 allowance given Archie by the British Empire Mission.

Christie devoted an entire chapter of *An Autobiography* to her world tour, and she described the journey as "one of the most exciting things that ever happened to me." The trip began inauspiciously: Christie, like Poirot, was prone to seasickness, and for four days on the *Kildonan Castle* she was prostrate in her cabin, while crossing the Bay of Biscay sailing south to the island of Madeira. She commemorated the episode by putting the *Kildonan Castle* into *The Man in the Brown Suit* as the *Kilmorden Castle*.

In Cape Town, South Africa, Christie got an inkling that "travelling with Belcher might not be as pleasant as it had seemed in prospect at our dinner table." At their hotel, Belcher became infuriated that he had been served unripe peaches at breakfast. He said he could bounce them and "they wouldn't come to any harm!" Christie said he then "bounced about five unripe peaches," and none of them squashed.

By the time the party reached Canada, there was a complete rift between the Christies and the irascible Belcher, and the couple vowed never to speak to their would-be benefactor again. But in the end, they discovered they "actually *liked* Belcher," and saw him on many occasions after the tour, when they would reminisce and then remind the major that "you really did behave atrociously, you know."

Before the trip, while dining with Belcher at Mill House, Dorney, their host suggested that Agatha write a book called *The Mystery of Mill House*. Agatha agreed the title had possibilities, but she balked when Belcher insisted that she put him in the book.

"I don't think I could put you in it," she protested. "I can't do anything with real people. I have to imagine them."

When she wrote her next book, after the trip, she gave in to the major's insistence that he be written in.

Christie began sketching the thriller when she was in South Africa, and the locale figures heavily in the book. Belcher became Sir Eustace Pedler ("Give him a title," suggested Archie. "I think he'd like that").

"[Pedler] wasn't Belcher," Christie wrote, "but he used several of Belcher's phrases and told some of Belcher's stories. He too was a master of the art of bluff, and behind the bluff could easily be sensed an unscrupulous and interesting character." She then added, "It is, I think, the only time I have tried to put a real person whom I knew well into a book, and I don't think I succeeded. Belcher didn't come to life, but someone called Sir Eustace Pedler did."

Not surprisingly, *The Man in the Brown Suit* is dedicated "To E.A.B.—in memory of a journey, some lion stories, and a request that I should some day write the 'Mystery of the Mill House'!"

Before publication, Christie changed the title to *The Man in the Brown Suit,* as she thought *Murder at Mill House* sounded too much like *Murder on the Links* (#3, 1923).

Christie introduced the Secret Service agent Colonel Johnny Race in this book. Race would be in only four Christie novels, with his next appearance in *Cards on the Table* (#27, 1936), then *Death on the Nile* (#30, 1937), and the 1945 *Sparkling Cyanide* (#45). Race, about thirty-eight years old, was described as "a dark, handsome, deeply bronzed man . . . usually to be found in some outpost of empire—especially if there were trouble brewing." Christie made no mention in her memoirs of Colonel Race or the reasons that might have led her to create him. It's possible that she got the idea for his creation while traveling around the world, where she would surely have had opportunities to meet and observe the Colonel Race types that could be found in foreign outposts of the British Empire in the 1920s.

The *Evening News* paid Christie the handsome sum of £500 for the serial rights to the new book. Though the author was distressed that the *News* changed the title to *Anna the Adventuress* ("as silly a title as I ever heard") she took the serial money anyway, and bought her first car, a Morris Cowley. (Refer to *The Listerdale Mystery,* #20, 1934.)

Christie did not find the book an easy one to write, though she did not reveal in her memoirs just why (it was completed after her return to England), and she considered it "rather patchy." The critics, however, found the new Christie to their liking.

The *Times Literary Supplement* (London) wrote, "The author sets so many questions to the reader in her story, questions which will almost certainly be answered wrongly, that no one is likely to nod over it, and even the most experienced reader of romances will fail to steer an unerring course and reach the harbour of solution through the quicksands and shoals of blood, diamonds, secret service, impersonation, kidnapping, and violence with which the mystery is guarded" (9/25/24).

Saturday Review of Literature thought, "Although the structure of this novel follows the beaten track of the average machine made mystery story, its action, after the first fifty pages, maintains a swiftness of pace we have never seen surpassed" (12/13/24).

"*The Man in the Brown Suit* is the best of its kind I have met for a long time," wrote J. Franklin in *New Statesman*. "It is remarkable especially for a brand new device for concealing the villain's identity to the very end. I defy the most practiced hand to discover him" (10/11/24).

PLOT:

Madame Nadina, "the dancer who had taken Paris by storm," is met in her dressing room by the elegant Count Sergius Paulovitch. In private the two are not what they outwardly seem: their talk is of the war, espionage, and of a mysterious man called simply "the Colonel . . . [who] has organized crime as another man might organize a boot factory."

Nadina reveals that she knows the supposedly infallible Colonel's weak point: his superstitious belief that his downfall will be through a beautiful woman. Nadina also has incriminating evidence on the Colonel and is on the way to blackmail him out of part of the vast fortune he has amassed from crime.

In a change of scene, clever, pretty young Anne Beddingfeld is left an impoverished orphan by the death of her anthropologist father. Lacking anything better to do, Anne moves to London, where she proposes to "have adventures and see the world."

Anne unexpectedly finds adventure on the platform of the Hyde Park Corner tube station. Returning from an unsuccessful job interview, she notices a small, thin man whose overcoat reeks of mothballs. He glances at her, then looks behind her. To her horror, the man recoils in fear, loses his balance, and falls to the tracks. He is electrocuted by the third rail.

In the hubbub that follows, a man wearing a brown suit who identifies himself as a doctor examines the body, then leaves hurriedly, dropping a piece of paper as he races off. Anne retrieves the paper, which contains the words *17-122 Kilmorden Castle*.

The death is ruled accidental. Anne, however, suspects foul play and contacts Scotland Yard.

The Yard doesn't pay much attention to Anne's evidence of murder, so she takes matters into her own hands. She coolly barges her way into the office of Lord Nasby, millionaire owner of the *Daily Budget,* and manages to convince the press tycoon that she should investigate the case for his paper because she has a vital clue—the piece of paper dropped by the "doctor."

With Lord Nasby's blessing ("I rather like cheek—from a pretty girl") Anne is off in search of a solution to the death in the station. Her search leads her to Mill House, a second murder, and to a mysterious man in a brown suit.

Principal Characters: Batani, Anne Beddingfeld, Suzanne Blair, L. B. Carton, Mr. & Mrs. Fleming, Anita Grünberg, Caroline James, Harry Lucas, Arthur Minks, Lord Nasby, Guy Pagett, Sir Eustace Pedler, Colonel Johnny Race, Harry Rayburn.

First Editions: British: John Lane, London, August 1924. 310 pp., 7s. 6d. **American**: Dodd, Mead & Co., New York, 1924. 275 pp., $2.00.

Adaptation: None.

◈ 6 ◈

THE SECRET OF CHIMNEYS (1925)

Christie described *The Secret of Chimneys* and its sequel *The Seven Dials Mystery* (#10, 1929) as "the light-hearted thriller type," which was "always easy to write, not requiring too much plotting and planning." The young author's career to this point—on the eve of her milestone book *Roger Ackroyd*—was evenly divided between "pure" detective novels like *The Mysterious Affair at Styles* (#1, 1920) and *Murder on the Links* (#3, 1923) and loosely constructed thrillers such as *The Secret Adversary* (#2, 1922) and *Chimneys*.

Critic Robert Barnard in *A Talent to Deceive* (1980) describes *The Secret of Chimneys* as "by far the least awful of the early thrillers . . . a farrago of comic foreigners and international jewel thieves . . . if you can take all the racialist remarks, which are very much of their time, this is a first class romp."

In the same vein, Christie bibliographer Nancy Blue Wynne warns that "certainly no one who happens to choose [this book] as his first taste of Christie would be able to form a true opinion of her detective stories."

Most Christie readers will agree that *Chimneys* and its companion thrillers can barely hold their own against the early Christie detective novels. Yet in their time they were well received by critics.

The *Times Literary Supplement* (London) described "a thick fog of mystery, cross purposes, and romance, which leads up to a most unexpected and highly satisfactory ending" (7/9/25). *Literary Review* said, "Here's another capital detective story by Miss Christie, which will keep the reader guessing until the very end, not only as to the identity of the arch villain—the murderer—but also that of the hero, Anthony Cade" (10/31/25). The *Boston Transcript* commented, "The usual ingredients of a mystery yarn are herein cleverly handled in the usual way" (9/23/25).

Superintendent Battle of Scotland Yard makes his first appearance in *The Secret of Chimneys*. The "big, square, wooden-faced" Battle appears in five Christie novels, *Towards Zero* (#43, 1944) being his last.

In 1925 Agatha and Archie Christie purchased their first home, "a sort of millionaire-style Savoy suite transferred to the country." The Berkshire house was especially attractive to the couple because it was priced below market value, and because it was located near the exclusive Sunningdale golf course, where the Christies played, and where they had been renting a house. Their new home was christened Styles House after Christie's first novel.

The book is dedicated "To my nephew in memory of an inscription at Compton Castle and a day at the zoo." Christie's nephew was James Watts, Jr. (Jack), the son of Madge Miller, Christie's older sister, and James "Jimmy" Watts, Sr. Jack was in his early twenties at the time *The Secret of Chimneys* was dedicated to him.

PLOT:

Anthony Cade, a good-natured drifter, is making ends meet by escorting Castle's Select Tours, consisting in the current case of "seven depressed-looking females and three perspiring males" through Bulawayo, Africa. By chance Anthony bumps into his old friend Jimmy McGrath, a footloose adventurer who offers Anthony a bit of adventure of his own. It seems that Jimmy once helped out an old man being mugged by a gang of toughs, only to find out that the codger was none other than Count Stylptitch of Herzoslovakia, a rather troubled Middle European nation. Jimmy has just read that the count has recently died in Paris. Before his death, the count mailed Jimmy the manuscript of his memoirs, with the promise that a thousand-pound reward would await him on delivery of the scandalous autobiography to a certain London publisher.

Jimmy is already headed for a newly discovered gold field, so he offers the highly paid messenger job to Anthony, who dumps the tourists in his care for a mission of historic import in the world of scandal and publishing. Jimmy also has another packet in his care—a batch of letters with which a now-deceased scoundrel friend of his was blackmailing an Englishwoman, Virginia Revel. Jimmy, though an adventurer, is not a blackguard, and he wants to return the damaging letters to the distressed and financially drained woman. As long as he's going to England to deliver the Stylptitch manuscript, Anthony will be happy to drop off Virginia's letters.

Anthony gets into more than he bargained for. Count Stylptitch was up to his neck in trying to restore the deposed Obolovitch dynasty of his nation, though his faction is getting stiff competition from Comrades of the Red Hand, a radical leftist group. When Virginia Revel's blackmail letters are stolen from Anthony's London hotel room, Anthony discovers that Mrs. Revel's husband, now dead, was once British minister to Herzoslovakia. What's more, Anthony finds the thief who stole the letters dead in her apartment. A slip of paper on the dead man's clothes notes an 11:45 meeting at Chimneys, a rambling Berkshire estate, which is often used for hush-hush diplomatic weekends. Anthony goes to Chimneys only to be confronted with another murder and a struggle for control of the Herzoslovakian throne and the Herzoslovakian oil fields.

Principal Characters: Boris Anchoukoff, Chief Inspector Badgworthy, Superintendent Battle, Clement Edward Alistair Brent, Daisy Brent, Dulcie Brent, Lady Eileen (Bundle) Brent, Anthony Cade, Dr. Cartwright, Bill Eversleigh, Hiram P. Fish, Herman Isaacstein, Constable Johnston, Monsieur Lemoine, Baron Lolopretjzyl, Hon. George Lomax, Giuseppe Manelli, Jimmy McGrath, Prince Michael of Herzoslovakia, Colonel Melrose, Angèle Mory, Prince Michael Obolovitch, Dutch Pedro, Virginia Revel, Count Stylptitch, Tredwell, King Victor, Professor Wynwood.

First Editions: British: John Lane, London, 1925. 306 pp., 7s. 6d. **American**: Dodd, Mead & Co., New York, 1925. 310 pp., $2.00.

Adaptation: None.

◈ 7 ◈

THE MURDER OF ROGER ACKROYD (1926)

This is the book that made Agatha Christie famous, and today, almost sixty years after its publication, it remains one of the most famous books in all detective writing, and certainly one of the most controversial.

On the surface, *Roger Ackroyd* is a conventional mystery, set in the peaceful village of King's Abbot, and peopled with the usual assortment of village murder-mystery characters. Christie handles her cast of stock characters with great skill and flair. The village doctor, his gossipy sister, the handsome, irresponsible stepson, the bluff former military big-game hunter, the nervous butler, are all presented in a manner that is a cut above the ordinary in characterization. Even if *Ackroyd* had a more conventional twist at the end, it would still rank as a classic Christie.

But therein lies the difference. For it is Christie's brilliant deception as to the murderer's identity that caused gasps among critics, fellow writers, and the public, followed by camps divided about equally into those who cried "Bravo!" and those who cried "Foul play! Cheating!"

The solution to the mystery (and we're not revealing anything) was so controversial because it broke the traditional rules of mystery writing, as set down by the Detection Club, that select organization of crime writers, of which Christie was a member, dedicated to the preservation and encouragement of the high standards and strict regulations of classic detective fiction.

Dorothy L. Sayers, that most erudite of mystery writers, and herself a member of the Detection Club, came publicly to Christie's defense (as quoted by Christie biographer Gwen Robyns) by saying that the book was "Fair! And fooled you . . . it is the reader's business to suspect everybody."

Contemporary mystery writer Julian Symons described *Ackroyd* as "the blandest, most brilliant of deceptions. When we look back to see how it was done—well, as so often with Dame Agatha, it is a matter of some assumptions that we are led to make because making them is customary, plus a few carefully chosen phrases intended to deceive without ever being positively untrue."

In her own behalf, Christie said, "I thought it was a good idea, and considered it for a long time. It had enormous difficulties, of course . . . a lot of people say that *The Murder of Roger Ackroyd* is cheating; but if they read it carefully they will see that they are wrong. Such little lapses of time as there have to be are nicely concealed in an ambiguous sentence, and [the narrative] contains 'nothing but the truth, though not the whole truth.'"

The idea for the deception in *Roger Ackroyd* came to Christie from two independent sources, as she recalled in *An Autobiography*. James Watts, husband of Agatha's sister, Madge, got the idea started by complaining that "almost everybody turns out to be a criminal nowadays in detective stories," and then went on to propose his own variation on the theme.

The second contributor to the *Roger Ackroyd* plot was none other than Louis Mountbatten, first Earl Mountbatten of Burma, the British naval commander, last Viceroy of India, and uncle of Prince Philip Mountbatten, the husband of Queen Elizabeth. Lord Mountbatten (who was assassinated in 1981 by Irish terrorists) was a young naval officer who dabbled in mystery writing on the side when, in 1924, he wrote to Christie—herself then just at the beginning of her career—with an idea for an out-of-the-ordinary murderer for a mystery novel.

Lord Mountbatten's role in *Ackroyd* was not publicly known until the 1970s when Christie biographer Gwen Robyns, during her research, noticed a published photograph of the Earl of Burma and the Queen of Crime. On asking Mountbatten about his heretofore unknown friendship with Christie, he replied that they had been brought together, not as friends, but because Mountbatten's family had not believed his claim that he had given Christie the germ of the *Ackroyd* plot many years before. So, in order to settle his family's doubts, after a lapse of forty-five years, Mountbatten wrote Christie, asking if she remembered his letter of many years before.

According to Mountbatten, Christie wrote back, with belated thanks for his help, and admitted "she had a load off her conscience and she could acknowledge the origin of the plot."

Christie and Mountbatten finally got acquainted during the premiere of *Murder on the Orient Express* in 1974 (the film happened also to be produced by Lord Brabourne, Mountbatten's son-in-law), and the photos were taken outside the Savoy Grill during a dinner celebrating the film premiere.

Mountbatten's contribution should not really be made too much of. He merely suggested the character that should be made the murderer; the plot as Christie worked it out could only have come from her. And, given her continuous search for new tricks to pull on her readers, it is very likely that, sooner or later, she would have come up with the idea herself.

Coming when it did, however, *The Murder of Roger Ackroyd* marked an important point in Christie's career, for it was her first book with William Collins Sons & Co. In 1920 she had signed a six-book contract with John Lane/the Bodley Head. At the time, she was only too happy to sign anything that would get her book published, and she paid little attention to the royalty provisions and to the option she gave Lane on her next five books.

When *The Mysterious Affair at Styles* (#1, 1920) and her subsequent books did well, it soon became apparent that she was bound to a very unsatisfactory contract. While still under contract to the Bodley Head, she took on as her agents Hughes Massie, Ltd. She had been steered to Massie several years before by Eden Phillpotts, the Devon novelist who had been the first professional to encourage her career, and when Agatha realized that the contract she had signed with the Bodley Head—without benefit of an agent's advice—was a mistake, she went to Massie to handle her affairs.

Massie, who still represents the Christie literary estate, saw the potential in the young author, who they had interviewed before *Mysterious Affair at Styles* (#1, 1920) was published, and wisely negotiated a much more favorable contract with a new publisher, a full two years before her contractual obligations to Lane/Bodley were fulfilled.

William Collins was noted primarily as a publisher of Bibles, but during the 1920s they began building a list of detective writers as well. Christie signed a three-book contract with Collins in January 1924. The Bodley Head in the meantime published *Poirot In-*

vestigates (#4, 1924), *The Man in the Brown Suit* (#5, 1924), and *The Secret of Chimneys* (#6, 1925).

Christie was probably quite pleased that the next book, her first with Collins, was such a success, for she seems to have harbored no little resentment against the Bodley Head for their original contract. "They had not treated a young author fairly," Christie wrote in her autobiography years later. "They had taken advantage of her lack of knowledge and her eagerness to publish a book. . . . If you have trusted people once and been disappointed, you do not wish to trust them any more."

Roger Ackroyd—the brilliance of its final twist aside—holds a great deal of charm for the reader. Within the familiar framework of the village murder, Christie has drawn some of her most delightful character sketches, all from the stock repertory of village inhabitants. The most noteworthy is Caroline Sheppard, the epitome of the gossipy village spinster, and one of Christie's best comic creations, whose obsession with gossip is brilliantly depicted in the Mah-Jongg scene in chapter 16, where Caroline speculates about possible murderers while laying down her tiles. For more information on the character of Caroline Sheppard and how it influenced Christie in the creation of Miss Marple, refer to *The Murder at the Vicarage* (#13, 1930).

"She plays fair, as always," wrote *The Nation and Athaneum*, "concealing from the reader no facts known to the incomparable Poirot; and as always she contrives to keep her secret just so long as she wishes—which is until the very end. But this time the secret is more than usually original and ingenious, and is a device which no other writer could have employed without mishap. The plot is disclosed with detached exactitude, but at the same time the characters are entertaining and the human interest never flags" (7/8/26).

The *New York Times* said, "There are doubtless many detective stories more exciting and blood curdling than *The Murder of Roger Ackroyd*, but this reviewer has recently read very few which provide greater analytical stimulation" (7/18/26).

Books (*New York Herald Tribune*) enthused, "The truly startling denouement is uncommonly original and will restore a thrill to the most jaded reader of detective stories. It is obtained, however, at a slight sacrifice of plausible character portrayal"

(7/25/26). The *Daily Sketch* complained mightily: "Tasteless, unforgivable letdown by a writer we had grown to admire."

As for the author, *The Murder of Roger Ackroyd* was one of the books she mentioned time and again as among her favorites.

This book, among the most unorthodox of all classic mysteries, is dedicated to Christie's sister, Madge "Punkie" Miller Watts, with more than a touch of irony: "To Punkie, who likes an orthodox detective story, murder, inquest, and suspicion falling on every one in turn!"

PLOT:

In the village of King's Abbot, a place "rich in unmarried ladies and retired military officers," a wealthy widow named Ferrars is found dead, and the local physician, Dr. Sheppard, determines that she died of an overdose of veronal—an apparent suicide. On returning home from his examination of the body, the bachelor doctor discusses, or rather, tries to avoid discussing, the death with his sister Caroline, a woman who "can do any amount of finding out sitting placidly at home." Even at this early hour Caroline is already up on the situation, and asserts that Mrs. Ferrars committed suicide out of remorse for having poisoned her alcoholic husband the year before. Caroline further speculates that the suicide left a letter confessing her undiscovered crime, but Dr. Sheppard passes this off as nonsense and idle gossip.

Attention focuses on Roger Ackroyd, a prominent King's Abbot resident who, it was rumored in the village, was to have married Mrs. Ferrars in the near future, probably right after the year of mourning for her first husband was over.

Dr. Sheppard is invited to dinner at Ackroyd's home, Fernly Glen, the following night, and Ackroyd makes it clear to Sheppard that he wants to talk to the doctor about something of importance —presumably about Mrs. Ferrars's death. After a dinner with the Ackroyd household and guests, the two men talk privately. Ackroyd is distressed, and admits that he blames himself for his fiancée's death: on the eve of the announcement of their marriage, Mrs. Ferrars had confessed that she couldn't marry Ackroyd because she had in truth poisoned her drunken and hateful husband. What's more, someone in King's Abbot was blackmailing her.

Ackroyd didn't hide his revulsion from his murderess-fiancée—

clearly he couldn't marry her now—but he didn't foresee that she would do herself in that very night, and without revealing the blackmailer. As Ackroyd and Sheppard are talking, the butler delivers a letter from Mrs. Ferrars, posted before her death. Ackroyd won't read the letter in front of Sheppard, but the doctor suggests it contains the name of the blackmailer.

Sheppard leaves and returns home, but an hour later he is recalled. Ackroyd has been found stabbed to death in his study.

Ackroyd was heard talking in his study more than a half hour after the doctor had left, so he *must* have been killed in the half hour between nine thirty and ten. There are a number of suspects with possible motives: Major Blunt, a big-game hunter who has known the victim for years; Ackroyd's poor sister-in-law and her daughter, Flora, living with their rich but penny-pinching relative; Ursula Bourne, the parlormaid with questionable references; Ralph Paton, Ackroyd's estranged stepson, who was secretly visiting King's Abbot; and Miss Russell, the Fernly Glen housekeeper who had had a shot at marrying Ackroyd until Mrs. Ferrars came on the scene.

The mystery begins unraveling when Dr. Sheppard's next-door neighbor turns out to be none other than Hercule Poirot, living in King's Abbot for a year now, where he has given up detection for cultivating vegetable marrows.

Principal Characters: Flora Ackroyd, Mrs. Ackroyd, Roger Ackroyd, Major Hector Blunt, Ursula Bourne, Mrs. Richard Folliott, Charles Kent, Parker, Captain Ralph Paton, Hercule Poirot, Inspector Raglan, Geoffrey Raymond, Miss Russell, Caroline Sheppard, Dr. James Sheppard.

First Editions: **British**: Collins, London, June 1926. 312 pp., 7s. 6d. **American**: Dodd, Mead & Co., New York, 1926. 306 pp., $2.00.

Adaptations: *The Murder of Roger Ackroyd,* Christie's first work to reach the stage, was adapted by Michael Morton under the title *Alibi.* The play, which was directed by Charles Laughton, opened May 15, 1928, at Prince of Wales's Theatre, London. Charles Laughton also starred as Hercule Poirot. An American production that again starred Laughton opened in New York with the title *The Fatal Alibi* in 1932. *Alibi,* a film derived from *Roger Ackroyd,* was made in England in 1931 and starred Austin Trevor as Poirot.

8

THE BIG FOUR (1927)

This is a book that justifiably falls in the shadow of its masterly predecessor, though it was a solid commercial success. After the success of *Roger Ackroyd* (#7, 1926), which sold about 4,000 copies of its first printing (a good sale in those days), and after the tremendous stir *Ackroyd* caused in critical circles because of its skill and audacity, William Collins no doubt hoped that their second publishing venture with rising star Agatha Christie would be even more successful. And so it was, though for reasons that could not have been anticipated.

The author's personal life intervened in a spectacular way, however, for between the publication of *The Murder of Roger Ackroyd* in June 1926 and *The Big Four* in January of 1927 came the dissolution of her marriage, and the author's famous disappearance of December 3, 1926.

The events leading up to the personal crisis of 1926 began some time earlier, perhaps as early as 1924, when Agatha's marriage to Archie Christie began to show signs of strain. The focal point of the strain was Archie's passion for golf, which by 1925 Agatha was beginning to feel was of greater interest to him than his family.

Christie is always circumspect about personal matters, and in her memoirs she gives few revealing details about this period of her life. Early in 1926 she took a holiday without Archie, to Corsica, which may indicate a growing distance between the pair. Agatha returned to England to find her mother seriously ill with bronchitis, and a week or two later, while Archie was away in Spain on business, Mrs. Miller died. Archie, who Agatha recognized had "a violent dislike of illness, death, and trouble," promptly went back to Spain after he'd returned to England and found his mother-in-law dead. Agatha was left essentially alone because of her sister's prior obligations to settle her mother's estate. Even after Archie returned from his second trip to Spain, he remained in London or at Styles House, the Christies' newly acquired Berkshire home, rather than with Agatha at Ashfield.

Agatha had been extremely devoted to her mother, and Ashfield, where Agatha had been born and raised, was a home so full of memories that it appeared again and again in her novels until the very end of her career. The task of clearing the house cannot have been an easy one, physically or emotionally.

"I worked like a demon . . . ten or eleven hours a day," Agatha wrote, in recalling the task of clearing three generations of acquisitions from Ashfield. "I began to get confused and muddled over things."

A "terrible sense of loneliness" came over Agatha, not helped by Archie's refusal to come to Ashfield on weekends for a visit. Agatha had warnings of an impending nervous breakdown when she had trouble remembering her name when signing a check, and when she burst into tears just because her car wouldn't start.

By midsummer, Agatha's situation seemed to be improving. *The Murder of Roger Ackroyd* (#7, 1926) was published in June and brought her great professional acclaim, and affairs at Ashfield were settled enough for her to return home to Styles House in time for her daughter Rosalind's birthday on August 5.

Then, a devastating blow came. Archie announced that he had fallen in love with another woman, Nancy Neele, the former secretary of Major Belcher of the Christies' world tour days (see *The Man in the Brown Suit,* #5). Archie asked Agatha for a divorce as soon as possible.

The Christies separated for a short period, then Archie came back to Styles House for a trial reconciliation, out of consideration for their daughter. Agatha described the attempted reconciliation as "a mistake . . . a period of sorrow, misery, heartbreak."

Though the culmination of this crisis was not to come until December (see *The Mystery of the Blue Train,* #9), during the period from August through November Agatha was clearly not in shape to produce a new book. Yet her publishers and readers expected a new Christie, especially after the success of *Roger Ackroyd,* and Christie admitted in her autobiography that she badly needed the money to cover expenses while she and her husband were trying to sell Styles House. Agatha's brother-in-law

Campbell Christie, who was well aware of Agatha's marital problems, suggested that as a "stop-gap" (her word) she piece together a dozen stories that had appeared in the *Sketch* and sell the pastiche as a novel to Collins. Since the stories dealt with the same four arch-criminals, all that was required to do the job was the writing of opening and closing chapters, and a bit of connective material between the episodes to give the feeling of a continuous narrative. Christie admitted that Campbell had helped her with the patchwork, since she was "still unable to tackle anything of the kind" owing to her overwrought emotional state. It is not known how much of the patching together was done by Campbell.

What Collins got was indeed a patchwork: a series of interrelated Poirot and Hastings stories, with the two men making their way through a mishmash of international intrigue. At first it may seem odd for Hastings and Poirot to appear in a thriller of this type. However, readers should keep in mind that from time to time in Christie's work there are varying degrees of crossover between her world-domination, secret-weapon thrillers and her purer detective puzzles. Especially in later years, with the growing general paranoia of World War II espionage and the Cold War, she introduced spies and agitators into her classic murder mysteries. Clearly, the stories that became *The Big Four* provide a precedent for this; she had seen nothing wrong with putting Poirot and Hastings in the middle of a secret international power cartel, just for the fun of it.

Though *The Big Four* turned out to be a creative clinker, the bottom line for the publisher and author wasn't at all bad. Christie merely says, "It turned out to be quite popular," neglecting to mention that its popularity was probably due primarily to the publicity surrounding her disappearance the month before publication.

In spite of poor reviews—*Saturday Review* said, "As a detective story *The Big Four* is a failure" (2/5/27) and Leonard Woolf in *The Nation and Athaneum* said, "The theme is too hackneyed for even the most skillful composer to make anything original out of it" (2/26/27)—the book sold a remarkable 8,500 copies, more than twice those of its predecessor.

The book itself is notable for the appearance of several characters involved in Poirot's personal life. One is Poirot's brother?

[sic] Achille Poirot, the spiritual cousin of Holmes's mysterious sibling, Mycroft. Achille appears here for the first and only time in the Christie oeuvre. Achille Poirot is merely a disguise—a fictitious brother—created by the detective to serve his purposes. And Hastings is gullible enough to believe that his detective friend really does have a brother.

"Your brother," Hastings cried in astonishment. "I never knew you had a brother."

"You surprise me, Hastings," Poirot said. "Do you not know that all celebrated detectives have brothers who would be even more celebrated than they are were it not for constitutional indolence?"

Hastings has an even greater shock in *The Big Four* when Poirot falls in love with Countess Vera Rossakoff, a flamboyant Russian jewel thief and member of the underworld. In spite of her criminal activities, Poirot thinks the countess is "a remarkable woman" while Hastings remarks that "small men always admire big, flamboyant women."

Though Poirot admires beautiful women on many occasions in his career, the Countess Rossakoff is the only woman he loses his heart to. They first met in the short story "The Double Clue," printed in a magazine c. 1925 (published in book form in *Double Sin and Other Stories,* #66, 1961). When Poirot meets her for the last time in "The Capture of Cerberus" from the *Labours of Hercules* (#47, 1947), he has fond memories of his love of many years ago.

Chief Inspector James Japp, who was introduced in *The Mysterious Affair at Styles* (#1, 1920), here makes his second appearance in a novel. Japp appeared in seven novels and eight short stories, all of which featured his old friend Poirot. His association with Poirot dates back to 1904 when Poirot was still working for the Belgian police and Japp was with Scotland Yard. Both Japp and Poirot remained good friends despite their completely different methods of solving crimes. Poirot was methodical and orderly, while Japp tended to be haphazard.

Captain Hastings, on seeing Japp for the first time in the Styles case, described him as "a little, sharp, dark, ferret-faced man." Christie's creation of Japp, according to her autobiography, was influenced by the Sherlock Holmes tradition. Poirot represented the "eccentric detective," Hastings the "stooge assistant," and Japp the "Lestrade-type Scotland Yard detective."

Japp, who had a tendency to call his friend "Moosier Poirot," once said to Poirot: "I shouldn't wonder if you ended by detecting your own death. . . . That's an idea, that is. Ought to be put in a book."

PLOT:

When Captain Hastings returns from his retirement to ranch life in Argentina and pays a surprise visit to his old friend Poirot in London, he finds that the detective is about to set sail for Rio, on a high-paying assignment for Abe Ryland, the American soap magnate. But as Poirot is packing, an intruder causes a change in plans. The stranger, "coated from head to foot with dust and mud; his face . . . thin and emaciated," staggers into the apartment and collapses. In his half-crazed state, the man can only ask for Poirot, and write repeatedly on a piece of paper the number four. Poirot soon learns from the crazed man of a powerful, ruthless international cartel called "the Big Four," a group with sinister but secret intentions. The man then mentions Li Chang Yen—the only named member of the Big Four, who is known as "Number One." "Number Two" is an American; "Number Three" is a woman of French nationality. But the identity of "Number Four"—the man known as "the destroyer"—is totally shrouded in mystery.

The stranger is left alone in Poirot's apartment to recover under the watchful eye of the housekeeper, as Poirot and Hastings go to catch their train. Just outside London, Poirot realizes he is being set up, and he and Hastings hastily return to the flat, only to find the crazed visitor dead. Soon after, a cockney claiming to be an insane asylum attendant pursuing the "escaped" man, calls on Poirot. After he leaves, the detective realizes that he must be "Number Four"—a master of disguise.

Soon Poirot and Hastings are plunged into a world of international intrigue, secret weapons, kidnapped physicists, underground laboratories, and hairbreadth escapes, until, at great risk to his own life, Poirot finally uncovers the identity of "Number Four."

Principal Characters: Joseph Aarons, Sydney Crowther, Claud

Darrell, Monsieur Desjardeaux, Mr. & Mrs. Halliday, Captain Arthur Hastings, John Ingles, Chief Inspector James Japp, Captain Kent, Mr. McNeil, Flossie Monro, Madame Olivier, Mabel Palmer, Mr. Paynter, Gerald Paynter, Achille Poirot, Hercule Poirot, Dr. Ridgeway, Countess Vera Rossakoff, Abe Ryland, Dr. Teeves, Mr. & Mrs. Templeton, Jonathan Whalley.

First Editions: British: Collins, London, January 1927. 281 pp., 7s. 6d. **American:** Dodd, Mead & Co., New York, 1927. 276 pp., $2.00.

Adaptation: None.

9

THE MYSTERY OF THE BLUE TRAIN (1928)

"Easily the worst book I ever wrote," Christie once said of *The Mystery of the Blue Train.* "Each time I read it again, I think it commonplace, full of clichés, with an uninteresting plot. Many people, I am sorry to say, *like* it. Authors are always said to be no judge of their own books."

Christie's problems in writing *The Mystery of the Blue Train* are understandable, as it was the first book she wrote after her traumatic and much publicized disappearance in December of 1926. That entire year, which began with the death of her mother, followed by the breakup of her marriage (see *The Big Four,* #8), piled emotional blow upon emotional blow, until Agatha was on the verge of a nervous breakdown. The final blow came on December 4, a Friday, when Christie's husband, Archie, apparently announced that he was leaving her again, for good, to seek a divorce and remarriage with his paramour, Nancy Neele. On that day, Archie, after a series of arguments with Agatha, took advantage of her absence from Styles House to pack his bags and leave. Archie had been invited to Godalming, to the house of a Mr. and Mrs. James, for the weekend. The invitation was apparently for the sole purpose of allowing Archie to leave Agatha, since the only other guest was Miss Neele. According to Christie biographer Gwen Robyns, the party at the James house was described at the time as "an engagement party."

When Agatha arrived back home she learned that Archie had left. At 9:45 that evening, after packing a small suitcase and kissing her sleeping daughter good-bye, Agatha left Styles House in her car. At this point, there are various versions of what happened. One version is that Charlotte Fisher, Christie's live-in secretary, called Archie at the James house, perhaps to warn him that Agatha had left and might confront him and Miss Neele at Godalming. This version has Archie leaving the James house during dinner to try to intercept Agatha and prevent any confrontation.

A second version of the story says that Archie did not hear of his wife's departure from Styles until the next morning, when he left the Jameses' and returned home.

In any case, the following morning, a Saturday, Agatha's green Morris, which she had only recently learned to drive, was found over an embankment at Newlands Corner, Berkshire, with the hood up and the lights on. Inside was a fur coat and a dressing case with Agatha's belongings and an expired driver's license.

When the Surrey police issued a missing persons report, it attracted immediate press attention, as *Roger Ackroyd* (#7, 1926) was still a best-seller. During the next week, Agatha's disappearance became national news. The press claimed that as many as five hundred policemen in four counties were involved in the search for the missing author, and the *Daily Mail* offered a £100 reward for information leading to Agatha's discovery.

As Michael Gilbert describes the affair in *First Lady of Crime* (1977), "By the weekend, the search had escalated into realms of fantasy. Hundreds of policemen, thousands of enthusiastic amateurs, Scouts, dogs, aeroplanes and divers were scouring the countryside and the pools for clues and propounding theories for the press."

The disappearance came to a rather unspectacular end when Bob Tappin, a musician in the dance band at the Hydro Hotel at Harrowgate, claimed the £100 reward. He recognized a guest at the hotel—registered under the name Teresa Neele!—as Agatha Christie. The police and press were notified, and Archie went to the Hydro with police officials. There he met privately with Agatha and made a statement to the press that his wife "has suffered the most complete loss of memory and does not know who she is."

Once she was found, Agatha remained firmly away from direct contact with the press, and released only formal statements reconfirming that her disappearance had resulted from a loss of memory.

There are still many unanswered questions about the disappearance. Christie avoids *any* mention of it in her memoirs (she skips from the difficult fall of 1926, when Archie was still at

home, to February 1927, when she began writing *Blue Train*).
The private Christie papers are still unavailable to the public, and
many official police documents were destroyed during the war.
While all Christie researchers agree that she went through some
sort of nervous breakdown in December 1926, most agree that the
total amnesia theory is unconvincing.

The truth may never be known.

Not much is known of Agatha's activities in the weeks immediately following the disappearance. Archie had moved out of Styles
at this point, and Agatha had decided to go ahead with a divorce.
Agatha's brother-in-law James Watts suggested that Agatha and
her daughter, Rosalind, should go away. Agatha chose the Canary
Islands, where she went in February 1927. It was while staying
there in the town of Oratava, on Tenerife, that she wrote most of
The Mystery of the Blue Train.*

Agatha decided that once she had "got away and calmed
down, she could perhaps . . . write another book," with the help
of her secretary, Charlotte (also called Carlo or Carlotta) Fisher.

In *An Autobiography,* Christie gives a rare description of
writing a book. *Blue Train* was dictated to Charlotte Fisher in the
garden of the hotel—apparently Christie's first attempt at dictating
a book—with an impatient, bored young Rosalind worrying and interrupting her mother at work.

"Oratava was lovely. The big mountain towered up; there were
glorious flowers in the hotel grounds . . . but Rosalind's eye upon
me had the effect of a Medusa. . . . To begin with, I had no joy
in writing, no élan. . . . I could not see the scene in my mind's
eye, and the people would not come alive. I was driven desperately by the desire, indeed the necessity, to write another book
and make some money.

"That was the moment when I changed from amateur to a professional. I assumed the burden of a profession, which is to write
even when you don't want to. . . . I felt more strongly than ever

---

* Most books on Christie give February 1928 as the date of the trip to the
Canary Islands. Since it is virtually impossible that the book was published
within one month of its completion, and since Christie herself stated that the
success of *The Big Four* (which was published in January 1927) encouraged
her to do another book. *The Mystery of the Blue Train* was for the most
part written in February/March of 1927, and published in March 1928.

that everything I was saying was idiotic! I faltered, stammered, and repeated myself. Really, how that wretched book ever came to be written, I don't know!"

The book, in spite of the author's dislike of it, did well at the booksellers', with an initial sale of about 7,000 copies. Reviews were generally good. C. M. Purdy in *Bookmark* wrote, "As in all her stories, Mrs. Christie is a bit slow in getting under way, sacrificing speed to characterization, but in the end her technique justifies her delay" (10/28).

"This time Miss Christie pursues conventional detective story methods," warned the *Independent,* "and by following conventional guessing you will probably discover the murderer" (7/28/28).

Will Cuppy in *Books* (*New York Herald Tribune*) enthused, "Here is none of your fly-by-night dreadfuls, but a truly honorable thriller in the right classic tradition, warranted to restore the jaded reader's faith in clews" (8/12/28).

And the opinion of the *Times Literary Supplement* (London) should have reassured the doubting author. "The reader will not be disappointed when the distinguished Belgian on psychological grounds . . . builds up inferences almost out of the air, supports them by a masterly array of negative evidence and lands his fish to the surprise of everyone" (5/23/28).

The dedication of the book is something of an "in" joke: "Dedicated to Two Distinguished Members of the O.F.D., Carlotta and Peter."

In her memoirs Christie explains that O.F.D. stands for Order of the Faithful Dogs. "All that I had gone through [with the divorce] made for a kind of acid test" of friends; some were loyal, some abandoned their friend at the most difficult time in her life. As a half-serious, half-joking way of noting which friends went in which direction, Christie and Charlotte Fisher created the O.F.D., first class, for the faithful friends, and its counterpart, the Order of the Rats, third class, for those that Agatha felt had not stood by her in her time of need.

Her secretary, clearly, was an O.F.D. Peter, who shares the honors with Carlo, is the wirehaired terrier the Christies acquired after their return from the world tour. Peter, "of course, became the life and soul of the family. He slept on Carlo's bed."

Charlotte Fisher, "a tall, brown haired" woman of "about twenty-three," had been hired by Christie around the time *The Murder of Roger Ackroyd* (#7, 1926) was written. Miss Fisher, whom Christie had found through a "help wanted" ad in the paper, served both as secretary and governess; she took dictation, typed manuscripts, and handled correspondence for Agatha, and minded young Rosalind. Carlo became a close companion to Christie, and was especially valued for her support and companionship during the breakup of Agatha's first marriage, for which Carlo was awarded Christie's personal Medal of Honor. The two women remained friends for their entire lives.

Le train bleu itself is only slightly less famous than the Orient Express, and in its heyday exceeded its well-known rival in luxury and glamor. Whereas the Orient Express gained its aura of mystery and intrigue from its international route, the Blue Train was simply the most elegant possible way for the leisured, monied class to travel to the Riviera for the winter season.

Like the Orient Express, *le train bleu* was created by railroad genius Georges Nagelmackers. The train, officially known as the Calais-Paris-Nice Express, began service in December 1883. It was not until 1922 when the Compagnie Internationale des Wagons-lits introduced their first all-steel sleeping cars, enameled in dark blue and gold, that the train acquired its famous name. So luxurious was the service that only ten passengers were accommodated in a single coach. "Tourist class" was unheard of, and not added to the train until 1962! The train was noted for its late hours in the dining car, which seldom had more than a few patrons before 10:00 P.M. In the meantime, the rich and famous put themselves in a Riviera frame of mind in the cocktail lounge, the first ever on a train.

According to Christie biographer Gwen Robyns, Agatha and Archie traveled on the Blue Train in 1926; there is no mention of this journey in *An Autobiography*. From Robyns's reconstruction of this complex period in the author's life, it is possible that *The Mystery of the Blue Train* was already begun, or at least plotted, before the disappearance of the author in December 1926. Robyns quotes a *Daily Mail* interview with Archie Christie's mother in which she mentions her daughter-in-law's trip to Corsica to work on a book based on the Blue Train. Christie mentions this holiday, with her sister Madge, which was before her mother's death in 1926. It was just after her mother's death that Agatha learned that Archie was having an affair with Nancy Neele and wanted a divorce. Robyns also suggests that on the day of her disappearance, Christie met with her agents, Hughes Massie, Ltd., to discuss the upcoming Blue Train mystery. Robyns does not give any supporting evidence for the claim that Agatha began the book in Corsica early in 1926 other than the newspaper interview with Mrs. Helmsley, Archie Christie's mother. Mrs. Helmsley's memory is suspect (as is Christie's) since Mrs. Helmsley says the Corsica stay was "some months," while Agatha recalls it as "short."

In any case, if the book was begun in Corsica, early in 1926, "the best part," according to Christie, was written in the Canary Islands a year later, and not published until March 1928.

Though there is no published record, it is likely that Agatha and Madge took *le train bleu* from London to Nice en route to Corsica in 1926, most especially if she had in mind a book with a setting on the train.

What Christie did see on *le train bleu* at the height of its glory is pictured by Martin Page, in his *The Last Pleasures of the Great Trains* (William Morrow & Co., 1975).

"For the upper-classes of Europe and especially of Britain, the inauguration of the Train Bleu marked the beginning of a new kind of social season, and a new style of travel. The novelty was considerable. Previously one had gone abroad for a purpose—to view ancient monuments and galleries of pictures, or for the sake of one's health. The purpose of the annual winter retreat to the south of France was pleasure.

"The British began the journey at Victoria Station. Trunks filled with the new season's fashions from Bond Street were unloaded from the hansom and entrusted to a porter, not to be seen again until arrival in Nice. Then across the station yard to Overton's Restaurant for a luncheon of a dozen or two Whitstable Oysters, grilled sole, Stilton cheese and a bottle of Chablis, served by avuncular waiters in long white aprons. Then one returned to the station platform where the Club Train awaited, the precursor of the Golden Arrow. At the entrance to each carriage stood its conductor, dressed in the chocolate brown livery of La Compagnie

Internationale. He took one to one's reserved coupe, relieved one of one's passport and tickets so that one need not be disturbed during the journey, and offered champagne and other refreshments.

"The train passed through the green Kent countryside to Dover, where a steam packet of the London, Chatham and Dover Railway Company, for the exclusive use of Club Train passengers, was at the quayside. It took three hours to cross to Calais, where the Train Bleu itself awaited.

"Installed in a still more luxurious private compartment, one was rushed to Paris where, as the train passed around the ceinture to meet up with other carriages from Berlin, St. Petersburg, Warsaw, Vienna, and elsewhere, one spent a two-hour excursion, perhaps doing some last-minute shopping in the Rue de Rivoli.

"Boarding the now fully-sized Train Bleu, it was time to change for dinner and to go to the Pergola Restaurant to consume soup, fish, meat, cheese and dessert and, more attentively, to survey the other passengers for familiar faces and new fashions.

"The train reached the Mediterranean coast at Marseilles the next morning."

The Mystery of the Blue Train contains several references to the village of St. Mary Mead—Jane Marple's village—though there is no mention of the spinster sleuth herself. However, it is interesting to note that *The Mystery of the Blue Train* was published in March 1928—the same year that the first Jane Marple short stories were published in the *Sketch*.

PLOT:

On board the famous and luxurious Blue Train that runs from London to Nice are the usual assortment of famous and glamorous people, including Hercule Poirot and attractive Ruth Kettering, twenty-eight-year-old daughter of American millionaire Rufus Van Aldin and wife of Derek Kettering.

The Kettering marriage is in trouble: Ruth Van Aldin married Kettering on the rebound, after a messy affair with a phony French count, and of late the handsome Kettering has been seen more in the company of "that woman" Mirelle, a dancer, than with his wife. Ruth's father has advised divorce—the fellow's "rotten through and through"—and has attempted, through the intermediary of his secretary, Major Knighton, to buy off Kettering. To make his daughter feel a bit better, her millionaire dad presents her with a gift—the fabled Heart of Fire ruby, "like all famous stones . . . behind it a trail of tragedy and violence."

Thrilled with her priceless bauble, Ruth is en route to the Riviera for a reunion with her former lover, Comte Armand de la Roche. She has ignored her father's advice not to take the Heart of Fire abroad with her. On board Ruth strikes up a conversation with Katherine Grey, a pleasant, unmarried woman of thirty or so, who is enjoying the benefits of a recent large inheritance from her former employer, to whom she was companion. Katherine learns of Mrs. Kettering's distressing personal problems, and of her journey to visit the Comte de la Roche. But she is a bit puzzled when, just outside Lyons, she sees a man hesitate in the corridor outside Ruth Kettering's compartment, and then enter and close the door behind him. It is a man she has seen twice before—once in the Savoy, and once in the Cook's Tour offices.

The following morning there is a problem at the station at Nice. The police are there, questioning passengers, among them Katherine Grey, concerning the murder of Ruth Van Aldin Kettering.

Principal Characters: Joseph Aarons, Monsieur Carrege, Monsieur Caux, Comte Armand de la Roche, Olga Demiroff, Ellen, Charles "Chubby" Evans, Mr. Goby, Katherine Grey, Boris Ivanovitch, Derek Kettering, Ruth Kettering, Major Knighton, Ada Beatrice Mason, Pierre Michel, Mirelle, Demetrius Papopolous, Zia Papopolous, Hercule Poirot, the Honourable Lenox Tamplin, Lady Rosalie Tamplin, Rufus Van Aldin, Amelia Viner.

First Editions: **British**: Collins, London, March 1928. 295 pp., 7s. 6d. **American**: Dodd, Mead & Co., New York, 1928. 306 pp., $2.00.

Adaptation: None.

THE SEVEN DIALS MYSTERY (1929)

In her autobiography, Christie writes incorrectly that she "had followed up *The Murder of Roger Ackroyd* [#7, 1926] with *The Seven Dials Mystery*," forgetting that, in the personally terrible years of 1926–27 she had published *The Big Four* (#8, 1927) and *The Mystery of the Blue Train* (#9, 1928). She called *Seven Dials* a "sequel" to *The Secret of Chimneys* (#6, 1925) and it does share as its setting the country house of Chimneys, along with a batch of characters from the earlier book, including Superintendent Battle, Colonel Melrose (the chief constable for Market-Basing and King's Abbot), Bill Eversleigh, Hon. George Lomax, Clement Brent, and his daughter, Lady Eileen (Bundle) Brent.

In recalling the creation of *The Big Four* and *The Mystery of the Blue Train*, Christie stressed her desperate need during the breakup of her marriage to write for money. After 1928 (her divorce was granted in April of that year), her writing took on a less desperate, if still mercenary tone.

"I was gaining confidence over my writing now. I felt that I would have no difficulty in producing a book every year, and possibly a few short stories as well. The nice part about writing in those days was that I directly related it to money. If I decided to write a story, I knew it would bring me in sixty pounds. . . . This stimulated my output enormously."

Though Christie is honest about her financial problems during the period of her divorce from Archie Christie, she is characteristically reticent about her personal feelings during what must have been an extremely difficult transition period of her life. We have almost no information about Christie's personal life during 1927 (after her trip to the Canary Islands) and the greater part of 1928 (except for the granting of her divorce in April of that year).

The fall of 1928 is well documented, however, since Christie took the first of what were to be many journeys to the Middle

East, a part of the world that was to have enormous impact on her work and personal life.* By the fall of 1928 the newly divorced author's affairs had settled enough for her to consider a vacation. It was to be the first major trip she had taken without her husband or a traveling companion. In her autobiography Christie recalls that her daughter, Rosalind, was in boarding school until the Christmas holidays, and that she had decided to travel to the West Indies until the holiday break, when Rosalind would be at home. However, "Fate," as she described it, intervened in the form of Commander Howe and his wife, whom she met at a dinner party in London. The Howes lived in Baghdad, extolled its virtues at great length to Agatha, and convinced her to change her travel plans and go to the Middle East. "You can go by train—by the Orient Express."

Agatha took the Howes' advice, canceled her tickets to the West Indies, and booked herself on the Orient Express, the first of many trips she was to take on the famous train (see *Murder on the Orient Express,* #19, 1934). Christie arrived at Constantinople (not Istanbul till 1930), where she stayed at the Toklatian Hotel (where Poirot stays in *Murder on the Orient Express*). After her tour of the Bosporus city, she continued on into Asia Minor and

* Some of Christie's best and most popular works resulted from her Middle East travels, including *Murder on the Orient Express, Death on the Nile,* and *Appointment with Death.* In Christie's autobiography there are a number of contradictions as to the sequence and dates of events during the period 1926–1929. One of the most confusing is the exact date of this trip. In *An Autobiography,* Part 7, Chapter 7, Christie implies that the first Middle East trip was made *after* "things were put in train" for her divorce, but *before* it was final, which would place the trip in the fall of 1927. This is almost surely incorrect, since a) it is highly unlikely that Christie could leave England for an extended period of time during the months when her divorce decree was being processed, and b) all sources, including Christie and Max Mallowan, state that Christie's first journey to the Middle East and her first meeting with the Woolleys at Ur took place during the digging season before she met and married Max Mallowan in 1930. The implication in *An Autobiography* that the first journey was made while the divorce was in progress is either the result of faulty memory on Christie's part (perhaps she was thinking of the legal procedure of selling Styles House as part of the divorce settlement as what was "in train" during the journey), or result of faulty editing of the autobiography manuscript after Christie's death.

the Middle East—Aleppo, Damascus, then across the desert to
Baghdad. This was a long and rather adventurous journey for a
thirty-eight-year-old single woman, though Christie did take advantage of Cook's Tours to arrange transportation and accommodations, and Christie commented that "not until you travel by
yourself do you realize how much the outside world will protect
and befriend you."

Christie experienced this kindness abundantly when she visited
the ruins of the biblical city of Ur, near Baghdad. At the time Ur
was being excavated by the noted British archaeologist Leonard
Woolley and his team. When Christie arrived at Ur she received
what she called "the V.I.P. treatment"—primarily because Katharine Woolley, Leonard's wife, had read and liked *The Murder of
Roger Ackroyd,* and rolled out the red carpet for its visiting author. Agatha hit it off with the Woolleys, and they were to become
great friends (see *The Murder at the Vicarage* [#13] and *The
Thirteen Problems* [#16]). As originally planned, Christie returned to England in time for the Christmas holidays with Rosalind, but she had struck up such a friendship with the Woolleys
that she invited them to stay with her in London when they were
there the following summer.*

Christie had bought a little mews house in London at the beginning of 1929 (probably with the proceeds from the sale of Styles
House at the time of her divorce), and it was at this mews cottage
in Cresswell Place that Katharine and Leonard Woolley stayed
while they were in London during June of that year. Christie said
that she thought "it was a delightful house—one of four or five
houses in the mews which had been built like cottages: old-
fashioned country cottages."

During the Woolleys' stay they invited Christie to return to Ur
for a second visit the next digging season. She was to arrive late in
the season in March 1930, and stay for about a week with them at
the site before they would all return home together. Little did
Christie imagine that this next visit to Ur would mean the begin-

---

* The archaeological excavation season in the Middle East usually ran from
October or November through March; European digging teams returned
home during the hot desert months of April–September. Thus a season is
described as "the season of 1928–29" or "the season of 1929–30."

ning of a new life for her—the meeting of the man who would become her second husband (see *The Murder at the Vicarage*, #13, 1930).

The Seven Dials got good reviews, which, along with the now famous Christie name, brought sales in England to over 8,000 copies.

Will Cuppy in *Books* (*New York Herald Tribune*) said, "All signs indicate that Mrs. Christie has been reading P. G. Wodehouse, and she does it very well in spots; this is her gayest thriller and mustn't be missed" (3/17/29).

The *New York Times* wrote, with a note that was to be sounded often in Christie's career, "The author has been so keen on preventing the reader from guessing the solution that she has rather overstepped the bounds of what should be permitted to a writer of detective stories. She has held out information which the reader should have had" (4/7/29).

Outlook called *Seven Dials* "an amusing, exciting, well-written story," (3/20/29) while *The Nation and Athaneum* (Leonard Woolf was never too kind to Christie) took a jab that might have been made during the last decade of Christie's career. "Once Mrs. Christie was the queen of detective story writers. But her power has latterly declined" (2/23/29).

PLOT:

Sir Oswald Coote, a tycoon of humble origins and immense fortune, and his lonely, melancholy wife, Lady Maria, have taken a two-year rental on Chimneys, the historic house belonging to the Marquis of Caterham. The Cootes enjoy the company of houseguests younger than they, and so, for their final party before their lease expires, have invited half a dozen or so "bright young things" to Chimneys.

Lady Coote, who is as perplexed by the habits of her high-spirited guests as she is intimidated by the formidable house staff, finds none of the guests inclined to be punctual for breakfast. One in particular, Gerry Wade, usually breakfasts at about noon—"I suppose he will come down *sometime,* Tredwell," laments Lady Coote to the butler—and his late sleeping even becomes a topic of conversation among the guests, who hatch a plot to get lazy Gerry up a bit earlier.

Six of them troop into Market Basing, and principal merchant Mr. Murgatroyd is puzzled by the sudden flood of energetic upper-class young adults all wanting alarm clocks. After much judging of relative bell-power, they decide on one clock each, plus one purchased for another houseguest nicknamed Pongo, whose idea the clocks were in the first place, and one for Lady Coote.

Pongo is elected to place the clocks in Wade's room after he's asleep, and even the ticking of eight clocks doesn't disturb Gerry's heavy breathing. The clocks go off like the Day of Judgment, but Gerry doesn't appear, and for good reason. He is dead in his bed, of an overdose of chloral taken to induce sleep.

But Gerry's friend Ronny, on being told the cause of death by Dr. Cartwright, gets to the heart of things: Why would Gerry, of all people, take something to make him sleep?

Principal Characters: Alfred, Count Andras, Rupert "Pongo" Bateman, Superintendent Battle, Clement Edward Alistair Brent (Ninth Marquis of Caterham), Lady Eileen "Bundle" Brent, Dr. Cartwright, Lady Maria Coote, Sir Oswald Coote, Vera "Socks" Daventry, Ronny Devereux, Sir Stanley Digby, Herr Eberhard, Bill Eversleigh, Hon. George Lomax, Colonel Melrose, Mr. Mosgorovsky, Hayward Phelps, Countess Anna Radzky, Babe St. Maur, Jimmy Thesiger, Tredwell, Gerald Wade, Loraine Wade.

First Editions: British: Collins, London, January 1929. 276 pp., 7s. 6d. **American:** Dodd, Mead & Co., New York, 1929. 310 pp., $2.00.

Adaptation: A television dramatization of this novel was presented in the U.S. in April 1981. The drama was imported to the U.S. from Britain's London Weekend Television.

11

PARTNERS IN CRIME (1929)

For her collection of Tommy and Tuppence Beresford stories, which are interconnected into a novellike narrative, Christie chose to parody popular fictional detectives of the day. "It was fun to get back to them for a change," Christie wrote in her autobiography, suggesting that the Beresfords were a relaxation for their creator.

Tommy and Tuppence Beresford, happily married after their single, sleuthing days of *The Secret Adversary* (#2, 1922), are restless for adventure, which is thrust upon them when Tommy's boss, Secret Service Chief Carter, asks the Beresfords to go underground and pose as Mr. Blunt and his secretary, of Theodore Blunt's International Detective Agency. The Beresfords' job is to carry on the daily business of the agency in place of the real Mr. Blunt, who is now in official custody because of his involvement in international espionage.

Christie apparently wrote the entire collection "straight through," and though the various cases that the Beresfords solve are separate entities, they are woven into the continuous narrative of the book. For this reason, these stories were not serialized in magazines prior to publication, unlike most of Christie's stories.

The outstanding feature of this collection is the parodies it contains of various popular fictional detectives of the period. The Beresfords self-consciously adopt the methods and manners of a dozen sleuths, ranging from Holmes to Poirot.

It is difficult to tell if Christie first chose to write a series of parodies and then decided that Tommy and Tuppence, if landed in a detective agency, would suit her purposes, or if she decided to write a Tommy and Tuppence collection and then hit upon the idea of detective parodies for extra fun. In the book, the idea of parodying comes to Tuppence offhandedly, after she and Tommy are ensconced at Blunt's, and we suspect Christie's inspiration was just as casual. This is borne out in the book, where characters (and author) never take their mimicking too seriously.

In her autobiography, Christie said, "It is interesting in a way to see who of the twelve detective-story writers that I chose are still well known—some are household names, others have more or less perished in oblivion. . . . Some of [the detectives] I cannot even recognize; I remember Thornley Colton, the blind detective— Austin Freeman, of course; Freeman Wills Croft [sic] with his wonderful timetables; and inevitably Sherlock Holmes."

Critics generally liked Christie's conceit of detective-parodying. *Books* (*New York Herald Tribune*) said, "*Partners in Crime* is the kind of thing this department likes—a number of plots strung loosely together and gently spoofed the while, and preferably written either by Dorothy L. Sayers or Agatha Christie. Required reading" (8/28/29).

The *New York Times* wrote, "The entire book and the separate stories may be taken as hilarious burlesque or parodies of current detective fiction, or they may be taken as serious attempts on the part of the author to write stories in the manner of some of the masters of the art. Taken either way, they are distinctly worthwhile" (9/22/29).

"By no means as good a detective story [!] as we have a right to expect from Mrs. Christie," complained the critic for *Outlook,* "although it is amusing, and contains much good burlesque of modern sleuth yarns" (9/11/29).

The *Springfield Republican:* "It is soon apparent that in this book Miss Christie is having quiet fun with all the famous authors of mystery stories, including herself. Each story contains its quota of laughs, as well as thrills, or rather more than can ordinarily be expected from a well-turned-out mystery story" (8/25/29).

The *Times Literary Supplement* (London) wrote, "Holmes, Thorndyke, Father Brown, and even Poirot are amiably parodied, and once or twice the solution as well as the dialogue is deliberately facetious. The author is incorrect (in 'Finessing the King' and 'The Gentleman Dressed in Newspaper') in the explanation she gives of the printer's marks on newspapers, the distinction of dates which she makes really being one of editions" (10/17/29).

Readers should take note of Christie's attitude about divorce in this book—keeping in mind that in 1929, when the stories were written and published, the author was a newly divorced, single mother. In the chapter "A Pot of Tea," Tuppence says, "Ugh! . . . We shan't touch divorce cases. We must raise the tone of our new profession. . . . I've read in the papers for years that the divorce evil was growing. . . ."

Christie's Poirot parody, in the final chapter, is great fun. The Beresfords decide in true Poirot fashion that, after this one last case, they will retire to "vegetable marrow growing."

Tommy speaks in mock-Poirot fractured English. "Him whom I crushed like an egg shell in the Dolomites. . . . You comprehend, my friend? . . . mon ami, can you not part your hair in the middle instead of on one side? The present effect is unsymmetrical and deplorable."

When Tuppence jokingly boasts that her contribution to the case will be so important that it will be called the "Triumph of Hastings," Tommy rejoins, "Once the idiot friend, always the idiot friend."

And during the investigation, Tommy-Poirot makes a great point of examining the timing of people's movements, and of considering "the psychology" of the suspects.

PLOTS:

"A Fairy in the Flat"

This is an introductory chapter, in which the Beresfords' boredom and restlessness for adventure is dissipated by Chief Carter's call to duty at Blunt's. Their main concern at Blunt's is to be on the lookout for a letter bearing the number 16, part of a plot involving a spy ring, and to be on the lookout for any stranger who opens his conversation with the word *sixteen*.

"A Pot of Tea"

Ensconced in the offices of Blunt's International Detective Agency at 118 Haleham Street, London, W.C., the Beresfords meet their first client, Lawrence St. Vincent, who needs their help in finding his secret love, shopgirl Janet Smith, who has disappeared. Tuppence makes their assignment difficult by boasting to the customer that they can find the girl within twenty-four hours.

In this story the Beresfords have yet to adopt their imitation of famous detectives, though Tuppence mentions that she "has got sort of an idea" about methods of solving cases.

"The Affair of the Pink Pearl"

Tommy and Tuppence are approached by Beatrice Kingston-Bruce and her mother, who are distraught because a precious pink pearl has been stolen from their houseguest, Lady Laura Barton.

"I think I shall be Thorndyke today," says Tommy, indicating his intention of imitating Dr. John Evelyn Thorndyke, the great medico-legal detective created by R. Austin Freeman (1862–1943). Thorndyke is possessed of incomparable intellect, vast knowledge on a number of subjects, and great good looks. The *Encyclopedia of Mystery and Detection* (1976) describes Thorndyke as "a forensic scientist and lawyer whose methods are extremely technical and specialized . . . he is concerned with things, seeking clues from physical entities that will ultimately serve as irrefutable evidence . . . [he approached] each case with solemnity and painstaking exactitude."

"The Adventure of the Sinister Stranger"

The Beresfords receive the long-awaited letter from Russia, which they hope will have the crucial number 16 under its postage stamp. Unfortunately, before they can pry off the stamp they are interrupted by a strange, tall foreigner, Dr. Bower, who fears someone is trying to steal his research on "certain obscure alkaloids." Tommy goes off with Bower, leaving Tuppence alone with the valuable letter.

To deal with Dr. Bower's case, the Beresfords adopt the style and methods of Francis and Desmond, the Okewood Brothers, created by Valentine Williams (1883–1946), writing as Douglas Valentine. The Okewoods' methods typically involved Desmond getting into a life-threatening scrape, only to be rescued by Francis, who "turns up as the gardener or something in the nick of time, and saves the situation," and in this case Tuppence unwittingly takes Francis's role.

"Finessing the King" and "The Gentleman Dressed in Newspaper"

During a slack period at Blunt's, Tommy and Tuppence amuse themselves by scrutinizing the personal columns in the papers. One especially cryptic ad reads, "three hearts . . . 12 tricks . . .

Ace of Spades . . . finesse the king." Tuppence cleverly deduces that the ad refers to the Three Arts Ball (3 hearts) held at midnight (12 tricks) at the Ace of Spades, a smart Bohemian cafe. Since they can't figure out what "finesse the king" means in the ad, Tommy and Tuppence decide to attend the ball (in costume) to investigate. They discover that "finesse the king" means murder. The detectives Tommy and Tuppence impersonate are McCarty and Riordan, created by Isabel Ostrander (1885–1924).

"The Case of the Missing Lady"

When a famed arctic explorer, Gabriel Stavansson, asks the Blunt agency to find his missing fiancée, Hermione Crane, the Beresfords are led to a sinister nursing home and a disreputable doctor with questionable medical practices.

Tommy Beresford adopts a Holmesian mode for solving this case, even to the point of picking up a violin in his office and screeching out "a few chords from Mosgovskensky."

Beresford's technique is apparently pretty dreadful, for Tuppence, in the Watson role, cries out, "If you must be Sherlock Holmes . . . I'll get you a nice little syringe and a bottle labelled Cocaine, but for God's sake leave that violin alone." Of course Sherlock Holmes was created by Sir Arthur Conan Doyle (1859–1930).

"Blindman's Buff"

While lunching at the chic Gold Room of the Blitz, with Tommy masquerading as a blind detective, the Beresfords are approached by the elegant Duke of Blairgowrie for help in locating his missing daughter. Before going off to aid the duke, the "blind" Tommy dictates a vital menu to Tuppence.

Tommy is imitating Thornley Colton, "the blind problemist," the sightless detective created by Clinton Holland Stagg (1890–1916), who depends on what he hears, feels, and smells to solve his mysteries; Colton's "eyes" is his secretary, here played by Tuppence.

"The Man in the Mist"

Tommy—in the guise of a cleric—and Tuppence trail Gilda Glen, a glamorous actress, to her house on Morgan's Avenue, enshrouded in fog; en route, they meet an agitated would-be murderer, a mysterious policeman, Gilda's elderly sister, and a real murderer.

In this episode Tommy imitates Father Brown, the Catholic priest-detective created by G. K. Chesterton (1874–1936). Father Brown, who is described by the *Encyclopedia of Mystery and Detection* as "a quiet, gentle commonplace . . . priest who views wrongdoers as souls needing salvation . . . appears dull-witted before his adversaries, but possesses a sharp, subtle, sensitive mind . . . he used a psychological approach, aided by his deep understanding of human nature."

In his guise as the Father, Tommy also carries Brown's characteristically shabby umbrella.

"The Crackler"

At Inspector Marriot's behest, Tommy and Tuppence sleuth after a clever counterfeiter who has been flooding both sides of the Channel with phony bank notes. Tommy winds up in an alley with chalked X's over the doors as signals to the "gang," and traps his counterfeiter with, among other things, a jar of catnip.

This is the Beresfords as the Busies, in an Edgar Wallace-type adventure, which parodies Wallace's slapdash, action-laden thrillers. Wallace (1875–1932) was the prolific, immensely popular author of 173 books, most of them thrillers or mysteries. During the 1920s, when he often dictated a book a week, he was one of the most widely read authors in England.

"We need several hundreds of yards of extra book shelf if Edgar Wallace is to be properly represented," Tuppence says at one point, referring to Wallace's vast output. And the case that Scotland Yard assigns to Tommy and Tuppence (which they solve in the Wallace style) has strong connections with big-money gamblers and horse racing—appropriate enough since Wallace himself was a compulsive gambler and squandered a good deal of the fortune he made from his books. His losses ran as high as $500 a day.

"The Sunningdale Mystery"

When Captain Sessle is found stabbed through the heart with a hatpin while golfing on the Sunningdale links, a pretty blond is charged because she was wearing a bright red wool coat—and the deceased had a bit of red wool in his hand. But the Beresfords don't like how the investigation is being handled, and decide that there's more behind the killing than the pretty blond and the red wool.

Tommy Beresford imitates the Old Man in the Corner, the greatest of the armchair detectives, a character created by Baroness Emma Orczy (1865–1947). The Old Man, who remains nameless, solves his mysteries while sitting in the corner of a tea shop; information on cases is brought to him by Polly Burton, a young reporter for the *Evening Observer*. The Old Man ponders his cases while tying and untying knots in an old piece of string which he carries with him—a habit Tommy copies; Tuppence logically takes the role of Polly Burton.

"The House of Lurking Death"

Young Lois Hargreaves, who has recently become wealthy owing to the death of a maiden aunt, calls on Tommy and Tuppence when she is sent a box of poisoned chocolates. As it turns out, it's not the chocolates that are deadly.

For this case the Beresfords adopt the methods of Inspector Gabriel Hanaud, the great detective of the French Sûreté. Hanaud, who first appeared in a book in 1910, is the creation of Alfred Edward Woodley Mason (1865–1948). Hanaud's style tends toward straightforward police detection, aided by his sidekick Mr. Ricardo (Tuppence's role), who is characteristically left in the dark until the last moment as to the solution of a case.

"The Unbreakable Alibi"

Una Drake, a capricious Australian, has challenged her fiancé, wealthy Mr. Montgomery-Jones, to crack two unimpeachable alibis that she will establish to prove that she was in two different places at the same time. Despairing that Una will not marry him if he cannot guess how she managed this feat, Montgomery-Jones calls on Tommy and Tuppence for help.

This case is solved in the manner of Inspector Joseph French, the easygoing, happily married Scotland Yard detective created by Freeman Wills Crofts (1879–1957). French is apt to discuss cases with his wife, and to get valuable help from her, a situation Christie takes advantage of in her takeoff. Since French is noted for his expertise in breaking cases in which there is an unimpeachable alibi, Christie plots this story with an Inspector French-style plot.

"The Clergyman's Daughter" & "The Red House"

An old aunt has left Monica Deane and her mother a large house but no means by which to maintain it. The mother and daughter want to keep the lovely home, but find it necessary to take in lodgers to keep the place up. Unfortunately the house seems to be inhabited by poltergeists, which makes it difficult to keep lodgers, but the Deanes are besieged by a prospective buyer, who seems a bit *too* anxious to buy the "haunted" house. When Tommy and Tuppence investigate they find not only the spiteful spirits, but the reason the prospective buyer is so anxious to own the house.

This adventure is handled in the style of Roger Sheringham, the vain, talkative detective created by Anthony Berkeley Cox (1893–1970). Sheringham is described in *Twentieth Century Crime Writers* (1980) as "an amateur detective . . . loquacious, conceited, occasionally downright offensive . . . something of a man about town. Sheringham is noted for solving cases that involve several complicated puzzles. In his first book, *The Layton Court Mystery* (1925), for example, he proves that a "suicide" is in fact a locked-room murder.

A. B. Cox (who wrote under several pseudonyms) is notable as the founder of the Detection Club, the "keeper of the flame" of mystery writing standards, an organization to which Christie belonged. Cox's most famous books are *Malice Aforethought* (1931) and *Before the Fact* (1932), both written under the pseudonym Francis Isles.

"The Ambassador's Boots"

The American ambassador, Randolph Wilmot, consults Tommy and Tuppence when his kit bag, monogrammed RW, is switched by mistake or intent with that of Senator Ralph Westerman. The senator's valet shows up at the embassy to exchange the bags, but it later comes out that the senator has never heard of this valet, or of any confusion among kit bags.

The detective in this case is Dr. Reggie Fortune, the creation of H. C. Bailey (1878–1961). Fortune, the son of a middle-class doctor, is himself a surgeon and consultant to Scotland Yard; more important, Reggie is a consummate snob, prone to effete speech mannerisms, who proclaims himself a "man of the people" while consuming enormous gourmet meals or driving around in his Rolls-Royce.

Tuppence proclaims herself Reggie Fortune, "because I feel like a lot of hot butter."

"The Man Who Was No. 16"

In this final case, the Beresfords come face-to-face with their "secret adversary."

The case, which involves a certain amount of peril for the Beresfords, is solved by the use of "little gray cells" to arrange facts "neatly, and with order." At the end of the case, however, Tommy-Hercule is presented with some news from Tuppence that the real Poirot would not have found amusing.

First Editions: **British**: Collins, London, September 1929. 251 pp., 7s. 6d. **American**: Dodd, Mead & Co., 1929. 277 pp., $2.00.

Adaptation: A television adaptation is to be aired by London Weekend Television, in England, and by PBS Television in America during 1984. Francesca Annis and James Warwick star as Tuppence and Tommy Beresford.

12

THE MYSTERIOUS MR. QUIN (1930)

According to Christie's autobiography, these short stories, all of which were written for magazines during the 1920s, are her personal favorites among her more than one hundred short works. Given her fondness for Mr. Quin, it is all the stranger that he was dropped as a character for the rest of Christie's career, a fact for which Christie gave no explanation.*

If Christie's reasons for dropping Quin from her repertoire are mysterious, her reasons for creating him are better documented. As a girl, Agatha often attended theatre in London and Paris with her family, and she acted in amateur theatricals in Torquay. Agatha became fascinated with the characters of the commedia dell'arte: Harlequin, Columbine, Pierrot, Pierrette, Punchinello, and Punchinella. The character of Harlequin became her particular favorite, with his bright, multicolored costume and his mysterious comings and goings.

Harlequin, like all the commedia figures, has a long history on the stage. In the sixteenth century, Arlecchino was a sly, covetous, and cowardly servant. By the seventeenth century, he had become a faithful, patient valet. By the eighteenth century, when the English stage adapted the commedia characters into its own version of the harlequinade, Harlequin had become a romantic character, paired with Columbine. In English theatre, he evolved into a character whom the *Oxford English Dictionary* describes as having "many attributes of the clown . . . with the addition of mischievous intrigue." He also acquired the ability to be invisible at times, which helped in his "intrigues," and the harlequinade became, as the dictionary describes it, "a fantastic procedure," as in

* There is one stray Quin story, "The Love Detectives," which was published in *Three Blind Mice and Other Stories* (#51, 1950), but it dates from the 1920s also.

Edgar Allan Poe's line, "Every trick of thought and every harlequinade of phrase."

When Christie created Mr. Harley Quin, she incorporated these
aspects of the theatrical Harlequin. In every story, he appears and
disappears quickly and unexpectedly, almost as if into thin air. (In
a Quin story, if there is an unexpected rap at the door, one can be
sure it's Mr. Quin knocking.) And Quin's clothing often takes on
multicolored, harlequinlike patterns, always by some trick of light,
such as sun through a stained glass window, or flickering firelight.

Once Quin appears, he does not actually solve a case. That role
is left to Mr. Satterthwaite, Quin's longtime friend who is on hand
in every Quin story.* Satterthwaite is a rather dry, cerebral bachelor, an art connoisseur and amateur photographer. Christie's second husband, Max Mallowan, in his memoirs describes Satterthwaite as "a born snob, who moves preferably in the highest
aristocratic circles. . . . He is preoccupied with pushing aside the
shutter and looking through the window into the truth of people's
lives." In this respect, Satterthwaite is like the observer-character
found so often in Henry James: the man who fills the vacuum of
his own empty life with an intense interest in observing the lives of
others.

Satterthwaite is the prototypical cultured bachelor houseguest,
and it is in his hosts' homes that he most often encounters and observes the "problem" to be solved, whether it be stolen jewels, a
love triangle, or murder. Though Satterthwaite always collects the
facts and "the atmosphere" of a case, the solution always eludes
him, until Mr. Quin makes one of his sudden appearances. Quin
works what Satterthwaite calls his "magic" merely by asking a few
pointed questions, by making a few simple observations, which
cause the scales to fall from Satterthwaite's eyes. As Satterthwaite
describes it, Mr. Quin shows "you what you have seen with your
own eyes," and "makes clear to you what you have heard with
your own ears." Thus enlightened, Satterthwaite solves the mystery at hand.

This ability of Quin's to act as a mysterious, inexplicable cata-

---

* Satterthwaite makes a few appearances without Quin: *Three Act Tragedy*
(#23, 1935) and "Dead Man's Mirror" from *Murder in the Mews* (#28,
1937).

lyst in a case is Christie's translation of the commedia Harlequin's "mischievous intrigue" and "fantastic procedure" into the detective story. He is more of a conjuror than a real detective, and in this sense is the antithesis of the super-ratiocinator Hercule Poirot.

Christie's concept of the Harlequin figure that she evolved into Mr. Harley Quin is revealed in her first volume of poetry, *The Road of Dreams* (1924). This volume contains a series of poems on the commedia dell'arte figures, poems that predate the Quin stories. One of them, "Harlequin's Song," describes a clever, invisible, but ultimately sad trickster.

> I pass
> Where'er I've a mind,
> With a laugh as I dance,
> And a leap so high,
> With a lightning glance,
> And a crash and a flash
> In the summer sky!
> I come in the wind,
> And I go with a sigh . . .
>> And nobody ever sees Harlequin,
>> "Happy go lucky" Harlequin,
>> Go by. . . .

The poem concludes,

>> I must play my part. . . .
>> For never a soul has Harlequin,
>> *Happy go lucky Harlequin,*
>> Only a broken heart. . . .

Christie liked her Harlequin–Mr. Harley Quin character so much that she dedicated the collection of stories "To Harlequin, The Invisible," the only time in Christie's work that a character receives a book dedication.

The *Times Literary Supplement* (London) echoed the Jamesian theme. "A dozen episodes in the life of Mr. Satterthwaite who has never done much himself but has an insatiable interest in the doings of other people. . . . Mr. Harley Quin . . . has a queer

power of making him perceive a new significance in events"
(5/29/30).

Saturday Review of Literature predicted, "The book will give
you many problems to solve and a chuckle over Mrs. Christie's
entertaining and subtle humor" (5/24/30), while the *New York
Times* wrote, "The book offers a rare treat for discriminating
readers" (5/1/30).

PLOTS:

"The Coming of Mr. Quin"

Prim, cultured bachelor Mr. Satterthwaite meets the remarkable
Mr. Harley Quin for the first time on New Year's Eve, while visiting Mr. and Mrs. Tom Eversham at Royston Hall. Mr. Satterthwaite's attention focuses on Mr. and Mrs. Porter, two fellow
guests, she uncommonly magnetic, he uncommonly nervous. Just
after midnight—the weather is beastly—a stranger appears at the
door. Perhaps it's the effect of the stained glass above the door,
but the man appears to be dressed in every color of the rainbow.
When he steps in, it's a "thin dark man," Mr. Harley Quin, who
says "my car broke down." Soon the pleasant but mysterious
stranger mentions that he knew the former owner of Royston Hall,
Derek Capel, who unexpectedly shot himself one morning after
reading that a Mr. Appleton's body was going to be exhumed. Satterthwaite soon realizes that Mr. Quin is expertly setting the scene
for a drama having to do with the inhabitants, past and present, of
Royston Hall.

"The Shadow on the Glass"

When African hunter Richard Scott arrives at the Unkertons'
house party with his new wife, knowing a woman from his past
will be there, the result is double murder, a legendary cavalier's
head stain that mysteriously appears on a certain window, and the
sudden appearance of Mr. Quin, who points out all the right clues,
solving the murder with almost supernatural cleverness.

"At the Bells and Motley"

When Mr. Satterthwaite's chauffeured car breaks down in isolated Kirtlington Mallet, he seeks refuge at the local inn, the Bells
and Motley, where he finds only one other guest, Mr. Quin. The

problem at hand is poor Mary, the innkeeper's daughter, whose fiancé, Stephen, is being unjustly charged with doing away with his former employer at the Grange.

"The Sign in the Sky"

Mr. Satterthwaite attends the trial of young Martin Wylde for the murder of Lady Vivien Barnaby at her home, Deering Hill. Shortly after the guilty verdict is returned, Satterthwaite runs into his mysterious friend, Harley Quin. Together they unravel why the maid's report of an ominous pattern of smoke from a train smokestack the day of the murder landed her a high-paying job abroad.

"The Soul of the Croupier"

Mr. Satterthwaite, on his annual jaunt to Monte Carlo, finds himself, in the company of Mr. Quin, caught in an unhappy love triangle involving the charming, naive young American, Franklin Rudge; Elizabeth Martin, the pretty young American girl who obviously loves him; and the glamorous, fashionable Countess Czarnova, many years Franklin's senior.

"The World's End"

Mr. Satterthwaite has come to Corsica with his friend the Duchess of Leith, where they meet the duchess's cousin Naomi Carlton-Smith. Naomi is distraught, even suicidal, because her fiancé, Alec Gerard, has been accused of stealing a valuable opal from famed stage actress Rosina Nunn, who is herself in Corsica. On a drive around the rugged island, Satterthwaite and Naomi meet none other than Mr. Quin, who quickly puts things to right concerning the missing jewel.

"The Voice in the Dark"

In Cannes, Mr. Satterthwaite meets his old friend Lady Barbara Stanleigh, rich and remarkably beautiful for her years, who asks him to look into her daughter Margery's disturbing reports that the family seat, Abbot's Mead, is haunted. Back in England, after a not-unusual encounter with Mr. Quin, Satterthwaite finds himself looking into the tragedy of many years before, when Lady Barbara's elder sister was killed in the sinking of the liner *Uralia*. It's dead sister Beatrice that seems to be haunting her surviving relatives.

"The Face of Helen"

At Covent Garden for a performance of *Cavalleria Rusticana* and *Pagliacci,* Mr. Satterthwaite spots Mr. Quin during the interval. After the evening (the appropriateness of *Pagliacci* to Mr. Quin's persona not going unnoticed by his friend), they witness a fight outside the opera house: two men engaging in fisticuffs while a female companion cowers against a wall. The girl turns out to be Gillian West, caught in a life-or-death struggle between two men who love her.

"The Dead Harlequin"

Mr. Satterthwaite attends the London exhibit of up-and-coming artist Frank Bristow, where he sees a remarkable painting by the artist. The painting depicts a Harlequin, with a face resembling that of Satterthwaite's friend Mr. Quin, standing over his dead twin. The setting is the terrace room at Charnley, which Satterthwaite recognizes as the place where Lord Charnley shot himself fourteen years before.

"The Bird with the Broken Wing"

While guesting with the Keeleys at their country house, Laidell, Mr. Satterthwaite happens to be in the library while the younger guests are holding a table-turning and rapping séance. Among the garbled and somewhat nonsensical messages is one clear one: QUIN and LAIDELL. Before long there is a tragic death in the house, and Satterthwaite, with the help of a message from Mr. Quin, correctly determines that it wasn't suicide, but murder.

"The Man from the Sea"

Satterthwaite has deserted the Riviera for a Mediterranean island, where, in the garden of a villa called La Paz, he encounters a stranger, Anthony Cosden, just as Cosden is about to leap to his death. Satterthwaite learns that this was not Cosden's first attempt. Just the night before, a tall, dark, otherworldly character— Mr. Harley Quin, of course—had stayed his first attempt. Satterthwaite learns that Cosden's unhappy past is linked to a reclusive woman on the island, and helps bring some happiness into the man's life.

"Harlequin's Lane"

While visiting with the rather dull, conventional Denmans, Mr. Satterthwaite unexpectedly meets Mr. Quin on a road called Harlequin's Lane, which ends at a rubbish heap, the site of the Denmans' first and happier home. Later, a harlequinade at the Denmans' present home, complete with Pierrot, Harlequin, and Columbine, the classic characters from the commedia dell'arte, has a profound influence on the lives of those living on Harlequin's Lane.

First Editions: British: Collins, London, April 1930. 287 pp., 7s. 6d. **American:** Dodd, Mead & Co., New York, 1930. 290 pp., $2.00.

Adaptation: The first English-language film version of a Christie work was adapted from the short story "The Coming of Mr. Quin." The film, titled *The Passing of Mr. Quinn* (sic), was released in 1928.

13

THE MURDER AT THE VICARAGE (1930)

In *The Murder at the Vicarage,* Agatha Christie gives us our first view (in novel form) of St. Mary Mead, the typical English country village, and its leading citizen, the sharp-eyed, fluffy old spinster, Miss Jane Marple. The creation of Miss Marple was a turning point in Christie's career, and gained for her a new audience—the woman reader—the housewife and mother, the schoolmistress, the middle-class matron of English society. These were the readers who could identify with the intelligent "old pussy," Miss Marple, who from her vantage point in her much-loved garden saw and heard all the "goings-on" of St. Mary Mead. As Miss Marple was apt to say on many occasions, "There is a great deal of wickedness in village life," and St. Mary Mead was never to cease being a fertile field of wickedness—from scandal to murder.

The fictional village of St. Mary Mead is about twenty-five miles from London, and twelve miles from the coast. The main train station is in Much Benham, two miles away. Although this is the first novel which takes place in St. Mary Mead, the village itself was mentioned several times in her novel *The Mystery of the Blue Train* (#9, 1928). In chapter 7 of *Blue Train* a letter is addressed to "Miss Katherine Grey, Little Crampton, St. Mary Mead, Kent."

Agatha Christie noted in her autobiography that *"Murder at the Vicarage* was published in 1930, but I cannot remember where, when or how I wrote it, why I came to write it, or even what suggested to me that I should select a new character—Miss Marple—to act as a sleuth in the story." Christie went on to say that she "had no intention of continuing her for the rest of my life" or that Miss Marple would "become a rival to Hercule Poirot."

Miss Marple, whose passions in life were gossip, knitting, and seeing the worst side of human nature, had a very sweet and gentle appearance, faded blue eyes, and snowy hair. "Miss Marple was born at the age of sixty-five to seventy—which, as with Poirot, proved unfortunate," said Christie in her autobiography, "because she was going to have to last a long time in my life." (For more on Miss Marple, see *The Thirteen Problems*, #16, 1932.) The character arose, according to Christie, "from the pleasure" she'd had in creating Dr. Sheppard's sister Caroline in *The Murder of Roger Ackroyd* (#7, 1926). Caroline, Christie's favorite character in that book, was "an acidulated spinster, full of curiosity, knowing everything, hearing everything—the complete detective service in the home."

Miss Marple had some faint resemblance to Agatha Christie's grandmother. "Miss Marple was not in any way a picture of my grandmother," Christie wrote. "She was far more fussy and spinsterish than my grandmother ever was. But one thing she did have in common with her—though a cheerful person she always expected the worst of everyone and everything—and was with almost frightening accuracy usually proved right."

Although Christie makes no mention of this in her memoirs, another possible influence on her creation of Miss Marple is her reading of *The Leavenworth Case* when she was eight years old. When Christie's sister, Madge, recounted the story of this book to her, Christie found it fascinating and promptly read the book herself. (For more on the early reading habits of Christie, see *The Mysterious Affair at Styles*, #1, 1920.)

The Leavenworth Case, written by American-born Anna Katharine Green (1846–1935), was published in 1878. Green was the first woman to write detective fiction. It is quite possible then, that since the young Christie was so enthusiastic about this book, she might have gone on to read other detective fiction by Green, who wrote more than thirty detective novels. One of those novels was *That Affair Next Door*, published in 1897. In this book Green introduced to the world of fiction the very first elderly spinster busybody detective, the well-bred Miss Amelia Butterworth. Miss Butterworth, who possessed the Marple nosiness, was, like her literary descendant, able to utilize that trait by becoming an unofficial assistant detective. She appeared in six novels.

Miss Marple was not to appear again in a novel until 1942 when *The Body in the Library* (#40) was published. Miss Marple did appear however in the short story collection *The Thirteen*

Problems (#16, 1932). Six of these stories had previously been published in 1928 in the *Sketch*.

Agatha Christie has said that in "reading *Murder at the Vicarage* now, I am not so pleased with it as I was at the time. It has, I think, far too many characters, and too many subplots. But at any rate the *main* plot is sound." The critics' reviews were mixed, with R. I. Center, in *Saturday Review of Literature,* giving a positive notice: "Any book by Agatha Christie attracts attention but when she really hits her stride in a full length detective story, as she does in *The Murder at the Vicarage,* she is hard to surpass" (11/22/30). However, Bruce Rae in the *New York Times* said, "The talented Miss Christie is far from being at her best in her latest mystery story. It will add little to her eminence in the field of detective fiction" (11/30/30).

The Murder at the Vicarage, one of Christie's most popular books, was the first of her mysteries to be published as part of her publisher Collins's new Crime Club series, which was introduced in 1930 by Sir Godfrey Collins and his nephew, William Collins. The Crime Club was not a book club, but a series of mystery titles published and promoted under the name.

The Murder at the Vicarage was also the first title of a new six-book contract Christie signed with Collins in 1930. The first printing of *The Murder at the Vicarage* was 5,500 copies, as was the first printing of the first title to be released in the Crime Club series, *The Noose* by Philip Macdonald.

In addition to professional achievements, 1930 was an important year in Christie's personal life. In the autumn of 1928, when Christie first visited the Middle East and the archaeological site at Ur, she had become friends with the director of the dig and his wife, Leonard and Katharine Woolley, and they had invited her to return to Ur for the following digging season of winter–spring 1929–30. (Refer to *The Seven Dials Mystery,* #10, 1929.) It was during this second visit in March of 1930 that Christie first met Max Mallowan, the young twenty-six-year-old archaeologist and assistant to Leonard Woolley, who would within the year become her second husband.

Max had graduated from Oxford in 1925 and had only one career in mind. As he wrote in his memoirs, when asked by the dean of the college what his plans were, he answered, "Just one thing—Archaeology." The dean suggested he go see the warden (H.A.L. Fisher), who helped him find a position. There was a vacant post as an assistant to Leonard Woolley, who was about to reopen his excavation site of the Chaldees at Ur. Max said, "Woolley, always in a hurry, practically engaged me on site." Max arrived at Ur "on a dark night in October 1925, filled with great expectations." Max had been working at Ur for five seasons, gaining valuable experience which would eventually enable him to undertake his own excavations, when Christie arrived in 1930 for her second visit. (During Christie's first visit, Max had been absent with appendicitis.)

Christie arrived for her second visit at Ur in the middle of a fierce sandstorm, which, as she recalled in her autobiography, was "five days of near torture." The time, however, was spent having friendly talks with members of the team, including Max. Christie described him as a "thin, dark, young man, and very quiet—he seldom spoke, but was receptive to everything that was required of him." It was when Katharine Woolley "ordered" Max to take Christie on a sight-seeing trip so that Christie might see some of the desert and interesting sights along the way to Baghdad, that they both realized how much they enjoyed each other's company. The digging season was coming to a close now, and the Woolleys were to meet Christie in Baghdad. Christie protested to Katharine, thinking Max might not enjoy being forced to be a travel guide. However, Katharine was insistent, saying Max would enjoy the trip. Max recalled in his memoirs that he found Christie "a most agreeable person and the prospect pleasing," and that he never thought that "the short journey to Baghdad would lead to a longer union which was destined to last for the best part of fifty years."

The journey went well and they arrived in Baghdad in good spirits. From there, they traveled back to London together, since this was the end of the digging season. Part of the trip home took place on the Simplon–Orient Express. Max wrote that the journey home "at the end of March was wholly enjoyable and gave me the firm intention of seeking Agatha's hand when we reached home."

They were married on September 11, 1930, in a quiet ceremony at St. Columba's* Church in Edinburgh, Scotland. Christie was forty years old and Max was twenty-six. (However, on their marriage certificate, Christie listed her age as thirty-seven and Max thirty-one.) The ceremony was very quiet and private with the only guests present being Christie's secretary and friend Charlotte Fisher, her sister, Mary Fisher, Christie's eleven-year-old daughter, Rosalind (from her marriage to Archie Christie), and Christie's dog, Peter. Christie recalled the wedding in her autobiography as being "quite a triumph—there were no reporters and no hint of the secret had leaked out." Christie was very shy of any type of publicity pertaining to her private life, especially after the sensational and much publicized headlines she created with her disappearance in December 1926. The marriage lasted forty-six years, until Christie's death in 1976. This marriage was to be for both Christie and Max one of great joy and contentment.

Another event of interest in 1930 was the publication of a romantic novel titled *Giant's Bread* by an unknown author named Mary Westmacott. It was not until fifteen years later that the public learned Miss Westmacott was actually Agatha Christie (see Miscellaneous Christie Books, #1).

The Murder at the Vicarage is dedicated "To Rosalind." Rosalind Christie Prichard Hicks, Agatha Christie's only child, was born in 1919, and would have been about ten or eleven when the first Jane Marple book was dedicated to her. Christie considered Rosalind to be one of her severest critics, one "who has had the valuable role in life of eternally trying to discourage me without success." Rosalind's first husband, Hubert Prichard, was killed in World War II. They had one son, Mathew, who was born in 1943. Rosalind later married Anthony Hicks.

PLOT:
One day at luncheon at the vicarage in St. Mary Mead, the vicar mentions to his wife that "any one who murdered Colonel Protheroe would be doing the world at large a service."

---

* In Christie's autobiography, she said that she was married in St. Columba's Church. Her biographer Gwen Robyns in *The Mystery of Agatha Christie* (1978) wrote that the ceremony took place in St. Cuthbert's Church.

Colonel Protheroe, the "pompous old brute" who inhabits Old Hall with his wife, Anne, and a son and daughter, is not a popular man in St. Mary Mead. In his capacities as magistrate and church-warden, he espouses a philosophy of "firmness," and thinks what the world needs is "a little militant Christianity."

That afternoon, the vicar learns that Lettice, the colonel's daughter and "something of a minx," is having her portrait done, in her bathing suit, by Lawrence Redding, the handsome young artist who lets a studio on the vicarage grounds. Old Protheroe has created quite a "shemozzle," as Lettice calls it, over the por-trait sitting.

Later, over "tea and scandal" in the drawing room, talk turns to the latest gossip in St. Mary Mead. Among the callers to tea is Miss Jane Marple, the vicar's next-door neighbor, who "always sees everything" and for whom "Gardening is as good as a smoke screen, and the habit of observing birds through powerful glasses can always be turned to account." Talk turns to Lawrence Red-ding and Lettice Protheroe, whom Miss Marple thinks innocent of hanky-panky—with one another at least.

The observant spinster is proven right, for the vicar stumbles on the handsome painter in passionate embrace, not with Lettice, but with her mother, Anne Protheroe. Their secret out, Lawrence Redding confesses to the vicar that he wishes the colonel were dead, and "good riddance to everybody."

On Thursday, the vicar has an appointment with the colonel at the vicarage. When the vicar arrives late, he discovers the body of Colonel Protheroe sprawled across the vicar's own writing table, shot through the head. Lawrence Redding is implicated.

Though the investigation is handled officially by Dr. Haydock, the village physician, and Inspector Slack, it is Miss Marple who successfully unravels the confusing clues and weaves them into a solution to the murder.

Principal Characters: Dennis Clement, Griselda Clement, Leonard Clement, Gladys Cram, Gladys (Gladdie), Mr. Hawes, Dr. Hay-dock, Mrs. Lestrange, Jane Marple, Colonel Melchett, Martha Price Ridley, Anne Protheroe, Lettice Protheroe, Colonel Lucius Protheroe, Lawrence Redding, Reeves, Inspector Slack, Dr. Stone, Raymond West, Caroline Wetherby.

First Editions: British: Collins, London, October 1930. 254 pp., 7s. 6d. **American:** Dodd, Mead & Co., New York, 1930. 319 pp., $2.00.

Adaptation: *The Murder at the Vicarage* was dramatized by Moie Charles and Barbara Toy as a play with the same title. It opened December 14, 1949, in the Playhouse Theatre, London.

14

THE SITTAFORD MYSTERY / MURDER AT HAZELMOOR (1931)

The Sittaford Mystery was probably written in 1929, before Christie's second journey to Ur in the Middle East. This novel was her first published work after her whirlwind courtship and marriage to Max Mallowan in September 1930.

When the honeymoon was over, Max and Agatha had to separate for a while. They were in Athens when Max had to return to Ur to help finish building additions to the burnt-brick expedition house that expedition leader Leonard Woolley wanted ready for them when they returned to Ur. So off Max went, and Christie returned to England on the Orient Express. She returned to her London house at 22 Cresswell Place, where she spent her lonely hours separated from her new husband, playing the piano in the music room on the top floor of the house. Christie was reunited with Max at Ur in March 1931. Since they were married for only a brief time before they had to separate, Christie wondered if she would feel shy when meeting again. Her fears were unfounded; "rather to my surprise it was as if we had met the day before," she recalls in her autobiography.

Christie uses Dartmoor as the setting, an area of England very familiar and nostalgic for the author. It was at the Moorland Hotel at Hay Tor, "a large dreary hotel," on Dartmoor that Christie completed the manuscript of her first mystery novel, *The Mysterious Affair at Styles* (#1, 1920).

It was sometime during this period that the Mallowans purchased Winterbrook House, a "delightful, small, Queen Anne house" on the Thames River in Wallingford, Berkshire. Christie wrote in her memoirs that this house was "Max's house, and always has been. Ashfield was my house, and I think Rosalind's."

This is the first time that Christie, who had a keen interest in the supernatural, touches upon that theme in one of her novels, although some of her earliest and finest short stories have supernatural themes (see *The Hound of Death*, #18, 1933).

"An excellent book to take away for a weekend reading," said the *New York Times* (8/16/31). The *Boston Transcript* wrote, "As a story it is nearly right for a summer holiday as anything can well be. As a novel it suffers from the author's very definite aim of preventing you from guessing the outcome. Her technique is clumsy. . . . But then, this is for pastime and as such it is excellent" (9/15/31). Will Cuppy in *Books* (*New York Herald Tribune*) wrote, "You can't go wrong with this one, certainly the best of the always high-grade Christie items in quite some time" (8/23/31).

PLOT:

A rare blizzard has struck England, and in the tiny village of Sittaford, high on the fringe of Dartmoor, the powder has accumulated to depths of several feet, effectively isolating the place from the nearest town, Exhampton, six miles away.

Retired army man Major Burnaby, still hale and athletic for his sixty-odd years, leaves his cottage for an afternoon visit to Sittaford House, a retirement place built ten years before by his old friend and fellow sportsman, Captain Joseph Trevelyan, R.N. But Trevelyan has rented Sittaford for the winter and taken a cheaper cottage in Exhampton. The seasonal tenants are Mrs. Willett, a wealthy widow, and her twenty-year-old daughter, Violet. Residents of the village find it odd that a woman of Mrs. Willett's means would want to winter in as isolated a spot as Sittaford.

Major Burnaby misses his bachelor evenings with Trevelyan and he doesn't care much for the Willetts or their other guests, but society is limited in a lonely place like Sittaford. As the evening gets on, a séance is proposed, and the group gathers around a table, with the usual mixture of giggles and disbelief. A series of rappings starts coming through and, after several unimportant messages, spells out TREVELYAN DEAD and then MURDER. This casts a pall on the group, and the séance is halted. Even though "I don't believe in this tommy rot," Major Burnaby is still concerned about Joe Trevelyan. Finally, he tells Mrs. Willett he has decided to leave the party—there are no phones in Sittaford—and trek to Exhampton to check on Trevelyan.

Mrs. Willett warns him about the weather, but he insists on going, saying the trip will take him only about two hours. Two and a half hours later, "emitting the loud sighing gasps of an utterly exhausted man," Major Burnaby rings the bell at Hazelmoor, Trevelyan's rented cottage in Exhampton. There is no answer. He makes his way to the police station and summons Constable Graves. Reluctantly Graves goes to Hazelmoor, where they find Trevelyan dead, for two, possibly three, hours . . . about the time of the message from the "spirit world."

Principal Characters: Major John Edward Burnaby, Martin Dering, Sylvia Dering, Mr. Duke, Charles Enderby, Rebecca Evans, Robert Henry Evans, Jennifer Gardner, Captain Robert Gardner, Ronald Garfield, Constable Graves, Inspector Narracott, Brian Pearson, James Pearson, Caroline Percehouse, Sergeant Pollock, Mr. Rycroft, Emily Trefusis, Captain Joseph Arthur Trevelyan, Mrs. Willett, Violet Willett, Captain Wyatt.

First Editions: **British**: Collins, London, January 1931. 250 pp., 7s. 6d. **American**: Dodd, Mead & Co., New York, 1931. 308 pp., $2.00.

Adaptation: None.

15

PERIL AT END HOUSE (1932)

In 1932, Christie went with her husband Max to the prehistoric mound Arpachiyah, near Mosul, where he was to conduct a dig of his own, "wholly free of servitude to others," as he recalled in his memoirs. Beginning with the dig at Nineveh, the year before, Max and Agatha remained inseparable, and she joined Max on all his expeditions to the Middle East, where she lent able support as a field assistant.

During these past three years of Christie's life, she'd been through a divorce and a remarriage, traveled to the Middle East on archaeological digs, and turned out seven books—four novels and three short story collections. The four novels were *The Seven Dials Mystery* (#10, 1929), *The Murder at the Vicarage* (#13, 1930), *The Sittaford Mystery* (#14, 1931), and *Peril at End House*. The short story collections were *Partners in Crime* (#11, 1929), *The Mysterious Mr. Quin* (#12, 1930), and *The Thirteen Problems* (#16, 1932). With such productivity from the "sausage machine," as Christie often referred to herself, it's easy to understand why she said in her autobiography that *"Peril at End House* was another of my books which left so little impression on my mind that I cannot even remember writing it. Possibly I had already thought out the plot some time previously, since this has always been a habit of mine, and often confuses me as to when a book was written or published."

Christie wrote that at this point in her career she still didn't consider herself a "bona fide author," even though she could count on her writing as a source of income. Her occupation was that of "married woman" and "as a sideline" she wrote books. However, she "wanted to be a good detective-story writer," and by this time in her career Christie said she was beginning to be "conceited enough to think that I *was* a good detective-story writer."

Peril at End House may have been a vague memory to Christie, but the critics took notice and were full of praise. The *Times Literary Supplement* (London) wrote, "The actual solution is quite unusually ingenious, and well up to the level of Mrs. Christie's best stories" (4/14/32). Will Cuppy in *Books* (*New York Herald Tribune*) wrote, *"Peril at End House* is a most agreeable time-killer" (3/6/32). The *Springfield Republican* wrote, "Those that like a good Christie mystery will find this the best of the lot," (4/3/32) and the *New York Times* critic Isaac Anderson said, "This person who is responsible for the dirty work at *End House* is diabolically clever, but not quite clever enough to fool the little Belgian detective all the time. A good story with a most surprising finish" (3/6/32).

Christie's dedication for this book was "To Eden Phillpotts, to whom I shall always be grateful for his friendship and the encouragement he gave me many years ago." The story of how Phillpotts encouraged and helped Christie in the early stages of her career can be found in the chapter on *The Mysterious Affair at Styles* (#1, 1920).

PLOT:

Hercule Poirot and Captain Hastings are at the Hotel Majestic at St. Loo, the "Queen of Watering Places," for a proposed week's stay. As they walk along the terrace of the hotel on their first morning, Poirot stumbles on some steps, twisting his ankle and falling at the feet of a pretty, dark-haired girl with dark blue eyes. To Hastings's delight, Poirot regains his composure and insists that the girl join them for a cocktail on the terrace. She turns out to be Nick Buckley, the last of a long line of Buckleys inhabiting End House, perched in isolation on a rocky point visible from the hotel. Hastings finds it "rather eerie and imposing standing by itself far from anything."

Nick reassures the men that life isn't at all gloomy at End House—"usually a cheery crowd coming and going"—and if there's a ghost, it's a "beneficent one. I've had three escapes from sudden death in as many days so I must bear a charmed life."

Poirot perks up at this, but further questioning is interrupted when a bee buzzes past Nick's head, causing her to jerk suddenly. Before they can get back to her scrapes with death, Nick is greeted by Commander George Challenger, one of the men she is at the Majestic to meet, and is whisked off to the bar.

Her hat is left behind. Poirot picks up the wide-brimmed felt chapeau and points out to an amazed Hastings the bullet hole in the brim. The bee was a bullet.

Poirot declares that it was *la mauvaise chance* for the would-be murderer who "shot at his victim within a dozen yards of Hercule Poirot!" With Hastings in tow, the Belgian sets out to unmask the *Peril at End House*.

Principal Characters: Reverend Giles Buckley, Jean Buckley, Maggie Buckley, Nick Buckley, Commander George Challenger, Bert Croft, Milly Croft, Captain Arthur Hastings, Chief Inspector James Japp, Jim Lazarus, Hercule Poirot, Mr. Rice, Frederica Rice, Charles Vyse, Dr. Whitefield, Ellen Wilson.

First Editions: **British**: Collins, London, March 1932. 252 pp., 7s. 6d. **American**: Dodd, Mead & Co., New York, 1932. 270 pp., $2.00.

Adaptation: *Peril at End House* was adapted for the stage by Arnold Ridley. The play opened May 1, 1940, at the Vaudeville Theatre, London, and starred Francis L. Sullivan as Poirot.

16

THE THIRTEEN PROBLEMS / THE TUESDAY CLUB MURDERS (1932)

Though Jane Marple made her first appearance in a full-length novel in 1930 in *The Murder at the Vicarage* (#13, 1930), the spinster of St. Mary Mead was created in 1928 with the publication of six short stories which eventually became the first half of the baker's dozen of *The Thirteen Problems*.

"I wrote a series of six stories for a magazine and chose six people whom I thought might meet once a week in a small village and describe some unsolved crime. I started with Miss Jane Marple, the sort of old lady who would have been rather like some of my grandmother's Ealing cronies—old ladies whom I have met in so many villages where I have gone to stay as a girl" (refer to *The Murder at the Vicarage,* #13 for detailed discussion on Miss Marple).

Christie structured her collection around the "Tuesday Night Club" (hence the American title). The six members of this impromptu crime-solving club included two characters who were to be with Marple to the very end: her nephew Raymond West, "a modern novelist who dealt with strong meat in his books, incest, sex, and sordid descriptions of bedrooms and lavatory equipment." From their beginnings in *The Thirteen Problems,* right up to *Nemesis* (#78, 1971), nephew Raymond was to treat his Aunt Jane "with an indulgent kindness as one who knew nothing of the world," in spite of her four decades of murder-solving. Second was Joyce Lemprière, a flapperish young modern painter, "with her close-cropped black head and queer hazel-green eyes." Joyce, who was "just getting on very special terms" with Raymond West, was to undergo a name change in later books—to Joan Lemprière West, Raymond's wife.

The opening of "The Tuesday Night Club" has the earliest description of Jane Marple, a picture quite different from that gotten by most Christie readers from jacket illustrations and film representations. In 1928, Jane Marple was a Victorian relic, with "a black brocade dress, very much pinched in round the waist. Mechlin lace was arranged in a cascade down the front of the bodice. She had on black lace mittens, and a black lace cap surmounted the piled-up masses of her snowy hair."

Even in the first scene of her long career she was knitting "something white and soft and fleecy." In the history of the novel Jane Marple is rivaled as a knitter only by Madame Defarge, and it is ironic that these two indefatigable knitters and purlers are both bound up with so much misery and death.

In the last seven stories of the collection, written to flesh out to book length the six stories serialized in the *Sketch,* Christie introduced new characters to the Tuesday Club, notably Colonel and Mrs. Bantry, who were to be lifelong companions of Marple's. In 1932, however, the Colonel and Dolly had yet to appreciate Jane's sleuthing skills.

"Know Miss Marple? Who doesn't?" exclaims Dolly Bantry. "The typical old maid of fiction. Quite a dear, but hopelessly behind the times. Do you mean you would like me to ask *her* to dinner?"

Dolly, of course, had no idea what a long friendship she was to have with Miss Marple, and that she would find the "typical old maid" of help a decade later, when the Bantrys were to find a body in their own library. And how was Mrs. Bantry to know that the spinster she was so reluctant to have to dinner in 1932 would prompt her to say in 1962, in *The Mirror Crack'd from Side to Side* (#68, 1962), "Why don't you come out boldly and call yourself a criminologist and have done with it?" Dolly Bantry's late sentiment echoed that of Isaac Anderson in his *New York Times* review of Marple's maiden voyage. "The stories are slight in structure, but they present some very pleasant problems and introduce us to some truly interesting people. Miss Marple . . . is in a class by herself. She does not call herself a detective, but she could give almost any of the regular sleuths cards and spades and beat him at his own game" (3/5/33).

In *Books* (*New York Herald Tribune*), Will Cuppy wrote, "The fact that these thirteen tales are extremely amusing in spots is nothing against them in our eyes, and we trust all good fans to rally round and enjoy them. You'll be delighted with Miss Marple, the capped and mittened spinster in whose house at St. Mary Mead most of the yarns are told" (5/5/33).

The comments of the *Times Literary Supplement* (London) about Marple's detections were to be echoed again and again by critics for the next five decades: "It is easy to invent an improbable detective like this elderly spinster who has spent all her life in one village, but by no means so easy to make her detections plausible. Sometimes Miss Marple comes dangerously near those detectives with a remarkable and almost superhuman intuition who solve every mystery as if they knew the answer beforehand, but this is not often, and Mrs. Christie shows great skill in adapting her problems so that she can find analogies in Miss Marple's surroundings . . . these are all problems to try the intellect rather than the nerves of the reader" (9/8/32).

Why Christie chose to drop Jane Marple for a decade after *The Thirteen Problems* is a mystery. True, Poirot was immensely popular at the time, and Christie recognized that she was "stuck" with him because her readers demanded it. However, during the 1930s, Christie's career was firmly established enough to allow her the luxury of deviation from an all-Poirot diet, as evidenced by Poirot-less books such as *Why Didn't They Ask Evans?* (#21, 1934), *The Sittaford Mystery* (#14, 1931), and *Parker Pyne Investigates* (#22, 1934). It was probably only with the approach of her own middle age that Christie began to appreciate fully the possibilities and appeal of an elderly female detective.

Christie dedicated *The Thirteen Problems* to archaeologist Leonard Woolley and his wife, Katharine, who were responsible for introducing the divorced writer to their young associate Max Mallowan during Christie's second trip to the Middle East in 1930. Katharine Woolley was later to have the rare privilege of being depicted—if not flatteringly—as a Christie character in *Murder in Mesopotamia* (see #26, 1936).

Sir Charles Leonard Woolley was born in London on April 17, 1880. He achieved early success as an archaeologist, and was chosen by the British Museum, London, and the University of Pennsylvania to direct the joint excavation of Ur (1922–1934). His findings at the ancient Sumerian city greatly advanced the historical knowledge of the ancient civilization of Mesopotamia. Woolley died in London on February 20, 1960. For additional information on Ur see the chapter on *Murder in Mesopotamia* (#26, 1936).

PLOTS:

"The Tuesday Night Club"

One evening a group is gathered at Jane Marple's house in St. Mary Mead: the hostess; her writer-nephew, Raymond West; his fiancée, Joyce Lemprière; "well-groomed man of the world" Henry Clithering; Dr. Pender, the elder clergyman of the parish; and Mr. Petherick, "the solicitor, a dried-up little man."

Conversation turns to unsolved mysteries and Joyce suggests that, being a representative group, they form a club, "The Tuesday Night Club." "It is to meet every week, and each member in turn has to propound a problem."

Sir Henry Clithering has the first round, and tells of a traveling salesman, Mr. Jones and his wife, and her stout, cheery companion, Miss Clark. One night after dinner, all three are taken ill, but Mrs. Jones dies while her husband and Miss Clark recover. Clithering sets the puzzle for the club, which hinges on a message found half-printed (in reverse, of course) on a piece of blotting paper, but only Miss Marple deduces what really happened.

"The Idol House of Astarte"

Old Dr. Pender tells a story of a costume party at Sir Richard Haydon's house, Silent Grove, on Dartmoor. In a mysterious grove on the grounds stands a stone summerhouse the host calls "the Idol House of Astarte," where sacred rites were once performed. That evening, a death occurs in the grove. It looks like murder, but it seems impossible for anyone present to have done the deed—until Miss Marple figures out a way.

"Ingots of Gold"

Raymond West tells of a visit to the village of Polperran, on the Cornwall coast, to visit his friend John Newman, who is searching for treasure in sunken Spanish ships offshore. Someone else in Polperran is looking for treasure as well, and finding it, and Aunt Jane easily guesses who and why.

"The Bloodstained Pavement"

Joyce Lemprière's story concerns a dowdy wife, her husband, and a good-looking woman acquaintance whom the husband meets while they are all staying in a small inn in Cornwall. Joyce is painting the front view of the inn when she realizes she has painted in bloodstains that were on the pavement in front. When she goes to look closer, the stains have disappeared. There is only water dripping from the balcony where two bathing suits are drying in the sun. A few days later, Joyce reads in the paper that the dowdy wife has drowned. Miss Marple quickly deduces the correct solution, and the part the bathing suits played in the crime.

"Motive vs. Opportunity"

Mr. Petherick, the solicitor, tells the tale of Simon Clode, a rich old client of his, who never got over the death of the orphaned granddaughter he was raising. After the girl's death, even though Simon had a niece and nephew on whom to lavish his attentions, he turned instead to spiritualism, and came under the influence of Mrs. Spragg, a medium. Before his death, Simon cut the niece and nephew off without a cent, and gave Mrs. Spragg everything. The only problem: the will turned out to be only a blank paper. Once again, Jane Marple figures out how this came to be.

"The Thumb Mark of St. Peter"

Miss Marple tells of her unfortunate niece Mabel, whose unpleasant husband, Gregory Denman, dies and leaves her a comfortable estate. But that hasn't solved Mabel's problems, since folks seem to think she poisoned Denman, and are keeping their distance as a result. Mabel, now left alone with only the servants and her late husband's impossible old father, admits she *did* buy arsenic, but swears it was intended for herself. Seizing on the words "heap of fish"—Denman's words on his deathbed, as reported by the maids—Miss Marple undertakes to clear her niece's name.

"The Blue Geranium"

A year after the six Tuesday Night Club meetings, Sir Henry Clithering is back in St. Mary Mead, guesting with Colonel and Mrs. Bantry, when he asks his hosts to invite Miss Marple to be the sixth guest for dinner. Clithering wants to try Jane's acumen at solving another mystery, this time that of George Pritchard and his impossible, demanding, semi-invalid wife. Neurotic Mrs. Pritchard has been warned by a spiritualist that the "Blue Geranium means death," and the old lady gets a bit excited when one of the geraniums on her bedroom wallpaper turns blue on the night of a full moon. This happens again a month later, and by the time of the third full moon, Mrs. Pritchard is almost hysterical—and near death. Once again Miss Marple shows up her less-gifted dinner companions, and explains the blue geranium.

"The Companion"

Dr. Lloyd, another guest at the Bantrys' dinner, relates the strange case of wealthy Miss Barton and her companion, Miss Amy Durrant, two rather nondescript English ladies traveling in the Canary Islands. One afternoon Miss Durrant drowns while the women are swimming, but a witness swears Miss Barton deliberately killed her employee in the water. Miss Marple correctly deduces the reason, and the means, of this apparently motiveless crime.

"The Four Suspects"

Sir Henry Clithering has a case for the assembled group at the Bantrys'. A Dr. Rosen, having worked successfully as a counterspy against the Germans, finds it wise to retire in obscurity in the small town of King's Gnaton, Somerset, with his maid of many years, his niece, a local gardener, and a Scotland Yard-appointed male secretary. Unfortunately, the "Black Hand" of the Germans penetrates Dr. Rosen's security and he is killed. The Yard knows it must be one of his companions—and Jane Marple unerringly zeroes in on the right one.

"A Christmas Tragedy"

Miss Marple tells of an unfortunate incident from her past, when she becomes convinced that Mr. Sanders, of St. Mary Mead, has decided to do away with his wife. When Miss Marple finds herself at the Keston Spa Hydro with the Sanderses, and actually in the company of Mr. Sanders when his poor wife is found murdered, it is up to the shrewd spinster to show how the murderous husband's alibi is not as airtight as it seems.

"The Herb of Death"

Dizzy Dolly Bantry makes an awkward stab at telling her own mystery. One day at Clodderham Court with Sir Ambrose Bercy, "a lot of foxglove leaves were picked with the sage" and put in the stuffing, causing everyone to be ill, and Sir Ambrose's ward, Sylvia Keene, to die. Miss Marple pounces on the story's weak point: why had only Sylvia died, if all had eaten the stuffed ducks?

"The Affair at the Bungalow"

At the Bantrys', beautiful actress Jane Helier tells her story. A young playwright, Mr. Faulkener, who has written to her for an appointment to discuss his play, finds himself charged with robbery after meeting a woman who definitely was *not* Jane Helier. For once even Miss Marple seems to be stumped by a case.

"Death by Drowning"

In a murder case that occurs while Sir Henry Clithering is staying at the Bantrys', Miss Marple intervenes in the police investigation of the death of Rose Emmot, an unwed mother-to-be. The evidence points to Rex Sanford, a London architect and probable father of the child. So sure is she of the truth that Miss Marple writes the name of the murderer on a slip of paper and hands it over to Clithering at the outset of the investigation.

First Editions: British: Collins, London, June 1932. 250 pp., 7s. 6d. **American**: with U.S. title *The Tuesday Club Murders:* Dodd, Mead & Co., New York, 1933. 253 pp., $2.00.

Adaptation: None.

17

LORD EDGWARE DIES / THIRTEEN AT DINNER
(1933)

Lord Edgware Dies was written while Agatha Christie accompanied her husband, Max Mallowan, on an archaeology dig to Nineveh in northern Iraq during 1931–32. Max had finished his work with Leonard Woolley at Ur, and was now assisting Reginald Campbell Thompson (1876–1941), the "bluff, hearty, free-and-easy-going" archaeologist who was in Nineveh, according to Max in his memoirs, "to demonstrate that there was no such thing as a flood at Nineveh." Barbara, a "delightful, kindly and altogether unselfish character," wife of Campbell Thompson, was also at Nineveh.

Christie loved her seasons of writing in the desert, where she and Max lived in a simple native-style house near the dig site at the mound of Nineveh. Christie described the house, with its garden of rosebushes to brighten the desert, as "altogether charming—one that I shall always think of with love and affection."

Besides knowing *where* and *when* Agatha Christie wrote *Lord Edgware Dies,* we know on what she wrote it. The house where Max and Agatha were living in Nineveh was furnished very economically. But Agatha, who could live with the bare necessities, could not write unless she had a "solid table at which I could typewrite, and under which I could get my knees." Orange crates would and could be used for sitting, storing clothes, etc., but a solid table was a must. Christie eventually found one at the bazaar, which cost, according to her, ten pounds (Max Mallowan, in his memoirs, said the table cost three pounds). Whatever the amount, Campbell Thompson thought it was much too expensive for the expedition budget. "I had one battle with C.T. He gave in to me with courtesy, but I think I went down in his estimation . . . it took him quite a fortnight to forgive me for this luxurious extravagance." After Agatha had bought the table, she proceeded to write *Lord Edgware Dies.*

The main idea for writing this book came, according to Christie, after she had seen a performance by Ruth Draper (1884–1956), the monologuist. "I thought how clever she was and how good her impersonations were; the wonderful way she could transform herself from a nagging wife to a peasant girl kneeling in a cathedral. Thinking about her led me to the book *Lord Edgware Dies*." Ruth Draper, who was born in New York, began her career writing and acting out sketches of people she knew. She made her London debut in 1920, in a program of her own sketches. This was a triumph, and she went on to achieve worldwide fame.

Lord Edgware Dies is considered one of the better efforts of Christie's early career. Ralph Partridge in the *New Statesman and Nation* said, "Mrs. Agatha Christie is quite beyond criticism, unless it be that she does not write enough novels. *Thirteen at Dinner* (American title) is the best detective story published this year" (10/14/33). Isaac Anderson in the *New York Times* wrote, "This story presents a most ingenious crime puzzle and a still more ingenious solution, all set forth with the consummate skill of which Agatha Christie is mistress" (9/24/33).

The *Times Literary Supplement* (London) wrote, "In *Lord Edgware Dies* we are introduced to an old friend, M. Hercule Poirot. The eminent Belgian detective himself feels a little doubtful about his latest case, for he says that it was the chance remark of a stranger in the street that put him on the right track. Three such murders, however, are enough to tax the powers of the most superhuman sleuth, and we do not grudge him one stroke of good fortune. The large number of suspects—some of them actors and one a trained impersonator—adds to his difficulties and our enjoyment. The mystery is finally elucidated before an astonished audience in one of M. Poirot's familiar speeches; and the whole case is a triumph of his special qualities, "the order and the method" (9/21/33).

Christie dedicated this book to Dr. and Mrs. Campbell Thompson. In her autobiography, Christie revealed that she read the manuscript aloud to Campbell and his wife Barbara, apparently the only people other than her family to receive this honor. Thompson was an Oriental scholar and Oxford Professor of Assyriology as well as archaeologist. He and his wife remained close friends of the Mallowans—in spite of the friction caused by the "sturdy writing table."

PLOT:

In London, Poirot and Hastings attend a one-woman theatrical by Carlotta Adams, "quite the rage in London at that moment." The brilliant young American is gaining note for her "amazing talent for single-handed sketches unhampered by make-up or scenery." Among the evening's monologues is a stunning imitation of the famous American stage actress Jane Wilkinson. Wilkinson had gained notoriety in England three years before when she left the stage to marry the "wealthy but slightly eccentric" Lord Edgware, whom she left shortly afterward to resume her career in Hollywood. By chance, Jane Wilkinson herself is in the audience that night.

After the performance Poirot and Hastings go to supper at the Savoy, where they see both Jane Wilkinson and Carlotta Adams with their escorts, though the women are at separate tables and apparently do not know one another. Hastings senses that Jane Wilkinson is watching Poirot, and sure enough Lady Edgware rises and comes to Poirot's table, introducing herself to the famous detective, and insists that Poirot and Hastings come immediately to her suite, their dinner plans notwithstanding.

Upstairs, Lady Edgware announces that "M. Poirot, somehow or other I've just *got* to get rid of my husband!"

It seems Lady Edgware is in love with, and wants to marry, the Duke of Merton, one of England's supremely eligible bachelors. But Lord Edgware refuses to even consider giving Jane a divorce.

She has exhausted every conventional channel, lawyers and the like, and in desperation is asking Poirot's help. She's heard he's "the cat's whiskers." To Hastings's surprise, Poirot accepts the challenge and makes an appointment with the estranged husband.

The interview with Lord Edgware takes place. Lord Edgware tells Poirot he has decided that his marriage to Jane Wilkinson was a grave mistake, and he is most willing to divorce her. Poirot is also told by Edgware that he wrote his wife six months before that he would in fact divorce her. That same day Poirot goes to the Savoy to pass on the good news to Jane Wilkinson. She is immensely pleased—but astonished to hear that her husband had written her about a divorce.

The following day, Lord Edgware is found dead in his library, stabbed at the base of the skull. Lady Edgware is arrested, since the previous evening she had been admitted by the butler, to whom she clearly identified herself, and had gone into the library to see her husband.

But Lady Edgware couldn't possibly have murdered her husband, since at the time the butler claims to have admitted her to the house, she was having dinner with a group at Sir Montague Corner's house—an unimpeachable alibi.

Principal Characters: Carlotta Adams, Alton, Alice Bennet, Miss Carroll, Sir Montague Corner, Jenny Driver, Ellis, Captain Hastings, Dr. Heath, Chief Inspector James Japp, George Alfred St. Vincent Marsh (the fourth Baron Edgware), Geraldine Marsh, Captain Ronald Marsh (the fifth Baron Edgware), Dowager Duchess of Merton, Duke of Merton, Hercule Poirot, Donald Ross, Mrs. Wilburn, Jane Wilkinson.

First Editions: **British**: Collins, London, 1933. 252 pp., 7s. 6d. **American**: with U.S. title *Thirteen at Dinner:* Dodd, Mead & Co., New York, 1933. 305 pp., $2.00.

Adaptation: A film of *Lord Edgware Dies* was made in England in 1934, with Austin Trevor portraying Hercule Poirot.

18

THE HOUND OF DEATH AND OTHER STORIES
(1933)

Christie's seventh* collection of short stories is of special interest because most of the twelve stories deal with the supernatural, either as a real force in the plot or as a means of deception perpetrated by one of the characters.

Christie critic Robert Barnard in *A Talent to Deceive* (1980), places these supernatural tales very early in Christie's career, probably from the early years of World War I when the young bride was still living at home and working in the local hospital dispensary while Archie Christie was in the service. Thus they fall between Christie's first novel, a still unpublished (and lost or destroyed?) romance, written before her marriage, and *The Mysterious Affair at Styles* (#1, 1920), written in 1916. Several of these occult tales are quite effective, and it's unfortunate Christie chose not to continue writing in this vein from time to time.

The Hound of Death marks the first publication of what was to become one of her most famous works: "The Witness for the Prosecution." The 1953 play, and the 1957 film, starring Marlene Dietrich and Charles Laughton, have become so famous that the short story on which they were based, a work that predates the play and film by more than twenty years, has remained relatively obscure.

The Hound of Death has never been published in America. All of its stories have been anthologized in U.S. collections, however: *Witness for the Prosecution and Other Stories* (#49, 1948) contains "The Red Signal," "The Fourth Man," "SOS," "The Mystery of the Blue Jar," "Wireless" (retitled "Where There's a Will"), and the title story. *Double Sin and Other Stories* (#66, 1961) contains "The Last Séance." *The Golden Ball and Other Stories* (#77, 1971) contains "The Hound of Death," "The

---

* If *The Big Four* (#8, 1927) is considered a collection of interrelated stories.

Gipsy," "The Lamp," "The Strange Case of Sir Arthur Carmichael," and "The Call of Wings."

Reviews of this British collection were not available. For reviews, see the later U.S. anthologies, listed above, which contain the same stories.

PLOTS:

"The Hound of Death"

Anstruther, a young Englishman visiting his sister in Cornwall, finds himself delving into the legend of a Belgian nun, possessed of supernatural powers, who is said to have caused her entire convent to explode when it was occupied by invading Germans during World War I. The invaders perished in the blast, but Sister Angelique survived, and is now living as a refugee in Folbridge, Cornwall. Once in Folbridge, Anstruther meets Dr. Rose, who is investigating the nun's powers, and Sister Angelique herself.

"The Red Signal"

Dermot West is invited to dinner at the home of Jack and Claire Trent, who happen to be, respectively, his best friend and the woman he loves. During the evening the conversation turns to the supernatural, and Dermot admits that he frequently gets what he calls "the red signal" to warn him of impending danger. He neglects to mention that he is getting the signal strongly that night. Among the other guests are Sir Arlington West, a famous psychiatrist, and a medium. A séance is held after dinner, during which the medium gets a portentous message: "Better not go home . . . Danger! Blood!"

"The Fourth Man"

Three men on a train, Sir George Durand, Cannon Parfitt, and Dr. Campbell Clark, discuss the strange case of Felicie Bault, a Brittany peasant of severely limited mental capacity who suddenly developed a multiple personality at age twenty-two. The men find her death even stranger until the fourth man in the compartment comes up with an explanation.

"The Gipsy"

Dickie Lawes has a phobia about gipsies, based on a frightening childhood encounter with a gipsy with a red scarf. As an adult, he has visions of a gipsy who warns him of imminent danger, though in his mind he confuses the gipsy with the fair-haired, cultured Mrs. Haworth.

"The Lamp"

Widowed Mrs. Lancaster, her father, and her son, Geoffrey, rent a charming old house, No. 19, knowing full well that it's reputed to be haunted, and that there was a tragedy some years before involving an unfortunate young boy. Before long little Geoffrey has a new playmate, though his mother and grandfather can't seem to see him.

"Wireless"

Wealthy Mrs. Harter, who lives with her nephew, Charles Ridgeway, is in delicate health, but her doctor says she'll live for years if she avoids all excitement. Charles buys a radio to keep his confined, semi-invalid aunt happy, but she soon starts receiving most distressing messages from her dead husband, who says he's on the way to get her.

"The Witness for the Prosecution"

Leonard Vole is arrested for the murder of his elderly friend Emily French, a woman who depended on his advice in managing her money. Because Emily made him her principal heir, not aware that he was a married man, things look bad for Leonard's defense. But the final blow comes when his wife, Romaine, agrees to testify, not in Leonard's defense, but as a witness for the prosecution.

"The Mystery of the Blue Jar"

One morning while Jack Hartington is playing his customary round of golf he hears across the links a cry of "Murder!" When he goes to investigate he finds only an attractive French girl, Felise, weeding the garden of her cottage. She hasn't heard what Jack has. He hears the same cry of distress on the golf course several days in a row. When Jack connects with Dr. Ambrose Lavington, an investigator of psychic phenomena, Jack discovers that his auditory hallucinations are connected with events in the cottage, and with an antique Chinese jar.

"The Strange Case of Sir Arthur Carmichael"

When Sir Arthur Carmichael, young heir to a title and a large estate, starts behaving strangely, psychiatrist Edward Carstairs is summoned to the family seat. Poor Arthur seems to be behaving like a cat, but it seems that's not all that's strange at Wolden, Hertfordshire. Lady Carmichael, Sir Arthur's stepmother, is rumored by the servants to have recently killed a cat, and she seems as well to have some sort of supernatural powers.

"The Call of Wings"

Millionaire hedonist Silas Hamer encounters an itinerant street musician, a man without legs, who plays hypnotic music on his flute. Though their encounter is brief, the man's music haunts the wealthy Hamer, and pulls him from the material world into the spiritual.

"The Last Séance"

Raoul Daubreuil insists that his fiancée, Simone, give up her activities as a talented and successful medium when they marry, but he does attend what is to be her last séance, conducted by another medium, Madame Exe. Madame Exe attempts to contact the spirit of her only child, Amelie, but complications arise when Madame is too eager to touch the manifestation of Amelie conjured up by Simone's powers.

"SOS"

When motorist Mortimer Cleveland finds himself stranded on the Wiltshire Downs, he takes refuge with the Dinsmead family, Mr. and Mrs., son Johnny, and daughters Magdalen and Charlotte. But Mortimer learns all is not well with the Dinsmead household. He finds an SOS written in the dust on the nightstand in his room. Mortimer, who feels he has mediumistic talents, thinks Charlotte may have scrawled the message, perhaps without realizing it. But his discovery of a large inheritance in the family complicates the puzzle.

First Editions: **British**: Collins, London, February 1933. 247 pp., 7s. 6d. **American**: None.

Adaptations: Based on the short story of the same name, *Witness for the Prosecution* was adapted for the stage by Agatha Christie.

This very successful production opened in London at the Winter Garden Theatre, October 28, 1953. The American production, which was received by the critics and public with the same enthusiasm, opened in New York at the Henry Miller Theatre, December 16, 1954. The film version of this play, which was directed by Billy Wilder and starred Charles Laughton, Marlene Dietrich, Tyrone Power, and Elsa Lanchester, was released in 1957. A 1982 television adaptation of the play featured Sir Ralph Richardson, Deborah Kerr, Diana Rigg, and Beau Bridges.

The stories "The Red Signal," "The Mystery of the Blue Jar," and "The Fourth Man" were adapted for television as part of the Thames Television series, *The Agatha Christie Hour*.

19

MURDER ON THE ORIENT EXPRESS / MURDER IN THE CALAIS COACH (1934)

The fabled Orient Express, the world's most famous luxury train, made its maiden voyage from the Gare de Strasbourg, Paris, on October 4, 1883, en route to Constantinople (since 1930, officially named Istanbul, or Stamboul, as Christie preferred). For the next ninety-four years, until the final run of regularly scheduled service in May 1977, the Orient Express set a standard of style, luxury, and glamor in travel that is rivaled only by a few other trains of the period and by the greatest ocean liners of the twentieth century.

The Orient Express was the brainchild of Georges Nagelmackers (1845–1905), member of a wealthy Belgian banking family. Georges grew up in the early days of railroads, when tracks were spreading like spiderwebs across Europe and America. He was always fascinated by trains, and believed in their great future. The turning point came in a trip to the United States in the 1860s, when he saw some of George Mortimer Pullman's early sleeping cars. Nagelmackers returned to Europe, determined that he, using Pullman's ideas, would create a luxury passenger service spanning the European continent.

It took almost twenty years of knocking on doors, negotiating, and engineering—along with generous help from the family's banking firm, which was heavily involved in rail finance, and from King Leopold of Belgium—before the first Orient Express, under the auspices of the Compagnie Internationale des Wagons-lits, was ready to roll.

The Orient Express was an immediate success, especially among Europe's wealthy and fashionable. And with good reason. Before the Express, a land crossing of Europe had been a long, arduous, and often dangerous journey. Now, even women and children could cross the Continent in a few days' time, in surroundings of utmost luxury. Interiors were planned by the most famous designers in Europe: inlaid paneling, silk lampshades, velvet upholstery, handmade lace antimacassars, crystal chandeliers, plush carpets, linen bedsheets, marble bath fixtures. The dining car turned out gargantuan *cordon bleu* meals, accompanied by the finest wines, served on bone china with sterling flatware, all presented by waiters in full livery.

During its long lifetime, the Orient Express numbered among its passengers almost every famous name in Europe and America, from kings and queens to actors, musicians, artists, and diplomats. There was always a strong flavor of the exotic. With its ultimate destination mysterious Stamboul, the gateway to the East, the Express had more than its share of sheiks, Eastern potentates, international financiers, thieves, smugglers, and, of course, spies.

This marvelous blend of glamor, luxury, and mystery provided an incomparable setting for books and films, the most notable being Hitchcock's *The Lady Vanishes,* Graham Greene's *Stamboul Express,* Ian Fleming's *From Russia with Love,* Eric Ambler's *The Mask of Dimitrios,* and, of course, *Murder on the Orient Express.*

Agatha Christie first journeyed on the Orient Express in the fall of 1928.* She was not a good ocean traveler; like Poirot, she had a tendency to seasickness. But trains were another matter. In her autobiography she wrote, "Trains have always been one of my favorite things. It is sad nowadays that one no longer has engines that seem to be one's personal friends. I entered my wagon-lit compartment at Calais, the journey to Dover and the tiresome sea

---

* NOTE: Gwen Robyns in *The Mystery of Agatha Christie* and E. F. Cookeridge in *The Orient Express* both give incorrect information on the writer's first journey on the O.E. Robyns mentions 1930—clearly an error, since Christie had taken the Orient Express on her first journey to the Middle East in 1928. Cookeridge writes incorrectly that Agatha traveled to the Middle East with first husband Archibald Christie, when in fact her first O.E. trip was after their divorce. Cookeridge goes on to write that "the Colonel, after distinguished service in the Royal Flying Corps in the first World War [correct], spent most of his later life as a senior officer in British Intelligence [wrong: he was an executive with Austral Trust Limited]. His wife thus gleaned many real-life secret-service plots, which she used as background for some of her thrillers" [wrong: their contact after the divorce was practically nil].

For more on Christie's first trip to the Middle East via the Orient Express see *The Seven Dials Mystery* (#10).

voyage disposed of, and settled comfortably in the train of my
dreams . . . All my life I had wanted to go on the Orient Express.
When I had travelled to France or Spain or Italy, the Orient Express
press had often been standing at Calais, and I had longed to climb
up into it. *Simplon–Orient Express—Milan, Belgrade, Stamboul.*"

On this and subsequent journeys, Christie took the Simplon–
Orient Express, the southernmost of the three Orient Express
routes that crossed Europe. The Simplon originated at Calais
(with boat-train connections to London, of course), then began
the three-day journey across Europe via Paris, Lausanne, the
seven-mile Simplon tunnel under the Alps (completed in 1909),
Milan, Venice, Trieste, Belgrade, Sofia, to Stamboul.

Two real events were used by Christie as "inspirations" for
Murder on the Orient Express.

The first is easily recognized by most readers: the Lindbergh
kidnapping. Its counterpart in the book, the Armstrong kidnapping, provides the revenge motive for the murder on the train.

In 1927 Charles Augustus Lindbergh (1902–1974) achieved
international fame when he made the first solo plane crossing of
the Atlantic in *The Spirit of St. Louis.* In 1932 a son was born to
Lindbergh and his wife, writer Anne Morrow (b. 1906). On
March 21 of that year, the infant was abducted from the Lindbergh home in Hopewell, New Jersey; a ransom of $50,000 was
paid, but on May 12 the child's battered body was found near
Hopewell. On September 19, 1933, Bruno Richard Hauptmann,
a German-born carpenter, was found with a portion of the ransom
money. Though he claimed innocence until the end, Hauptmann
was electrocuted in 1936.

When Christie wrote *Orient Express* in 1933, the Lindbergh
case was still very much a part of international headlines, though
Hauptmann had still to be discovered and arrested. The Lindberghs both came from prominent families, and Agatha gave the
tragic Armstrong couple a similar background, though with
stronger British ties to suit her setting. Christie made John
Armstrong a British colonel, half American, married to the daughter of a famous American actress, and both living in America. To
heighten the tragedy of the kidnap/murder, and strengthen the
motive for revenge, Christie causes the young mother to die from
the shock of her child's murder, and the husband to shoot himself

in grief from his double loss. Ironically, the Lindberghs, who were both American, moved to England in 1935, where they lived until World War II.

The second actual event drawn upon by Agatha Christie occurred on the Simplon–Orient Express itself in 1929, just a few months after the author's first journey.

Nineteen twenty-nine is famous as the year of the great crash, which came in October. But the winter of 1928–29 was the worst in Europe in decades, a harsh prologue to the financial disasters to come. For weeks, all of Europe was swept by blizzards and gale-force winds; the north of the Continent was virtually frozen solid; in southern Italy, temperatures dipped to ten below zero; in Yugo-slavia and Turkey the mercury went as low as forty below zero. The snow and ice storms brought almost all transportation to a halt.

The Orient Express train which left Paris on January 29 made a slow journey across the Continent, hampered all along the route by snow and ice on the tracks. However, the engineers and managers in the home office in Paris seemed to believe their own publicity about the infallibility of the Orient Express service, and in spite of questioning telegrams from the train and stations along the way, they continued to send go-ahead messages to the Express.

The train made it across the Turkish border, but at that point encountered massive, impassable snowdrifts. To make things worse, as soon as the train stopped, the engine froze, preventing the train from backing up. Within minutes the train was snowed in, and soon became completely buried in the snow.

Some readers might question the plausibility of a luxury train's being marooned in a snowdrift, cut off from all communication with the outside world. However, in real life this is not only exactly what happened, but the train was stuck for six days. In the beginning, services were as usual, including the full-course dinners, but as food and fuel ran low, the passengers were reduced to eating scraps of cold chicken (served on bone china). Attendants stoking furnaces had to use pickaxes to break the lumps of frozen coal, and several attendants suffered severe frostbite. When the passengers and crew realized that help was *not* on the way, and that they would soon freeze to death, crew members tunneled out of the fifteen-foot drifts—a project that took forty-eight hours—and struggled across the snowbound Turkish countryside, where they bargained with hostile peasants for food and help.

With additional food, the group was able to hold out until the snowplows from Stamboul freed them. One can easily imagine Agatha Christie reading the accounts in the papers, saying to herself, "Marooned in the snow, a group of travelers, each with his secret. Now what if . . ."

The real-life train was trapped near Cherkeskoy between Luleburgaz and Stamboul; in the novel, Christie chose a spot between Vincovci and Brod, in north-central Yugoslavia. The reason is simple: a certain amount of time was required to set up the murder, and the original site in Turkey would have come too soon after leaving Stamboul (Christie was quite scrupulous about following timetables). Second, there is a time change on the Bulgaria-Yugoslavia border at Tsaribrod (modern Dmitrovgrad) that is necessary for the plotting of the book. (It is this change from Eastern European to Central European time that Mr. Ratchett overlooks in the novel.)

It's interesting that, at the conclusion of the book, no word has been mentioned by M. Bouc or the other staff that rescue is definitely on its way. But when M. Bouc says, "the Jugo-Slavian police when they arrive," does he know they are indeed on their way? Perhaps the group are in for a few more days of one another's company.

With few exceptions, Christie mysteries are contemporary. The author is careful to weave enough current events and attitudes into her books to give them the correct flavor, but is just as careful to avoid too many hard dates to keep the books from becoming dated.

However, several references in *Murder on the Orient Express* allow us to place within a few weeks the probable time of Hercule Poirot's trip. The conductor mentions the 1929 blizzard as "once," indicating that it occurred more than one season past. The Lindbergh kidnapping was in 1932 and Prohibition (the Volstead Act) which McQueen and Colonel Arbuthnot discuss the night of the murder was not repealed until late 1933, after the novel was completed.

Provided the Armstrong kidnapping occurred simultaneously with the Lindbergh tragedy, the train trip would have to be in the

1932–33 winter season. In fact, the first sentence of the novel places the journey in winter, so the earliest would be December 21, 1932, and the latest March 20, 1933 (which would be the eve of the first anniversary of the Lindbergh kidnapping). Since at no time does any character refer to the Christmas holidays, it's safe to assume the trip took place between January 1 and March 20 of 1933. This allows one year from the time of the kidnapping until Ratchett's murder. In Poirot's interviews with the passengers, Hector McQueen mentions that he has been in Ratchett's employ "just over a year," while Edward Masterman has worked for Ratchett, "Just over nine months, sir."

As always, Christie was precise in her planning.

Isaac Anderson in the *New York Times* said, "Although both the murder plot and the solution verge upon the impossible, Agatha Christie has contrived to make them appear quite convincing for the time being, and what more than that can a mystery addict desire?" (3/4/34).

Mortimer Quick in the *Chicago Daily Tribune* wrote, "It has been a long time since Mrs. Christie has written so good a book or one that moves so smoothly and entertainingly to its surprise conclusion" (4/17/34). With less enthusiasm the *Saturday Review of Literature* commented, "*Sauce piquante* of super-deduction brilliantly disguises fact that dish itself is largely moonshine" (4/3/34).

"One of Mrs. Christie's charms is, of course, that she writes in the civilized manner, and that always helps," wrote Will Cuppy in *Books* (*New York Herald Tribune*). "Then, her mystery technique is nothing short of swell. She's probably the best suspicion scatterer and diverter in the business. If you find your old friend, credibility, seeming to slip in the later stages of this exciting tale, don't worry—for Mrs. Christie is working up to something most unusual by this very means" (4/4/34).

The *Times Literary Supplement* (London) wrote, "Need it be said—the little grey cells solve once more the seemingly insoluble. Mrs. Christie makes an improbable tale very real, and keeps her readers enthralled and guessing to the end" (1/11/34).

The original hardcover editions contain the following, very personal dedication: "To M.E.L.M., Arpachiyah, 1933." M.E.L.M. is Max Edgar Lucien Mallowan. The Mallowans celebrated their third anniversary on September 11, 1933, probably about the time the book was completed. The couple had traveled on the Orient Express on their first trip together, from the Middle East to England in March 1930, and on their honeymoon later that same year.

Arpachiyah is one of the archaeological sites at Calah (or Nimrud), Iraq, which Mallowan excavated and studied during the 1930s, with his wife's help. The Arpachiyah site is especially important in Mallowan's career: it had long been considered an archaeological site of minor potential, but under Mallowan's supervision, it yielded a treasure house of pottery and ivories from the fourth millennium B.C. Christie discusses the Arpachiyah digs at length in her autobiography and in *Come, Tell Me How You Live* (1946), her short book of reminiscences about her trips to the Middle East.

Orient Express is a Poirot tour de force: he's on the scene from the first page to the last, meets the victim just hours before he becomes the victim, and in fact is asleep in the next compartment when the murder takes place.

There is a marvelous pun on Poirot's name which is lost on most of today's readers. When Poirot is interviewing Hector McQueen, the young American secretary-companion, he says, "My name is Hercule Poirot . . . you know the name, perhaps?" McQueen replies that the name is familiar, but that he "always thought it was a woman's dressmaker." Poirot cringes, for McQueen has innocently confused Poirot with Paul Poiret, the famous Parisian couturier of the early decades of this century.

A final point of interest: Poirot doesn't show a flicker of guilt at the fact that, had he overcome his dislike of the unpleasant Mr. Ratchett, he might have saved the man's life. Poirot's attitude toward this murder ties in with the conclusion of the book, where Christie reveals that in her moral system, justice is not always identical with the letter of the law.

PLOT:
Having finished "a little affair in Syria," Hercule Poirot arrives at the Tokatlian Hotel in Stamboul for a sight-seeing tour of the city. However, a telegram informs him he must return to England

at once on business. Poirot books passage on the next Orient Express. While dining at the Tokatlian, Poirot unexpectedly runs into his old friend, Monsieur Bouc, a director of the Compagnie Internationale des Wagons-lits, which runs the Express. To their delight, they will be traveling together to Paris.

At the station, Poirot and Bouc discover to their surprise that the sleeping car, containing the first- and second-class accommodations, is fully booked, a most unusual situation in the winter months. However, one passenger fails to appear and Hercule obtains a berth. The Belgian finds himself traveling with a curious assortment of passengers of all nationalities, social classes, and occupations—all in the off-season.

One traveler attracts Poirot's attention: a smartly dressed, outwardly respectable, obviously wealthy American. Something about the man displeases Hercule greatly, though "all seemed to speak of a benevolent personality. Only the eyes belied this assumption."

The next day out, after luncheon, the detective is approached in the dining car by the same American, Samuel Edward Ratchett, who informs Poirot that his life has been threatened. He offers Poirot "*big* money" if the famous Belgian will protect his life.

Poirot refuses, saying, "If you will forgive me for being personal—I do not like your face."

The next morning the American is found dead of multiple stab wounds in the compartment next to Poirot's. The situation is complicated because of the weather. The train has become marooned in a snowdrift between the towns of Vincovci and Brod in Yugoslavia.

Naturally Monsieur Bouc, with the local police unavailable because of the snow, calls upon Poirot to conduct the investigation. The suspects are quickly narrowed to individuals who spent the night in the Calais coach. Fifteen began the journey: Poirot, the victim, and thirteen others. Within twenty-four hours, as the train is about to be freed, Poirot has arrived at not one, but two solutions to the crime.

Principal Characters: Countess Elena Maria Andrenyi, Count Rudolph Andrenyi, Colonel Arbuthnot, Monsieur Bouc, Dr. Constantine, Mary Hermione Debenham, Princess Natalia Dragomiroff, Antonio Foscarelli, Cyrus Bethman Hardman, Caroline

Martha Hubbard, Hector Willard McQueen, Edward Henry Masterman, Pierre Michel, Hercule Poirot, Greta Ohlsson, Samuel Edward Ratchett, Fräulein Hildegarde Schmidt.

First Editions: British: Collins, London, January 1934. 254 pp., 7s. 6d. **American**: with U.S. title *Murder in the Calais Coach:* Dodd, Mead & Co., New York, 1934. 302 pp., $2.00.

Adaptation: The film version of *Murder on the Orient Express,* released in the U.S. in November 1974, was the most successful and ambitious adaptation of a Christie work up to this time. The film, directed by Sidney Lumet, had an all-star cast which included Sean Connery, Sir John Gielgud, Lauren Bacall, Wendy Hiller, Ingrid Bergman, and Albert Finney as Hercule Poirot.

20

THE LISTERDALE MYSTERY (1934)

The dozen stories in this collection show Christie in her most "unbuttoned" mood. There are no feats of ratiocination here, no Herculean gray cells or Marpleian insights, merely a box of clever bonbons that are better called amusing problems than detective stories, though there is a mystery of the lightweight sort in each one.

All of the stories in this British collection have been included in the later American collections, *Witness for the Prosecution and Other Stories* (#49, 1948) and *The Golden Ball and Other Stories* (#77, 1971).

Two of these stories, "Philomel Cottage" and "Accident," are among Christie's best-known works in the genre. Two others in the collection are of interest for other reasons.

"The Rajah's Emerald," features as its hero an underpaid clerk thrust unwittingly into international jewel-thievery. Many years later, Christie's thrillers were compared, always unfavorably, with those of Ian Fleming. The irony: the meek self-effacing hero of "The Rajah's Emerald" is named James Bond.

A real event in Christie's life was the basis for the short story "The Manhood of Edward Robinson." In 1924, Christie was offered five hundred pounds by *The Evening News* for the serial rights to her novel *The Man in the Brown Suit* (see #5, 1924). An enormous sum for Christie at the time, she wondered what she would do with this windfall. At first her practical side took control, and she thought of putting the money aside "for a rainy day."

However, her then husband Archie suggested that she buy a car. Christie was startled by this extravagant suggestion, since "cars were for the rich." But the idea gradually found favor and she decided, as she recalled in her autobiography, "Why not indeed? It was possible. I, Agatha, could have a car, a car of my own. I will confess here and now that of the two things that have excited me most in my life the first was my car; my grey bottle-nosed Morris Cowley."

The second event happened about forty years later: she dined with Queen Elizabeth II at Buckingham Palace.

The *Times Literary Supplement* (London) wrote, "After a heavy meal of full-course detective stories these *friandises* melt sweetly—perhaps a shade too sweetly—on the tongue; but they are, without exception, the work of an experienced and artful cook, whose interest it is to please. And just as one accepts and swallows without misgiving a green rose, knowing it to be sugar, so one can accept the improbabilities and the fantasy with which Mrs. Christie's stories are liberally sprinkled. The little kernel of mystery in each tale is just sufficient to intrigue the reader without bewildering him. Here is no Hercule's vein; indeed Poirot would find little worthy of his great gift for detection in the situations, where one knows from the start that everything will come delightfully right in the end" (7/5/34).

PLOTS:

"The Listerdale Mystery"

On the death of her husband, genteel Mrs. St. Vincent, her daughter, Barbara, and teenage son, Rupert, are forced to live in less-than-genteel poverty in a cheap London flat. When Mrs. St. Vincent finds an elegant town house for a suspiciously cheap rent —it even includes staff—the family moves in. But there is something curious about the house. Why is the owner, wealthy Lord Listerdale, who has slipped from sight (rumored to be on extended holiday, though some say possibly a victim of foul play), allowing the house to be let so cheaply?

"Philomel Cottage"

Dick Windyford has been engaged to Alix King for years, but he puts off marriage until he can support her properly. Even when Alix comes into an unexpected small fortune he still won't marry her. Then Alix meets good-looking Gerald Martin, who sweeps her off her feet. They're soon married, and living in isolated Philomel cottage, with wills in each other's favor. When ex-fiancé Dick Windyford comes to vacation nearby, Alix refuses to see him, mainly because of her recurrent nightmares of Dick murdering her husband.

"The Girl in the Train"

George Rowland, a rather bored playboy, recently disinherited by his uncle, is on board a London-bound train for a few days of knocking about. Suddenly a girl bursts into his compartment, frantically begging to be hidden. George slips her under his seat, only to be accosted by an infuriated man at the carriage window, demanding "his niece." George puts off the pursuer, but the girl, Elizabeth, soon has George holding a packet of valuable papers, and chasing after a dark-haired man, spies, and a Grand Duchess in love.

"Sing a Song of Sixpence"

Retired Scotland Yard detective, Sir Edward Paliser, is called upon by Magdalen Vaughn for help in solving the murder of her wealthy, eccentric aunt, Miss Crabtree. The authorities believe only members of the household could have committed the crime, and Magdalen is distraught because the suspicion is tearing her family apart at a time when they could be enjoying the money Miss Crabtree left them.

"The Manhood of Edward Robinson"

Prim, unaggressive Edward Robinson, a store clerk engaged to the domineering Maud, decides to go on a frivolity binge when he wins £500 in a newspaper contest. He buys an expensive sports car and learns to drive. His car soon gets him involved with a beautiful adventuress named Noreen and a diamond necklace, and effects a remarkable change in his personality.

"Accident"

Evans, a retired inspector, at a friend's for a holiday, meets Mr. and Mrs. Marrowdene, he quiet and absentminded, she handsome but familiar. Evans soon becomes convinced that Mrs. Marrowdene is really someone else, a husband killer, and sets about trying to unmask her.

"Jane in Search of a Job"

When Jane Cleveland answers an ad for a job requiring someone of her physical description—a job she desperately needs—she finds herself masquerading as the Grand Duchess of Ostrova, with dangerous results.

"A Fruitful Sunday"

Edward Palgrove, thrilled with his new secondhand Austin motorcar, takes his girl friend, Dorothy Pratt, for a drive in the country. But a stop at a fruit stand for a basket of cherries turns their motoring holiday into an adventure. There is a ruby necklace hidden among the cherries.

"Mr. Eastwood's Adventure"

Mr. Eastwood, successful writer of newspaper thrillers, while writing his latest story, "The Mystery of the Second Cucumber," gets a mysterious phone call and a chance to take part in a real-life mystery. He soon finds himself arrested for murder.

"The Golden Ball"

George Dundas, recently disowned by his rich uncle for not keeping his nose to the grindstone, is picked up on a London street corner by pretty Mary Montresor, who proposes a ride in the country and marriage. But the offer leads to an unfortunate encounter with a revolver-brandishing tough.

"The Rajah's Emerald"

Young James Bond, an underpaid clerk, has been persuaded by Grace, his rather ambitious fiancée, who earns more money than he, to vacation with her at Kempton-on-Sea, a posh watering hole. Among the notables in the resort are Lord Campion and his houseguest, the Rajah Maraputna, owner of an egg-sized emerald. James, who is staying at a cheap guest house, is upset to find Grace checked into the fancy Esplanade Hotel fronting the water. Matters get worse when she starts paying attention to Claude Sopworth, obviously a man of means. After a morning's swim, James finds himself changing by accident into the wrong pair of shabby gray flannel slacks. He discovers his mistake when he finds the Rajah's emerald in the pants pocket.

"Swan Song"

Famed soprano Paula Nazorkoff, on a tour of England, accepts an invitation to sing privately at Rustombury Castle only because she knows the castle is near the retreat of retired baritone Breon, a man who had, through cruelty and callousness, allowed her first love to go to the gallows many years before.

First Editions: British: Collins, London, June 1934. 251 pp., 7s. 6d. **American:** None.

Adaptations: The short story "Philomel Cottage" was adapted for the stage, under the title *Love from a Stranger,* by Frank Vosper. The play opened in London on March 31, 1936, at the New Theatre. The American production opened in New York on September 21, 1936. Two film versions of this dramatization of "Philomel Cottage" were produced. The first version, filmed in England in 1937, starred Ann Harding and Basil Rathbone. The second version was released in 1947. The stories "The Girl in the Train," "Jane in Search of a Job," and "The Manhood of Edward Robinson" were adapted for television as part of the Thames Television series, *The Agatha Christie Hour.*

21

WHY DIDN'T THEY ASK EVANS?/THE BOOMERANG CLUE (1934)

Why Didn't They Ask Evans? is a lighthearted murder romp with two young, enthusiastic, but bumbling amateur detectives, Bobby Jones and Lady Frances Derwent, who get themselves involved in a murder and a romance. By 1934, after four years of marriage, Christie was beginning to share more and more her husband Max's archaeological career, and it is possible that *Evans* was written in late 1933 or early 1934 when she was with Max in Arpachiyah, Iraq. Arpachiyah was Max Mallowan's first independent dig, and as he wrote in his memoirs, it "stands out as the happiest and most rewarding: it opened a new and enthralling chapter and will forever stand as a milestone on the long road of prehistory."

In 1934 Christie also published *Unfinished Portrait,* the second of her pseudonymous Mary Westmacott romantic novels (see Miscellaneous Christie Books, #2). The critics enjoyed *Evans.* Will Cuppy in *Books* (*New York Herald Tribune*) wrote, "Thoroughly entertaining in a not too solemn way" (9/25/35). Mortimer Quick in the *Chicago Daily Tribune* said, "In spite of a murder or two there is scarcely a grim moment so light hearted are all concerned" (9/28/35). Agreeing with the American critics, the reviewer in the *Times Literary Supplement* (London) said, "Mrs. Christie describes the risks they ran in her lightest and most sympathetic manner, playing with her characters as a kitten will play with a ball of wool, and imposing no greater strain on her readers than the pleasure of reading at a sitting a story that tickles and tantalizes but never exhausts their patience or ingenuity" (9/27/34).

PLOT:

Young Bobby Jones, fourth son of Rev. Thomas Jones of Marchbolt, Wales, is playing a round of golf in his usual forceful if erratic style with Dr. Thomas, a middle-aged physician friend.

Bobby slices terrifically on one hole and sends his ball over the edge of a cliff into a sea chasm. Bobby knows the course well enough to know the ball may not have landed in the water, but instead on the shelf of land opening out at the foot of the cliff. He walks around to the top of the path that winds down the cliff face, but is startled to see "some forty feet below . . . a dark heap of something that looked like old clothes."

Dr. Thomas and Bobby scramble down the path. At the bottom is a man "of about forty . . . still breathing, though unconscious." Dr. Thomas quickly examines the stranger—"His number's up, poor fellow"—noting that his back has been broken in the fall. The doctor goes to notify the authorities about the accident, while Bobby stays with the dying man. Bobby is studying the handsome features of the poor fellow and thinking what rotten luck, when the man regains consciousness for a moment. His eyes open, and he says in a clear voice, "Why didn't they ask Evans?" Then he goes limp, dead.

Bobby reaches in the man's pocket to remove a handkerchief to cover his face. As he does so, a photo is pulled out as well—a woman's face "strangely haunting in quality . . . not easy to forget."

A few days later, on a return trip from London, Bobby bumps into his friend Frankie, Lady Frances Derwent, a very modern, fun-loving, down-to-earth girl. Talk turns to Bobby's recent tragic discovery, and Frankie shows him an item in the papers. The victim was identified by means of a photograph found on the body. He was Alex Pritchard, brother of a Mrs. Cayman.

As they reach their destination, Frankie suggests that someone might have pushed Pritchard over the cliff because "it would make it much more exciting, wouldn't it?"

But the inquest is routine, accidental death the ruling. The unfortunate death is about to be forgotten, until Bobby mentions the dying man's last words in front of the wrong people, and soon finds himself and Frankie off on a wild, if dangerous, gambit to discover who Evans is, and why Evans wasn't asked.

Principal Characters: Dr. George Arbuthnot, Henry Bassington-ffrench, Roger Bassington-ffrench, Sylvia Bassington-ffrench, Tommy Bassington-ffrench, Badger Beadon, Alan Carstairs,

Amelia Cayman, Leo Cayman, Lady Frances (Frankie) Derwent, Robert "Bobby" Jones, Reverend Thomas Jones, Lord Marchington, Dr. Nicholson, Moira Nicholson, Gladys Roberts, Frederick Spragge, Inspector Williams.

First Editions: British: Collins, London, September 1934. 252 pp., 7s. 6d. **American:** with U.S. title *The Boomerang Clue:* Dodd, Mead & Co., New York, 1935. 290 pp., $2.00.

Adaptation: A television dramatization of this novel was presented in the U.S. in May 1981. The drama was imported to the U.S. from Britain's London Weekend Television.

22

PARKER PYNE INVESTIGATES /
MR. PARKER PYNE, DETECTIVE (1934)

Though by no stretch of the imagination can he be considered one of Christie's important detectives, Mr. Parker Pyne displays as much charm in his own small way as more famous cousins in the Christie family. Mr. Pyne is what might be called a Detective of the Heart. Like any good private eye, he advertises in the personal columns, but his "come on" reads, ARE YOU HAPPY? IF NOT, CONSULT MR. PARKER PYNE.

Not unexpectedly, the bulk of his clients are having romantic or marital problems (though in a few of the stories he gets involved in a more traditional criminal-detection case). But Pyne's greatest skill is in devising methods, some of them quite theatrical, for solving personal problems.

As Max Mallowan put it in *Mallowan's Memoirs,* in his discussion of his wife's short stories, Pyne is "possessed of scientific skill in dealing with affairs of the heart."

The origins of Christie's "romantic" detective, and her reasons for dropping him from her repertoire of detectives, remain a mystery.

Pyne is by far the most deceiving of Christie's sleuths. His usual method of operation involves a certain amount of hoodwinking the involved parties; he's not above hiring accomplices to assume disguises and false identities, and he takes an active, even manipulative, role in solving the client's problem.

Yet because he is dealing most often with affairs of the heart and because his cases have happy endings, his deceptions are easily forgiven by the reader. And they are forgiven all the more easily because of Pyne's charming, gentlemanly, *concerned* style.

"Undoubtedly one of Mr. Parker Pyne's greatest assets was his sympathetic manner," Christie writes. "It was a manner that invited confidence." Pyne's sympathetic and charming manner is tempered somewhat by a slightly tongue-in-cheek, fey wisdom, as when one client remarks, "I've a great deal to be thankful for," to which Pyne replies, "We all have. . . . But when we have to remind ourselves of the fact it is a bad sign."

The twelve stories in the collection fall into two groups. The first six (all beginning "The Case of . . .") are Pyne as the personal problem solver, and all have English settings. This first group is notable also because of the cameo appearances of Ariadne Oliver and Miss Felicity Lemon. Miss Lemon works as Pyne's private secretary before settling into a long career in the employ of Hercule Poirot. These six stories were first published in magazine form in 1932; by the mid-thirties (the time of "How Does Your Garden Grow?" from *The Regatta Mystery* (#34, 1939), Miss Lemon had been hired by Poirot, and in later books and stories was the subject of some of Christie's funniest character descriptions.

Felicity Lemon appears in six Christie short stories, and four novels, the first being *Hickory Dickory Dock* (#60, 1955). Why Christie waited so long to use Felicity Lemon in a full-length novel remains a mystery. Her appearances in these novels and short stories are usually brief and have no significance to the story, except in *Hickory Dickory Dock* (see #60).

Mrs. Oliver achieved fame in the Christie pantheon as the author's parody of herself (actually Ariadne is Christie's parody of Christie's public image). In later books she was to become a frequent Poirot companion, and something of a spokeswoman for Christie's views. Mrs. Oliver makes her first appearance in a novel in *Cards on the Table* (#27, 1936).

The second group of stories in the volume have foreign settings; their plots are more conventional detection than the first six, since they revolve around theft and murder instead of romantic problems. The settings (the Orient Express, Baghdad, Shiraz, the North African desert, the Nile River, and Delphi) reflect Christie's frequent Middle Eastern trips with her second husband, archaeologist Max Mallowan. In his memoirs, Mallowan mentions in particular "The House at Shiraz," which uses as its setting an empty house the Mallowans visited about 1933. He also notes that the house later became a summer residence of the Shah of Iran.

The Mallowans' visit to Petra, in present-day Jordan, made at about the same time, provided the setting for "The Pearl of Price."

Most of the exotic settings in this second sextet were used in later, and more famous, mysteries. *Murder on the Orient Express* (#19, 1934), of course, and *They Came to Baghdad* (#53, 1951). Petra was the setting for *Appointment with Death* (#31, 1938). Mr. Pyne's short story encounter with "Death on the Nile" shares the title and setting (though not the plot) with Agatha's 1937 novel.

Parker Pyne makes only two other brief appearances outside this collection, in the stories "Problem at Pollensa Bay" and "The Regatta Mystery" in the 1939 American collection *The Regatta Mystery and Other Stories* (#34).

PLOTS:

"The Case of the Middle-Aged Wife"

When Mrs. Packington, whose husband is paying more attention to a secretary in his office than to his wife of many years, answers an ad in the papers reading, ARE YOU HAPPY? IF NOT, CONSULT MR. PARKER PYNE, she soon finds herself being dazzled and swept off her feet by the handsome Mr. Luttrell.

"The Case of the Discontented Soldier"

Major Wilbraham, recently retired after a life of action in the military, finds himself bored and unhappy enough to answer Parker Pyne's newspaper ad. Before long the major finds himself rescuing blond Freda Clegg from two burly attackers, and, with Freda in tow, searching for treasure buried in Africa.

"The Case of the Distressed Lady"

Pretty Daphne St. John enlists Parker Pyne's aid in returning a valuable diamond she has stolen from her friend Lady Dortheimer, which she replaced with a paste copy, and pawned to pay off gambling debts. Now, repenting her rash act and having redeemed the pawned jewel, Daphne needs help in getting the real diamond back on Lady D's finger, without the owner's detecting the substitution.

"The Case of the Discontented Husband"

Good-natured, athletic, but rather inarticulate, Reginald Wade goes to Parker Pyne when he learns that his wife has decided to leave him for long-haired, artsy young Sinclair Jordan. Reggie's only hope is that his wife has declared a six-month grace period. If she's still of like mind at the end, she wants a divorce. Pyne decides that dark, glamorous Madeline de Sara is just what Reggie needs to console him. But Mrs. Wade gets a bit upset when her husband and his girl friend start kissing in front of her, right in her own house.

"The Case of the City Clerk"

While his wife and children are on holiday with his mother-in-law, mild, conventional Mr. Roberts goes to Parker Pyne, looking for whatever excitement can be brought into his drab clerk's life, for the meager five pounds he can afford. Pyne decides that Mr. Roberts is just the man to travel to Geneva with secret plans, and Roberts finds more romance and intrigue than he'd bargained for.

"The Case of the Rich Woman"

Mrs. Abner Rymer goes to Pyne for help. Her wealthy new friends and her old working-class friends shun her, and she is widowed and childless, so she is desperately lonely. After Pyne takes her to see Dr. Constantine, an Oriental sage, Mrs. Rymer passes out and awakens with a totally different identity.

"Have You Got Everything You Want?"

Elsie Jeffries, married a year and a half to successful businessman Edward, meets Parker Pyne by chance on the Simplon–Orient Express. She has seen Pyne's ads and feels he may be of help. She tells him that she has seen a fragment of a letter left on Edward's blotting pad, which points to some sort of plot against her while on the train to Stamboul.

"The Gate of Baghdad"

While Parker Pyne is on tour of the Middle East, traveling across the desert from Damascus to Baghdad with his tour and a group of RAF officers, one of the officers, Smethurst, tells Pyne he's worried about something. But Smethurst is killed before he can reveal exactly what's on his mind. The death turns out to be linked with the disappearance of Samuel Long, stock-market millionaire and embezzler.

"The House at Shiraz"

On tour in Persia, Parker Pyne is approached by Herr Schlagel, the pilot who has flown the detective to the small town of Shiraz, about a personal matter. The young German pilot has become romantically involved with an Englishwoman, Lady Ester Carr, an expatriate living in Shiraz, but Lady Carr has become an eccentric recluse, shut up in her villa, since her maid, Muriel King, fell to her death from the terrace some time ago.

"The Pearl of Price"

While on tour of the African desert, Parker Pyne investigates the theft of a valuable pearl earring from pretty Carol Blundell. Though Carol's father has stressed how valuable the earrings are, the theft seems to make little impression on Miss Blundell's traveling companions, an archaeologist, a detective, a jaded suitor, and an ex-convict.

"Death on the Nile"

Parker Pyne travels on a Nile charter boat with the Grayle party, a group of wealthy Britishers and their companions. Lady Grayle soon lets Pyne know that someone is trying to poison her. The evidence points to her husband, since she's ill only when he's with her.

"The Oracle at Delphi"

Well-to-do widow Peters takes her quiet, bookish son, Willard, to Greece, where the boy pores over antiquities all day while his mother strikes up a friendship with Parker Pyne. When Willard is kidnapped by bandits, and a ransom of £10,000, or Mrs. Peters's jewel necklace, is demanded, Pyne helps the distraught mother concoct a ruse that will save the jewels and get her son safely back to her.

First Editions: British: Collins, London, 1934. 248 pp., 7s. 6d. **American**: with U.S. title *Mr. Parker Pyne, Detective:* Dodd, Mead & Co., New York, 1934. 245 pp., $2.00.

Adaptation: The stories "The Case of the Discontented Soldier" and "The Case of the Middle-Aged Wife" were adapted for television as part of the Thames Television series *The Agatha Christie Hour*.

◈ 23 ◈

THREE ACT TRAGEDY / MURDER IN THREE ACTS
(1935)

In 1935, as Christie began her fifteenth year as a professional novelist, husband Max began his archaeological excavation at Tell Chagar Bazar in Syria. Max, who spent two seasons at this site, had a staff that included Agatha, assistants Robin Macartney and Richard Barnett, and about one hundred and forty men, consisting of Arabs, Kurds, Christians, and the devil-worshiping Yezidis.

The seasons spent at Chagar Bazar were to figure prominently in the author's reminiscences of the Middle East, *Come, Tell Me How You Live* (1946). In spite of her travel schedule and her active participation in the archaeology at Chagar Bazar and other sites during this period, Christie's literary productivity was remarkable. She published three novels in 1935 alone.

Three Act Tragedy is a far cry from the Middle Eastern desert that had so much influence on Christie's work. It is set in England and was influenced by another of her great loves, the theatre. Her sister Madge and brother Monty went to the theatre almost every week, and young Agatha would be allowed to tag along. The three usually sat in the pit stalls, which cost a shilling. One of the first plays Christie remembered seeing is *Heart and Trumps,* written by Cecil Raleigh (1856–1914), which opened at the Drury Lane Theatre, London, in September 1899. She was nine years old and she recalled the play as "a roaring melodrama of the worst type."

In 1906 Agatha went to Paris to attend Miss Dryden's, a fashionable "finishing" school on the Avenue du Bois near the Arc de Triomphe in Paris. Agatha enjoyed her stay and her studies there, especially, as she recalls in her autobiography, the drama class where members of the Comédie-Française (the national theatre of France), would come to give "talks on Molière, Racine and Corneille." Her class often went to the Comédie-Française to see many of the classics performed, as well as an occasional modern play.

Agatha Christie saw the legendary Sarah Bernhardt perform in Edmond Rostand's *Chantecler* in Paris in 1910. She said of Madame Sarah, "she was old, lame, feeble, and her golden voice was cracked, but she was certainly a great actress, she held you with her impassioned emotion." Christie was also impressed with another French actress, Réjane, whom she thought was "even more exciting than Sarah Bernhardt" when she saw her perform in the Paul Ernest Hervieu play *La Course du Flambeau.*

Given her early love of the theatre, it was only a matter of time before the author tried her own hand at stage writing. Although Christie could not remember when she wrote her first detective play, she remembered the "terrible suffering" she endured with the project. For one thing the play wasn't approved by her agent, Hughes Massie, who told the potential playwright "to forget it entirely." She did for a while, but eventually the play titled *Black Coffee* was pulled together and in 1930 opened in the West End and had a modest run. (For more on *Black Coffee,* see Part Two.)

Christie's love of the theatre also spilled over into her mystery novels, as evidenced by *Three Act Tragedy,* which is divided into three "acts" of several chapters each. The original hardcover editions also begin with a lot of production credits, such as those found in a theatre program. One of these credits is "Illumination by Hercule Poirot." The book also stars Hercule Poirot; supporting cast of players includes "A dried-up little pipkin of a man," who is a "very shrewd observer of people and things." This is Mr. Satterthwaite, who also appears in all of the Harley Quin stories, as that detective's companion and observer.

Agatha Christie turns in one of *her* superb performances by applying her in-depth knowledge of poisons. The poison she selects is nicotine, a pure liquid alkaloid which causes respiratory failure and paralysis and kills the unfortunate person almost instantly. Before the final curtain falls on *Three Act Tragedy,* Poirot reminds Mr. Satterthwaite and the reader, that he, Hercule Poirot, could have fallen victim to the nicotine poison and been killed—one of the rare instances of Poirot himself being in danger.

Without giving away too much, it's interesting that *Three Act Tragedy* shares a plot device with *The ABC Murders* (#25, 1936). Though Christie's works show an enormous variety of murder plot inventions, there are several types of plot devices that she used more than once: the locked-room murder, murder in retrospect, and a series of murders in which only one death is really significant. *The Mysterious Affair at Styles* (#1, 1920), and *Hercule Poirot's Christmas* (#32, 1938) are locked-room murders; *Five Little Pigs* (#41, 1943), *Sparkling Cyanide* (#45, 1945), and *Sleeping Murder* (#83, 1976) are examples of murders in retrospect; and *The ABC Murders* (#25, 1936) and *Three Act Tragedy* fall into the third category, which might be called red-herring murders.

One of Christie's best lines about one of her favorite character types, the village spinster, appears in this book. When Sir Bartholomew hints to Sir Charles that there's a romance between Sir Charles and his not-too-attractive housekeeper, Miss Milray, Sir Charles says, "The most scandal-loving old cat in the neighborhood couldn't seriously connect sexual passion with a face like that." Sir Bartholomew sums it all up with his response: "You underrate the imagination of the British spinster."

The reviews were mixed for this Christie performance. "Not so good," wrote the *Saturday Review of Literature* (10/6/34). Isaac Anderson in the *New York Times* said, "Since this is an Agatha Christie novel having Hercule Poirot as its leading character, it is quite unnecessary to say that it makes uncommonly good reading" (10/7/34); and Mortimer Quick in the *Chicago Daily Tribune* wrote, "A very readable and amusing story, but, my! how the denouement does let you down" (10/20/34).

Despite the reviews, *Three Act Tragedy* became Christie's first book to achieve sales of 10,000 copies in its first year of publication. This record established Christie, once and for all, as a best-selling author. From then on, sales would increase with each new publication. Christie could hardly be considered an overnight success. It took her fifteen years and twenty-three books to set that record. Her first book, published in 1920, *The Mysterious Affair at Styles* (#1) sold a meager 2,000 copies its first time around.

The dedication for *Three Act Tragedy* was ". . . to My Friends, Geoffrey and Violet Shipston."

PLOT:

Dry, cultured, perceptive Mr. Satterthwaite is guesting at Sir

Charles Cartwright's place overlooking the sea about a mile outside Loomouth. There are to be thirteen for dinner that night, though Miss Milray, Sir Charles's secretary, volunteers to be the fourteenth guest at the table because "so many people are superstitious." The guests include Lady Mary Lytton Gore and her beautiful daughter, nicknamed Egg, who seems to be quite a bit in Sir Charles's company these days, and a man whose name almost escapes the host, Hercule Poirot.

The guests assemble in the dining room, and the parlormaid makes her round with a tray of cocktails. The Reverend Stephen Babbington, rector of Loomouth, chokes on his first sip, and becomes ill. Before the eyes of the startled guests, he falls to a couch and dies.

Sir Charles suspects that the vicar's unexpected demise was not due to natural causes, and asks that the deceased's martini glass be sent for chemical analysis. When asked his opinion about this procedure, Poirot remarks that "they will find only the remains of an excellent dry Martini." This proves to be the case, though as the second act of the tragedy takes place, it becomes clear that poor Rev. Babbington acted well his part upon the stage, until Poirot rings down the final curtain.

Principal Characters: Mrs. Margaret Babbington, Reverend Stephen Babbington, Sir Charles Cartwright, Doris Cocker, Superintendent Crossfield, Cynthia Dacres, Margaret de Rushbridger, Colonel Johnson, Hermione "Egg" Lytton Gore, Lady Mary Lytton Gore, Oliver Manders, Mrs. Milray, Violet Milray, Hercule Poirot, Mr. Satterthwaite, Sir Bartholomew "Tollie" Strange, Angela Sutcliffe, Miss Temple, Muriel Wills.

First Editions: **British**: Collins, London, January 1935. 252 pp., 7s. 6d. **American**: with U.S. title *Murder in Three Acts*: Dodd, Mead & Co., New York, 1934. 279 pp., $2.00. (Note that the American edition was published before the British edition, an unusual occurrence for a Christie book.)

Adaptation: None.

DEATH IN THE CLOUDS / DEATH IN THE AIR
(1935)

Part of Agatha Christie's education at Miss Dryden's finishing school in Paris was various outings designed to enrich the pupils' awareness: the Eiffel Tower, the Louvre, the Bois de Boulogne, and now and again, a few "modern" sights calculated to keep these pubescent daughters of the British gentry informed about progress in science and technology. Among these was a demonstration of that newfangled gadget, the aeroplane.

"We were taken one day to see Santos-Dumont endeavor to get up off the ground in the Bois de Boulogne," Agatha recalled in her autobiography. "As far as I remember, the aeroplane got up, flew a few yards, then crashed. All the same, we were impressed."

What Agatha and her fellow finishing-school girls had seen was an important event in the history of world aviation. The flight was made on November 12, 1906, by Brazilian-born aviator Alberto Santos-Dumont (1873–1932). The Wright brothers' epochal flight had been made at Kitty Hawk on December 17, 1903, and it was Santos-Dumont who duplicated their achievement of sustained engine-powered flight for the first time in Europe, with Agatha and the other girls from Miss Dryden's looking on.

Agatha's fascination with flight continued: "Then there were the Wright brothers. We read about them eagerly." In 1911 when Agatha and her mother were visiting friends in the country they attended one of the barnstorming flying exhibitions that were so popular during the early days of aviation. While at the exhibition, Agatha, who was about twenty-one at the time, couldn't resist going up for a spin in one of the exhibition planes, and cajoled her mother into paying the rather steep fare of five pounds (about twenty-five dollars at the time) so she could take a five-minute flight in an open cockpit biplane.

"Five minutes of ecstasy—and a half crown extra for a photograph" was how she described it. She kept the photograph her entire life, "a dot in the sky that is *me* in an aeroplane," with the date inscribed, May 10, 1911.

By the time Christie came to write *Death in the Clouds* in 1935, much of the novelty of flight had worn off, though every year brought innovations and developments. Passenger travel by air burgeoned after World War I. The first Paris–London airline service flight was flown on February 18, 1919, by a converted bomber; on this flight the passengers were all military officers because civilian flying was still prohibited by wartime restrictions.

Regular London–Paris service began in August of that year, when Air Transport and Travel Limited, again using converted bombers, offered service from Hounslow Aerodome to Paris.

Cross-channel routes soon became popular with businessmen and tourists, and airlines began to offer more and more extras to encourage passenger travel, such as hot meals, flight attendants, and decorated cabins.

By the 1930s, there were numerous flights daily between London and Paris. The airfield at Croydon, in one of London's outer boroughs, was built in 1915, and designated in March 1919 as the London terminus for air traffic from the Continent; by 1930, it had become a bustling metropolitan airport, the Heathrow of its day.

When Hercule Poirot and his fellow passengers landed at Croydon in 1935, at the end of their death-marred flight from Le Bourget airfield in Paris, they were undoubtedly flying in the greatest of the British passenger planes of the day, the Imperial Airways H.P. 42 Hannibal-class biplane. The H.P. 42 was a slow-flying plane of rather ungainly proportions. The craft averaged a modest 100 m.p.h., and the upper of the two wings was considerably longer than the lower. But the plane had many features that appealed to commercial travelers. The fuselage suspended beneath the two wings and four engines was spacious by the day's standards; the enclosed cockpit enabled the flight crew to wear blue suits and gold braid instead of leather flight jackets and goggles; and the thirty-odd passengers enjoyed the luxury of full-course hot meals and washrooms.

The H.P. 42 was so successful that during the 1930s it flew more passengers between London and the Continent than all other aircraft combined; during its remarkable career, the plane (there were only eight of them built) flew over ten million miles, without a single passenger injury.

Though Christie does not specifically mention the H.P. 42 in *Death in the Clouds,* there is little question that it is the plane that carried Madame Giselle on her death flight. (Would this make her the only passenger fatality in the H.P. 42's history?) Aside from the fact that the plane was the most common passenger plane on the London–Paris route during the 1930s, Christie named her plane the *Prometheus,* and the actual H.P. 42s all had names taken from classical sources: *Hercules, Helen,* and so on. In addition, the cabin plan that Christie drew for the fatal flight shows the two-cabin, central pantry/washroom configuration of the H.P. 42.

As for the plot itself, Christie tackles the problem of a murder—call it a closed-cabin murder, if you will—committed right across the aisle from the great Belgian. The problem is tackled fairly, and with all the deftness and skill one expects from this decade of her work. The period interest provided by the details of the flight, and by the charming assortment of characters in the second cabin, only add to the book's strength and appeal.

"A crime puzzle of the first quality, and a mighty entertaining story besides," said Isaac Anderson in the *New York Times* (3/24/35), while Mortimer Quick in the *Chicago Daily Tribune* thought the book was "entertaining, swift, plausible to a degree, but pretty hard to swallow at the latter end" (3/23/35).

"Very good," pronounced *Saturday Review* (3/23/35), while Will Cuppy in *Books* (*New York Herald Tribune*) said, "Where the plot is a bit thick, you can take it with a smile" (3/24/35).

Finally the *Times Literary Supplement* (London) said, "It will be a very acute reader who does not receive a complete surprise at the end" (7/4/35). Christie dedicated the book "To my old friend Sybil Healey, with affection."

PLOT:

Twenty-one passengers board the *Prometheus* at Le Bourget aerodome in France in preparation for a day flight to Croydon airfield outside London. The rear compartment, with eleven passengers, is the odd assortment of characters one might expect to be thrown together during air travel, some traveling singly, others in pairs. The midday flight is routine, a meal and coffee served aloft by the two stewards, the passengers absorbed in their various interests. The only event out of the ordinary is a wasp buzzing in the cabin, which is finally killed by one of the passengers. As one of the stewards collects money from the passengers after the meal service, he notices that two are asleep: a little man, wearing unnecessary mufflers and sporting a big mustache, and "a stoutish, middle-aged woman dressed in heavy black," whom the steward recognizes as having made the crossing several times before.

The little muffled man awakes and pays for his mineral water and biscuit, but about five minutes out of Croydon, the steward is forced to awaken the sleeping woman.

He is unsuccessful, because she is dead.

Among the passengers is a doctor, who inspects the woman's body, and pronounces that she has been dead at least half an hour. The doctor is joined in his inspection by the muffled passenger, who points out that there is a small puncture on the deceased woman's neck.

Of course, the wasp is suspected; that is, until the diminutive, mustachioed gentleman points with the tip of his patent leather shoe to a small orange-and-black object on the floor of the cabin, "very like a wasp, but it is not a wasp."

The object is determined to be a blowgun dart and, as the *Prometheus* lands, the discoverer of the object, none other than Poirot, of course, is challenged with discovering who killed the woman in the closed compartment in full view of the other passengers.

Principal Characters: Raymond Barraclough, Dr. Roger James Bryant, Daniel Clancy, Lord Dawlish, Armand Dupont, Jean Dupont, Monsieur Fournier, Norman Gale, Madame Giselle, Elise Grandier, Jane Grey, Lady Cicely Horbury, Lord Stephen Horbury, Chief Inspector James Japp, the Honorable Venetia Anne Kerr, Andrew Leech, Henry Charles Mitchell, Ruth Mitchell, Anne Morisot, Jules Perrot, Hercule Poirot, Miss Ross, James Bell Ryder, Maitre Alexandre Thibault, Dr. James Whistler, Detective Sergeant Wilson, Henry Winterspoon, Monsieur Zeropoulos.

First Editions: British: Collins, London, July 1935. 252 pp., 7s. 6d. **American:** with U.S. title *Death in the Air:* Dodd, Mead & Co., New York, 1935. 304 pp., $2.00.

Adaptation: None.

25

THE ABC MURDERS (1936)

"A masterwork of carefully concealed artifice . . . most stunningly original," crime novelist and critic Julian Symons said of *The ABC Murders* in *Agatha Christie: First Lady of Crime* (1977). Since its publication, critics and readers alike have shared Symons's enthusiasm and admiration for this, one of Christie's slickest, classiest deceptions.

As was pointed out earlier, the ploy used is similar to that in the 1935 *Three Act Tragedy* (#23). A series of murders is committed, apparently related. The deception is that only one of the murders has real significance; the others are merely deadly diversions. The ABC of the title is taken from the familiar British railway guide, known as *The ABC Rail Guide,* which derives its name from the alphabetical listings of station stops it contains.

Christie cleverly structures her murders so they correspond with the guide. The first victim's initials are A.A., and the body is found at a station stop in the "A" listings, with an ABC guide found near the body as a deliberate clue. And so the sequence goes, though as Christie critic Robert Barnard writes in *A Talent To Deceive—an Appreciation of Agatha Christie* (1980), it was "a total success—but thank God she didn't try taking it through to Z." (This might have been difficult without cheating, since the British rail guide has no Z listings.)

During the mid-1930s, Christie spent several months a year with husband Max on archaeological digs in the Middle East, and it is possible that *The ABC Murders* was written at Chagar Bazar, Syria. "I enjoy writing while I am in the desert," Christie said. "There are no distractions such as telephones, theatres, operas, houses and gardens." Though there is no hard evidence, it is possible that all or most of Christie's books between 1933 and 1938 were written at least in part in Syria and Iraq.

The critics were lavish with praise for this novel. Isaac Anderson in the *New York Times* wrote: "This story is a baffler of the first water, written in Agatha Christie's best manner. It seems to us the very best thing she has done, not even excepting 'Roger Ackroyd'" (2/16/36). Ralph Partridge in the *New Statesman and Nation* said, "Once more our half-yearly homage is due to Mrs. Christie, who has held the throne of detection for the last ten years, and brooks no rival near her. There have been old pretenders, but where are they now? 'Where (gaudy) Night and Chaos hold eternal anarchy'" (1/25/36). Will Cuppy in *Books* (*New York Herald Tribune*) wrote, "The slickest baffler we've read in months. It's Agatha Christie at her best, than which there isn't anything superior in the mystery racket" (2/16/36). C. W. Morton, Jr., in the *Boston Transcript* wrote, "It seemed to us that the murderer's characteristics were just a bit too firmly postulated by all concerned for things to turn as they did, otherwise it is one of those beautifully put-together Christie yarns with the stamp of expert, sound taste and intelligence on every page" (2/15/36). The *New Yorker* said, "Recommended highly for this writer's admirers" (2/23/36).

Agatha Christie dedicated this classic "To James Watts—one of my most sympathetic readers."

James Watts, husband of Christie's sister, Madge, had an important influence on several of his sister-in-law's novels (see *The Murder of Roger Ackroyd, #7*). It was he who once said, "Almost everybody turns out to be a criminal nowadays in detective stories—even the detective. What I would like to see is a Watson who turned out to be the criminal." This was a suggestion Agatha was to use in slightly varied form in one of her most famous books. And it was James's complaint about Christie's murders being too bloodless that led to the throat-slashing murder in *Hercule Poirot's Christmas* (#32, 1938).

PLOT:

In June 1935, Captain Hastings returns to England from his ranch in South America for a six months' stay. The first order of business is to look up Hercule Poirot. The famous detective is now of an age to find a dye bottle handy in maintaining the jet blackness of his hair, but as for his official retirement from crime, Poirot says, "I am like the Prima Donna who makes positively the farewell performance! That farewell performance, it reveals itself an indefinite number of times!"

Poirot then tells Hastings that a matter at hand has him perplexed, whereupon he produces a note addressed to him: "MR. HERCULE POIROT—You fancy yourself, don't you, at solving mysteries that are too difficult for our poor thick-headed British police? Let us see, Mr. Clever Poirot, just how clever you can be. Perhaps you'll find this nut too hard to crack. Look out for Andover on the 21st of the month. Yours, etc., ABC."

Poirot has shown the note to Inspector Japp of Scotland Yard, who thinks it's merely a crackpot hoax. But something in the note worries Poirot. Early on the morning of the 22nd, the body of Alice Ascher, a shopkeeper in Andover, is found in the modest shop she kept. She has been struck over the back of the head with a blunt object. From questioning shop customers, the police determine that the murder took place between 5:30 and 6:05 on the 21st. And a British railway guide listing stations in alphabetical order, known popularly as an ABC guide, is found open on the counter next to Mrs. Ascher's body, turned to the page listing trains from Andover.

Principal Characters: Colonel Anderson, Alice Ascher, Franz Ascher, Mr. Barnard, Mrs. Barnard, Elizabeth Barnard, Megan Barnard, Sir Carmichael Clarke, Lady Charlotte Clarke, Franklin Clarke, Inspector Crome, Alexander Bonaparte Cust, Mary Drower, George Earlsfield, Donald Fraser, Thora Grey, Tom Hartigan, Captain Hastings, Milly Higley, Jameson, Chief Inspector James Japp, Dr. Kerr, Sir Lionel, Hercule Poirot, Dr. Thompson.

First Editions: **British**: Collins, London, January 1936. 252 pp., 7s. 6d. **American:** Dodd, Mead & Co., New York, 1936. 306 pp., $2.00.

Adaptation: The film based on this novel, titled *The Alphabet Murders,* was released in 1966. Tony Randall starred as Poirot, and Robert Morley was featured as Hastings.

26

MURDER IN MESOPOTAMIA (1936)

Murder in Mesopotamia is an outgrowth of Christie's yearly visits to the Middle East on her husband's archaeological expeditions, beginning in 1930, the year of their marriage, until 1938 and the disruptions of World War II.

Max Mallowan's first major archaeological work was done as an assistant on the expeditions conducted by Leonard Woolley, who gained fame for his important work at the biblical site of Ur in Mesopotamia. Mesopotamia, much of which is now in the Republic of Iraq, is the area between the Tigris and Euphrates rivers. It was at the dig at Ur that Woolley and his wife, Katharine, introduced Christie to Mallowan in 1930 (see chapters on *The Murder at the Vicarage,* #13, 1930, and *The Thirteen Problems,* #16, 1932). Christie had visited Ur in 1928 and "fell in love" with the ancient city.

Ur of the Chaldees, as it was called in biblical times, was an important city of Sumer, southern Mesopotamia. It is described in the Bible as the home of Abraham. The findings by Leonard Woolley enabled scholars to trace the history of Ur, from its last days during the fourth century B.C., back to its beginnings in the fourth millennium B.C. Woolley's work in this area, known as "the cradle of civilization," was important because it provided a great deal of information about much of the everyday life in Ur, including art, architecture, literature, government, and religion.

In his memoirs Max wrote that Christie modeled the character of Mrs. Leidner on that of the "masterful" Katharine Woolley, who was known as a demanding, difficult, but fascinating woman. "Here perhaps Agatha touched rather near the bone and for once was apprehensive about what this *dramatic persona* might say. Fortunately, and perhaps not unexpectedly, Katharine did not recognize certain traits which might have been taken as applicable to herself, and took no umbrage in this book. I figured as Emmott, a minor but decent character."

Whatever Katharine Woolley's opinion of this book was, she kept it to herself. The critics were divided. The *Saturday Review of Literature* wrote, "No Poirot story can be dull, but this one has the most improbable plot and the weakest characterization of all" (10/17/36). Kay Irvin in the *New York Times* said, "This latest Christie opus is a smooth, highly original and completely absorbing tale" (9/20/36). Nicholas Blake wrote in the *Spectator* that "Mrs. Christie writes with her usual humour and economy, and Poirot is in good form. I felt, however, that too many of the discoveries are left to the end" (8/7/36).

Murder in Mesopotamia was dedicated by Christie "To my many archaeological friends in Iraq and Syria."

PLOT:

Amy Leatheran, an English nurse, age thirty-two, finds herself in Baghdad when she is hired to accompany a new mother and infant to the Middle East. Leatheran is about to return to England when she learns that Dr. Leidner, a Swedish-American archaeologist currently excavating a nearby site, is looking for a nurse-companion for his wife, who is subject to fits of "nervous terrors."

Amy is hired by Leidner, and travels four hours from Baghdad to the town of Hassanieh, on the Tigris River, at the dig site of Tell Yarimjah.

Mrs. Leidner, who both demands and commands attention from those around her, is clearly a woman under great strain. She likes Amy and takes her into her confidence. Her first husband, a German spy, was supposedly killed in a train wreck years before. But she is convinced he is alive, and determined to wreck her new marriage. There have been warning letters and even been an attempt against the couple's lives.

Even after Leatheran's arrival there are incidents, but the members of the expedition attribute them to Mrs. Leidner's nervous and imaginative nature.

However, one afternoon Louise Leidner is murdered by a blow from a heavy object. Due to circumstances, and to the closed arrangement of the rooms at Tell Yarimjah, the murder must have taken place within a ten-minute period, and been committed by someone living and working in the building. Fortunately Hercule

Poirot is passing through the area, and, at the request of the baffled local authorities, looks into the case.

Principal Characters: Ali Yusuf, Frederick Bosner, Richard Carey, Bill Coleman, David Emmott, Anne Johnson, Major Kelsey, Mary Kelsey, Father Lavigny, Amy Leatheran, Dr. Eric Leidner, Louise Leidner, Captain Maitland, Raoul Menier, Joseph Mercado, Marie Mercado, Major Pennyman, Hercule Poirot, Dr. Giles Reilly, Sheila Reilly, Carl Reiter, Monsieur Verrier.

First Editions: **British**: Collins, London, July 1936, 284 pp., 7s. 6d. **American**: Dodd, Mead & Co., New York, 1936. 298 pp., $2.00.

Adaptation: None.

❖ 27 ❖

CARDS ON THE TABLE (1936)

Agatha Christie states in her foreword to this book that this was one of Poirot's "favourite cases," a sentiment not shared by his friend Captain Hastings, who thought this case "very dull." Christie warns her readers that there will be only four suspects who, *"given the right circumstances,* might have committed the crime . . . the deduction must, therefore, be entirely *psychological."* The solution to this crime can also *possibly* be reached by a reader who has a good knowledge of bridge, and like Poirot, is able to analyze the bridge scores of the four players.*

Christie arranges her tour de force around an evening of bridge at the home of the manipulative, mysterious Mr. Shaitana, who has invited two quartets of bridge players. One group of four players contains the suspects in the murder. In the second group are four crime experts: Hercule Poirot, Superintendent Battle of Scotland Yard, Colonel Race of the British Secret Service (Battle and Race had been featured in earlier Christie novels), and Mrs. Ariadne Oliver, the feminist writer "of detective and other sensational stories." This is Mrs. Oliver's debut in novel form. She made two brief appearances in the 1934 short story collection, *Parker Pyne Investigates* (#22, 1934). By bringing together four criminologists at the scene of the murder-to-be, Christie is clearly telling her readers that they are about to be presented with a virtuoso murder puzzle, which she will unravel with her virtuoso skill.

The ABC Murders (#25, 1936) contains a description of the crime in *Cards on the Table.* "Supposing," murmured Poirot, "that four people sit down to play bridge and one, the odd man out, sits in a chair by the fire. At the end of the evening the man

---

* The author's foreword cannot be found in the latest Dell paperback edition (1979). Instead, the reader will find a teaser on the first page (not written by Christie), which suggests there are seven possible suspects instead of four.

by the fire is found dead. One of the four, while he is dummy, has gone over and killed him, and, intent on the play of the hand, the other three have not noticed. Ah, there would be a crime for you! *Which of the four was it?"*

When Christie wrote that passage in *The ABC Murders,* did she not yet know that would be the plot of this mystery, or did she already have *Cards on the Table* thought out or written and decide to amuse herself and give her readers a hint of the masterpiece to come?

Max Mallowan, Christie's husband, wrote in his memoirs that Mrs. Oliver was "lightly sketched, but a portrayal of Agatha herself." Christie was a lover of apples and would sometimes think out her next plot while eating them in her bathtub. Mrs. Oliver, too, had a passion for apples. She had "been known to eat as many as five pounds" of the fruit while conjuring up a plot. Mrs. Oliver "was an agreeable woman of middle age, handsome in a rather untidy fashion with fine eyes, substantial shoulders and a large quantity of rebellious grey hair with which she was continually experimenting." Mrs. Oliver, a feminist, who believed a woman should be the head of Scotland Yard, would appear in six more Christie novels, mostly with Poirot. Her next appearance, however, wasn't until 1952 when she appeared in *Mrs. McGinty's Dead* (#55).

Like Christie, Mrs. Oliver was the creator of a foreign detective. Christie's Poirot was Belgian, and Oliver's Sven Hjerson was Finnish. Another similarity was that both ladies would eventually tire of their successful detectives. Also, Mrs. Oliver, like Christie, was shy in crowds, and had a successful career; her books were best-sellers in England and America, and were translated into many languages.

Max points out that there is a passage in *Cards on the Table* describing "the pain and toil of writing" that Christie endured. "One actually has to *think,* you know. And thinking is always a bore. And you have to plan things. And then one gets stuck every now and then, and you feel you'll never get out of the mess—but you do! Writing's not particularly enjoyable. It's hard work, like everything else."

Another item of interest appears at the beginning of *Cards on the Table,* when one of the dinner guests sees Mrs. Oliver and asks Poirot if she is "The one who wrote *The Body in the Library.*" Poirot replied "That identical one." Agatha Christie's own book with that title was published in 1942, with Miss Marple at the helm.

A word of caution to any eagle-eyed readers who pick up *Cards on the Table* before *Murder on the Orient Express* (#19, 1934). The solution to that crime is revealed in *Cards on the Table.* It's a small reference, but nonetheless the observant may resent having the solution to one of Christie's most popular and exciting works revealed to them.

References are made by Christie in this book to that "damned dago, Shaitana." There is a reference to a solicitor's being "rather alert and Jewish," and there's the remark, "I never forget a face—even a black one—and that's a lot more than most people can say." It is not unusual while reading the early Christie novels to come across some racial and ethnic slurs. Christie was a product of her times, reflecting the middle- and upper-middle-class English attitude toward foreigners. Many of the American editions of these novels had the slurs deleted. Though offensive, perhaps the slurs shouldn't have been excised in the American editions because they do provide an insight into Christie's prejudices and those of her contemporaries. It's interesting that in the American edition of this novel only the anti-"dago" and anti-Semitic remarks were removed. The insulting reference to blacks was left in.

It was during the 1930s that an incident occurred in Christie's life that would cause her to cease inserting anti-Semitic remarks in her books. The incident, related by Christie in her autobiography, took place while she was in Baghdad. She was having tea at the home of Dr. Jordan, the German director of antiquities, whom she described as a "gentle and considerate" man. However, when Jews were mentioned "his face changed; changed in an extraordinary way that I had never noticed on anyone's face before." Dr. Jordan told Christie, "They should be exterminated. Nothing else will really do but that." Christie had met her first Nazi and soon discovered that his wife was even worse than he.

An interesting footnote about the character of Mr. Shaitana appears in a *Time* magazine review of *Come, Tell Me How You Live,* the informal, autobiographical description of Christie's years with her husband on his digging expeditions in Iraq and Syria.

"Christie fans will find some clues to the origin of various matters in her mystery stories of the period. There is, for example, the gentle cult of the yezidis, some of whom are hired as diggers. They worship Shaitana (Satan) whom they believe God has placed in charge of the world. No Christie reader will fail to recognize the prototype of Mr. Shaitana, a curiously devilish figure in Christie's *Cards on the Table*" (10/28/46).

Cards on the Table was one of Max Mallowan's favorites because of the ingenious technique which makes use of no more than four suspects, only one of whom has committed the murder, and the difficulty in spite of the apparent simplicity of the circumstances, in determining which is the guilty party. The critics agreed with Max. Ralph Partridge in the *New Statesman and Nation* wrote, "Mrs. Christie is forever Mrs. Christie. *Cards on the Table* is one of her inimitable chess problems. The only information Mrs. Christie does not impart is whether this time she has constructed a two-mover or a three-mover. And it is just there you may go wrong. But if you do join the lugubrious ranks of 'incorrect solvers,' you must blame yourself; Mrs. Christie remains impeccable though without cunning" (11/12/36). Will Cuppy in *Books* (*New York Herald Tribune*) wrote, "We always say there's nobody quite like Agatha Christie when she puts her mind to it, and that's what she has done in *Cards on the Table*" (2/21/37). Nicholas Blake in the *Spectator* was impressed and wrote, "Her opening situation in *Cards on the Table* is, I think, the best she has ever devised. The book lags a little in the middle, but it gathers pace again with a second murder, and—as usual—the author savagely tweaks our legs at the end" (11/20/36).

A later article from the *Times Literary Supplement* (London) perhaps sums up *Cards on the Table* best. "If the most intelligent detective story so far written is Dorothy Sayers's *Five Red Herrings*, it is certain that Mrs. Christie's *Cards on the Table* whose solution depends on the study of bridge hands runs it close" (9/18/70).

PLOT:

At an exhibit of snuffboxes at Wessex House, Hercule Poirot encounters Mr. Shaitana, the Mephistophelian man "of whom nearly everybody was a little afraid," though his parties, "large parties, small parties, *macabre* parties, respectable parties and definitely queer parties" were always well attended, even by guests who were thoroughly uneasy about their host.

Shaitana arouses in Poirot "an emotion that he seldom had occasion to feel," but even so, the detective accepts an invitation to dinner at Shaitana's house because the host boasts that he will invite no less than four murderers—four *successful* murderers—to join them for dinner.

When Poirot arrives at Shaitana's elegant flat, he finds four guests unknown to him, and who seem innocent enough: Dr. Roberts, a successful physician; Anne Meredith, a sweet young girl; Mrs. Lorrimer, a middle-aged widow; and Major Despard, a well-known explorer. To Poirot's surprise, there are three other guests, unquestionably *not* murderers: Colonel Race, British Secret Service; Superintendent Battle, crack Scotland Yard investigator; and Mrs. Ariadne Oliver, famous, if a bit eccentric, writer of mystery novels.

After dinner Mr. Shaitana suggests bridge, though he declines to play himself, and with a Mephistophelian smile on his lips, settles down in a chair by the fire while two tables, four possible murderers and four representatives of the law, begin their bidding.

After the fifth rubber, Race, Battle, Oliver, and Poirot take a break. Later, when Race goes to say good night to his host, he finds Shaitana dead, stabbed with a slender dagger.

It's soon clear that one of the four guests at the other table slipped over to Shaitana while sitting out a dummy hand and coolly murdered him.

Principal Characters: Superintendent Battle, Mrs. Benson, Mrs. Craddock, Charles Craddock, Rhoda Dawes, Major John Hugh Despard, Gerald Hemmingway, Mrs. Lorrimer, Mrs. Luxmore, Anne Meredith, Sergeant O'Connor, Mrs. Ariadne Oliver, Hercule Poirot, Colonel Johnny Race, Dr. Roberts, Mr. Shaitana.

First Editions: **British**: Collins, London, November 1936. 286 pp., 7s. 6d. **American**: Dodd, Mead & Co., New York, 1937. 262 pp., $2.00.

Adaptation: *Cards on the Table* was adapted for the stage by Leslie Darbon. The play opened at the Vaudeville Theatre, London, on December 9, 1981.

MURDER IN THE MEWS / DEAD MAN'S MIRROR
(1937)

This collection of Poirot novellas was published in America as *Dead Man's Mirror,* a title change that seems, like most title changes for American editions, capricious and unnecessary. One can only surmise that Dodd, Mead was worried that non-British readers wouldn't know what a mews was, and therefore wouldn't buy the book. Also, for no clear reason, one story, "The Incredible Theft" was jettisoned while crossing the Atlantic, and has never been published in an American edition.

All four novellas are among Christie's better works in short form. The novella length seems to have given Christie the "breathing space" for characterization and detail which she did not have in her true short stories; yet the novellas are a fast read, without the subplots and excursions of the full-length novels.

The four novellas are also of interest to students of Christie's craft because each exists in another version.

The title story shares the same murder puzzle with a short story "The Market Basing Mystery" (see #54, #81), and reading the two together is an excellent opportunity to see how Christie handled the same problem in different settings. The basic puzzle concerns a "suicide" in a locked room. Poirot and Japp, who appear in both versions, investigate several clues which throw doubt on the suicide theory. Some clues are common to both stories, though in some cases Christie will use the same clue in a different way, as with the cigarette stubs and the closed window. Other clues are different, but are used to prove the same point, such as the victim's wristwatch in "Mews" and the handkerchief in the victim's sleeve in "Market Basing." "Murder in the Mews" also has a long "red-herring" segment, which logically did not appear in the much shorter, earlier "Market Basing Mystery."

"The Incredible Theft," the story omitted in U.S. editions, is a very close revision of "The Submarine Plans" (see #54, #81), which had been published in a magazine in Britain in the 1920s. When Christie expanded her story for the present collection, she changed the stolen plans from submarine to bomber; character names are changed as well, and new dialogue and descriptions added. The major structural change concerns Poirot. In the earlier story, he and Hastings are summoned to the scene of the crime on page one, after the theft of the plans. In the later version, the reader sees the events leading up to the theft, then Poirot and Hastings are called to investigate. This change is logical for the longer version, since Christie now has the time to develop the characters surrounding the crime. The details of the actual puzzle and its solution are virtually identical in both stories.

"Dead Man's Mirror" is an expanded version of "The Second Gong" (see #54). The basic plots of the two versions are the same, as are the clues. Character names and locales are changed, and dialogue and description added. Poirot, of course, appears in both.

"Triangle at Rhodes" is very similar to the novel *Evil Under the Sun* (#38, 1941) in its basic outline. Both are set in seaside resorts, both have Poirot and various curious hotel guests observing a very visible love triangle among fellow guests (the opening of the novel in particular is a close rewrite of the opening of the earlier novella). Given the similarity of setting and situation, a comparison of the two works is especially interesting, because Christie uses two totally different murder puzzles.

The first reviews were lukewarm. Will Cuppy in *Books* (*New York Herald Tribune*) wrote, "All four are expert goods and easy to read—none of your high pressure Christie, but fairly sure fire" (7/4/37). E. R. Punshon in the *Manchester Guardian* found it "perhaps enough to say they are all good but not outstanding" (4/9/37). Isaac Anderson in the *New York Times:* "The four stories in the book are fully up to the Agatha Christie–Hercule Poirot standard, and are about as varied in plot and in the characters involved as it is possible for detective stories to be" (6/27/37).

The *Times Literary Supplement* (London) thought, "The ideas are not highly original, but to all M. Poirot finds an unexpected solution—in three cases not only unexpected by the reader, but unpredictable. The last story has the additional fault that the psychology of the characters is insufficiently developed to make the solution either predictable or plausible: but the first allows the reader to participate just enough for him to foresee if he is very acute, what Poirot will make of it" (3/27/37).

PLOTS:

"Murder in the Mews"

Jane Plenderleith returns from a weekend holiday to find her housemate, the widow Barbara Allen, murdered in their mews apartment. Inspector Japp of Scotland Yard, greatly aided by M. Poirot, tackles the problem of how a woman holding a pistol in her right hand could possibly shoot herself in the left temple. The scent of stale Turkish tobacco, and a man's cuff link found in the closed room, add to the mystery.

"The Incredible Theft"

Lord Charles Mayfield, Minister for Armaments, summons Hercule Poirot to his estate when vital secret bomber plans disappear from his desk during a weekend conference. Poirot soon learns that one of the guests is the glamorous Mrs. Vanderlyn, a suspected enemy agent.

"Dead Man's Mirror"

The eccentric Sir Gervase Chevenix-Gore sends a letter to Hercule Poirot, asking the famous Belgian to come down to his place, Hamborough Close, to investigate a matter of fraud. On Poirot's arrival, Sir Gervase is found dead in his locked study. The most perplexing clue is a mirror in the room, apparently shattered by a bullet, but not directly in the line of fire. In addition to assessing the family members and houseguests, all with dubious alibis, Poirot must tackle a curious twist in Sir Chevenix-Gore's will, growing out of the childless peer's passion for family tradition.

"Triangle at Rhodes"

While vacationing in sunny Rhodes, Hercule Poirot runs across an intriguing love triangle: the renowned beauty Valentine Chantry, married six times and at thirty-nine as seductive as ever; her powerful, moody, and sinister husband, Tony, who obviously adores his wife; and Douglas Gold, a dazzling, if not too bright, resort Adonis, much taken with Valentine, to the chagrin of his mousey wife, Marjorie. As the vacation progresses, the triangle becomes more complicated, and Poirot wisely suggests that Valentine leave Rhodes to save her life. But she stays long enough to effect what appears to be a reconciliation between her husband and her suitor.

First Editions: **British**: Collins, London, March 1937. 280 pp., 7s. 6d. **American**: with U.S. title *Dead Man's Mirror and Other Stories*: Dodd, Mead & Co., New York, 1937. 290 pp., $2.00.

Adaptation: None.

❖ 29 ❖

DUMB WITNESS / POIROT LOSES A CLIENT (1937)

Christie used the plot of the short story "How Does Your Garden Grow?" not published in book form until 1939 in *The Regatta Mystery* (#34, 1939) as the starting point for *Dumb Witness*.

The "witness" of the title is a dog belonging to Emily Arundell, mistress of Littlegreen House in Market Basing, a town an hour and a half from London.

Market Basing, the village in which Littlegreen House is located, is also the setting for *The Secret of Chimneys* (#6, 1925), and *The Seven Dials Mystery* (#10, 1929). Bob, the wirehaired terrier whose ball provides such an important clue in the plot, with his "short, staccato barks of delight and expectation," is clearly patterned after Peter, Agatha's own terrier. He had shared the dedication of *The Mystery of the Blue Train* (#9, 1928) for his loyalty during the disintegration of Christie's first marriage. Now he received the rare honor of a second Christie dedication: "To Dear Peter—most fruitful of friends and dearest of companions, a dog in a thousand."

Dumb Witness is Hastings's last appearance until *Curtain* (#82, 1975), published almost forty years later. At the end of the book, Poirot is given Bob the terrier, though Hastings, with an unusual show of independence, announces that *he* intends to keep the dog. Poirot reminds Hastings that the dog was given to him, and Hastings counters, "you're not really any good with a dog, Poirot. You don't understand dog psychology!" Perhaps Poirot was just as glad to be rid of both dog and companion.

Christie admitted that she grew tired of Poirot and Hastings, and though Poirot couldn't be gotten rid of because of his popularity, Hastings at least was dispensable without too much fuss. "Truth to tell," she wrote in *An Autobiography,* "I think I was getting a little tired of him. I might be stuck with Poirot, but no need to be stuck with Hastings, too."

Will Cuppy in *Books* (*New York Herald Tribune*) wrote,

"Don't be discouraged by the slightly threadbare materials with which Mrs. Christie starts this grade A Poirot tale. . . . All in all, it's a slick job in the admirable Christie manner" (9/12/37).

The *New York Times* thought, "Agatha Christie is not doing her most brilliant work in *Poirot Loses a Client,* but she has produced a much-better-than-average thriller nevertheless, and her plot has novelty, as it has sound mechanism, intriguing character types, and ingenuity" (9/26/37).

The *Times Literary Supplement* (London) in their review latched on to one weakness in the plotting that is still criticized in the book. "It is not at all easy, as the experienced reader knows, to catch M. Poirot out; but it is good fun to trip him up, when one can on trivial details . . . One need not be very quick witted to detect a weakness in the incident on the stairs outside the companion's bedroom. Who, in their senses, one feels, would use hammer and nails and varnish in the middle of the night within a few feet of an open door! . . . a door that was deliberately left open at night for observation! And, incidentally, do ladies wear large brooches on their dressing-gowns? These are small but tantalizing points which it would not be worth raising in the work of a less distinguished writer . . . but they are worth recording, if only as a measure of the curiosity and interest with which one approaches her problems and attempts to anticipate their solutions" (7/10/37).

Inconsistencies such as those mentioned in the *Times* review are fortunately rare at this point in Christie's career, when she was in top form. But in later years such flaws would become more common, and damaging to the plots, especially in *Elephants Can Remember* (#79, 1972) and *Postern of Fate* (#80, 1973).

PLOT:

On a hot summer morning Arthur Hastings, back from Argentina, is visiting Poirot in his London flat. Poirot is reading his mail, when one letter in particular catches the detective's attention. It is from Miss Emily Arundell, mistress of Littlegreen House, Market Basing, Berkshire. Its contents are typical of the reticent, dramatic inquiries Poirot receives from hysterical spinsters, asking his assistance in unnamed matters of grave personal importance, which Hastings imagines to be "some upset to her fat lapdog."

One detail, however, catches Poirot's eye: Miss Arundell's letter is dated April 17—and it's now June 28. His curiosity piqued, Poirot decides to go to Littlegreen House. When he and Hastings arrive there they find that the house is up for sale and Miss Arundell is dead.

Clearly there was more behind Miss Arundell's letter than "some upset to her fat lapdog." The late spinster was heir to a sizeable fortune left to her by her father, General Arundell. It had always been assumed in Market Basing that the Arundell money would be left to the nieces and nephews.

However, Poirot soon discovers that Emily Arundell, just before her death, had remade her will, cutting off her family and leaving everything to her spiritualist-leaning companion, Miss Minnie Lawson. The unassuming Miss Lawson, a rather gray, dull woman, had become legatee of the Arundell estate because Miss Arundell had become convinced that one of her family was trying to murder her. The most blatant incident had come in April, when Emily had nearly been killed in a fall down the stairs. The apparent cause of her fall had been a rubber ball left at the top of the stairs by her terrier, Bob, but Emily, in spite of the shock of her near-fatal tumble downstairs, had suspected foul play, since the dog had been out of the house all night and his ball had been put safely away in a drawer before he had been let out.

It was this near-miss that prompted Miss Arundell to write to Poirot for assistance. Unfortunately, her death from a sudden attack of "jaundice" prevented her letter from being posted, though it was mysteriously mailed a month later.

Principal Characters: Angus, Charles Arundell, Emily Arundell, Theresa Arundell, Nurse Carruthers, Dr. Rex Donaldson, Ellen, Dr. Grainger, Captain Hastings, Wilhelmina Lawson, Caroline Peabody, Hercule Poirot, William Purvis, Bella Tanios, Dr. Jacob Tanios, Isabel Tripp, Julia Tripp.

First Editions: **British**: Collins, London, July 1937. 316 pp., 7s. 6d. **American**: with U.S. title *Poirot Loses a Client*: Dodd, Mead & Co., New York, 1937. 302 pp., $2.00.

Adaptation: None.

30

DEATH ON THE NILE (1937)

This is Agatha Christie's favorite among her books with a foreign background, and the exotic setting, strong characterization, and superb plotting of *Death on the Nile* have made it a perennial favorite among her readers as well. The lush, all-star 1978 film version further ensured that this would remain one of Christie's most famous mysteries.

Agatha's acquaintance with Egypt began in her teens when, after her father's death, she and her mother were left in what were politely called "reduced circumstances." Clara Miller, faced with the problem of a large house to maintain, and a daughter to bring out in society, did what so many women of her social station did at that time: she rented Ashfield, the Miller home in Torquay, at a handsome profit (staff included), and spent a season in a fashionable but affordable winter resort. Her choice was Cairo, and she and Agatha, then about eighteen years old, spent three months in a "moderately expensive" residential hotel. It was in Cairo that Agatha had her "coming out." She went to as many as five dances a week in the various hotels, and in her memoirs admits to numerous flirtations with the young officers of the British regiments stationed in Cairo (Egypt was at that time a British protectorate).

"Those were still great days for the purity of young girls," she wrote of these flirtatious, much chaperoned days. "Romantic friendships, tinged certainly with sex or the possibility of sex, satisfied us completely . . . In Cairo I didn't even get as far as falling slightly in love. . . . There was so much going on, and so many attractive, personable young men."

Christie admits that her preoccupations during her first visit to Egypt were social; it was not until the 1930s, during her Middle East journeys with Max Mallowan, that she took an interest in the historical Egypt.

The journey aboard the Nile steamer *Karnak* made by the characters in the book is probably identical to one made by the Mallowans, the details of the geography between Assuan and Wadi Halfa, the details of the ruins at Abu Simbel, and even the cabin plan of the *Karnak,* are all authentic.

The journey proper begins at Assuan, the city of 128,000 located about 600 miles south of Cairo at the point in the Nile's 4,132-mile course where the first of the six cataracts obstructs the river's navigability for a length of 1,200 miles. The *Karnak* sailed up the Nile as far as Wadi Halfa, on the Egyptian border, the site of the second cataract. This stretch of the Nile is not suitable for farming, and the banks of the river are generally rocky and barren.

Steamers like the *Karnak,* long, flat-bottomed boats, usually with a single smokestack and two or three open-galleried decks, were an important means of transportation along the slow-moving stretches of the river between the cataracts. The voyage south of Assuan was also popular with tourists because of the many ruins of temples and tombs along the river's banks, the most impressive being those at Abu Simbel, built by Ramses II during his reign (1292–1225 B.C.).

Between 1899 and 1902, during the first years of the British protectorate, a dam was built at Assuan to provide a reservoir for irrigation, and later for hydroelectric power. The first Assuan dam was built with four locks to allow river traffic to pass the barrier, and Christie mentions that "the *Karnak* was a smaller steamer than the *Papyrus* and the *Lotus* [the steamers that traveled from Cairo to Assuan] . . . which are too large to pass through the locks of the Assuan dam."

The reservoir created by the dam naturally caused flooding of a large area of the Nile basin upstream, and the enlargement of the dam, in 1908–1911, and later in 1929–1934, which raised the level of the reservoir 120 feet, submerged even more acres of land, including formerly habitable villages and many ancient ruins. During the time of Poirot's trip on the *Karnak* there was still fresh evidence of the recent flooding of new areas, as Poirot observes in this passage from the novel:

"There was a savage aspect about the sheet of water in front of them, the masses of rock without vegetation that came down to the water's edge—here and there a trace of houses abandoned and ruined as a result of the damming up of the waters. The whole scene had a melancholy, almost sinister charm."

Between 1950 and 1979 the Assuan High Dam was constructed about four miles upstream from the original dam; this mammoth earthworks enlarged the older reservoir into the world's largest man-made lake (Lake Nasser), which extends past the second cataract at Wadi Halfa and more than three hundred miles farther into Sudan. The enormous increase of the reservoir engulfed hundreds of ruins along the river, and necessitated the relocation of more than fifty thousand people in the Sudan alone. Virtually everything seen by the passengers on the *Karnak* in *Death on the Nile* is now under the waters of Lake Nasser.

One major exception is the temple of Ramses II at Abu Simbel, the site of Linnet Doyle's near brush with death while the *Karnak* party was on shore touring the ruins. Once the construction of the High Dam began, the temple, one of the most significant in Egypt, was doomed to be submerged. While other important buildings were dismantled and moved to higher ground or to reconstruction in museums, Abu Simbel's plight seemed hopeless because the entire construction, the four monumental seated reliefs of Ramses, and the frescoed temple they guarded, was carved out of the rocky cliffs overlooking the Nile.

In an engineering feat almost as impressive as the construction of the temple itself, the entire section of the mountain containing the temple was sawn into 950 sections and then hoisted to a new site higher up and farther back from the river, well above the eventual high water level of Lake Nasser; the reconstructed stone jigsaw is now virtually indistinguishable from the temple in its original setting. The project, sponsored by UNESCO, was funded by fifty-two nations.

Christie must have been impressed by Abu Simbel, for she takes her passengers there twice during their voyage, once by day, once by torchlight, and she gives unusually detailed (for her) descriptions of the architecture. And the influence of Christie's archaeologist husband can be detected throughout the book. She accurately tosses out the names of the figures in the reliefs, for example, and Signor Richetti's passion for side trips to obscure archaeological sites ("Semna . . . he explained, was of paramount interest as being the gateway of Nubia in the time of Amenemhet III") are probably drawn from her own experiences with Max.

Before departure on the *Karnak,* Poirot and the other tourists stay at the Cataract Hotel, which is situated directly on the river opposite Elephantine Island. From the balcony of the hotel, Jacqueline de Bellefort watches Simon and Linnet Doyle setting off in one of the native sailboats, while Poirot goes across the river to the Elephantine with the talkative Guido Richetti, to visit the archaeological museum and the ruins of ancient Yeb. The Cataract Hotel is still in operation, and the 1980 price of forty dollars for a double room with bath is comparable with what Christie's characters paid in 1937 currency.

In spite of the strong period flavor of the book (especially in Christie's descriptions of clothing and of methods of travel), the book has surprisingly few contemporary references. The Great Depression is passed over with a mere, "I suppose, though, that the recent slump is bound to affect any stocks, however sound they may be?" And the worsening European political situation is brought in only by means of the mysterious X, one of Christie's terrorist-agitator types.

"It isn't the people who ostensibly lead the rioters that we're after," says Colonel Race, who is hot on the mystery man's trail. "It's the men who very cleverly put the match to the gunpowder. . . . He's one of the cleverest paid agitators that ever existed."

Christie's use of subversive characters, which earlier in her career had been limited to the Tommy and Tuppence type of thrillers, now begins to appear in her "pure" detective novels. Unfortunately, these secret agitators seldom if ever work, and as often as not detract from the plausibility of the mystery. Why Christie introduced these "crossover" characters isn't clear—though it may have been a response to the very real subversives active in Europe and the Middle East during the years just before and during the war.

"Trust Agatha Christie to turn out the rightest and generally slickest mystery currently at hand," wrote Will Cuppy in *Books* (*New York Herald Tribune*). "Once more she makes most of her rivals look a bit silly with her skill in every department of the puzzler's art—or is it a science?" (2/6/38).

"Slightly transparent plot, plethora of action, but all is handled with customary Christie expertness. Very good" (12/19/38). This from the *Saturday Review of Literature.*

Nicholas Blake in the *Spectator* thought, "There's too much coincidence; also, I doubt if one could really work the red ink business with any certainty of success. However, there's a very hot alibi; and Mrs. Christie's *denouement,* as usual, plays us all for suckers" (12/17/37).

In the *Manchester Guardian,* E. R. Punshon wrote, "M. Poirot's little grey cells had been obliged to work at full pressure to unravel a mystery which includes one of those carefully worked-out alibis that seem alike to fascinate Mrs. Christie and to provide her with the best opportunities for displaying her own skill. A fault-finding critic may, however, wonder whether M. Poirot is not growing just a little too fond of keeping to himself such important facts as the bullet-hole in the table. If he is to enjoy all, a reader should also know all" (12/10/37).

Isaac Anderson in the *New York Times Book Review* glowed, "Poirot is traveling for pleasure, but the moment you see his name on the passenger list you know there is going to be a murder or two or three and that the little grey cells of the great Poirot are going to solve the mystery. That is precisely what happens, and if you want to know more, you will have to read the book, which is probably what you intend to do anyhow if you are at all familiar with Poirot and his methods and with the skillfully constructed stories that Agatha Christie tells about him. You have the right to expect great things of such a combination, and you will not be disappointed" (2/6/38).

Death on the Nile is dedicated "To Sybil Burnett, who also loves wandering about the world." Sybil, known as "Bauff" to her friends, was the wife of Sir Charles Burnett, an air vice-marshal stationed in Algiers. Christie and Bauff met on Agatha's second trip to the Middle East (the trip on which she was to meet her second husband), when Lady Burnett was a fellow passenger on the boat from Trieste to Beirut. Their first impressions of one another were not the best. Sybil found Agatha "one of the most unpleasant women I have ever seen," while Agatha recalled, "I don't like that woman. I don't like the hat she is wearing, and I don't like her mushroom-coloured stockings."

The two soon overcame their mutual dislike, and Christie in the end described "Bauff" as "a woman of great originality, who said exactly what came into her head . . . and [had] an inexhaustible enjoyment of life."

PLOT:

The villagers of Malton-under-Wode are a bit leery of Linnet Ridgeway, the girl who has everything: she's young, beautiful, stylish, single—and heir to American millions. She's just bought Wode Hall, an estate in Malton, and is reputed to have spent £60,000 on the refurbishing.

One day Linnet gets a call from Jacqueline de Bellefort, her oldest friend, now left penniless by the stock market crash. When Jackie arrives at Wode Hall, she immediately imparts the good news to Linnet: she's *engaged,* and to the most wonderful man, Simon Doyle. Simon is "big and square and incredibly simple and boyish and utterly adorable!"—and utterly broke. Jackie asks Linnet if she'd consider hiring Simon as her land agent—"he knows all about estates"—and Linnet agrees.

Some time later, Hercule Poirot is traveling in Egypt, staying at the Cataract Hotel in Assuan. Among his fellow guests are the newlyweds, Mr. and Mrs. Simon Doyle. Mrs. Doyle, however, is none other than the former Linnet Ridgeway. It seems that Simon was "so utterly adorable" that he won the heart of his employer and married her instead of Jackie de Bellefort. One afternoon, just before tea, Mr. and Mrs. Simon Doyle see a familiar face—none other than jilted Jackie de Bellefort. The couple are not startled, but enraged, because it is by no means their first encounter with Jackie. She is deliberately tailing them, trying to mar their happiness.

Distressed, Linnet Doyle calls on Poirot, whom she recognizes among the hotel guests, to ask his help in persuading Jackie to leave her and her husband alone. Poirot declines to take a commission from Mrs. Doyle, but he does say he will talk to Miss de Bellefort. When he does so, he cautions the wounded party, "Do not open your heart to evil," but Jackie confesses that she would gladly kill Linnet Doyle because "What have I got to live for . . . [she] has taken away everything [I had] in the world."

Things come to a head on board the *Karnak,* a river steamer that carries Poirot, the Doyles, and an assortment of British and

American travelers up the Nile on a tour of the ruins. An attempt is made on Simon Doyle's life, but that is only a prelude to the successful attempts soon to be made on more than one passenger on the Nile steamer.

Principal Characters: Mrs. Allerton, Tim Allerton, Dr. Carl Bessner, Monsieur Gaston Blondin, Louise Bourget, Miss Bowers, Jacqueline de Bellefort, Simon Doyle, James Fanthorpe, Mr. Ferguson, Mr. Fleetwood, Jules, Marie, Rosalie Otterbourne, Salome Otterbourne, Andrew Pennington, Hercule Poirot, Colonel Johnny Race, Signor Guido Richetti, Linnet Ridgeway, Cornelia Ruth Robson, Sterndale Rockford, Marie Van Schuyler, the Honorable Joanna Southwood.

First Editions: **British**: Collins, London, November 1937. 284 pp., 7s. 6d. **American**: Dodd, Mead & Co., New York, 1938. 326 pp., $2.00.

Adaptations: Released in 1978, the all-star movie of *Death on the Nile* was made by the same film company that produced the very successful film, *Murder on the Orient Express*. Peter Ustinov starred as Poirot; Bette Davis, Angela Lansbury, Maggie Smith, and David Niven were featured in the supporting cast.

Christie dramatized *Death on the Nile* as *Murder on the Nile*. The play opened in London on March 19, 1946, at the Ambassadors Theatre. The American production of this play, with the title *Hidden Horizon,* opened in New York at the Plymouth Theatre on September 19, 1946.

31

APPOINTMENT WITH DEATH (1938)

Appointment with Death holds its own among the mysteries produced in this, the greatest period of Christie's creativity, for two main reasons: its exotic setting amid the ruins of Petra, "the rose-red city," and the character of Mrs. Boynton, perhaps the most convincing and unforgettable evil figure in all of Christie's work.

Petra (which means "rock" in Greek), located in the Ma'an district of present-day Jordan, was in Hellenistic and Roman times the center of an Arab kingdom. The city was built on a mesa of the Wadi Musa, or Valley of Moses, an important trade route in ancient times, and traditionally one of the places where Moses, during the wanderings in the desert, struck a rock and brought forth water to quench the thirst of the Israelites. The entire area is characterized by craggy, gorge-broken, stony terrain with reddish-yellow sandstone cliffs and outcroppings that gave the city its colorful nickname.

Christie first visited Petra about 1933, while on one of her many Middle East journeys with archaeologist husband Max Mallowan, who no doubt shared a great deal of his professional knowledge of the city with his wife. She used Petra one other time as the setting for a story, "The Pearl of Price" from *Parker Pyne Investigates* (#22, 1934). However, in the book Agatha makes almost nothing of the history of Petra, and mentions only once the Nabataeans, the Arab tribe that dominated Petran culture and politics from about 312 B.C. to 106 A.D. when they were conquered by the Romans.

Christie was never one for elaborate, atmospheric description in her books, and *Appointment with Death* is no exception. Where many writers would have lavished pages to evoke the bizarre, almost lunar landscape of the red stone wasteland under the canopy of an empty, clear desert sky, Christie is content with a few sharp paragraphs describing the caravan of tourist-laden donkeys winding their way down through the narrow gorge (the Wadi as-Sik) that leads from the desert plateau to Petra, carved into the rocks of the Wadi Musa.

"The shapes of the rocks rose up around them—down, down, into the bowels of the earth, through a labyrinth of red cliffs. . . . Suddenly they came out into a wide space—the cliffs receded. . . . They could see a cluster of tents, a higher row up against the face of a cliff. Caves, too, hollowed out in the rock. Bedouin servants came running out."

Aside from the coloration of the terrain, one of the most distinctive features of Petra is its many buildings carved into the rock cliff faces. (These ruins—mostly tombs and temples—were hand-hewn out of the rock, some with elaborate facades constructed in front of caves and rock excavations.) Many of these caves and grottoes are now used as dwellings, and it is in one of the caves that the monstrous Mrs. Boynton sits "Buddha-like" and keeps her evil eye on her family and fellow tourists.

Christie's depiction of the Boynton family—the neurotic children caught in the emotional web of their stepmother's tyrannical bondage—is well done. The reader cannot help but be torn by the portrait of young adults helpless in the clutches of their bloated evil mother, unable to free themselves from her web.

In addition to the forceful portrait of the Boynton family, *Appointment with Death* has psychological "insights" provided directly by one of the characters, Dr. Gerard, an eminent French psychologist and fellow guest at the hotel in Jerusalem. Gerard's observation concerning Mrs. Boynton seem a bit facile by today's standards, but they are very much of their time.

"There is some deep underlying compulsion [in Mrs. Boynton]," says Dr. Gerard. "She does not love tyranny *because she has been a wardress*. Let us rather say that she became a wardress *because she loved tyranny*. In my theory it was a secret desire for power over other human beings that led her to adopt that profession . . . There are such strange things buried down in the unconscious. . . . They are all there . . . all the cruelty and savagery and lust! We shut the door on them and deny them conscious life, but sometimes they are too strong."

In the same vein, there is a curious passage (also spoken by Dr. Gerard) that bears close examination for what it may reveal about the author herself, and her behavior during the breakup of her first marriage and her much-publicized disappearance. This is especially so, since the "official" version of her disappearance (that is, the version Christie readers are most familiar with) has often been discounted in favor of versions that make the Christie disappearance an attempt to humiliate, or even incriminate, Archie Christie.

The passage, as Dr. Gerard speaks it, is awkwardly written, as if Christie had difficulty getting the words down clearly.

"Below the decencies and conventions of everyday life, there lies a vast reservoir of strange things—as, for instance, delight in cruelty for its own sake. But when you have found that [cruelty], there is something deeper still—the desire, profound and pitiful, to be appreciated. If that [desire to be appreciated] is thwarted, if through an unpleasing personality [!] a human being is unable to get the response it needs, it turns to other methods—it must be *felt* —it must *count*—and so to innumerable strange perversions. The habit of cruelty, like any other habit, can be cultivated, can take hold of one." Did Christie's "profound and pitiful" desire to be appreciated, and loved, by Archie Christie lead her to her irrational and melodramatic disappearance?

One character in *Appointment with Death* is clearly based on a recognizable individual. The character of Lady Westholme in reality is a wickedly funny, sharp parody of Lady Nancy Astor. Christie didn't often put "real" people in her books, though Katharine Woolley in *Murder in Mesopotamia* (#26, 1936) and Major Belcher in *The Man in the Brown Suit* (#5, 1924) are two good examples.

Nancy Witcher Langhorne (1879–1964) was born in Virginia. A famous Southern beauty in her youth, she was first married to the American millionaire, Robert Gould Shaw, whom she divorced in 1903. She moved to England, where in 1906 she married Waldorf Astor, the future second Viscount Astor. Waldorf, the grandson of the self-made multimillionaire John Jacob Astor, was the son of William Waldorf Astor, who moved (with his considerable fortune) from America to England in 1890, where he maintained two magnificent estates, Cliveden and Hever Castle, and became involved in politics, philanthropy, and publishing. W.W. was made a baron in 1916 and a viscount in 1917 in part because of his enormous financial contributions to the war effort. The latter title passed to his son Waldorf.

When Waldorf succeeded as second Viscount, he was forced to give up his seat in the House of Commons, and Nancy was elected in his place, the first woman in history to serve in Parliament. During her long political career (1919–1945), Lady Astor was noted for her sharp tongue and her passionate espousal of reform movements, especially those involving women's rights and child labor.

Like Lady Astor, Christie's Lady Westholme is American born. She meets Lord Westholme, a "simple-minded peer, whose only interests in life were hunting, shooting, and fishing," while the lord is returning from a trip to America. Their subsequent marriage is cited as an example of "the danger of ocean voyages."

Christie rather venomously traces the new Lady Westholme's political career: "The new Lady Westholme lived entirely in tweeds and stout brogues, bred dogs, bullied the villagers and forced her husband pitilessly into public life."

When Lady Westholme sees that her husband is not suited to politics, she retires him to the estate "to resume his sporting activities and herself stood for Parliament. . . . As a public figure she stood for the old-fashioned values of Family Life, Welfare work among Women, and had decided views on questions of Agriculture, Housing and Slum Clearance. She was much respected and almost universally disliked!"

Christie gets off some rather witty jibes at the more-British-than-British aggressive, insensitive MP: Lady Westholme enters a room "with the assurance of a transatlantic liner coming into dock." The lady politician complains about the size of her car, tells the hotel manager how he can improve the operations of the place, and berates the Bedouin servants on their dress and hygiene.

"Efficiency," she says, "is my watchword."

There are several references to other Christie novels of the period. Miss Pierce, during her conversation with Poirot, is thrilled to meet the man who solved the ABC murders (*The ABC Murders,* #25, 1936), as she had a post near Doncaster at the time. Colonel Carbury, the representative of British law and authority in

Appointment with Death, has heard about Poirot from his old associate Colonel Race, who wrote in glowing terms of Poirot's solution of the Shaitana murder (*Cards on the Table, #27, 1936*).

The most interesting of the cross-references, however, is in the scene between Nadine Boynton and Poirot. Nadine, like the rest of the Boynton family, has been freed from a horrid life by the murder of her mother-in-law. During the course of Poirot's investigation, Nadine reminds him of this beneficial aspect of the murder. She urges Poirot to cut short his investigation, to let the case rest as "death from natural causes" from an official standpoint, and as "justifiable homicide" from the standpoint of those who knew the monstrous Mrs. Boynton.

"I have heard, M. Poirot," Nadine pleads, "that once, in that affair of the Orient Express, you accepted an official verdict of what had happened?"

Poirot looked at her cautiously. "I wonder who told you that."

"Is it true?"

He said slowly, "That case was different."

"No, no, it was not different! The man who was killed was evil . . . as *she* was . . ."

Poirot seems to be caught in a moral dilemma, which he forcefully evades.

"The moral character of the victim has nothing to do with it! A human being who has exercised the right of private judgment and taken the life of another human being is not safe to exist."

"How hard you are," she replies.

"Madame, in some ways I am adamant. I will not condone murder! That is the final word of Hercule Poirot."

Interestingly, Poirot ignores the moral contradiction in his handling of the Orient Express affair.

The reviewers were generally enthusiastic about the book, though several pointed out some very real flaws in Christie's handling of the plot, especially in the denouement. Even in her golden age, there were occasional weak moments.

The *Saturday Review of Literature* wrote, "Starts well and progresses beautifully against rich background and interesting characters—but then the durned thing blows up in your face. Disappointing" (9/10/38). In the *Spectator,* Nicholas Blake said, "It is a criticism of *Appointment with Death,* though a tribute to Mrs. Christie's usual mastery of technique (she surely is the neatest plotter we have), that for once Poirot takes far too long—forty pages to be exact—in his summing up. Apart from this, and a superfluity of italics, this story . . . gets very fair marks" (6/17/38).

The *Times Literary Supplement* (London): "Poirot's examination of the family, the psychologists and the few others in the party, this sifting of truth from half-truth and contradiction, his playing off one suspect against another and gradual elimination of each in turn are in Mrs. Christie's most brilliant style. Only the solution appears a trifle tame and disappointing" (5/7/38).

"For ingenuity of plot and construction, unexpectedness of denouement, subtlety of characterization, and picturesqueness of background, *Appointment with Death* may take rank among the best of Mrs. Christie's tales." This from E. R. Punshon in the *Manchester Guardian* (5/27/38).

"When in doubt, read Agatha Christie," wrote Will Cuppy in *Books* (*New York Herald Tribune*). "You'll find *Appointment with Death* one of this author's slickest. . . . This seems to be the season for whopping tall solutions; at any rate, Mrs. Christie springs a fiend you aren't likely to guess. Which is all right with us. We like to be surprised" (9/11/38).

And finally, Ralph Partridge in the *New Statesman and Nation* complained, "For once I think Mrs. Christie has overcrowded her stage. There are too many balls to juggle with; and [the author] is so busy keeping all our suspicions in the air that she lands herself in a psychological tangle from which there is no plausible escape. No wonder then that Poirot brings down the curtain with a run, before we have time to analyse what has gone wrong with the performance. . . . For once Mrs. Christie has chosen too many ingredients to mix into one of her smooth puddings" (5/21/38).

The book is dedicated "To Richard and Myra Mallock to remind them of their journey to Petra."

PLOT:

On the first night of his vacation in the Holy Land, at the Hotel Solomon in Jerusalem, Hercule Poirot overhears talk of murder: a wisp of conversation drifting through the window, "You do see, don't you, that she's got to be killed?"

The detective is a bit amused—the overheard words are perhaps a collaboration on a play or book. But he recalls "a curious nervous intensity in the voice . . . A man's voice, or a boy's." He thinks to himself, "I should know that voice again."

Poirot is not the only person of note registered at the Hotel Solomon. There is Dr. Gerard, the famous French psychologist, an expert in schizophrenia, and attractive young Sarah King, an English medical student; but especially there is Mrs. Boynton and her family.

Mrs. Boynton, a wealthy American widow, is a remarkable woman—remarkable for the horrible impression she makes on all who behold her. In Dr. Gerard's words, *"What a horror of a woman!* Old, swollen, bloated, sitting there immovable—a distorted old Buddha—a gross spider in the center of a web!"

The other guests in the hotel soon notice the Boynton family, and if mother Boynton is a spider in her web, her children and stepchildren—all young adults—are flies caught in the web, waiting for the spider's deadly sting. For Mrs. Boynton is both mentally *and* physically repulsive: she holds her family in a sick, demeaning relationship with her.

The children clearly live in terror of their mother, and are showing signs of mental strain. The eldest, Lennox, has been completely crushed by his mother's maternal sadism; the youngest, Ginevra, is showing clear signs of schizophrenia and persecution mania.

After their stay in Jerusalem, the Boyntons journey *en suite* to Petra. While at Petra Mrs. Boynton exhibits what is, for her, remarkable behavior—she allows her children, or at least all but young Ginny—to go somewhere without her. Even more remarkable, however, is the discovery that evening, on the return of the tour group, that Mrs. Boynton has been murdered, in full view of the camp, by injection of digitoxin, a powerful cardiovascular drug.

Poirot, now stopping over in Amman, Jordan, calls on Colonel Carbury, armed with a letter of introduction from their mutual friend, Colonel Race. Carbury tells Poirot of the Boynton death—

until that time attributed to natural causes—and adds that, despite appearances, he thinks her family did her in.

Poirot, of course, recalls the Boyntons. Though he may think Mrs. Boynton's death was a blessing to all concerned, he is "alas, always incurably interested in one's own subject" and undertakes to discover what really happened among the ruins.

Principal Characters: Mrs. Boynton, Carol Boynton, Ginevra Boynton, Lennox Boynton, Nadine Boynton, Raymond Boynton, Colonel Carbury, Jefferson Cope, Dr. Theodore Gerard, Sarah King, Amabel Pierce, Hercule Poirot, Lady Westholme.

First Editions: **British**: Collins, London, May 1938. 252 pp., 7s. 6d. **American**: Dodd, Mead & Co., New York, 1938. 301 pp., $2.00.

Adaptation: Christie adapted *Appointment with Death* for the stage. The play opened March 31, 1945, at the Piccadilly Theatre, London.

◈ 32 ◈

HERCULE POIROT'S CHRISTMAS / MURDER FOR CHRISTMAS / A HOLIDAY FOR MURDER (1938)

Christie's dedication for this novel reads:

> My Dear James
> You have always been one of the most faithful and kindly of my readers, and I was therefore seriously perturbed when I received from you a word of criticism.
>
> You complained that my murders were getting too refined—anaemic, in fact. You yearned for a "good violent murder with lots of blood." A murder where there was no doubt about its being murder!
>
> So this is your special story—written for you. I hope it may please.
>
> > Your affectionate sister-in-law,
> > Agatha

When James Watts, husband of Agatha's sister, Madge, said he wanted a little more blood in Agatha's murders, he got not only that but a classic country-house, locked-room murder story that ranks among Christie's best for brilliance of plotting and masterly clues.

By the standards of today's television violence and Kung Fu movie mayhem, however, the death of Simeon Lee is tame indeed, and for Christie one paragraph of description was sufficient to fill James's request.

"There had clearly been a terrific struggle. Heavy furniture was overturned. China vases lay splintered on the floor. In the middle of the hearthrug in front of the blazing fire lay Simeon Lee in a great pool of blood. . . . Blood was splashed all around. The place was like a shambles."

Even at her most deliberately violent, Christie was still too removed, too ladylike, to get down to the business of butchery. For her, James Watts's blood lust had to be satisfied by the mere method of murder—throat cutting. But the crime itself is not depicted in descriptions of sliced flesh and severed tendons. A "good violent murder" is for Agatha best pictured in the disarray of furniture, irreparably stained Oriental rugs, and lovely Ming porcelains shattered into a million shards.

As Robert Barnard points out in his essay on *Hercule Poirot's Christmas* in *A Talent to Deceive* (1980), the author cannot be bothered with drawn-out descriptions of the throat slashing in the locked library, or of the romantic possibilities of an English country Christmas. "Everyone gets straight down to the job of interviewing the suspects and interpreting the clues. The puzzle is all."

The Mallowans returned from their annual Middle East archaeological expedition in the spring of 1938, sensing that, with the threat of war, they would not return to their beloved desert for an unknown number of years. *Hercule Poirot's Christmas* was probably written shortly after Christie's return to England.

"Poirot has solved some puzzling mysteries in his time," wrote Isaac Anderson in his *New York Times* review, "but never has his mighty brain functioned more brilliantly than in *Murder for Christmas*" (2/12/39). And in the *Manchester Guardian,* E. R. Punshon wrote, "In this kind of detective novel, depending most entirely for its interest on accuracy of logical deduction from recorded fact and yet with the drama played out by recognizable human beings, Mrs. Christie remains supreme. One may grumble that she depends a little too much upon coincidence and manufactured effect . . . but how small are such blemishes compared with the brilliance of the whole conception!" (1/13/39).

PLOT:

Simeon Lee, the master of Gorston Hall, is a "thin, shrivelled figure of an old man," with white hair and sallow complexion, and "long clawlike hands." Though he might at first appear to be insignificant, his "dark and intensely alive" eyes reveal him to be a man of "fire and life and vigour." His wife died many years before, allegedly because of her suffering over Simeon's flagrant unfaithfulness; his fortune was made in his youth when he struck it rich mining diamonds in South Africa, and as an old man he has a habit of taking a hoard of uncut diamonds from his safe and fondling them. To his friends and family, he is generous, though he enjoys nothing more than showing up those around him as greedy sycophants, even to the point of playing cruel jokes on them.

One Christmas Simeon concocts an elaborate and sadistic game at Gorston Hall. He brings together his large family—son Alfred, who has spent all his life living at home, catering to his father's every wish; daughter-in-law Lydia, who hates Simeon for the hold he has over her husband; Harry, the black sheep son, who hasn't been home for years, even though he's enjoyed a generous allowance; David, the youngest son, who hates his father for his mistreatment of his mother; son George and daughter-in-law Magdalene, who are extravagant, and in debt because of it despite their allowance from Simeon. Finally, there are the two dark horses—Pilar, Simeon Lee's half-Spanish granddaughter, an orphan all but unknown to the family, and Stephen Farr, who arrives uninvited at the hall just in time to see old Lee's game played out. The game itself begins when Simeon allows the far-from-disinterested group to overhear instructions to the lawyer to change his will. The second step is a thorough dressing-down, in which Simeon confronts each of his descendants with their greed, weakness, and stupidity.

"Your mother had the brains of a louse!" Simeon yells out. "And it seems to me she's transmitted those brains to her children. . . . You're not *men*! You're weaklings—a set of namby-pamby weaklings."

Simeon sends the family out of his study. Later, there is the sound of crashing and banging from upstairs, followed by a wailing scream and a deathly gurgle. The study door is locked, but once the door is broken in, Simeon Lee is found dead, his throat slashed . . . and his diamonds missing.

Unfortunately for the murderer clever enough to perpetrate the locked-room killing, the local chief constable has Poirot as a houseguest that Christmas.

Principal Characters: Mr. Charlton, Pilar Estravados, Stephen Farr, Sydney Horbury, Alfred Lee, David Lee, George Lee, Harry Lee, Hilda Lee, Lydia Lee, Magdalene Lee, Simeon Lee, Hercule Poirot, Superintendent Sugden, Tressilian.

First Editions: British: Collins, London, December 1938. 251 pp., 7s. 6d. **American:** with U.S. title *Murder for Christmas:* Dodd, Mead & Co., New York, 1939. 272 pp., $2.00. (The U.S. paperback edition appeared under the title *A Holiday for Murder.*)

Adaptation: None.

33

Murder Is Easy / Easy to Kill (1939)

A classic Christie recipe: a quiet English village, a gossipy vicar, an even more gossipy spinster, a nasty local lord with a beautiful fiancée, a retired army major, an effeminate antiques shopkeeper, all leading their quiet village lives while suspecting that several recent deaths in Wychwood have not been as natural or accidental as they appeared.

Murder Is Easy was written during the ominous months of early 1939, when following the German annexation of Czechoslovakia, Britain abandoned its appeasement policy toward Germany and began creating an "anti-aggression" front with Turkey, Greece, Rumania, and Poland. Two months after publication, on September 1, the war officially began with the German invasion of Poland.

An important personal event in 1939 was Christie's purchase of Greenway House, a secluded Georgian estate on the river Dart in Devon, which was to become her favorite home. The house was purchased in the spring of 1939 for the sum of £6,000. During the summer Greenway was renovated—a Victorian addition pulled down, bathrooms added—and the Mallowans moved in. Their pleasure in their new house was short-lived, though. "Just after we had done so," Christie writes in *An Autobiography,* "and were exulting in it, the second war came."

As with most of the novels from this decade, the handling of the plot and clues is superb, though for all its quality, *Murder Is Easy* has suffered anonymity because of flashier, more exotic mysteries from the same years: *Death on the Nile* (#30, 1937), *Appointment with Death* (#31, 1938), and *Ten Little Niggers* (#35, 1939).

Superintendent Battle, last seen in *Cards on the Table* (#27, 1936), is on the scene again, aided by a bright, entertaining character named Luke Fitzwilliam, who is unwittingly drawn into the role of detective when he stumbles on the Wychwood murders. Like Lucy Eyelesbarrow in *4.50 from Paddington* (#62, 1957), Fitzwilliam is a "natural" at mystery solving, and it is unfortunate that Christie chose not to use them in other books.

Reviews were mixed—not an unusual state of affairs with her better books. Throughout her career, Christie often got panned for her more brilliant performances, while her weaker detective novels and silly thrillers often got raves. This is due in part to the ingenuity of the plots in many of her best books, which left conservative critics feeling that Christie had broken the rules or lost credibility by her brilliance and experimentation.

In the *Spectator* Nicholas Blake claimed, "I had no difficulty in spotting the murderer though in Mrs. Christie's previous books I have seldom been within a mile of him. Still, the book opens very nicely and the love story is agreeably developed" (6/23/39).

"Even if the fiend seems hard to swallow," thought Will Cuppy in *Books* (*New York Herald Tribune*), "*Easy to Kill* contains some clever plotting and enough casting of suspicion to keep you guessing like mad" (9/24/39).

Kay Irvin in the *New York Times* found it "one of Agatha Christie's best mystery novels, a story fascinating in its plot, clever and lively in its characters and brilliant in its technique" (9/24/39).

"Altogether the story must be counted as yet another proof of Mrs. Christie's inexhaustible ingenuity," wrote E. R. Punshon in the *Manchester Guardian* (7/11/39).

The *Saturday Review of Literature:* "Dunder-headed detective and far-fetched finish pretty nearly spoil story that has authentic Christie touch in the characterizations. Irritating" (9/23/39).

PLOT:
Luke Fitzwilliam is back in England after years in the colonies. On the connecting train from Dover to London he finds himself sharing a compartment with a twinkling-eyed old woman who reminds him of one of his own elderly aunts. During their casual conversation it comes out that he is recently retired from police work in the East.

"Really, it's quite a coincidence," the woman dithers, adding that she herself is going up to London to see Scotland Yard to report a series of murders she has discovered in her village, Wychwood. Fitzwilliam is amazed, and thinks that Scotland Yard must need a special department to deal with all the old village ladies who come to report murders committed "in their nice quiet country villages."

The old dear—Miss Fullerton is her name—rattles on about all the "natural" deaths that she has deduced are really murder, and speculates that Dr. Humbleby is going to be the next to go.

Luke reads in the *Times* the next day that Miss Fullerton has been killed while crossing Whitehall by a hit-and-run driver; it seems an ironic coincidence until a week later when the paper's death notices carry an announcement about the unexpected demise of Dr. John Ward Humbleby of Wychwood. Luke realizes that the old pussy on the train may not have been dotty after all.

"Once a policeman, always a policeman," Luke says as he sets off for Wychwood. Through his London friend Jimmy Lorrimer, Fitzwilliam establishes contact in Wychwood-under-Ashe with Jimmy's young cousin, Bridget Conway.

When he arrives at the village, Fitzwilliam pretends to be researching and writing a book on folklore and superstitions, which gives him plenty of opportunity to interview the locals.

The recent series of deaths are still thought to be natural or accidental by the inhabitants of Wychwood, though Luke finds plenty of possible motives lurking under the surface.

The most convincing evidence comes from Miss Honoria Waynflete. She is a good friend of the late Miss Fullerton, and is as convinced as her late friend was that there are indeed murders being committed in the village. She points out loopholes in all the official death explanations, and alleges that she knows who the murderer is, though she won't tell.

Two developments color the situation: Luke becomes enamored of Bridget Conway, who is engaged to the snobbish, ruthless, self-made newspaper magnate Lord Easterfield, and Lord Easterfield's chauffeur is found with his head bashed in shortly after the victim and his employer are overheard arguing. Concerned that the situation is getting out of hand—and that Bridget might be in danger—Luke calls in Superintendent Battle from Scotland Yard.

Principal Characters: Mr. Abbott, Superintendent Battle, Bridget Conway, Lord Easterfield, Mr. Ellsworthy, Luke Fitzwilliam, Lavinia Fullerton, Major Horton, Jessie Rose Humbleby, Dr. John Ward Humbleby, Rose Humbleby, Jimmy Lorrimer, Sir William Ossington, Mrs. Pierce, Tommy Pierce, Dr. Geoffrey Thomas, Alfred Wake, Honoria Waynflete.

First Editions: **British**: Collins, London, June 1939. 254 pp., 7s. 6d. **American**: with U.S. title *Easy to Kill:* Dodd, Mead & Co., New York, 1939. 248 pp., $2.00.

Adaptation: A television adaptation of *Murder Is Easy* was aired on January 2, 1982, in the U.S., as a presentation of CBS "Saturday Night at the Movies." The cast was headed by Bill Bixby, Lesley-Anne Down, and Olivia de Havilland.

34

THE REGATTA MYSTERY AND OTHER STORIES
(1939)

The decade of the 1930s was the most productive of Christie's career. From 1930, the year of her courtship by and marriage to Max Mallowan and the publication of the first Jane Marple novel, to the beginning of the war in 1939, no less than twenty-four of her books were published, a record she was never to better.

The Regatta Mystery is the first of several short story collections assembled especially for the American market. Oddly enough, the grab bag of stories in this collection—two Parker Pynes, one Marple, five Poirots, and a lone "ghost" story for good measure—had not appeared in any of the earlier British short story collections, though most had been published in magazines, and this collection marks their first appearance in book form. As was the case with many of her short works, several stories of this group were to have later incarnations in full-length novels. "Yellow Iris" was rewritten during the war as *Sparkling Cyanide* (#45, 1945). "The Mystery of the Baghdad Chest" reappeared in an expanded version as "The Mystery of the Spanish Chest" in *The Adventure of the Christmas Pudding* (#65, 1960). (Why, in the revision, the chest in which the husband's body was found changed nationalities is something of a mystery.)

"How Does Your Garden Grow?", in which Poirot is summoned by letter to Littlegreen House for help with an unspecified problem, only to find on arriving that the woman who wrote the letter is dead, was considerably changed and expanded to become *Dumb Witness* (#29, 1937).

"How Does Your Garden Grow?" is also of interest because it contains the first appearance of Felicity Lemon as Poirot's secretary. She had appeared as Parker Pyne's secretary in two stories in *Parker Pyne Investigates* (#22, 1934), written circa 1932—her first published appearance. Christie's thumbnail sketch of the woman with "a passion for order almost equalling that of Poirot himself" is a fine and very funny example of Christie's ability to paint a character in few words: "Her general effect was that of a lot of bones flung together at random. . . . The contents of a letter meant nothing to Miss Lemon except from the point of view of composing an adequate reply . . . she was very nearly the perfect machine, completely and gloriously uninterested in all human affairs. Her real passion for life was the perfection of a filing system beside which all other filing systems should sink into oblivion."

When Christie expanded this plot into the full-length *Dumb Witness,* she eliminated Miss Lemon and brought in the bumbling Hastings, presumably because, for a full-length novel, someone was needed on hand most of the time as a foil for Poirot, and a male traveling companion was more appropriate than a female private secretary.

The *New Yorker* thought the collection "rather frothy but pleasant enough for summer-weekend readings" (6/24/39). Will Cuppy in *Books* (*New York Herald Tribune*) counseled, "Unless you are one of those stubborn fans who dislike short mysteries, these should serve your purpose nicely" (6/24/39).

The *Springfield Republican* wrote, "All of this is highly entertaining for the reader. The facts as presented to these two incomparable investigators [Poirot and Marple] leave him utterly baffled; when it all becomes clear as day, the reader can only say, 'Now why didn't I think of that?' But he never does. . . . Miss Christie at her best" (7/2/39).

PLOTS:

"The Regatta Mystery"

Wealthy diamond merchant Isaac Pointz and the party of guests from his yacht *Merrimaid* come ashore at Dartmouth to enjoy the fair after the yacht races. Over dinner at the Royal George, Eve Leathern bets that she can make Pointz's famous diamond, the Morning Star, disappear right at the dinner table. When the girl effects her sleight of hand in full view of the party, she discovers to her dismay that she has made the priceless gem disappear more completely than she'd intended.

Fortunately, detective Parker Pyne is able to divine what has happened to the Morning Star.

"The Mystery of the Baghdad Chest"

Poirot and Hastings take an interest in the much-publicized murder of Mr. Clayton, whose stabbed body was found stuffed inside an elaborate chest in the sitting room of his friend—and rumored lover of Mrs. Clayton—Major Jack Rich. The "horrible and macabre" angle of this love-murder is that Mrs. Clayton, Major Rich, and other friends had all danced and played cards in the Major's sitting room the evening of the murder, not knowing that the body was in the chest.

"How Does Your Garden Grow?"

Poirot receives a letter from a Miss Barrowby that urges him to help her in a matter of utmost secrecy and importance. Poirot replies that he will be happy to discuss the problem. But before Poirot receives a response from his would-be client, he learns through a newspaper clipping that she has suddenly died. The Belgian's curiosity is further piqued when Miss Barrowby's relations insist that this secret matter is "no longer of importance."

"Problem at Pollensa Bay"

Mr. Parker Pyne, on holiday from his problem-solving business in London, finds the Piños d'Oro, a quaint small hotel on Mallorca, the perfect spot to relax. Unfortunately, also staying at the hotel are two fellow countrymen, Mrs. Adela Chester and her dutiful young son, Basil. When Mrs. Chester discovers that Mr. Pyne is a "wizard" at solving human problems, she calls on him to save Basil from making a match with a most unsuitable young woman who lives in the local artists' colony.

"Yellow Iris"

Late one evening, Poirot receives an anonymous phone call, summoning him to the Jardin Des Cygnes, to the table with the yellow irises, on a matter of life or death. At the table set with yellow irises, Poirot finds a memorial dinner in progress, in honor of Iris Russell, who had mysteriously died of strychnine poisoning four years ago that night, while sitting at a nightclub table with the same men and women who are at the Jardin Des Cygnes for the memorial dinner.

"Miss Marple Tells a Story"

Aunt Jane tells her nephew Raymond and his wife Joan West about the "curious little business" some years back, when "just by applying a little common sense" she had solved a murder. Likable young Mr. Rhodes had been about to be charged with the murder of his wife in her room at the Crown Hotel, Barnchester, even though the investigating jury had originally ruled "murder by person or persons unknown."

"The Dream"

Poirot is summoned by letter to the dilapidated mansion of recluse and eccentric millionaire Benedict Farley, who makes the unusual request that Poirot help him interpret his recurrent nightmare of suicide.

"In a Glass Darkly"

A houseguest at Badgeworthy, the Carswells' country home, sees a reflection in his bedroom mirror: a scar-faced man strangling a beautiful fair-haired young woman. But the doorway to the adjoining room, which was reflected in the mirror, is in reality blocked by a heavy wardrobe. The houseguest is shocked and frightened when he goes downstairs that evening, and finds that the murderer and victim are staying with him at Badgeworthy.

"Problem at Sea"

A seasick Poirot is crossing the Mediterranean on his way to Egypt when he is thrown together with shipboard companions Colonel and Mrs. Clapperton. She is the bossy rich former Lady Carrington, he the former music-hall star who married well and had a military career of sorts mainly because of his wife's good connections. He's good-natured about his wife's sharp criticism of him, meek to the point of subservience . . . yet he knows a few too many flashy card tricks for a man of such passive demeanor.

First Editions: British: None. **American**: Dodd, Mead & Co., New York, 1939. 229 pp., $2.00.

Adaptation: The story "In a Glass Darkly" was adapted for television as part of the Thames Television series *The Agatha Christie Hour*.

35

TEN LITTLE NIGGERS / AND THEN THERE WERE NONE / TEN LITTLE INDIANS (1939)

Christie ended a decade of brilliant detective novels with one of her most brilliant deceptions. She was especially proud of the plot of *Ten Little Niggers*. "It was so difficult to do that the idea fascinated me. . . . It was well received and reviewed, but the person who was really pleased with it was myself, for I knew better than any critic how difficult it had been."

The so-called nursery rhyme on which Christie based her murder plot is actually a popular Victorian minstrel show song, which was written by Frank Green to music by Mark Mason and published in England in February 1869. Green wrote the song for G. W. "Pony" Moore, a comic tenor with the Christy Minstrels who performed at St. James's Hall, Piccadilly. The song became a classic and was especially popular among children, hence its "nursery rhyme" status.

Christie includes the complete rhyme in chapter 2 of the book. Vera Claythorne finds it written on parchment in a gleaming chromium frame hanging over the fireplace in her bedroom. The reader will find that the ensuing murders follow the poem quite closely and cleverly; the "red herring" which swallowed boy number four is not an alteration of the text, though Christie must have found the appearance of the phrase amusing.

Frank Green's lyrics were actually an adaptation of the American comic song and chorus *Ten Little Indians* by Philadelphia songwriter Septimus Winner. Winner's lyrics were published in London in July 1868 and (in the days before copyright) were soon adapted for British audiences. Mr. Winner, who sometimes wrote under the pseudonym Alice Hawthorne, his mother's maiden name, is also noted for "Listen to the Mockingbird" (1855) and "Where Oh Where Has My Little Dog Gone?" (1864); his brother Joseph had a big hit in 1867 with "Little Brown Jug."

TEN LITTLE INDIANS

by Septimus Winner, 1868

Ten little Injuns standin' in a line,
One toddled home and then there were nine;
Nine little Injuns swingin' on a gate,
One tumbled off and then there were eight.

> One little, two little, three little, four little,
>   five little Injun boys,
> Six little, seven little, eight little, nine little,
>   ten little Injun boys.

Eight little Injuns gayest under heav'n,
One went to sleep and then there were seven;
Seven little Injuns cutting up their tricks,
One broke his neck and then there were six.

Six little Injuns kickin' all alive,
One kick'd the bucket and then there were five;
Five little Injuns on a cellar door,
One tumbled in and then there were four.

Four little Injuns up on a spree,
One he got fuddled and then there were three;
Three little Injuns out in a canoe,
One tumbled overboard and then there were two.

Two little Injuns foolin' with a gun,
One shot t'other and then there was one;
One little Injun livin' all alone,
He got married and then there were none.

Green's rhymes follow the American version closely in structure, though the actual means of knocking off the boys are changed considerably.

TEN LITTLE NIGGERS

by Frank Green, 1869

Ten little Nigger boys went out to dine;
One choked his little self and then there were nine.

Nine little Nigger boys sat up very late;
One overslept himself and then there were eight.

Eight little Nigger boys traveling in Devon;
One said he'd stay there and then there were seven.

Seven little Nigger boys chopping up sticks;
One chopped himself in halves and then there were six.

Six little Nigger boys playing with a hive;
A bumblebee stung one and then there were five.

Five little Nigger boys going in for law;
One got in Chancery and then there were four.

Four little Nigger boys going out to sea;
A red herring swallowed one and then there were three.

Three little Nigger boys walking in the Zoo;
A big bear hugged one and then there were two.

Two little Nigger boys sitting in the sun;
One got frizzled up and then there was one.

One little Nigger boy left all alone;
He went and hanged himself and then there were none.

Christie actually devised two endings for *Ten Little Niggers*. In the novel, she uses the ending of the Frank Green version.

One little Nigger boy left all alone;
He went and hanged himself and then there were none.

When she adapted the book for the stage in 1943, she chose a "happier" ending based on the original Septimus Winner rhyme.

One little Nigger boy left all alone;
He got married and then there were none.

When the film version of the book was made in Hollywood in 1945, under the title *And Then There Were None,* some critics pounced on director Rene Clair for altering Christie's downbeat ending and giving the film a romantic denouement, not realizing that this was a version that came from Christie herself, and that she thought a romantic ending was more suitable for the stage.

Christie's story has even more titles than endings. When the American edition was published in 1940, Dodd, Mead rightly decided that the original title could be construed as racially offensive, even though it was taken directly from the British song. The book appeared as *And Then There Were None.* In the intervening years, American editions have also been titled *Ten Little Indians* and *The Nursery Rhyme Murders,* though as of this writing *And Then There Were None* is being used by U.S. publishers.

The change of title from British to American editions necessitated changes in the text as well, for the most part the mere substitution of Indian for nigger.

One of the interesting changes is the line "Nigger Island, eh? There's a nigger in the woodpile," which in the American editions becomes "Indian Island, eh? There's a nigger in the woodpile."

"He remembered Nigger Island* as a boy . . . Smelly sort of rock covered with gulls—stood about a mile from the coast. It had got its name from its resemblance to a man's head—a man with negroid lips."

"He remembered Indian Island as a boy . . . Smelly sort of rock covered with gulls—stood about a mile from the coast. It got its name from its resemblance to a man's head—an American Indian profile."

* The actual existence of Nigger Island is open to speculation. The Devon coast is fringed with many rocky outcroppings, some inhabited, some not, and Christie during her youth certainly would have spent summer days on boat trips to various picturesque spots near Torquay. It is very easy to imagine the young Agatha and her companions, as various perspectives of cliffs and crags came into view, looking for resemblances to faces or objects among the rocks.

The original title and text still appear in British editions, though Christie biographer Gwen Robyns points out that during a 1966 English revival of the play, an organized protest by a civil rights group resulted in the title of the play, during that run, at least, being changed to *And Then There Were None,* apparently with Christie's permission.

The critics recognized that *Ten Little Niggers* was one of Christie's more spectacular deceptions, though a few voiced reservations about the plot's credulity—understandable enough, given what happens on Nigger Island, and why. Fellow mystery writer Julian Symons, in his 1977 essay on Christie in *Agatha Christie: First Lady of Crime,* speculates that *Ten Little Niggers,* achievement that it is, is not as good as *The Murder of Roger Ackroyd* (#7, 1926) "because the trick played on the reader is deliberately artificial rather than fitting naturally into the story."

Will Cuppy in *Books* (*New York Herald Tribune*) wrote that "there is no doubt that this is a highly ingenious jigsaw by a master of puzzling, but don't try to believe it, or you'll be sunk at the half-way mark. Hercule Poirot does not appear. Nor any other detective, for that matter" (2/25/40).

"For absolute horror and complete bafflement Agatha Christie's *And Then There Were None* takes all prizes," wrote the *Boston Transcript* (2/24/40) while *Library Journal* shrieked, "It is Agatha Christie run wild" (2/1/40).

Ralph Partridge in the *New Statesman and Nation* found that "apart from one little dubious proceeding there is no cheating; the reader is just bamboozled in a straightforward way from first to last. If it were not for that iota of hanky-panky, [*And Then There Were None*] would be the most colossal achievement of a colossal career. As it is the book must rank with Mrs. Christie's precious best . . . on the top notch of detection" (11/18/39).

"The whole thing is utterly impossible and utterly fascinating," wrote Isaac Anderson in the *New York Times.* "It is the most baffling mystery Agatha Christie has ever written, and if any other writer has ever surpassed it for sheer puzzlement the name escapes our memory. We are referring, of course, to mysteries that have logical explanations, as this one has. It is a tall story, to be sure, but it could have happened" (2/25/40).

"Slick, tricky idea which somehow doesn't quite come off,"

wrote the *New Yorker,* "probably because of a forced emphasis on a group of manufactured people. Smart as anything, though, and you'll have to hand it to Miss Christie" (3/2/40).

The *Saturday Review of Literature* found the book had a "hair-raising and completely inexplicable build-up not matched by rather fantastic explanation—but most readers won't mind that. Spectacular" (2/24/40).

And with a certain finality, Rupert Hart-Davis in the *Spectator* pronounced, "Agatha Christie's masterpiece" (12/15/39).

PLOT:

Ten men and women, from all walks of life, have received summonses to Nigger Island, the much-talked-about private domain which is a mile off Sticklehaven, Devon. Built as a private retreat by an American millionaire, the house is reputed to have been bought by a film actress, or a certain Mr. Owen, or the Admiralty, or even by the royal family. No one seems to know for sure.

At the Sticklehaven dock, seven of the ten—strangers to each other—meet for the first time. They size one another up, and try to figure out just why they all are on their way to Nigger Island. The seven are: Mr. Justice Wargrave, lately retired from the bench, and known as "A hanging judge"; Vera Claythorne, a former governess who had an unfortunate incident with one of her charges; Emily Brent, a sixty-five-year-old spinster with questionable mental stability; Anthony Marston, a dazzlingly handsome young swell; Mr. Blore, a blustery and rather phony South African; Captain Philip Lombard, a gun-carrying soldier of fortune; and General Macarthur, a seasoned war veteran who harbors a strong death wish.

After they are ferried across the channel to the island, the guests arrive at the "low and square and modern-looking" house to find a reassuringly grave butler, Mr. Rogers, who informs the new arrivals that Mr. Owen, their host, has been delayed and will arrive the following day. Dr. Armstrong, another late arrival, is a man known to Justice Wargrave. They are to settle in, enjoy themselves, and have dinner at eight, prepared by Rogers and his wife.

There are ten souls on the island, eight guests and two staff—but no host. As the guests learn to their surprise, Mr. Owen is not known to any of them. They rather uneasily await his arrival. But before he comes, there is a death on Nigger Island. Then another. There is a murderer among them—one of the ten. But as fear and suspicion grip the island, it seems only the dead are above suspicion.

Principal Characters: Dr. Edward George Armstrong, William Henry Blore, Emily Caroline Brent, Vera Elizabeth Claythorne, Sir Thomas Legge, Captain Philip Lombard, General John Gordon Macarthur, Inspector Maine, Anthony James Marston, Fred Narracott, Ethel Rogers, Thomas Rogers, Mr. Justice Wargrave.

First Editions: **British**: Collins, London, November 1939. 252 pp., 7s. 6d. **American**: with U.S. title *And Then There Were None:* Dodd, Mead & Co., New York, 1940. 264 pp., $2.00.

Adaptations: *Ten Little Niggers,* adapted by Christie for the stage, opened in London on November 17, 1943, at the St. James's Theatre. The play, with the title changed to *Ten Little Indians,* opened in New York at the Broadhurst Theatre on June 27, 1944. Three film versions were made from Christie's adaptation of the novel. The first and most important version was released in 1945. The film, titled *Ten Little Niggers* (U.S. title: *And Then There Were None*), was directed by Rene Clair and starred Barry Fitzgerald, Walter Huston, C. Aubrey Smith, and Judith Anderson. The second film version was released in 1965 with the title *Ten Little Indians*. The third version was released in 1975, with the title *And Then There Were None* (in U.S., *Ten Little Indians*).

❖ 36 ❖

Sad Cypress (1940)

This is a book Poirot didn't belong in, or so Agatha Christie thought. In an article by Frances Wyndham that appeared in the *Sunday Times* (London), the author is quoted as saying, *"Sad Cypress* could have been good, but it was quite ruined by having Poirot in it. I always thought *something* was wrong with it, but didn't discover what till I read it again some time after" (2/27/66).

Critics have generally disagreed with the author. Robert Barnard in *A Talent to Deceive* (1980) described the book as "Elegiac, more emotionally involving than is usual with Christie, but the ingenuity and superb cluing put it among the very best of the classic titles." N. B. Wynne in *An Agatha Christie Chronology* (1976) named it "one of my three favorite Christie books."

At the time of publication, the *Times Literary Supplement* (London) found that, "Like all Mrs. Christie's work, it is economically written, the clues are placed before the reader with impeccable fairness, the red herrings deftly laid and the solution will cause many readers to kick themselves" (3/9/40). Rupert Hart-Davis in the *Spectator* wrote, "Mrs. Christie wastes no words, and her timing is accurate. Here is the modern English detective story in its most agreeable form" (3/8/40). The *New York Times* wrote, "Not the best of the Christie achievements, but it is better than the average thriller on every count" (9/15/40). Ralph Partridge in the *New Statesman and Nation* lamented, *"Sad Cypress* would be a most admirable piece of detection—by any other writer. The blueprint of the plot indicates the supreme architect; only the actual edifice has been hastily run up" (3/9/40). And finally, a classic review from none other than the *Saturday Review of Literature,* which commits the unpardonable sin: "[The] long *sans-Poirot* preamble may be slow for some but [the] French [!] sleuth has rarely done his stuff more admirably. Good—as usual!" (9/14/40).

The book is dedicated to Peter and Peggy MacLeod, a husband and wife physician team who ran the hospital in Mosul, Syria, during the 1930s, when the Mallowans were frequently in Syria on archaeological digs.

In *An Autobiography* Christie tells the charming story of the MacLeods' unusual surgical teamwork at Mosul. Under Moslem law, a male doctor could not perform surgery on a female patient. If a Moslem woman did require surgery, Dr. Peggy MacLeod would perform the procedure while her husband stood behind a screen next to the operating table. During the operation, they would describe symptoms and techniques back and forth across the screen, never once in sight of one another.

Back in England, the Mallowans remained friends with the doctors, and after the outbreak of the war, during the blitz, the MacLeods' children went west to Torquay to stay with Max and Agatha, away from the bombings in London and the Southeast. Young Peter MacLeod spent afternoons walking with Agatha, and taught her how to identify the various types of British and German planes flying overhead.

PLOT:

Elinor Carlisle stands in the dock as she pleads not guilty to the murder of Mary Gerrard, July 27 last, at Hunterbury, Maidensford. As she answers the indictment, she studies the courtful of faces: Sir Edward Blumer, counsel for the defense; Sir Samuel Attenbury, representing the Crown; many faces from her past; and one stranger in the courtroom standing out from the others, with his "big black moustache and shrewd eyes"—Hercule Poirot.

Miss Carlisle's road to the Old Bailey began some time before when she received a vicious anonymous letter. It warns her that some unnamed young girl is "sucking up to" Elinor's wealthy, stroke-invalided Aunt Laura with the alleged motive of manipulating herself into being named Laura Welman's beneficiary.

Elinor Carlisle and her fiancé, Roddy, concerned by the letter, hurry off to Hunterbury "to protect our interests *and* because we're fond of the old dear!"

When they arrive at the estate, they find that the would-be legatee is Mary Gerrard, the beautiful daughter of the estate's caretaker, and Roddy becomes madly taken with her.

Laura Welman dies during the night, leaving no will, and Elinor, as next of kin, inherits everything. As the estate is settled, Elinor has to bear up under the pain of seeing Roddy very much in love with Mary Gerrard, but she obeys her aunt's deathbed wish and gives Mary a large bequest.

Then Mary Gerrard dies of poisoning. Suspicion falls on Elinor, and she is arrested. The case against her is damning, until Dr. Peter Lord, the late aunt's doctor, who has fallen for Elinor Carlisle as headlong as Roddy Welman fell for Mary Gerrard, asks Poirot to look into the case.

Principal Characters: Inspector Brill, Sir Edwin Bulmer, Elinor Katherine Carlisle, Mary Draper, Mary Gerrard, Jessie Hopkins, James Arthur Littledale, Dr. Peter Lord, Chief Inspector Marsden, Hercule Poirot, Alfred James Wargrave, Laura Welman, Roderick Welman.

First Editions: **British**: Collins, London, March 1940. 252 pp., 8s. 3d. (the first British price hike since 1920!) **American**: Dodd, Mead & Co., New York, 1940. 270 pp., $2.00.

Adaptation: None.

37

One, Two, Buckle My Shoe / The Patriotic Murders / An Overdose of Death (1940)

World War II brought many changes to Christie's life. The Mallowans' favorite home, Greenway in Devon, was used as a home for refugee children and later requisitioned by the government as a "barracks" and headquarters for American naval men. Max Mallowan joined the Royal Air Force voluntary reserve, with the rank of Wing Commander to the British Military Administration, and went on to be made an advisor on Arab affairs; he was to spend most of the war in the Middle East. With Greenway unavailable and the prospect of Max being away, Christie took a small flat on Lawn Road, Hampstead, in a sleek, modern-style building—just the kind Poirot admired so and always chose to inhabit—which included among its residents the influential modern architects Marcel Breuer and Walter Gropius.

Like many British women whose husbands were in the service, Agatha volunteered for local service. Owing to her experience as a pharmacy dispenser in World War I, she began working at University College Hospital, London, working with the medicines—and poisons—she knew so well.

One, Two was probably written during the so-called "phony war," that ominous period of stagnation after the German invasion of Poland in September 1939. Though Britain declared war on Germany on September 3, there was no fighting for months, while Britain hurriedly prepared for war. The silence was broken suddenly on April 9, 1940, with the surprise German invasion of Denmark and Norway, and the invasion of Luxembourg, Belgium, and the Netherlands on May 10. The heroic evacuation of Dunkirk, between May 26 and June 4, was the British populace's first close contact with the fighting across the Channel.

The war itself is not mentioned in the book, though Hitler and Mussolini are named in passing. There is also reference to a British right-wing pseudo-military group called "the Imperial Shirts," obviously patterned after Oswald Mosley's British Union of

Fascists, who were active in Britain during the 1930s. This would indicate a probable time setting of the book before September 1939.

This time frame is further confirmed by the scene in which Poirot's dentist mentions King Leopold of Belgium when he discovers his patient's nationality. "Very fine man . . . so I've always heard." Unless Christie is being deliberately ironic, this statement places the probable completion of the book at the time of Dunkirk or before, as Leopold of Belgium's reputation suffered a tremendous setback after the German invasion on May 10, when he surrendered unconditionally to the Nazis against the wishes of his cabinet. He was accused of treasonous cooperation with the Germans and of harboring fascist leanings. Leopold spent the war in Germany, until freed by the Allies in 1945. He was not allowed to return to Belgium by parliamentary vote, and lived in Switzerland in exile after the war.

Though the American edition was published months before Pearl Harbor, its title, *The Patriotic Murders,* reflects American support of the British war effort. There is little in the book itself that is concerned with patriotism (although Alistair Blunt is head of the most powerful bank in England, and an important advisor to the government). In their choice of title, Dodd, Mead seems to have overlooked the rather unpleasant connotation that there is such a thing as *patriotic* murder (assassination? warfare?). In recent American editions the title has been changed to the more appropriate *An Overdose of Death.*

In the *Boston Transcript* Marian Wiggin wrote, "Agatha Christie is tops as you probably know, and I think you will agree that her latest . . . . is right at the head of the list" (3/15/41).

Kay Irvin in the *New York Times* thought, "It's a real Agatha Christie thriller: exceedingly complicated plot, briskly simple in narrative, with a swift course of unflagging suspense that leads to complete surprise. After closing the book one may murmur, 'far fetched,' or even 'impossible.' But any such complaint will be voiced only after the story has been finished; there won't be a moment to think of such things before" (3/2/41).

"In fine fettle, Poirot is always a jump or two ahead of Inspector Japp, one of those cops with a genius for picking the wrong motive," said Will Cuppy in *Books (New York Herald Tribune).*

"He arrives at a hair-raising solution after a third casualty by methods he alone can handle—so you probably won't guess it. As always, this author provides generous amounts of entertainment over and above the bare bones of a puzzle. This seems to be a major Christie, the best thing currently in sight for all-around mystery merit" (3/2/41).

And E. R. Punshon in the *Manchester Guardian:* "In today's slang a girl is said to be not pretty but 'easy to look at.' To adapt the phrase it may be said of Mrs. Agatha Christie that she is 'easy to read,' and to be 'easy to read,' if not the greatest of qualities a writer may possess, is one of the most valuable" (12/13/40).

PLOT:

At precisely eleven o'clock one morning Hercule Poirot alights from a taxi at 58 Queen Charlotte Street and enters a doorway, prepared to face one of those "certain humiliating moments in the lives of the greatest of men." The Belgian was about to be reduced to "that ordinary, that craven figure, a man afraid of the dentist's chair." Poirot manages to endure the humiliation of being drilled in Mr. Henry Morley's chair. "The ordeal of the drill was terror rather than pain."

In the afternoon, a call from Inspector Japp of Scotland Yard informs Poirot that Henry Morley has been found dead in his office, an apparent suicide.

Poirot returns to the dentist's the second time that day. He and Japp go over the evidence—Morley appears to be a suicide, but the circumstances don't ring true. The man was not depressed, not in financial trouble, not involved in any problematic affairs of the heart. And his death had occurred in the middle of a day of continuous appointments—hardly a likely time for doing oneself in.

Poirot immediately focuses on Morley's other appointments, and finds that Morley's patients that day were hardly run-of-the-mill. They included Alistair Blunt, a vastly powerful and wealthy financier with more than casual political importance, and the Greek, Amberiotis, a mysterious new patient who had called for an appointment from the Savoy Hotel.

Poirot soon discovers a few problems closer to home. Georgina Morley, the spinster sister with whom the dentist lived in the flat above his offices, kept her brother on a tight rein; Gladys Nevill, the young blond assistant, has taken up recently with Frank Carter, a ne'er-do-well suitor who resents Morley's disapproval of him; Reilly, Morley's associate dentist, is a capable professional, but has a drinking problem, and is considerably less successful than his older partner.

Evidence points to one likely suspect, until that suspect is murdered by an overdose of procaine and Adrenalin. Clearly, affairs at Morley's dental office are not as hygienic as they should be.

Principal Characters: Colonel Abercrombie, Mr. Amberiotis, Reginald Barnes, Alfred Biggs, Alistair Blunt, Frank Carter, Agnes Fletcher, Gerda Grant, Ram Lal, Mrs. Merton, Georgina Morley, Henry Morley, Gladys Nevill, Jane Olivera, Julia Olivera, Hercule Poirot, Mr. Reilly, Mabelle Sainsbury Seale.

First Editions: British: Collins, London, November 1940. 252 pp., 7s. 6d. **American:** with U.S. title *The Patriotic Murders:* Dodd, Mead & Co., New York, 1941. 240 pp., $2.00.

Adaptation: None.

38

EVIL UNDER THE SUN (1941)

The setting is the Devon coast of a summer, where tourists have come to a converted Georgian mansion called the Jolly Roger Hotel on Smuggler's Island, Leathercombe Bay, to partake of the salt air, the sea breezes, and the sun's tanning rays. The Devon coast was home surf to Christie,* since she was born in Torquay, one of the most famous of the Devon resorts. During her childhood, Torquay and the "English Riviera" had been a winter resort for the upper- and upper-middle classes, who maintained large private villas or luxury hotel accommodations during the relatively mild Devon winter.

This all changed after World War I. "In 1922 when the great cult of the Seaside for Holidays was finally established," Christie writes in the novel, "and the coast of Devon and Cornwall was no longer too hot in the summer," Devon became a haven for that new breed, the sunbather, who flocked to converted villas like the Jolly Roger to broil and baste themselves to a perfect brown.

It is with a certain amount of humor that Christie depicts Poirot at the beach, at his advanced age, wearing white suits and Panama hats, concerned that his mustache might droop in the heat, or his hair dye run onto his collar—a figure not at all unlike Aschenbach in Mann's *Death in Venice,* clinging to an illusion of youth while watching the *real* youth play on the beach.

"Regard them there," Poirot says of the tanned, near-naked beachgoers. "There is nothing personal about them. They are just . . . bodies."

Poirot longs for the old days, when there was the mystery of petticoated thighs, a half-revealed ankle, "a beribboned garter."

And one of Poirot's fellow guests, Mrs. Gardener, in response

---

* Devon always remained Christie's favorite part of England; Greenway, the home she bought in 1939, is on the river Dart, a few miles inland from the coast depicted in the book.

to Poirot's nostalgia, chimes in with her concern that all that sun-bathing will cause her daughter to grow hair—"hair on your arms, and hair on your legs, and hair on your bosom, and what will you look like then?"

Christie herself was an avid swimmer (she even surfed in Hawaii while on her world tour with Archie Christie), and in spite of her Victorian upbringing, she was not hesitant to wear "modern" bathing dress and to expose ample amounts of flesh at public beaches. She had probably received many dire warnings about "growing hair" from older female relatives.

Evil Under the Sun is one of Christie's classic (and classiest) triangle mysteries, and as such shares a lineage with the short stories "Triangle at Rhodes" (published in *Murder in the Mews,* #28, 1937) and "The Bloodstained Pavement" (published in *The Thirteen Problems,* #16, 1932), and with *Death on the Nile* (#30, 1937). Reviews were glowing.

Will Cuppy in *Books* (*New York Herald Tribune*) called it "a regular fireworks display of her technical abilities, with a surprise conclusion of high voltage. You can't go wrong with this one" (10/19/41).

Isaac Anderson in the *New York Times* thought, "The murder is an elaborately planned affair—a little too much so for credibility, in view of the many possibilities of a slip-up somewhere along the way—but Poirot's reasoning is flawless, as it always is" (10/19/41).

The *Times Literary Supplement* (London): "Everybody is well aware that any character most strongly indicated is not a likely criminal; yet this guiding principle is forgotten when Miss Christie persuades you that you are more discerning than you really are. Then she springs her secret like a land mine" (6/14/41).

"Agatha Christie does not disappoint her admirers in *Evil Under the Sun,*" wrote John Fairfield in the *Spectator.* "The puzzle is deftly mounted with the customary economy, and is then broken by Poirot with the precise pomp which so nearly resembles a Guards regiment manoeuvring at the slow march. . . . If one can make any objection it is that the weather is too good; a spell of unbroken fine weather outlasting a Poirot investigation on the Cornish [sic] coast strains the reader's credulity almost to the breaking point" (6/13/41).

PLOT:

While relaxing on the terrace of the Jolly Roger Hotel, Hercule Poirot familiarizes himself with his fellow guests, who are at the resort for sunning, sea air, and recreation. Among them are two Americans, the garrulous Mrs. Gardener and her long-suffering husband, Odell; Miss Brewster, a "tough, athletic" spinster; and Rosamund Darnley, a famous fashion designer. Among other guests are the Reverend Stephen Lane, who sublimates his passion for women only with difficulty; Horace Blatt, a pushy life-of-the-party sort of self-made millionaire; and Major Barry, a gossipy retired officer.

Special attention is focused on the honeymooning Redferns. Christine Redfern, who takes great pains to protect her milk-white skin from the summer sun, is a devoted young bride. Husband Patrick is a superb specimen of male attractiveness, so much so that even on the honeymoon there are signs that Christine will have problems in keeping women away from her husband.

Problems arise with the arrival of the Marshall family: Captain Kenneth, a man of forty, of good family; his daughter by previous marriage, Linda (an awkward adolescent); and his new wife, the startlingly beautiful Arlena Stuart Marshall. Arlena's beauty seduces Patrick Redfern, and the two's flagrant carryings-on are a pain and embarrassment to poor Christine and to Captain Marshall.

Soon, hidden connections are revealed: not only are Arlena and Patrick lovers, but fashion designer Rosamund Darnley has never gotten over her youthful love for Captain Marshall, and thus despises his beautiful and unfaithful wife.

One morning Arlena Marshall is discovered on the beach, strangled to death.

Principal Characters: Major Barry, Horace Blatt, Emily Brewster, Mrs. Castle, Inspector Colgate, Rosamund Darnley, Carrie Gardener, Odell Gardener, Reverend Stephen Lane, Arlena Marshall, Captain Kenneth Marshall, Linda Marshall, Hercule Poirot, Christine Redfern, Patrick Redfern, Colonel Weston.

First Editions: **British**: Collins, London, June 1941. 252 pp., 7s. 6d. **American**: Dodd, Mead & Co., New York, 1941. 260 pp., $2.00.

Adaptation: The film *Evil Under the Sun,* based on the novel, was released in the U.S. in March 1982. The screenplay was by Anthony Schaffer. Peter Ustinov starred as Hercule Poirot. Featured in the all-star cast were Maggie Smith, Diana Rigg, James Mason, and Roddy McDowall.

39

N OR M? (1941)

With husband Max in the Middle East and daughter Rosalind married, Christie stayed alone in London during the war. She was living in Lawn Road Flats, Hampstead, and working at University College Hospital as a dispenser.

"The rest of the time I wrote," she states flatly in her memoirs.

Christie's attitude toward London during the war is remarkably nonchalant, yet stoic and courageous, an attitude shared by many of her countrymen.

"It had become . . . natural to expect that you yourself might be killed soon, that the people you loved best might be killed, that you would hear of deaths of friends. Broken windows, bombs, land mines, and in due course flying bombs and rockets—all these things would go on, not as something extraordinary, but as perfectly natural."

It is interesting that Christie, who by 1941 was a wealthy woman, chose to live amidst the very real perils of besieged London when she easily could have afforded to rent or buy a house in the least-threatened parts of England, or to go to North America.

With the limitations of the war—blackouts, rationing, air raids—she found that she actually had time to spare. Before the war, while working on a novel, when she ran into the inevitable dry periods, she had "other things to do"—decorating houses, traveling, gardening. Now, during the long wartime nights, she found that working on two books at once was the best solution to writer's block.

"If . . . I alternated the writing of them, it would keep me fresh at the task."

The two novels she chose to work on simultaneously were *N or M?* and *The Moving Finger* (#42, 1943). *N or M?,* arguably the best of the Tommy and Tuppence Beresford books, is unusual for Christie in that it has a specific wartime setting. Tommy and Tuppence, as a middle-aged couple who don't know just *what* they can do to help the war effort, are a bit autobiographical. During the early months of the war, while still living in the country, Max Mallowan volunteered for the Torquay House Guard, by Christie's account a comic little militia, with one gun to eight men. Agatha for her part trotted down to the local dispensary to offer services.

Like the Mallowans' early involvement in the war effort, Tommy and Tuppence Beresford's adventure in *N or M?* is a pretty harmless affair, in spite of all the Nazis lurking around the Torquay-like resort that Christie christens Leahampton.

Reading the espionage high-jinks in *N or M?* was probably a welcome escape for besieged readers, for by the time of its publication in November 1941, Britain had suffered through "the Battle of Britain," and the quiet days of the "phony war" seemed long ago. The lighthearted book must have been an equally welcome escape for Christie, as it was written under less-than-ideal conditions during the blitz. During the raids she slept with a pillow over her face to ward off flying glass from nearby bomb hits. Her two most precious possessions—her fur coat and a real rubber hot water bottle (irreplaceable in wartime)—were kept on a chair beside the bed ready to be taken to an air-raid shelter. Christie didn't say if she kept the manuscript of *N or M?* close by as well.

"Here's exactly the thing for those who want some fairly dangerous non-combatant war atmosphere, slick spy-stuff, and a sufficiently baffling puzzle all wrapped up in an attractive package," (6/22/41) wrote Will Cuppy in *Books* (*New York Herald Tribune*). The *Saturday Review of Literature* found "engaging characters, bright dialogue, capital seashore boarding house scenery, and plenteous thrills—with one or two rather unbelievable bits. Good hunting" (6/28/41).

Kay Irvin in the *New York Times* wrote, "In a story whose mystery and excitement follow not unfamiliar—but always interesting—lines, Agatha Christie has found room for a wit which is both keen and significant (6/22/41).

The *New Yorker* said, "Crisp, quick reading in this story, but the reader should be able to put his finger on the guilty parties about halfway through the book" (7/5/41), while Ralph Partridge, in the *New Statesman and Nation* enthused, "It is exciting, full of surprises, laced with sentiment, and as good a Fifth Column thriller as is likely to be written" (12/20/41).

The *Times Literary Supplement* (London) in an uncharacteristic, dramatic review, described "fine, anxious rapture . . . troubling the mind . . . you begin to fear your own sanity on catching yourself wondering whether an ingratiating babe-in-arms might not be Herr Doktor in disguise. Yes, such is Miss Christie's skill in conjuring up the ominous that even infant prattle sounds uncommonly like a code for the Fifth Column" (11/29/41).

PLOT:

During the early years of World War II, as Britain struggles to recover from the early setbacks caused by German military superiority and British unpreparedness, Tommy and Tuppence Beresford are in the full flush of wartime patriotism. However, they are feeling a bit bored and "middle aged and past doing things," and they recall fondly the days of the "Great War" when Tommy was in the service and Tuppence did volunteer work at hospitals. The couple also long for the days when they "adventured" in service of their country, tracking down secret agents and dangerous criminals and rescuing abducted girls.

The answer to their ennui comes when Mr. Carter, Tommy's former intelligence boss, sends a government agent, Mr. Grant, to their flat. Grant asks Tommy to go on assignment for Intelligence to the seaside resort of Leahampton, where the government suspects a group of spies and saboteurs are operating out of the resort hotel Sans Souci. Recently, a government secret agent was murdered, and his last words were "N or M Song Susie," which Mr. Grant interprets as code for the secret Nazi agent and the Sans Souci Hotel.

Tommy agrees to go on a mission in pursuit of the spies, though Tuppence has been kept in the dark about the affair and is left behind.

When Tommy arrives at the hotel, he finds a predictable assortment of resort-hotel guests: the quarrelsome retiree Mr. Cayley; the obese, nosy Mrs. O'Rourke; Miss Minton, a knitting spinster; the long-winded Major Bletchley; bland Mrs. Sprot and her young daughter Betty. But there are less-than-usual characters as well, including Carl von Deinim, a hostile young German refugee, and

Mrs. Perenna, the hotel's owner, who as it turns out has changed her name and has a history of radical political involvement.

The biggest surprise among the guests, however, is Mrs. Blenkensop, who the other guests think is a mother with three sons away in the war; Mrs. Blenkensop is Tuppence Beresford incognito.

Tommy is surprised by his wife's unexpected appearance—she overheard Tommy's arrangements with Mr. Grant, and decided on her own to go adventuring with her husband—but they decide to keep up the facade anyway. Soon, Mrs. Blenkensop's room is being searched by persons unknown, little Betty Sprot is abducted and nearly tossed over a cliff, and Tommy Beresford himself disappears.

Principal Characters: Albert Batt, Tommy Beresford, Tuppence Beresford, Dr. Binion, Major Bletchley, Alfred Cayley, Elisabeth Cayley, Lord Easterfield, Mr. Grant, Commander Haydock, Anthony Marsdon, Sophia Minton, Mrs. O'Rourke, Eileen Perenna, Sheila Perenna, Vanda Polonska, Betty Sprot, Millicent Sprot, Carl von Deinim.

First Editions: **British**: Collins, London, November 1941. 192 pp., 7s. 6d. **American**: Dodd, Mead & Co., New York, 1941. 289 pp., $2.00.

Adaptation: None.

40

THE BODY IN THE LIBRARY (1942)

"The best opening I ever wrote," Christie said in a 1956 *Life* magazine article of the memorable beginning of *The Body in the Library* in which Dolly Bantry tries to convince her sleepy husband that there is the body of an unknown woman downstairs in front of the library hearth. Though we know from the article that Christie liked the opening scene, and from her autobiography that *Body* was written during the London bombings, what we don't know is why Christie waited more than a decade to get back to Jane Marple after *The Murder at the Vicarage* (#13, 1930) and *The Thirteen Problems* (#16, 1932).

Perhaps it was her preoccupation with the brilliant series of books, most dominated by Poirot, that filled the decade of the 1930s. And perhaps it was Christie's own sense of growing older (she turned fifty in September 1940), combined with her growing boredom with Poirot, that made her turn to the possibilities of the spinster of St. Mary Mead, and to return to her often during the remaining thirty-five years of her career.

The title is, of course, a cliché which, tongue in cheek, was to be subjected to Christie's own special brand of detective magic. (Given the nature of the young woman found cooling her cells on the Bantrys' hearth rug, is there possibly an intentional pun on *bawdy* lurking in the title?)

Though Christie thought in retrospect that there were too many characters in *The Murder at the Vicarage* (#13, 1930), her first Marple book, she wisely kept a few of the St. Mary Mead folks around for this and future Marple mysteries: Colonel Melchett, Leonard Clement, the vicar, the Bantrys, of course, and good Dr. Haydock, who was to guard Jane's health to the very end of her career.

"When the time comes to release a sensational twist near the end," wrote Will Cuppy in *Books* (*New York Herald Tribune*), "as she is expected to do in every major story, Mrs. Christie delivers with a pronounced impact, thus adding one more to her list of undoubted successes. How is it done? Mostly, we'd say, by guarding a special kind of secret better than any one else in the business. We didn't believe a word of it, ourself, yet we were fascinated by the whole thing in no uncertain manner" (3/1/42).

"Some devoted souls may sigh for Hercule Poirot," said the *Times Literary Supplement* (London). "But there are bound to be others who will be glad to find his place taken in the 'new Agatha Christie' by Miss Marple. What this relief signifies is that professional detectives are no match for elderly spinsters . . . with some training in looking under the antimacassar. . . . We find it hard not to be impressed by old-maid logic. When Miss Marple says, 'The dress was all wrong,' she is plainly observing facts hidden from the masculine eye—facts which are of a very lively interest" (5/16/42).

Time called *The Body in the Library,* "Genuine old-crusted Christie" (3/2/42), an interesting remark about a writer not yet at the halfway point in either years of her career or in number of books published.

And in the *Spectator,* John Fairfield voiced a criticism that is still leveled at Christie, that some of her solutions are so amazing that surely she has revealed the *wrong* person as the criminal: "The solution seems so improbable that the reader is left with a very strong feeling that Miss Marple has succeeded in pinning the killings on the wrong people and that the dear old owner of the library ought to swing" (8/7/42).

PLOT:

In the early morning hours at Gossington Hall, St. Mary Mead, Dolly Bantry, mistress of the house, is having a delightful dream, which takes "a very odd turn" when the voice of the housemaid Mary breaks in, breathless and hysterical: "Oh ma'am, oh ma'am, there's a body in the library!"

After a few confused moments, Dolly realizes that Mary really did say there was a body in the library. She manages to rouse her husband, Colonel Bantry, and sends him scouting downstairs to see what's afoot. He finds a clutch of servants huddling in the hall, and sure enough, in the library there is a body of a young blond woman in evening dress, sprawled on the floor. The incongruity is striking. The library is "dim and mellow and casual. It spoke of long occupation and familiar use and of links with tradition." The corpse is "the flamboyant figure of a girl . . . with unnaturally fair hair . . . the face was heavily made up, the powder standing out grotesquely on its blue, swollen surface, the mascara of the lashes lying thickly on the distorted cheeks."

At the unlikely hour of 7:45 A.M., Jane Marple's phone rings. It is her dear friend Dolly Bantry, announcing that "we've just found a body in the library" and that she's called the fluffy spinster because "you're so good at bodies."

The official investigation begins under Colonel Melchett, the chief constable, and Inspector Slack. But it is Jane Marple, of course, who gets to the heart of things and unravels the puzzle.

Principal Characters: Colonel Arthur Bantry, Dolly Bantry, Mrs. Bartlett, George Bartlett, Basil Blake, Peter Carmody, Leonard Clement, Griselda Clement, Sir Henry Clithering, Mark Gaskell, Superintendent Harper, Dr. Haydock, Adelaide Jefferson, Conway Jefferson, Ruby Keene, Dinah Lee, Jane Marple, Colonel Melchett, Martha Price Ridley, Pamela Reeves, Inspector Slack, Raymond Starr, Josephine Turner, Caroline Wetherby.

First Editions: **British**: Collins, London, May 1942. 160 pp., 7s. 6d. **American**: Dodd, Mead & Co., New York, 1942. 245 pp., $2.00.

Adaptation: None.

41

FIVE LITTLE PIGS / MURDER IN RETROSPECT
(1943)

Though not among Christie's best-known books, *Five Little Pigs* is at the very top rung of her creative ladder. At the time of publication, Isaac Anderson wrote in the *New York Times,* "another triumph for Agatha Christie, perhaps the greatest in her career" (6/28/43). And as recently as 1980, critic Robert Barnard wrote in *A Talent to Deceive* that *Five Little Pigs* "is a beautifully tailored book, rich and satisfying. The present writer would be willing to chance his arm and say that this is the best Christie of all."

The respect that critics have shown for *Five Little Pigs* is due in no small part to the exceptional—and for Christie unusual—depth of characterization and richness of writing. This is the first of Christie's "murder in retrospect" mysteries, in which the detective seeks to solve a murder which has taken place some time in the past,* and though Christie was to use this plot device in several other books, this is by far the most successful. Barnard, who analyzes *Five Little Pigs* in his book on Christie, makes the interesting, and to our minds valid, observation that the love triangle in the book has strong emotional parallels to the triangle that broke up Christie's first marriage.

In *Five Little Pigs* Poirot is asked to reopen the case of Amyas Crale, who was to all appearances poisoned by his wife, Caroline, sixteen years before, out of jealousy over his involvement with Elsa Greer. As Barnard points out, in addition to the shared initials (Amyas Crale–Archibald Christie), the traumatic breakup of Agatha's marriage to Archie Christie took place in 1926–27, sixteen years before the book was written. In both book and life, the couple had been married ten years before the fatal affair, and in both cases the divorcing couple had a young daughter.

---

* *Sleeping Murder* (#83), written during World War II but withheld from publication until 1976, may actually predate *Five Little Pigs.* Other murder-in-retrospect books are *Sparkling Cyanide* (#45, 1945), *Ordeal by Innocence* (#63, 1958), and *Elephants Can Remember* (#79, 1972).

Though these parallels between the love triangles in the plot and in Christie's life exist, how Christie saw the parallels must remain purely speculative, since she left no comments on record about *Five Little Pigs*. Christie did discuss the period of her divorce, 1926–28, in her autobiography, but she says virtually nothing about her first husband or her feelings about him after 1928. Given the greater-than-usual depths of characterization, it's safe to assume Christie was putting a lot of her own personal feelings into the book. Whether or not she was also getting vicarious revenge by murdering the philandering Amyas Crale, or merely using a classic love triangle in the most logical way for the purposes of a murder mystery, is difficult to guess. Sixteen years after the breakup of her marriage, Christie may still have been bitter, or she may just have been giving Archie Christie a poke in the ribs.

Another remarkable aspect of *Five Little Pigs* is its complex structure. In order to delve into a murder sixteen years old, Poirot hears the story of Crale's murder and Caroline's trial many times, each time from a differing point of view as seen by characters who were involved in the events at the time. This *Rashomon*-like technique, while by no means exclusive to *Five Little Pigs,* is here used to best effect: the characters—as well as the crucial facts revealed by the recollections—are presented beautifully.

The *New Yorker* thought the book had "beautiful deducting and better writing than you'll find in the average mystery" (6/27/42). And the *Times Literary Supplement* (London) said, "No crime enthusiast will object that the story of how the painter died has to be told many times, for this, even if it creates an interest which is more problem than plot, demonstrates the author's uncanny skill. The answer to the riddle is brilliant" (1/16/43).

The dedication is to Stephen Glanville, noted professor of Egyptology and close personal friend of Agatha and Max Mallowan. Glanville received the rare honor for a nonfamily member of receiving two book dedications from Christie: *Five Little Pigs* and *Death Comes as the End* (#44, 1945).

PLOT:

Miss Carla Lemarchant, a strikingly handsome young woman from Canada, calls on Hercule Poirot to ask his help in solving an unusual case. She reveals that her real name is Caroline Crale, and that she is the daughter of Amyas Crale, a famous painter who was murdered sixteen years before by her mother, Caroline, who was sentenced to life for the murder and who died after a year in prison. Carla had not known of her family history until she turned twenty-one, when she was given a letter that her mother had written before her death, in which the dead Caroline said that she was innocent of killing her husband.

Carla believes the old letter, and wants Poirot to reinvestigate the case. Intrigued by the possibility of solving a case in which all the tangible evidence has disappeared and only the psychology of the participants remains to be examined, Poirot readily agrees.

Poirot begins delving, first by interviewing the attorneys and the police, then by examining the "five little pigs"—Philip Blake, Crale's best friend; Meredith Blake, a country squire who dabbled in poisons; Elsa Greer (now Lady Dittisham), Crale's mistress, who has married well three times since her lover's death; Angela Warren, Caroline's younger sister, whom Caroline had disfigured for life in a fit of rage; and Cecelia Williams, Angela Warren's governess, now an old woman.

Poirot finds that each story is in basic agreement: Amyas Crale, though talented, was a womanizer who took advantage of his wife's loyalty. His latest fling had been with the beautiful Elsa Greer, who made it clear that she wanted Crale to divorce Caroline and marry her.

Meredith, the herbalist, had given the Crales a tour of his hobby lab and had pointed out a bottle of coniine, a strong poison extracted from hemlock. The next morning Caroline brought her husband a bottle of beer while he was painting his mistress, Elsa. After lunch, Crale was found dead in the garden—of coniine poisoning. A quantity of coniine was missing from Blake's lab, and a bottle with traces of the poison was found in Caroline's dresser drawer.

The consensus is that the case against Caroline was damning, though Poirot says, "I must satisfy myself on that point," which he indeed does.

Principal Characters: Meredith Blake, Philip Blake, Caleb, Amyas Crale, Caroline Crale, Sir Montague Depleach, Lord Dittisham,

Quentin Fogg, Elsa Greer, Jonathan, Carla Lemarchant, Hercule Poirot, John Rattery, Angela Warren, Cecelia Williams.

First Editions: British: Collins, London, copyright 1942, publication, January 1943. 192 pp., 8s. **American:** with U.S. title *Murder in Retrospect:* Dodd, Mead & Co., New York, 1943. 234 pp., $2.00.

Adaptation: *Five Little Pigs* was adapted for the stage by Christie in 1960 as *Go Back for Murder.*

42

THE MOVING FINGER (1943)

"Rather to my surprise . . . I find that another one [of my books] I am really pleased with is *The Moving Finger,*" Christie wrote in her autobiography, putting this classic novel of hatred and "poison pen" letters among the half dozen or so of her books that she mentioned as her personal favorites. In the chapter in *Mallowan's Memoirs* on his wife's writing, Max also recalls that, though her opinions changed from time to time, *The Moving Finger* was one of the favorites that his wife mentioned as a rule.

Mallowan is of the opinion that "the latent study of good and evil is never far from absent in most of Agatha's books together with an original and intuitive understanding of the associated psychology." He goes on to describe the village of Lymstock as "a small closed society engaged in simple worthy avocations; gossip is of course the breath of life . . . a poison pen has been at work and brought tragedy in its train. A series of baffling murders is resolved with the help of 'someone who knows a great deal about wickedness,' alias Miss Marple . . . this is deservedly a favorite with many."

There is more attention paid to romance than is usual with Christie; perhaps the author couldn't help harking back to the days of the first war when she had been in love with a dashing young airman; Mallowan merely describes the romance in *Moving Finger* as adding "gilt to the gingerbread."

It is interesting to compare the dashing airman figure of Jerry Burton with the character of Amyas Crale in *Five Little Pigs* (#41, 1943). Both characters share traits with Archibald Christie, yet the traits of her first husband Agatha chose to utilize in these two characters are so different in each case that the characters emerge as totally different from one another. This provides an interesting example of how an author's mind can transform real people and experiences to suit its purposes.

Christie chose as her setting the familiar Devon countryside of her youth. The fictional town of Lymstock, "a little provincial market town with a sweep of moorland rising above it," is typical of the area. The name is obviously taken from Lyme Bay, on which most of the coast of Devon fronts, and Lyme Regis, the sea-coast town on the Dorset-Devon line.

According to Christie's autobiography, she wrote *The Moving Finger* in London, at the same time as *N or M?* (#39, 1941), during the long, blacked-out wartime nights in which she had nothing to do, unless there was a bombing raid which would send her to the air-raid shelters.

The book has a wartime setting—Jerry Burton has presumably been injured in a crash during the Battle of Britain—though there are few other period references. As for Mr. Burton's injuries, the *Times Literary Supplement* (London) rightly pointed out that they seem to be of varying severity—the man clearly has good days and bad days. "He is an airman who has crashed and walks with two sticks," wrote the *TLS*. "That he should make a lightning recovery is all to the good, but why, in between dashing downstairs two at a time and lugging a girl into a railway carriage by main force, should he complain that it hurts to drive a car? . . . [The book] would grip more if Jerry Burton . . . were more credible. . . . And why . . . does he think in this style, 'The tea was china and delicious and there were plates of sandwiches and thin bread and butter, and a quantity of little cakes'?"

These kinds of inconsistencies, which crop up occasionally even in Christie's best works, are forgivable (given the volume of her work) when, as in *The Moving Finger,* they do not substantially detract from the book's plausibility. The *Times* went on to say, "Beyond all doubt the puzzle in *The Moving Finger* is fit for experts. . . . Though odd, thwarted characters live round every corner, the number who can be suspected of bloodshed is so closely limited that it ought not to be difficult to find the guilty. . . . But it is. . . . There has rarely been a detective story so likely to create an epidemic of self-inflicted kicks" (6/19/43).

The review in the *New York Times* said, "The story is swift-moving and highly original: one of the better productions by a writer whose work is always good" (10/18/42).

PLOT:

Young airman Jerry Burton, who "took a bad crash flying," has, on his doctor's orders, rented Little Furze, a house on the outskirts of the quiet town of Lymstock, where he will be undergoing the last stages of recuperation and rehabilitation under the care of his sister, Joanna. One day during breakfast the morning mail arrives. In it is a letter with a local postmark and a typewritten address. Inside Jerry finds a letter composed of printed words, cut out and pasted on a sheet of paper. It is "a particularly foul anonymous letter," which crudely intimates that Jerry and Joanna are not brother and sister.

That morning Dr. Griffith arrives at Little Furze to give Jerry his weekly checkup. When the good doctor notices that Jerry is "a bit under the weather," Jerry mentions the letter, only to have the doctor reply, "Do you mean to say that *you've* had one of them?" It turns out that Dr. Griffith, Symmington, the solicitor, and one or two of Griffith's poorer patients, have all received poison pen letters.

The letters, all of which feature "a definite harping on the sex theme," soon create much talk and more trouble in Lymstock— several hit rather close to home, or so rumor has it. But the first major shock is the suicide of one of the recipients. Fortunately, as the web of rumor and suspicion entangles all of Lymstock, Mrs. Dane Calthrop, the vicar's wife, sends for her old friend Jane Marple, who is finally able to point out who is really behind *The Moving Finger*.

Principal Characters: Emily Barton, Jerry Burton, Joanna Burton, Rev. Dane Calthrop, Maud Dane Calthrop, Florence, Miss Ginch, Inspector Graves, Aimee Griffith, Dr. Owen Griffith, Elsie Holland, Megan Hunter, Dr. Marcus Kent, Jane Marple, Superintendent Nash, Mr. Pye, Mona Symmington, Richard Symmington, Agnes Woddell.

First Editions: British: Collins, London, June 1943. 160 pp., 7s. 6d. **American:** Dodd, Mead & Co., New York, 1942. 229 pp., $2.00.

Adaptation: None.

43

TOWARDS ZERO (1944)

Christie's dedication of this novel to poet and novelist Robert Graves reads:

> Dear Robert,
>   Since you are kind enough to say you like my stories, I venture to dedicate this book to you. All I ask is that you should sternly restrain your critical faculties (doubtless sharpened by your recent excesses in that line!) when reading it.
>   This is a story for your pleasure and *not* a candidate for Mr. Graves' literary pillory!
>
> Your friend,
Agatha Christie

Robert Graves and Christie became friends during World War II when the two authors, who knew one another's work, found themselves neighbors. According to Robert Graves's biographer, Martin Seymour-Smith,* Graves first met Christie and Max toward the end of 1940, a meeting which Graves described in a letter written the same year.

> A large impressive Mrs. Mallow or Mellon or something "from Greenway House" walked in to call with an archeological little husband. After 20 minutes Beryl & I realised that she was . . . Agatha Christie herself.

During their conversation that day, Christie apparently confessed that she was not a very observant person, which prompted Graves

* *Robert Graves: His Life and Work;* New York: Holt, Rinehart & Winston, 1983.

to ask why she had become a writer. As Graves recalled in his letter

> She said, very simply and fairly, that she had been an only child [!] and told herself stories, all plots & no characterisation.

Christie visited Graves often at Vale House Farm but Graves "became much fonder of her archeologist husband Max Mallowan than of her." Graves (b. 1895), poet, novelist, critic, essayist, and translator, is best known for his two novels of ancient Rome, *I, Claudius* (1934) and *Claudius the God* (1935). Though the two writers are artistically worlds apart, they shared many of the problems of a writer's life, and no doubt shared their thoughts on the subject during long nights of wartime blackout. In particular, Christie recalled Graves's humorous but practical belief "that washing up was one of the best aids of creative thought." It was a technique Christie herself used; she would often clean house to help break down writer's block. Interestingly, recent scientific research on frontal lobe functions of the human brain—the portion of our "little gray cells" that handle most of our conscious, rational thought—has revealed that loosely structured, intuitive activities like cooking and gardening do indeed allow the part of the brain that handles analytical, structured thought to relax and refresh itself.

As Christie's dedication makes clear, Graves told her he liked her work, at least prior to 1944. But Christie's plea for her literary neighbor to restrain his critical faculties was to no avail. In an article titled "After a Century, Will Anyone Care Whodunit?" published in the *New York Times Book Review,* August 25, 1957, Graves attacked the question of whether or not literature courses in the year 2057 would include the crime novel.

Graves's answer was a resounding no. His negative assessments ran from Sherlock Holmes—"on close examination many of his plots fall to pieces"—to Dorothy Sayers, "at one time Miss Christie's most formidable rival, [she] will, I surmise, sink without a trace."

As for Agatha, Graves launched into her work with a mixture of venom and guilt:

Will the twenty-first century English literature course include Agatha Christie—statistically the most popular detective-writer today? An embarrassing question, because she was my country neighbor during the last war, and I have the greatest affection for her; besides, she has dedicated one of her books to me. And when I once asked why she wrote, she answered: "I was an only child and told stories to amuse myself; I still do." The pure pleasure of self-amusement communicates itself to her readers, and she shines at the ingenious distractions of their attention. Yet though she knows the Devonshire countryside well and is not only a qualified pharmacist, an enthusiastic gardener, but a capable archaeological worker, nobody could promise Agatha immortality as a novelist. Her English is school-girlish, her situations for the most part artificial, her detail faulty. Nevertheless, the novels are sure-fire stage successes—on the stage, critical judgment is mercifully suspended—and she may well figure in future histories of the theatre.

Towards Zero shares a similarity in theme with the story "The Man from the Sea" from *The Mysterious Mr. Quin* (#12, 1930). In both works Christie reveals her attitude about suicide while using suicide as a plot device.

Christie said in an interview,* "Life is a gigantic drama under the order of a divine producer . . . any moment before the end might be the important one. This I believe."

In addition to this theme of an averted suicide having an important unexpected influence on future events, *Towards Zero* is noteworthy for its complex portrait of the workings of the mind of a psychopathic killer.

Though *Towards Zero* is an original, solidly realized mystery of Christie's classic period, it has never achieved the popularity of the other top-rung novels of the 1940s. This may be because the detective, Superintendent Battle (making the last of his five novel appearances) does not have the "star appeal" of Poirot and Marple, whose presence is almost invariably necessary to elevate even a top-notch Christie to the status of "reader favorite."

---

* *New York Times,* 27 October 1966, "Quiet Murders Suit Miss Christie" by Howard Thompson.

The book was called "superb" by Robert Barnard, the crime novelist and author of *A Talent to Deceive* (1980). He added that the book was "intricately plotted and unusual." The *Times Literary Supplement* (London) wrote, "Undiscriminating admirers of Miss Christie must surely miss the thrill of realizing when she is at her best. If this argument is sound, then *Towards Zero* is for the critical. By virtue of masterly storytelling it makes the welfare of certain persons at a seaside town seem of more importance at the moment than anything else in the world. . . . As an exhibition of the modern brand of human nature *Towards Zero* deserves higher praise than any that can be awarded to it as an excellent detective story" (7/22/44). Isaac Anderson in the *New York Times* said, "Agatha Christie has surpassed herself—and without the aid of Hercule Poirot" (6/11/44).

The murder takes place late in the story of *Towards Zero*. Some of the critics found fault with the late payoff. The *Saturday Review of Literature* wrote, "Worked out with characteristic Christie finesse, but plot develops very leisurely and dramatic payoff doesn't make up for earlier chapters. Poirot, come home!" (6/17/44). And the *New Yorker* wrote, "The solution, by Superintendent Battle, is fine, but you may be left with the feeling that orthodox readers, who insist on a corpse early in the game, have something on their side after all" (6/10/44).

PLOT:

A series of apparently unrelated events—a thwarted suicide, a fireside gathering at a famous solicitor's house, and a thievery problem involving Superintendent Battle's daughter—are all steps leading toward a zero point: murder.

Behind the scenes, an unknown psychopathic killer picks as his zero point a seaside house called Gull's Point, high on a cliff overlooking the river Tern, near Easterhead Bay. The house is occupied by elderly, widowed Lady Camilla Tressilian and her secretary-companion, Mary Aldin, who is a distant cousin. Lady Tressilian has no close relations, but over the years Gull's Point has acquired a group of regular visitors who are related to Camilla in various ways.

This particular September, the guests include handsome tennis star Nevile Strange, a ward of the late Sir Matthew Tressilian, and his wife Kay. Nevile's first wife, Audrey, who has remained on good terms with Camilla, is a guest too, a situation which creates a certain awkwardness. Also on hand are Thomas Royde, a Malay planter and former flame of Audrey's, and Ted Latimer, an old beau of Kay's.

Though the personal relationships are all sticky at Gull's Point, they hardly seem sticky enough for murder, until the "zero" of the killer is reached with the unexpected and apparently unmotivated murder of Camilla Tressilian.

Principal Characters: Mary Aldin, Miss Amphrey, Superintendent Battle, Sylvia Battle, Lord Cornelly, Detective Sergeant Jones, Ted Latimer, Inspector James Leach, Andrew MacWhirter, Olive Parsons, Thomas Royde, Audrey Strange, Kay Strange, Nevile Strange, Lady Camilla Tressilian, Mr. Treves.

First Editions: **British**: Collins, London, July 1944. 160 pp., 7s. 6d. **American**: Dodd, Mead & Co., New York, 1944. 242 pp., $2.00.

Adaptation: *Towards Zero* was dramatized by Agatha Christie and Gerald Verner. The play, with the same title, opened in 1956 at the St. James's Theatre, London.

DEATH COMES AS THE END (1945)

It was Stephen R. K. Glanville, noted Egyptologist and close personal friend and professional associate of Max Mallowan, who suggested to Mrs. Mallowan that she write a murder mystery set in ancient Egypt. The book that resulted from Glanville's prompting is dedicated to him, with acknowledgment that without his "active help and encouragement this book would never have been written."

Death Comes as the End is Christie's only book with a historical setting. All of her mysteries save this one are firmly rooted in a time frame not too long before the copyright date. Her excursions into the past (the present book excepted) are limited to the occasional flashback in her murder-in-retrospect books, and even these episodes are in books with late-enough settings that the flashbacks take place contemporaneously with Christie's adult years.

These firm roots in the present are part and parcel of Christie's creative world. Her readers expected contemporary settings, though there is no question that, in the last decades of her career, part of Christie's appeal lay in the cozy-chintz nostalgia of her books from the 1920s through the 1930s and 1940s. Christie may also have been wise in keeping her books out of the historical past, since the historical details that are necessary to create a sense of the past may distract the reader from the real issue of the plotting and clues.

Finally, as Christie pointed out in *An Autobiography*, writing *Death Comes as the End* required an enormous amount of research about Egyptian history, an undertaking which required a good deal of encouragement and persuasion from Glanville and Max Mallowan.

Once Christie was persuaded to delve into the ancient world for a setting, she opted to take her characteristic domestic-intrigue murder plot, with its family wealth, jealous in-laws, rival siblings, and so on, with her. After all, though names and clothing styles and gods may change over time, human nature and the conflicts it causes are the same anywhere, anytime—as Jane Marple was quick to point out.

In her Author's Note at the beginning of the book, Christie states that the inspiration for the characters and plot came from "two or three Egyptian letters of the XI Dynasty," which had been found by one of the archaeological expeditions sponsored by the Metropolitan Museum of Art (New York) and published in the museum's bulletin during the 1920s. In addition to these letters, Christie was given other historical and research material by Glanville so that her character names, domestic details, and religious and cultural facts would be accurate.

The Old Kingdom, that remarkable period which began c. 2686 B.C. and culminated in the Pyramids at Giza, fell into a long decline, and ended in 2160 B.C., at which time political power became scattered among many local rulers. This situation, called the First Intermediate period, lasted for about 120 years (2160–2040) during which time Thebes, which had been a relatively obscure city south of Giza and Memphis during the heyday of the Old Kingdom, began a rise to wealth and power. The XI Dynasty, in which the book is set, began in 2134 B.C. at the point in the Intermediate Period when a powerful Theban aristocratic family established a new ruling lineage under the Theban leader Sehertowy Intef. With this dynasty began the second flourishing of Egyptian culture and civilization that led in an almost unbroken chain to the Middle Kingdom (2040–1786) and to the glories of the later days of Ramses and Tutankhamen. The Thebes that Christie uses for her setting is this newly powerful city, which was prominent not only as the royal residence, but as the center of worship of the god Amon. Also located at Thebes was the Necropolis in the Valley of the Tombs, where kings and nobles were entombed in great splendor in crypts hollowed out of cliffs on the Nile's East Bank.

Death Comes as the End is unique among Christie's books for two reasons: because of the historical setting, and because (according to her) it is the only ending she was ever persuaded to change. After the book was written, Stephen Glanville, as its "godfather," was apparently allowed to read the manuscript. For reasons Christie never revealed, he didn't like her solution, and suggested a "better" ending. Oddly (for Christie knew her own mind when it came to her craft), she complied, though she was later to regret the new denouement.

"If I think I have got a certain thing *right* in a book—the way it should be—I'm not easily moved," she recalled. "In this case, against my better judgement, I *did* give in. . . . I still think now, when I reread the book, that I would like to rewrite the end of it —which shows that you should stick to your guns in the first place . . ." Unfortunately for her readers, Christie never revealed her original ending.

Critical reaction to Agatha and the XI Dynasty was mixed. The *Times Literary Supplement* (London) wrote, "When a specialist acquires unerring skill there is a temptation to find tasks that are exceptionally difficult. The scenes in *Death Comes as the End* . . . are . . . painted delicately. The household of the priest, who is depicted not as a sacred personage but as a humdrum landowner, makes instant appeal because its members are human. But while the author's skill can cause a stir over the death of an old woman some thousands of years ago, that length of time lessens curiosity concerning why or how she (and others) died" (4/28/45).

In the *New York Times* Isaac Anderson said, "Besides giving us a mystery story quite up to her own high standard, Agatha Christie has succeeded admirably in picturing the people of ancient Egypt as living persons and not as resurrected mummies" (10/22/44).

Will Cuppy in *Books* (*New York Herald Tribune*): "Mrs. Christie, wife of an archaeologist, knows whereof she speaks when it comes to ancient lore, so you needn't feel that Egyptology has taken a beating. It's an amusing lark and a decided novelty—startling in all directions" (10/15/44).

Finally, eminent American critic Edmund Wilson, who made no secret of his loathing of detective novels—he once roasted the entire genre in an article written in 1945 for the *New Yorker* entitled, "Who Cares Who Killed Roger Ackroyd?"—launched into *Death Comes as the End:* "I did not guess who the murderer was, I was incited to keep on and find out, and when I did finally find out, I was surprised. Yet I did not care for Agatha Christie. . . . Her writing is of a mawkishness and banality which seem to me literally impossible to read. You cannot read such a book, you run through it to see the problem worked out; and you cannot become interested in the characters because they never can be allowed an existence of their own even in a flat two dimensions but always have to be contrived so that they can seem either reliable or sinister, depending on which quarter, at the moment, is to be baited for the reader's suspicion."

PLOT:

Imhotep, a wealthy farmer-priest of Thebes, sows discord in his family and household when he brings home Nofret, a "young, arrogant, and beautiful" girl to be his concubine. Yahmose and Sobek, the eldest sons, have yet to receive their share of the family lands, and fear that Nofret may usurp their rightful legacies. Satipy, Yahmose's ambitious and domineering wife, is immediately set against Nofret. Kait, the other daughter-in-law, is a docile, dull woman, whose only concern is that her beloved children may be cut out of their grandfather's will if Nofret gets her way.

Nofret convinces Imhotep to have his grandchildren kept out of his presence when he is at home. Youngest son Ipy, spoiled, vain, and arrogant, is embarrassed and shown up by the willful, manipulative concubine and soon comes to hate her. Even Renisenb, Imhotep's widowed daughter, the only family member who attempts to befriend Nofret, is set against her father's concubine when there is evidence of a romantic flirtation between Nofret and a handsome young scribe of the household. To make matters worse, Nofret always tells Imhotep that his family is intriguing against her. Imhotep finally becomes angered with his family, and accuses them of ingratitude and disobedience to his wishes to make Nofret welcome.

Imhotep is called to the south to attend to his property there. While he is away, Nofret writes to him with continual stories of the family's enmity toward her. Finally, Imhotep decides to disinherit his uncooperative and disobedient sons in favor of Nofret.

The same day that the letter arrives, Nofret is found dead at the foot of a cliff below a narrow, deserted path. The fall could have been accidental—perhaps she was frightened by a snake while running on the barren rocks—but there is little doubt among the family that Nofret was murdered.

Principal Characters: Esa, Henet, Hori, Imhotep, Ipy, Kait, Kameni, Divine Father Mersu, Nofret, Renisenb, Satipy, Sobek, Yahmose.

First Editions: **British**: Collins, London, March 1945. 159 pp., 7s. 6d. **American**: Dodd, Mead & Co., New York, 1944. 223 pp., $2.00.

Adaptation: None.

45

SPARKLING CYANIDE / REMEMBERED DEATH
(1945)

Sparkling Cyanide, a good standard 1940s Christie, based on the short story "Yellow Iris," first published in *The Regatta Mystery and Other Stories* (#34, 1939),* once again utilizes the murder-in-retrospect type of plot, which was to be of continued interest to Christie for the rest of her career. As in Christie's previous retrospect novel, *Five Little Pigs* (#41, 1943), the reader is given different versions from the people involved in the events of the crime. However, the span of time linking the events in *Sparkling Cyanide* (one year) is short in comparison to the time span in *Five Little Pigs,* which was sixteen years.

Sparkling Cyanide was probably written during the summer or fall of 1944, in the period after the Allied landing in Normandy on June 6 when the British and American forces pushed across France and Belgium, to the crossing of the Rhine in October. Christie was to write only one more book, *The Hollow* (#46, 1946), before the end of the war, and these two books bring to seventeen the total number of full-length works Christie produced during the war: the eleven mysteries from *Sad Cypress* (#36, 1940) to *The Hollow; Curtain* and *Sleeping Murder,* the two mysteries withheld from publication (#82, 1975, and #83, 1976); one Mary Westmacott romance, *Absent in the Spring;* her reminiscences *Come, Tell Me How You Live;* and the stage adaptations of *Ten Little Niggers* and *Appointment with Death.*

The book sold 30,000 copies within its first year of publication —her first book up to that point to reach such a sales figure, a barometer of the steadily escalating Christie popularity. The long wartime nights that gave Agatha plenty of time to write also gave her fans plenty of time to read.

Colonel Johnny Race, the Secret Service agent who made his

---

* For more on how Christie rewrote and expanded shorter works, see *Murder in the Mews* (#28, 1937).

debut in *The Man in the Brown Suit* (#5, 1924), makes his fourth and last appearance in this novel. Race, who is over sixty years old now, has known George Barton, the husband of the apparent suicide victim Rosemary Barton, from Barton's boyhood days.

In an article that appeared in the *Times Literary Supplement* (London), dated February 25, 1955, and titled "Five Writers in One: The Versatility of Agatha Christie," C.H.B. Kitchin wrote in part, "Of all the books written by our quintet of Mrs. Christies . . . I think *Sparkling Cyanide* is the one . . . in spite of keen competition from *Roger Ackroyd, Death on the Nile, Murder on the Orient Express,* and *Death in the Clouds*—which I should take with me to a desert island; for I find in it a seriousness and a psychological insight unparalleled in the author's other works." Kitchin continued, "It is true I have a moment of scepticism as to the climax. But I have never yet read a detective story worth reading which did not at some time call for a willing suspension of disbelief."

Some critics were not overly impressed with this work, but felt as Will Cuppy did, who said in his review in *Books* (*New York Herald Tribune*), "Any Christie, we always say, is better than none" (2/11/45). Elizabeth Bullock in *Book Week* wrote, "This is not Agatha Christie's best, certainly, but a satisfactory tale, nonetheless" (3/18/45). Isaac Anderson in the *New York Times* was pleased with the book: "So skillfully has Agatha Christie told the story that the denouement will probably come as a surprise to nine readers out of ten" (2/11/45).

PLOT:

Beautiful heiress Rosemary Barton died unexpectedly at a birthday dinner held in her honor at the Luxembourg, a posh London restaurant. The death was dramatic: Rosemary had slumped forward at the table with "blue cyanosed face . . . [and] convulsed clutching fingers," during the floor show, when the house lights were turned down.

The inquest ruled suicide. Cyanide was found in Rosemary's purse, and the young beauty was known to have been severely depressed following a bout of influenza.

Nine months after the tragedy, widower George Barton receives two poison pen letters which imply that Rosemary was murdered. The letters alarm George, since he had nursed a deep doubt that his fun-loving, if unfaithful, wife was the sort for suicide. Barton goes to see his old friend Colonel Race for advice. Race, after hearing the facts, points out that Rosemary was a likely murder victim. After all, George had long suffered her infidelities; her sister Iris had been left out of the will that had given Rosemary a fortune; Ruth Lessing, George's devoted secretary, had personal reasons for getting her beloved employer's wife out of the way; and Lady Alexandra Farraday, wife of one of Rosemary's lovers, had obvious reasons. So did Anthony Browne, another of Mrs. Barton's suitors, who was afraid of what she knew about his tarnished past.

Given these possibilities, Race decides to try and solve a murder in retrospect.

Principal Characters: George Barton, Rosemary Barton, Patricia Brice-Woodworth, Anthony Browne, Charles, Lucilla Drake, Victor Drake, Lady Alexandra Catherine Farraday, Stephen Farraday, Chief Inspector Kemp, Lady Victoria Kidderminster, Lord William, the Earl of Kidderminster, Ruth Lessing, Iris Marle, Colonel Johnny Race, Chloe Elizabeth West, General Lord Woodworth.

First Editions: **British**: Collins, London, December 1945. 160 pp., 8s. 6d. **American**: with U.S. title *Remembered Death:* Dodd, Mead & Co., New York, 1945. 209 pp., $2.00.

Adaptation: A television adaptation of this novel is to be aired by CBS Television in the fall/winter season of 1983–84.

46

THE HOLLOW / MURDER AFTER HOURS (1946)

The war in Europe officially ended in May 1945, and England began the long slow process of rebuilding its damaged towns and cities in the face of severe postwar shortages. Agatha and Max were able to move back to their beloved Greenway House, which had been requisitioned by the Admiralty for most of the war. There were repairs to make at Greenway, the gardens were masses of weeds and the trees needed pruning, but overall the house was not in as much disrepair as Christie had feared.

Christie recalled in her autobiography that it was the United States Navy which took over Greenway. The negotiations were made through the English Admiralty. Maypool, a big house on a hill above Greenway, accommodated the enlisted men, and Greenway became home to the "officers of the flotilla." Christie said of the Americans: "I cannot speak too highly of the kindness of the Americans, and the care they took of our house." Christie's own war memorial, as she put it, was in Greenway's library, which was used as the Americans' mess room. It was in the form of a fresco, which someone painted "round the top of the walls [showing] all the places where that flotilla went, starting at Key West, . . . finally ending with a slightly glorified exaggeration of the woods of Greenway and the white house showing through the trees." "Beyond that," Christie continued, was ". . . an exquisite nymph, not quite finished—a pin-up girl in the nude—which I have always supposed to represent the hopes of houris at journey's end when the war was over." The commander wrote to Christie to see if she wanted the fresco painted out, but Christie said no, she was very pleased to have this "historic memorial," which also had the heads of Winston Churchill, Stalin and President Roosevelt sketched over the mantelpiece. Christie wished she "knew the name of the artist."

Greenway survived the war untouched, with no bombs destroying it as Christie had feared might happen. However, fourteen lavatories had been added, and she had "to fight the Admiralty to take them away again."

The major loss of the war was Christie's son-in-law Hubert Prichard, who was killed while fighting in France. Though the war years had brought personal sacrifice and tragedy, the period was a remarkable one for Christie professionally. She said in her autobiography, "It is only now that I fully realize, looking back over my wartime output, that I produced an *incredible* amount of stuff during those years; I suppose it was because there were no distractions of a social nature; one practically never went out in the evening."

Agatha Christie described *The Hollow* as the book "I had ruined by the introduction of Poirot. I had got used to having Poirot in my books and so naturally he had come into this one, but he was all wrong there. He did his stuff all right, but how much better . . . would the book have been without him."

With Hercule Poirot appearing in thirty-three full-length Christie novels (twenty-two up to the publication of this book), it's quite understandable why Christie would feel the way she did about having Poirot appear so often. She'd felt the same way six years earlier with *Sad Cypress* (#36, 1940), but up to this point she really had no substitute detective in her repertoire that could rival Poirot in popularity. Miss Marple, who would come into her own in the early 1950s, had only appeared in three novels up to this time: in the 1930 *The Murder at the Vicarage* (#13), in the 1942 *The Body in the Library* (#40), and in the 1943 *The Moving Finger* (#42). Poirot had become a staple ingredient in a Christie mystery, and his presence was expected in her books by her publishers and the public. It was only after Miss Marple's popularity began to rival Poirot's (in the 1950s and 1960s) that Christie was able to use less of her Belgian. And even though Marple was later to become a rival for Poirot, his books still outnumbered hers by three to one.

On reading the book, it is understandable why the author felt Poirot could be dispensed with (he was in fact written out of Christie's stage adaptation of the book in 1951): *The Hollow*, especially in its opening chapters, is the most romantic and interior of Christie's mysteries, and in many ways is an attempt to integrate a murder mystery with a romantic novel.

The scenes between Henrietta Savernake and Edward Angkatell, for example, are highly reminiscent of the full-blown romantic novels Christie wrote under the name Mary Westmacott, one of
which, *Absent in the Spring* (1944), was written during the same
productive war years in which *The Hollow* was penned.

Many readers will find some of the dialogue a bit soppy, with
lines like, "Sometimes I think I want to be peaceful more than
anything in the world, Edward!" but this rather saccharine side of
The Hollow is balanced by the character of Lady Angkatell, the
scatty, loquacious social mistress of the Hollow, who ranks with
Caroline Sheppard of *The Murder of Roger Ackroyd* (#7, 1926)
as one of Christie's most memorable comic creations.

"I've asked the crime man to lunch on Sunday," Lady Angkatell says, announcing her invitation of Poirot, and then goes on in
a typical non sequitur, "Like an egg. . . . He was in Baghdad,
solving something . . . I don't remember much about it because I
never think it's very interesting who killed who. I mean once they
are dead it doesn't seem to matter why, and to make a fuss about
it all seems so silly."

The Hollow, the Angkatells' country house which gives the book
its title, is one of the rare instances in Christie's work in which an
actual house can clearly be identified.* The book's dedication,
"For Larry and Danae, with apologies for using their swimming
pool as the scene of a murder," provides the clue.

Larry and Danae are Mr. and Mrs. Francis L. Sullivan. Sullivan, the well-known British stage actor, portrayed Poirot in Christie's first original play, *Black Coffee,* in 1930, and the actor and
author met at that time. A decade later, when Sullivan portrayed
Poirot in *Peril at End House* (1940), the Mallowans and the
Sullivans became friendly, and weekended at the Sullivans' country
home at Hazlemere, Surrey.

In her biography of Christie (*The Mystery of Agatha Christie,*
1978), Gwen Robyns tells how Sullivan had the opportunity to
watch Christie in the midst of plotting a book.

"At the back of the house my wife, in a moment of insane opti-

---

* Other identifiable homes are Ashfield, Christie's birthplace (see #80), her
sister's home Abney (see *After the Funeral,* #57, 1953), and Christie's own
favorite house, Greenway (see *Dead Man's Folly,* #61, 1956).

mism of the English weather, had caused a swimming pool to be made, with half a dozen paths leading down to it through the chestnut wood. One fine Sunday morning I discovered Agatha wandering up and down these paths with an expression of intense concentration."

When *The Hollow* was published, an advance copy was sent to Sullivan, who only then discovered that his house had been used as the setting for the book, even down to the chestnut wood through which John Christow walks on his late night visit to Veronica Cray, and to the swimming pool murder site, "a kind of nucleus with paths radiating from it in every direction."

Christie makes very effective use of the layout of the Sullivans' pool in the murder scene, when several guests happen upon the pool area from the various paths, just after the murder has taken place.

In chapter 6, the anecdote about the pet squirrel is based on an incident from Christie's childhood as recorded in her autobiography, when her sister and brother kept a squirrel that had been brought in with a hurt paw. Agatha's grandmother, who seemed to her granddaughter to be prophetic, predicted that the squirrel would one day escape up the chimney, and after a year of captivity it indeed did. The incident appears almost verbatim in *The Hollow*.

Reviews of *The Hollow* were enthusiastic. "Hercule Poirot returns in fine form" (10/28/46) said the *New Republic,* while Isaac Anderson in the *New York Times* proclaimed, "This is Agatha Christie at her best" (9/29/46).

"Admirers of Mrs. Christie's mysteries ought to like this one because it is more fairly plotted than most," wrote the *New Yorker* (10/5/46), while Anthony Boucher in the *San Francisco Chronicle* thought, "A grade-A plot combined with a much solider novel than usual makes this the best Christie in years" (10/6/46).

Finally, Will Cuppy in *Books (New York Herald Tribune)*: "There's no possible doubt whatever that *The Hollow* is a splendid mystery bet for fans of almost any grade, including those of loftiest brow" (9/29/46).

PLOT:

Lady Lucy Angkatell, mistress of the Hollow, has planned a weekend house party. In her usual fashion, she has put together her guest list without giving much thought as to whether or not the guests will get along, and only at the last minute does she realize that her household for the next two days may be nothing more than "a lot of discordant personalities boxed up indoors."

In addition to the hosts, Lucy and Sir Henry Angkatell, the personalities boxed up at the Hollow are the handsome, brilliant Dr. John Christow and his plain, dull, insecure wife Gerda; beautiful redheaded sculptress Henrietta Savernake, who happens to be Dr. Christow's mistress; and Midge Hardcastle, a rather plain unmarried young cousin of Lady Angkatell. Also up for the weekend are Sir Henry's quiet bookish cousin Edward Angkatell, the principal heir to the family titles and fortunes—who happens to have a long-standing and unrequited love for Henrietta Savernake. The last guest is the rebellious, surly young David Angkatell, who will inherit Edward's estate and title if Edward dies childless.

An after-dinner bridge game is interrupted by the unexpected appearance of Veronica Cray, a famous and very glamorous film star, who has leased one of the nearby cottages as a country getaway. She makes her appearance at the Hollow ostensibly to borrow matches, but the fact that she and John Christow had an affair many years before throws some suspicion on Veronica's motives.

As she leaves the interrupted bridge party, the beautiful actress insists that Christow accompany her and her borrowed matches back through the wood to her cottage. Christow and his former mistress disappear, and he doesn't return for three hours, long after the household has gone to bed.

The next morning Christow receives a note from Veronica, summoning him to her cottage, and against his better judgment, he goes.

A while later Poirot arrives at the Hollow for Sunday luncheon, and is escorted through the house and down to the pool, where he sees a rather "tasteless" *tableau vivant* staged for his amusement. John Christow is sprawled awkwardly beside the pool, bleeding. His wife, Gerda, is standing over him, with a gun in her hand, while the other guests stand in shocked poses around the pool, apparently just having stumbled on the murder scene. In an instant,

Poirot realizes that it is not a theatrical tableau, but that the man by the pool is in fact shot and dying. Poirot goes to the victim, who manages to say only "Henrietta" before he expires. Then, as the shocked watchers converge on the body, the gun slips from Mrs. Christow's hand and falls into the pool.

Principal Characters: David Angkatell, Edward Angkatell, Sir Henry Angkatell, Lady Lucy Angkatell, Gerda Christow, Dr. John Christow, Zena Christow, Beryl Collins, Veronica Cray, Inspector Grange, Mr. Gudgeon, Midge Hardcastle, Elsie Patterson, Hercule Poirot, Doris Saunders, Henrietta Savernake.

First Editions: **British**: Collins, London, 1946. 256 pp., 8s. 6d. **American**: with U.S. title *Murder After Hours:* Dodd, Mead & Co., New York, 1946. 279 pp., $2.50.

Adaptation: Christie turned *The Hollow* into a stage play, which opened June 7, 1951, at the Fortune Theatre, London.

47

THE LABOURS OF HERCULES (1947)

Often cited as the best of the Christie short story collections, *The Labours of Hercules* as the title implies is patterned after the twelve famous exploits of the ancient strongman, with his Belgian namesake taking on twelve "heroic" cases, each with a parallel to the Greek's mythic labors.

Christie was in fine fettle while writing these stories. Her take-offs on the classical labors are cleverly worked out, and more than a little tongue-in-cheek; the stories also feature some of her best comic writing.

As always, Poirot is on the verge of retirement (only opera singers announce their farewell appearances with greater regularity than Poirot). But before he settles down to cultivate vegetable marrows once and for all, he decides to take on twelve last cases, in honor of his fabled predecessor.

Hercule makes it quite clear that he, with his love of order and symmetry, with his magnificent mustache and incomparable gray cells, considers himself far superior to the ancient, muscle-bound adventurer.

"Hero indeed?" Poirot proclaims with no little indignation. "What was he but a large muscular creature of low intelligence and criminal tendencies!"

He then goes on to condemn the general demeanor of classical gods on the whole. "These gods and goddesses—they seemed to have as many different aliases as a modern criminal. Indeed, they seemed to be definitely criminal types. Drink, debauchery, incest, rape, loot, homicide, and chicanery. . . . No decent family life. No order, no method."

A good deal of Hercules's behavior would make headlines these days, as much for his murderous temper as for his heroic exploits. The mythological Hercules (whose legend probably grew out of the feats of an actual tribal chieftain-warrior) was involved in scandal and controversy from his birth. The son of Alcmeme, wife of King Amphitryon, Hercules (or properly, Herakles) was actually the illegitimate son of Zeus. Hera, who was not one to easily tolerate her husband's infidelities, went to great lengths to make her husband's illegitimate son's life a misery.

In one of her first plots to get rid of Hercules, Hera commanded two serpents to slither into the infant's cradle, but the baby, in his first show of strength, strangled them.

By the time he was an adult, Hercules's strength and temper had earned him quite a reputation—he killed his music teacher in anger when the old man boxed his ears for clumsy lyre technique—but his heroic hunting down and killing of the marauding Thespian lion so impressed the King of the Thespians that the king gave all fifty of his daughters to Hercules. Forty-nine of the maidens bore Hercules sons, while the one who resisted his charms was condemned to death.

Hercules eventually married Megara, the daughter of King Creon, and had children by her, but his vengeful stepmother Hera caused Hercules to go insane, and he killed Megara and their children.

It was in part because of this crime that Hercules was forced to perform the twelve labors. His scrapes weren't over, however.

Hercules then fell in love with Iole, but when her father refused him the maiden's hand (and with good reason, considering Hercules's track record with women), Hercules went into another of his rages and killed Iphitus, his bride-to-be's brother. To make matters worse, when Hercules was refused absolution for *that* murder, he sacked the kingdom of Pylos, and killed all the sons of the local king.

Now Hercules found himself in real hot water, and the all-powerful oracle at Delphi stepped in and meted out a punishment designed to put the muscle-bound Greek in his place: he was bound in servitude to Queen Lydia, and forced to wear women's clothing and to pass the days spinning yarn with the girls in Queen Lydia's court.

Little wonder that Poirot deplored certain personality traits of his namesake, while admitting that there was "one point of resemblance. Both of them . . . had been instrumental in ridding the world of certain pests."

Isaac Anderson in the *New York Times Book Review* commented, "Before embarking on these adventures Poirot has announced his intention to return to the country and devote the rest of his life to the cultivation of vegetable marrow with a view to improving its flavor, a truly laudable ambition, but one which might better be left to others. Poirot's little grey cells are sorely needed here and now for more important work. We sincerely hope and trust that he will change his mind about retiring" (7/6/47).

"Twelve short stories of the brisk, workmanlike type that Mrs. Christie's admirers have come to expect," wrote the *New Yorker*. "All right if you happen to like Poirot, or mysteries in this abbreviated vein" (7/12/47).

Anthony Boucher in the *San Francisco Chronicle:* "A finely shaped book, richly devious and quite brilliant—by far the best volume of Poirot shorts" (7/6/47).

PLOTS:

"The Nemean Lion"

In the myth, the Nemean lion, which could not be killed by iron, bronze, or stone, was trapped in its lair by Hercules, who then strangled the beast, and took its skin as a trophy, which he wore as a trademark.

Poirot's Nemean lion is Shan Tung, the Pekingese dog belonging to Sir Joseph and Lady Hoggin, which has been kidnapped while Lady Hoggin's companion, Miss Carnaby, was walking him, and is being held for ransom.

"The Lernean Hydra"

The many-headed hydra terrorized the Lernean swamp, devastating the surrounding area with its breath; the beast could not be killed because as soon as one head was chopped off, two grew in its place. Hercules's solution was to enlist the aid of Iolaus, who seared the hydra's neck-stumps as Hercules lopped off the monster's heads.

Poirot's hydra is the many-headed monster of gossip and rumor, which in this case is wrecking the life of Dr. Charles Oldfield, who is unjustly rumored to have poisoned his wife.

"The Arcadian Deer"

Another of Hercules's labors was the capture of the golden-horned hind that lived near the Cerynean River in Arcadia. He managed this by pursuing the deer for one year, finally catching her as she drank from a river, though he was reprimanded by the goddess Artemis, to whom the hind was sacred, because he'd captured the elusive creature by piercing her forelegs with his bow.

Christie's golden hind is a lovely deerlike young woman, who meets by chance Ted Williamson, a handsome, charming working-class man, a garage mechanic of "perfect physique . . . a Greek God—a young shepherd in Arcady." Ted falls in love with the golden, elusive young woman, and thinks she feels the same way about him.

Young Ted, in his coveralls, cap in hand, approaches "Mr. Hercules Pwarrit," asking his help in finding the girl, who said her name was Nita. Nita had told him she was a lady's maid to one of the houseguests, and that she could meet him again in a fortnight, when her mistress would again be a guest there. Ted had gone to the house on the Thames after a fortnight but Nita wasn't there, though her mistress was. When Ted was told that Nita had been discharged, he had gotten her new address and written to her, but his letters had been returned.

In this story Christie makes much of the resemblance between graceful does and certain types of feminine physiques; the simple love between Ted Williamson and the "Arcadian Deer" is one of her most touching romances.

In most versions of the myth, "The Arcadian Deer" is the fourth labor of Hercules.

"The Erymanthian Boar"

Hercules's next labor was the pursuit of the Erymanthian boar, which he chased "to the North" and eventually captured in a snowdrift.

Christie's "boar" is the unsavory underworld gambling hood, Marrascaud, whom Poirot pursues into the snowy Alps, and finally captures alive.

This story has a careless misattribution, which appears when Poirot is a little giddy from the thin Alpine air.

"The lines of a nursery rhyme ran idiotically through his mind. *Up above the world so high, Like a tea tray in the sky.*"

What Christie calls a nursery rhyme is actually Lewis Carroll's brilliant parody of "Twinkle, twinkle, little star," which appears in *Alice's Adventures in Wonderland.*

The original nursery rhyme has the line, "Up above the world so high, like a diamond in the sky." Carroll's parody, which is sung by the Dormouse at the tea party, begins, "Twinkle, twinkle, little Bat, How I wonder where you're at. . . ."

"The Augean Stables"

In most classical series, this is the sixth of the labors, in which the hero has the task of mucking out the stables of King Augeas of Elis, who, though he had a magnificent herd of cattle, didn't pay much attention to cleanliness. Hercules offered to clean up the mess, in one day, in exchange for one-tenth of the herd. Augeas accepted the offer, never thinking for a moment that Hercules could do the job in such a short time. But Hercules cleverly did the trick by building a dam that diverted the Alpheus and Peneus rivers from their courses, sending their waters through the stables.

Christie equates the Augean manure to political scandal which is about to destroy the career of a prime minister and the reputation of his wife. The "stink" has been fermented by a muckraking journal called *X-ray News.* Poirot saves the situation by a clever diversion made by slinging mud (here Christie was enjoying plotting on puns), and the "tide" of public opinion sweeps away the scandalous filth.

"The Stymphalean Birds"

These pestilential creatures (which resemble B-52 bombers more than birds, from the classical descriptions) were huge bronze-beaked birds with iron feathers. They inhabited the Stymphalean marshes, and flew on "missions" over the countryside, during which they dropped their feathers, killing people and destroying crops.

Hercules shook a bronze rattle (or castanets) and frightened the creatures up from the swamp, which enabled him to shoot down most of them with bow and arrow.

Christie's destructive birds are female blackmailers, who are frightened away by the metallic "rattling" of the telegraph that Poirot uses to learn their true identity from police officials.

"The Cretan Bull"

The seventh labor was to bring back the Cretan bull beloved by

Pasiphae; this Hercules accomplished by riding the bull as it swam from Crete to Greece. Once the bull was returned, it was set free to roam the Greek countryside.

Christie's Cretan bull is Hugh Chandler, whose "magnificent physique . . . impressed Hercule Poirot more than anything else." Here, the loving Pasiphae is Diana Maberly, who is distraught and who enlists Poirot's aid because her magnificent young bull of a boyfriend is going insane and terrorizing the countryside.

"The Horses of Diomedes"

Diomedes of Thrace raised his mares to be man-eaters by feeding them human flesh. Hercules tamed them by feeding them the flesh of Diomedes.

Poirot captures the four daughters of retired General Grant of Mertonshire—wild, flashy girls ("man-eaters") who run around with a fast new-money crowd in Mertonshire, much to the dismay of their gruff military father.

The diet of human flesh that made Diomedes' mares so dangerous is changed by Christie into cocaine, which she describes as "stuff that starts off making you feel just grand and with everything in the garden lovely. It peps you up and you feel you can do twice as much as you usually do."

"The Girdle of Hyppolita"

Hercules's ninth labor was to travel to the land of the warrior women, the Amazons, and bring back the girdle (or golden belt) that belonged to Queen Hyppolita. When Hercules arrives, the Queen of the Amazons gladly gives the girdle to him, though in the meantime the ever-meddlesome Hera starts the rumor among the Amazons that Hercules is attacking their queen. The Amazon women march against Hercules at the palace where he is paying a call on Hyppolita.

Hercules, thinking he has been tricked by Hyppolita, kills her and escapes from the advancing horde of angry women, taking the girdle with him.

Christie's "Amazons" are the teenage girls who attend Miss Pope's, an exclusive finishing school in Paris that is closely modeled on Miss Dryden's finishing school, which Christie attended as a girl.

"We specialise here, M. Poirot," says Miss Pope, "in art and

music. The girls are taken to the Opera, to the Comédie-Française, they attend lectures at the Louvre. . . . The broader culture, that is our aim."

The girdle in question—which Miss Pope surrenders freely to
Hercule—is a stolen Rubens painting, a miniature gem called *The
Girdle of Hyppolita.*

"The Flock of Geryon"

Hercules's tenth labor was to set free the cattle owned by
Geryon, which were herded on the island of Erythea. In order to
loose the herd, Hercules had to kill Orthus, the hound that guarded
the flock, then Eurytion, the herdsman, and finally Geryon himself.

Christie's herd of cattle is a group of women who have been
"captured" into bovine submission by a religious cult, "The Flock
of the Shepherd," which is led by the mesmerizing, otherworldly
Dr. Anderson.

There are several points of interest in this story. First, to free
the flock, Poirot enlists the aid of Miss Carnaby, who appeared in
the first of the labors. Also of note is Christie's use of Cannabis
Indica or hashish as a part of the religious group's ritual. ("This
gives delusions of grandeur and pleasurable enjoyment. It bound
his devotees to him.")

Finally, "The Flock of Geryon" is a rare instance in Christie's
fiction of Hitler's being mentioned by name.

"The Apples of the Hesperides"

The eleventh labor sent Hercules to fetch the golden apples,
which had been given to Hera as a wedding gift, and which were
guarded by the daughters of Atlas, the Hesperides, and by the
hundred-headed dragon, Ladon.

Hercules had been advised not to pick the apples himself, so he
asked Atlas, in whose garden the tree with the apples grew, to let
him take over Atlas's job of holding up the heavens while Atlas
fetched the golden fruit. Atlas agreed only after Hercules had
killed the dragon, Ladon. Atlas duly fetched the apples, and was
selfishly planning to leave Hercules with the tiring job of holding
up the heavens and take the apples himself, but Hercules pre-
vailed upon him to hold the heavens just a moment, so Hercules

could pad his shoulders to make the heavy burden more comfortable.

Atlas shouldered the heavens again, and thus tricked, was left by Hercules, who took the apples to Eurystheus. Since the apples were sacred, and belonged to Hera, they were eventually returned to the garden of the Hesperidean daughters.

Poirot's "golden apples" is a priceless gold goblet, in the form of a tree, with apples of emerald. The art object, which has been sought after by a number of ruthless, wealthy collectors, is said to have been made by Benvenuto Cellini for Pope Alexander VI, the "Borgia" pope, and the goblet in fact contains a secret poison chamber.

Christie has a good time with her retelling of the tale—including a drunk Irish gambler as the Atlas character, and a group of nuns as the modern Hesperidean daughters, to whom the goblet, like the golden apples, is returned in the end.

One glaring factual error has been pointed out by Robert Barnard in *A Talent to Deceive* (1980). Roderigo Borgia, Pope Alexander VI, for whom the goblet was supposedly made, was elevated to the Papacy in 1492, and died in 1503, possibly by poisoning. Cellini, alas, was only three at the time. Still, it makes a nice story.

"The Capture of Cerberus"

For his final labor, Hercules was required to descend into the underworld and bring back Cerberus, the three-headed dog which guarded the entrance to Hades. Hercules was allowed to take the dog back to Earth with him only on the condition that he capture the dog without weapons. This Hercules managed to do by choking the infernal dog until he submitted.

Christie depicts two underworlds in her story. The first shows Poirot battling a rush-hour crowd in the London subways. While ascending one of the long escalators for which the London tubes are famous, he sees, descending on the other escalator, the magnificent Countess Rossakoff, his great love of two decades before (see *The Big Four*, #8, 1927).

When Poirot cries out, "Where . . . can I find you?" Vera Rossakoff replies, "In Hell."

Poirot finds that her answer is not enigmatic at all, since the flamboyant countess, more overdressed and overpainted than ever, is now the proprietress of a fashionable but oh-so-decadent nightclub called Hell, complete with naughty murals, an artificial stream at the entrance which patrons must cross like the river Styx, and a live dog named Cerberus, which guards the entrance.

First Editions: British: Collins, London, 1947. 256 pp., 8s. 6d. **American:** Dodd, Mead & Co., New York, 1947. 265 pp., $2.50.

Adaptation: None.

48

TAKEN AT THE FLOOD / THERE IS A TIDE (1948)

In 1947, Max Mallowan had just completed the final work on a book that dealt with his excavations at Tell Brak and Chagar Bazar: Max uncovered the third-millennium shrine now called the "Eyed Temple." He had started the writing project in 1945, when he and Agatha returned to Greenway, after the war.

When visited by a professor friend at Greenway, Max said in his memoirs, "My good friend Professor Sidney Smith . . . saw the manuscript and was, I think, suitably impressed, for he set about, together with Stephen Glanville, finding me an academic post." The post to which Max was appointed was that of the first occupant of the Chair of Western Asiatic Archaeology at the Institute of Archaeology in the University of London. Max stayed at the Institute until 1960. This position enabled Max to divide his time equally between home, the Institute, and field work.

It was at this time that the Iraqi authorities and the Iraqi Department of Antiquities were offering "fair terms" to archaeologists who would return to Iraq for archaeological digs. The conditions were favorable now for Max and Agatha, and after a period of ten years of not working on digs, they were once again, "with enormous pleasure," able to resume work in Iraq. Max also took over the directorship of the British school. However, the Mallowans' method of traveling to the Middle East had changed. Christie, in her autobiography, commented, "No Orient Express this time, alas! It was no longer the cheapest way—indeed one could not take a through journey by it now. This time we flew—the beginning of a dull routine, traveling by air." Even sadder for Christie was that flying meant going directly from London to Baghdad, which eliminated the journey across the desert which she had relished on earlier expeditions.

But even though there would be no more Orient Express train journeys for Christie, the next ten years for her and Max were to be most rewarding—especially for Max. They reached Baghdad, and together with Robert Hamilton, who had once spent time digging with the Campbell-Thompsons, went out visiting sites in the north of Iraq.

As Christie recalled in her autobiography, "The result of this tour was that Max finally came into the open and said firmly that all he wanted to do was to dig Nimrud. 'It's a big site, and an historical site—a site that *ought* to be dug.'" With financial contributions forthcoming—the Metropolitan Museum of New York was the biggest contributor—Max began with Christie's help and encouragement the preliminary arrangements for this dig which Max thought would rank "with Tut-ankh-amun's Tomb, with Knossos in Crete, and with Ur" in historical importance and which would "add to the world's knowledge." The excavations at Nimrud continued until 1958, and among the many finds was a rich deposit of Assyrian ivories.

Not considered one of the major Christies of the period, *Taken at the Flood* was probably written during the preparations for the long-awaited return to the Middle East. It is easy to imagine that, at the time of its publication in 1948, Agatha and Max were much preoccupied with the important new events in the archaeological side of their lives, which were to lead to the great achievements of the next decade in Mallowan's career.

Taken at the Flood has more intricate plotting than most Christie novels. Characters are not who they say they are; there are murders, attempted murders, murder that looks like suicide, a problem about a will, and other plot complexities that Hercule Poirot must sort out before the final page. Christie, in one of the few instances of her career, touches upon an actual time of events with this book. She begins her story during the London blitz, when a bomb strikes the house where some of the book's major characters live.

The title for this novel was taken from act IV of *Julius Caesar*. Poirot murmurs the lines at the end of the book when the last piece of the puzzle is put in place.

> "There is a tide in the affairs of men
> Which, taken at the flood, leads on to fortune."

Will Cuppy in *Books* (*New York Herald Tribune*) said, "*There Is a Tide* is no *Roger Ackroyd* when it comes to a final surprise, but it's one of the better Christies most of the way. Don't miss" (3/28/48). The *New Yorker* said, "A covey of nice, upper-class murder suspects . . . comes to the attention of Hercule Poirot, who incidentally, seems to be a little less self-consciously Gallic [!] of late. The case involves some tricky business . . . all of which Poirot explains with great fluency. A pleasant, workmanlike job" (3/27/48).

PLOT:

Sixty-two-year-old Gordon Cloade, eldest and wealthiest of the Cloade family of Warmsley Vale, is killed during an air raid just after returning to England from America on government business. While crossing the Atlantic, Cloade had met and married an attractive young widowed actress, Rosaleen Underhay. The newly-weds had just arrived in England and were on their way to Cloade's estate, Furrowbank, to introduce Rosaleen to her new family, when the air raid occurred and left the bride in full posession of the Cloade fortune.

The Cloade family, Gordon's brothers Jeremy, Lionel, and Rowley, are successful men in their own right, being respectively a lawyer, a doctor, and a farmer. But they and their families have always depended on Gordon for financial backing in a pinch, and had counted on inheriting his large estate.

Rosaleen arrives at Furrowbank with her brother, David Hunter, and mistrust and resentment naturally spring up on both sides. Hunter is wary of the Cloade clan—he tells his sister she had better beware strychnine in her soup—and the Cloades are put in the awkward position of having to ask a near stranger, Rosaleen, for the loans her late husband was in the habit of extending them.

A new complication arrives in the form of Rosaleen's former husband, Robert Underhay, who was presumed to have died in the African bush. The Cloades learn by letter that Underhay may be alive—a fact that would nullify Rosaleen's marriage and inheritance—and that someone named Enoch Arden, who is at an inn at the village, knows of him. The mysterious Arden is found dead in his room, though he did have visitors before his death.

In the meantime, Rowley Cloade makes an appointment with Poirot to ask him to help find Underhay. Unbeknownst to Rowley, Poirot already has an interest in the case. By coincidence he has heard of the connection between Underhay and Arden during a recent conversation at his club. The case leads Poirot to Warmsley Vale, more deaths, and the unmasking of several people who are not what they appear to be.

Principal Characters: Francis Cloade, Gordon Cloade, Jeremy Cloade, Katherine Cloade, Dr. Lionel Cloade, Rosaleen Cloade, Rowley Cloade, Eileen Corrigan, David Hunter, Mrs. Leadbetter, Beatrice Lippincott, Adela Marchmont, Lynn Marchmont, Hercule Poirot, Major George Douglas Porter, Superintendent Spence, Charles Trenton, Captain Robert Underhay.

First Editions: **British**: Collins, London, 1948. 192 pp., 8s. 6d. **American**: with U.S. title *There Is a Tide*: Dodd, Mead & Co., New York, 1948. 242 pp., $2.50.

Adaptation: None.

◈ 49 ◈

Witness for the Prosecution and Other Stories (1948)

After World War II, with Christie's popularity (and sales figures) gathering the force of a publishing title wave, the combination of author-agents-publishers that was by then "Agatha Christie" once again took up the idea of publishing separate American collections of short stories, something they had done in 1939 with *The Regatta Mystery and Other Stories* (#34). Stories from early British anthologies that had never been published by Dodd, Mead in America were reshuffled (sometimes incorporating tales from decades apart) and dealt out to the American market as the "latest" hand from the Queen of Crime. Except for "The Second Gong," which features Poirot, none of the other stories in this random collection features any of Christie's popular detectives.

Witness was the first of this very successful set of deals. It includes six titles from *The Hound of Death* (#18, 1933) and the fine pairing of "Philomel Cottage" and "Accident" from *The Listerdale Mystery* (#20, 1934).

The odd story in the collection is "The Second Gong," which is an early unpublished version of "Dead Man's Mirror," which appeared in *Murder in the Mews* (#28, 1937). Christie apparently decided that the early manuscript that had been gathering dust in the back of her desk drawer for a dozen years or so could be included in the new collection for the Yanks. She apparently liked the idea of having an outlet for old, unpublished short story manuscripts, because several of the American collections that followed *Witness for the Prosecution* included stories or versions of stories that had never been published in England.

"Where There's a Will" was titled "Wireless" in its original collection.

Nancy Blue Wynne, in *An Agatha Christie Chronology* (1976), claims *Witness for the Prosecution* is "probably the finest single collection of Christie short stories available. If one were allowed only one, this would be the one to choose."

At the time of the book's release, however, critics were less impressed.

Will Cuppy in *Books* (*New York Herald Tribune*) wrote, "Some of the tales are fairish, running largely to mystery psychology, with little or no professional detection, but the volume picks up with the last three selections" (9/12/48).

"A pretty routine sampling of Mrs. Christie's short stories from the past twenty-odd years," said the *New Yorker*. "The title story, about a wife's testimony at her husband's trial for murder, is ingenious, if improbable. In 'The Second Gong' Hercule Poirot solves a nicely cut-and-dried locked-room puzzle." The review continues, "None of the stories has appeared in a book before [incorrect], but some have been published in magazines. The majority have a familiar and somewhat dated ring" (9/11/48).

"Witness for the Prosecution"
"The Red Signal"
"The Fourth Man"
"SOS"
"Where There's a Will" ("Wireless")
"The Mystery of the Blue Jar"
   Published in *The Hound of Death* (#18, 1933)

"Philomel Cottage"
"Accident"
   Published in *The Listerdale Mystery* (#20, 1934)

"The Second Gong" ("Dead Man's Mirror")
   Published in *Murder in the Mews* (#28, 1937)

First Editions: British: None. **American:** Dodd, Mead & Co., New York, 1948. 272 pp., $2.50.

Adaptations: See *The Hound of Death* (#18) for information.

50

CROOKED HOUSE (1949)

In an interview which appeared in the *Daily Mail* on September 1, 1970, on the occasion of her eightieth birthday, Agatha Christie responded to interviewer Godfrey Winn's question if *Three Blind Mice* was her favorite of her works.

"No, it isn't my favorite," she replied. "That's *Crooked House.*"

Christie reconfirmed that opinion in her autobiography when she listed *Crooked House* and *Ordeal by Innocence* (#63, 1958) as the two books which satisfied her most. She added that *Crooked House* had been pure pleasure in writing. One reason for her fondness for the book was given in a February 27, 1966, interview in the *Sunday Times* (London), in which Christie said that she enjoyed best writing the *Crooked House*-type novel, "which depends on a family and the interplay of their lives." In the same interview Christie reiterated that, "Yes, *Crooked House* is one of my favorites. But I had difficulty with that one—the publishers wanted me to change the end . . ." because "you couldn't have the murder done" the particular way Christie had written it. As always, with the single exception of *Death Comes as the End* (#44, 1945), Christie didn't budge from her original ending; one suspects that Christie's fondness for this particular book is due in part to its unexpected and controversial denouement.

The title of the book is taken from the nursery rhyme "There was a crooked man," which ends with the line "and they all lived together in a crooked house." This is an example, like *Hickory Dickory Dock* (#60, 1955), of Christie's use of a nursery rhyme for a title or beginning idea for a mystery, without structuring the book around the content of the rhyme, as she did in *Ten Little Niggers* (#35, 1939).

In *Crooked House* Christie draws a parallel between the wizened little tycoon Leonides and the crooked man, and between the eclectic storybook half-timbered mansion his family shares with him and the crooked house of the rhyme. Beyond that parallel in the beginning of the novel, the rhyme has little connection with the plot.

Crooked House lacks one of Christie's usual detectives. Instead of Poirot, Marple, or another of her regular stable, she creates a "one time only" sleuth named Charles Hayward, a second-generation Scotland Yarder who is personally involved with the Leonides family. Though Christie's basic puzzles do not change appreciably whether or not a Poirot or Marple is on hand, the manner of solving the puzzle often does. Her "regular" detectives almost always stand on the sidelines of the puzzles and gather information, while using their gray cells or making comparisons to solve the mystery. Christie's one-shot detectives, however, are more closely involved in the actual plot. In this regard Hayward is much like Dr. Calgary in *Ordeal by Innocence*—a detective who has some personal stake in solving the crime. Perhaps this is one reason why *Crooked House* and *Ordeal by Innocence* (#63, 1958) are at the top of Christie's list of personal favorites.

There is one minor inaccuracy in the book which escapes most critics and readers, but which is typical of the kind of errors that were to appear more frequently in Christie's books during her later years. Sophia Leonides is twenty-four years old in *Crooked House,* which means she was born about 1923–24. Her grandmother, so the book states, died in 1905. Yet Sophia says, "And then there was my grandmother. I only just remember her, but I've heard a good deal about her."

About six months after the publication of *Crooked House,* Agatha and her husband Max Mallowan renewed their annual archaeological expeditions to the Middle East, which had been interrupted by the war. For a decade beginning in the fall of 1949, the Mallowans spent winter and early spring in Iraq, excavating at Nimrud.

Nimrud is the modern name of the site of the ancient capital of Assyria, Calah, which is situated south of Mosul in Nineveh, Iraq. The city was first excavated by A. H. Layard during 1845–1851, but it was not until Max Mallowan's excavations of Nimrud during the years 1949–1958 that the history of this ancient capital city came alive. It was Agatha's job during these excavations to photograph, clean, and help with the registration of the small finds, a job she thoroughly enjoyed. The historical discoveries found at Nimrud by Max were recorded in his book, *Nimrud and Its Remains,* published in two volumes in 1966, the crowning achievement of his lifelong work in the field of archaeology.

Critics were quite pleased with this Christie. Beatrice Sherman in the *New York Times* wrote, "The Greek-English eccentrics in their prodigiously overgrown English cottage are entertaining, but the story moseys along at a mild pace with the thrills packed in the swift finish" (4/17/49). Ralph Partridge, in the *New Statesman and Nation* said, "Mrs. Christie is a marvel. *Crooked House* is her forty-ninth contribution to detection, and her sleight of hand is still impeccable" (9/3/49). The *New Yorker* wrote, "Sticklers for mystery conventions will be disappointed to find that everything is finally explained by a series of documents rather than by any great amount of deductive work on the part of the enamored detective. The countryhouse trimmings are beautifully handled, though" (3/19/49). And, one-word praise in the *Saturday Review of Literature:* "Knock-out" (4/2/49).

PLOT:

Octogenarian Aristide Leonides, who worked his way up from penniless Greek immigrant to head of a large fortune based on the restaurant and catering business, is found dead in his home in the affluent London suburb of Swinley Dean. The cause of death: eserine, a barbiturate, which had been substituted for the insulin which the diabetic tycoon regularly injected.

The Leonides family had lived together in a sprawling gabled half-timbered mansion jokingly referred to as "a little crooked house," all under the patriarchal rule of old Leonides. The family includes Leonides's two sons and their wives, the children of the oldest son, Leonides's sister-in-law from his first marriage, and his second wife, Brenda, a woman fifty years her husband's junior.

Given Brenda Leonides's age, the wealth she stands to inherit, and her rumored affair with a young tutor living in the house, suspicion for Leonides's death naturally falls on the young widow.

Charles Hayward, whose father is with Scotland Yard, is by chance the fiancé of Sophia Leonides, a granddaughter of the late millionaire. Charles's familiarity with criminology, and with the inhabitants of the crooked house, naturally lead him to search for the culprit who did in old Leonides.

Principal Characters: Laurence Brown, Edith de Haviland, Mr. Gaitskill, Sir Arthur Hayward, Charles Hayward, Mr. Johnson, Detective Sergeant Lamb, Aristide Leonides, Brenda Leonides, Clemency Leonides, Eustace Leonides, Josephine Leonides, Magda Leonides, Philip Leonides, Roger Leonides, Sophia Leonides, Janet Rowe, Chief Inspector Taverner.

First Editions: **British**: Collins, London, May 1949. 192 pp., 8s. 6d. **American**: Dodd, Mead & Co., New York, 1949. 211 pp., $2.50.

Adaptation: None.

51

THREE BLIND MICE AND OTHER STORIES/
THE MOUSETRAP AND OTHER STORIES (1950)

This fine American collection of stories is dominated by the no-vella-length title story, which achieved its greatest fame in its stage version, *The Mousetrap*. Christie's famous tale of the snowbound occupants of Monkswell Manor being terrorized by a homicidal maniac had its beginnings in a twenty-minute radio play written in 1947 expressly for the eightieth birthday of Queen Mary, mother of King George VI.

For the occasion, the BBC offered to do any special broadcast whatsoever at the queen's request. Like many members of the royal family (including her granddaughters Elizabeth and Margaret), the queen was an avid Christie fan, and requested a radio play by Christie. The BBC contacted Christie. Given her love of things royal and the importance of the commission, she was hardly likely to say no, and the radio play titled *Three Blind Mice,* lasting less than thirty minutes, was written in about one week's time.

Christie related in her autobiography that Queen Mary listened to the broadcast from Marlborough House, and expressed her liking for the birthday present enough for the modest author to say, "As far as I know Queen Mary was pleased with it."

After the broadcast someone (Christie does not say who) suggested that *Three Blind Mice* be turned into a short story. She followed the advice, while at the same time mulling over the possibility of turning the radio play into a full three-act play. *The Hollow* had already been produced by Peter Saunders in the West End, with success, and Christie was starting to feel "theatre" in her blood.

"Why not write a play instead of a book?" Christie wondered. "Much more fun. One book a year would take care of finances, so I could now enjoy myself in an entirely different medium."

By the time the short story was ready for publication Christie must have begun writing the stage version, or at least planning it, because she withheld the publication of the short story in Britain, presumably because it would cut into the box-office draw of a murder mystery play. In fact, "Three Blind Mice" never has appeared in a British short story collection.

This story is another example of Christie's use of nursery rhymes in her works. In this case the tune "Three Blind Mice" is the "theme song" of the psychopathic killer who terrorizes Monkswell Manor. Christie does not structure her plot around the rhyme, as she did in *Ten Little Niggers* (#35, 1939). Instead, the image of the blind mice, running in fear from the knife of the farmer's wife, is used to parallel the blind terror of the characters who know there is an unseen killer among them.

The balance of the stories in the collection are Poirot and Marple forays that appeared in British magazines from 1925 through 1942, but which had not been published in book form in England or North America. The final story, "The Love Detectives," features the only appearance of Harley Quin outside the 1930 collection, *The Mysterious Mr. Quin* (#12).

"Deft, entertaining long title story and eight short mysteries, neatly propounded and solved," thought *Bookmark* (5/19/50). The *New York Herald Tribune* remarked, "Each one of them is a good puzzle and well up to Miss Christie's usual standard" (3/5/50).

"Some of these are rather old-fashioned," thought the *New Yorker,* "but the book as a whole is well above average" (3/11/50).

Hillis Mills in the *New York Times* wrote, "Any reader who plows through a great many good, bad, and so-so mysteries welcomes a new volume by Agatha Christie. At last, he says to himself, I am in the capable hands of an experienced entertainer who knows her craft. With a Christie book, it is possible to relax in the comfortable knowledge that there will be a tidily constructed plot, reasonably lifelike, adequately motivated characters and no flimflam or loose ends" (2/26/50).

PLOTS:
"Three Blind Mice"
The guests and residents of the newly opened guest house, Monkswell Manor, find themselves trapped by a snowstorm and threatened by a psychopathic killer.

"Strange Jest"

Miss Marple helps Edward and Jane Helier find the "hidden treasure" that their practical-joking Uncle Matthew left them when he died. The problem: they know his money is somewhere, but no one can find it.

"The Tape-Measure Murder"

When Miss Politt arrives at Mrs. Spenlow's house to do a fitting on her client's dress, she finds Mrs. Spenlow dead—strangled. Mr. Spenlow, who stood to inherit a good bit, is a likely suspect, but villager Jane Marple takes a measure of the case and finds the real murderer.

"The Case of the Perfect Maid"

When the Skinner sisters' maid, Gladys, is sacked on suspicion of having pinched one of her employers' brooches, Jane Marple draws on her knowledge of serving girls to clear Gladys's name and find the real thief.

"The Case of the Caretaker"

To help his patient Jane Marple get out of a postinfluenza depression, Dr. Haydock brings her a manuscript of his own creation, detailing a village mystery, but without a solution. Jane's prescription is to find the solution to Haydock's problem.

"The Third Floor Flat"

Two young couples, back from a date, find themselves locked out of one of the girls' apartments. They cleverly decide to gain access by riding up in the dumbwaiter from the basement, though by mistake they get out on the third instead of the fourth floor, and find a body.

"The Adventure of Johnnie Waverly"

Steel magnate Marcus Waverly and his wife come to Poirot when their three-year-old son, Johnnie, is kidnapped and held for ransom, in spite of the police's efforts to prevent the kidnapping.

"Four and Twenty Blackbirds"

While dining at the Gallant Endeavour, Poirot and a friend notice a fellow diner, a lone bearded man, who they learn has been eating there on Tuesday and Thursday nights for a decade. When Poirot hears that the diner came in on a Monday the week before, he is intrigued, and is soon on the trail of a murder involving eating habits.

"The Love Detectives"

While visiting Colonel Melrose, effete Mr. Satterthwaite hears of the murder of Sir James Dwighton, a friend and neighbor of his host. The Dwightons have recently been in a messy love-triangle business, and the wife and lover are immediately suspect. While on their way to Dwighton's to investigate, Melrose and Satterthwaite have a minor auto accident—with none other than Harley Quin—who brings his usual uncanny insights to solving the case.

First Editions: British: None. American: Dodd, Mead & Co., 1950. 250 pp., $2.50.

Adaptation: Christie turned the short story "Three Blind Mice" into the play *The Mousetrap,* which has become the longest running play in theatre history. The play had its London opening at the Ambassadors Theatre on November 25, 1952, and is still playing to capacity audiences. The American production of *The Mousetrap* opened (off-Broadway) in New York on November 5, 1960, at the Maidman Playhouse.

52

A MURDER IS ANNOUNCED (1950)

There was much hoopla in England and America surrounding the publication of *A Murder Is Announced*. The book had a first printing of 50,000 copies, the first time one of Christie's books achieved that figure with its initial printing, and the publishers pushed the "50" theme by touting 1950 as the year of Christie's fiftieth book.* The novel was well received by the critics, and Christie's fans flocked to their favorite bookstores to purchase copies of her latest masterpiece of crime. The Queen of Crime was off and running on solid footing into the 1950s with this book, considered one of the best efforts of her later years.

A new era of postwar books by Christie would now reflect the changing times and social attitudes of her middle-class English social milieu. One reason why Christie was a good social historian was because over the decades she was able to incorporate these changes accurately into her English village novels. *The Murder of Roger Ackroyd* (#7, 1926), *The Murder at the Vicarage* (#13, 1930), *Murder Is Easy* (#33, 1939), and *The Mirror Crack'd from Side to Side* (#68, 1962) are just some of the other novels which supply the reader with good descriptions of village life from the 1920s through the 1960s.

The archetypal English village in this book is Chipping Cleghorn, where in 1950 the local inhabitants are just beginning to adjust to the new ways which are fast replacing the old customs and morals. Servants are disappearing at a fast pace after the war, being replaced by "dailys," women who live out and come in "daily" to clean and cook. Young women now smoke in public, are getting

---

* Both Collins and Dodd, Mead inaccurately advertised this as Christie's fiftieth mystery "novel." The advertisement should have said Christie's fiftieth book, as there are short story collections among the total number of books. In our chronology of her books, this is volume #52; our list includes two short story collections published only in England, and two short story collections published only in America.

better educations, and are starting to work in jobs that at one time were not considered proper for them. The citizens in Chipping Cleghorn have to deal with food rationing and shortages of all types, including housing. Strangers are suddenly moving into a population that at one time was stable and devoid of new faces.

We can imagine the characters in this novel sitting down to breakfast, picking up their favorite morning papers, glancing at the headlines, and eagerly turning to the local news. And here is where Christie introduces one of her most imaginative, memorable, and successful plot devices. An announcement that a murder will occur is placed in the "personals" column of the newspaper where most of the village residents will spot it immediately. Instead of the ordinary "A marriage is announced" or "An engagement is announced," there's the eye-opening "A murder is announced." Some of Christie's books are memorable because of their endings; others stand out because of the exotic setting, but *A Murder Is Announced* is unforgettable because of the premise contained in its title and opening chapter.

Robert Barnard, the critic and crime novelist, wrote an excellent analysis of *A Murder Is Announced* in *A Talent to Deceive* (1980). In his appraisal of the book, Mr. Barnard speaks of Christie's "ability to conceive and work through 'a good idea for a murder'—a circumstance which makes her crimes stand out from run-of-the-mill coshings and stabbings." He says the title is easy to remember because Christie took a familiar statement and "used it creatively."

Miss Marple returns in *A Murder Is Announced* after an absence of seven years, last appearing in the 1943 *The Moving Finger* (#42). Marple, much to the delight of her fans, would now begin to appear with more regularity in the Christie novels of the 1950s and 1960s, and from this point on she would rival Poirot in popularity. Poirot had his Hastings in his early career, then went solo as a detective, with occasional assistance from Mrs. Oliver in later books. Marple had Chief Inspector Craddock (a detective inspector before his promotion at New Scotland Yard) to assist her with detection in three books. For Marple's other cases, Christie introduced a variety of different detectives, and assistants to help her.

Chief Inspector Dermot Eric Craddock was the nephew and

godson of Sir Henry Clithering, the former commissioner of Scotland Yard who held a special respect for the talents of the "old pussy" Miss Jane Marple.

Sir Henry Clithering had known Miss Marple from the very early days when Miss Marple and he both belonged to the "Tuesday Night Club" (see #16, 1932). His only other appearance in a Christie work was in the 1942 *The Body in the Library* (#40). Of Miss Marple, Sir Henry said, "She's just the finest detective God ever made. Natural genius cultivated in a suitable soil." And Inspector Craddock, after a few encounters with the fragile old lady of crime, was soon to share his uncle's high opinion of Miss Marple.

Chief Inspector Craddock and Miss Marple teamed up in two more novels, *4.50 from Paddington* (#62, 1957) and *The Mirror Crack'd from Side to Side* (#68, 1962). He also appeared in the short story "Sanctuary," which featured Miss Marple (from *Double Sin and Other Stories,* #66, 1961). "Craddock . . . not only had brains and imagination, he had also . . . the self-discipline to go slow, to check and examine each fact and to keep an open mind until the very end of a case."

Although the characters of *A Murder Is Announced* were pretty much the straightforward village types that Christie loved to portray, she did throw a surprise in this novel. Miss Murgatroyd and Miss Hinchcliffe were quite obviously an elderly lesbian couple and Miss Hinchcliffe had very masculine characteristics. Christie treated them very delicately, but this was the first time Christie ever went this far portraying obviously "gay" people in one of her full-length novels. In her short story "Three Blind Mice" (#51, 1950) Christie also had as a character an obvious homosexual. Christie was definitely falling into step with the changing times.

Christie dedicated *A Murder Is Announced* "To Ralph and Anne Newman, at whose house I first tasted . . . Delicious Death!" Delicious Death refers to an incident in the book when a cake is prepared by the housekeeper at Little Paddocks for Dora Bunner's birthday. Patrick, Letitia Blacklock's nephew, teases the housekeeper by calling her chocolate cake "Delicious Death," but Miss Blacklock reassures the upset girl by saying, "He meant it was worth dying to eat such a cake." Readers can easily imagine

Christie's hearing the name applied to a rich chocolatey concoction at the Newmans' dinner party, and noting it for use in her next mystery.

An article written by the mystery writer Margery Allingham appeared as a front cover story on Christie in the *New York Times Book Review,* in celebration of Christie's fiftieth book. A review of this book, written by C. V. Terry, accompanied the article. The review in part said, "Here's a super-smooth Christie—three neat murders in an English village only faintly shadowed by the reign of Attlee, the customary constables very amusingly winded and Miss Marple (that amateur sleuth) always a good stride in the lead. It goes without saying that most readers will guess in vain, though the author lays her facts scrupulously on the line, along with an assortment of her famous red herrings, all beautifully marinated. By no means neglect Miss Marple's remarks on those faded letters, and the rope of pearls that turn out to be false, after all" (6/4/50). Ralph Partridge in the *New Statesman and Nation* wrote, "*A Murder Is Announced* is a heady wine that will stand comparison with the Christies of any but the best vintage years" (8/5/50). Robert Barnard in *A Talent to Deceive* (1980), expressing a dissenting opinion, said, "For two-thirds of its length *A Murder Is Announced* is as good as Agatha Christie ever wrote. In the last fifty pages it suffers a damaging collapse into something approaching absurdity."

E. D. Doyle from the *San Francisco Chronicle* said, "You'll find the old Christie magic as potent as ever" (6/4/50). The review from the *Times Literary Supplement* (London) was perhaps the best tribute of all: "A new novel by Miss Agatha Christie always deserves to be placed at the end of any list of detective fiction and her fiftieth book, *A Murder Is Announced,* establishes firmly her claim to the throne of detection. The plot is as ingenious as ever, the writing more careful, the dialogue both wise and witty; while suspense is engendered from the very start, and maintained very skillfully until the final revelation: it will be a clever reader indeed who anticipates this, and though Miss Christie is as usual scrupulously fair in scattering her clues, close attention to the text is necessary if a correct solution to the mystery is to be arrived at before the astute Miss Marple unmasks the culprit" (6/23/50).

PLOT:

On Friday, October 29, Mrs. Swettenham opens the freshly delivered copy of the Chipping Cleghorn *Gazette* and, as is her habit, immediately peruses the personals columns. The advertisements are of the usual sort: antique cars for sale, puppies for adoption, posts sought, false teeth purchased, star-crossed lovers seeking reunions. As she reads these predictable but eminently interesting listings, exchanging comments with her son Edmund (who prefers reading the socialist-oriented *Daily Worker*), Mrs. Swettenham stumbles on an extraordinary personal: *A murder is announced and will take place on Friday, October 29, at Little Paddocks, at 6:30 p.m. Friends please accept this, the only intimation.*

Edmund puts the unusual listing down to a gimmicky party announcement, "The Murder Game—that kind of thing." But his mother finds it highly out of character for the mistress of Little Paddocks, Letitia Blacklock, "such a sensible woman," to resort to "these new-fangled ways of giving invitations."

Of course Mrs. Swettenham, with Edmund reluctantly in tow, arrives at Little Paddocks at the appointed hour, to find that more than a few friends and neighbors have decided to pay a call on Letitia Blacklock, including Colonel Easterbrook and his young wife, dithery Bunch Harmon and her husband, Julian (vicar of Clipping Cleghorn), and Hinchcliffe and Murgatroyd, the tweedy spinsters who share a cottage.

The curious respondents to the announcement find the Little Paddocks household as much in the dark as they. The members of the household—Letitia, the stylish unmarried mistress of the place; Dora Bunner, her old school friend and current "charity" houseguest; Miss Blacklock's distant cousins Patrick and Julia Simmons; Mitzi, the emotional and rather paranoid Middle European housekeeper; Phillipa Haymes, the Paddocks' gardener—are all as puzzled by the newspaper item as their neighbors. But with her customary cool and style, Letitia welcomes the unexpected guests—all waiting for something to happen. As the clock chimes the half hour, the lights at Little Paddocks go out, amid "Delighted gasps and feminine squeaks of appreciation."

In the sudden darkness, a door swings open, and a flashlight beam plays around the room. A voice calls out, "Stick 'em up!"—

followed by two gunshots. With a third report, the intruder's body slumps to the floor.

This extraordinary sequence of events sets Chipping Cleghorn on its ear, but fortunately Jane Marple is on hand to find out just who it was who announced this particular murder.

Principal Characters: Charlotte Blacklock, Letitia Blacklock, Dora Bunner, Sir Henry Clithering, Chief Inspector Dermot Eric Craddock, Colonel Archie Easterbrook, Laura Easterbrook, Belle Goedler, Diana "Bunch" Harmon, Reverend Julian Harmon, Myrna Harris, Phillipa Haymes, Miss Hinchcliffe, Jane Marple, Mitzi, Amy Murgatroyd, Rudi Scherz, Julia Simmons, Patrick Simmons, Emma Jocelyn Stamfordis, Edmund Swettenham, Mrs. Swettenham.

First Editions: British: Collins, London, June 1950. 256 pp., 8s. 6d. **American**: Dodd, Mead & Co., New York, 1950. 248 pp., $2.50.

Adaptations: *A Murder Is Announced,* adapted for the stage by Leslie Darbon, opened at the Vaudeville Theatre, London, on September 21, 1977. A one-hour dramatization of this novel by William Templeton was shown on American television, December 30, 1956, with Gracie Fields as Miss Marple.

53

THEY CAME TO BAGHDAD (1951)

Agatha Christie visited Baghdad on her first trip to the Middle East in the fall of 1928—the fateful journey that led to her introduction to archaeologist Leonard Woolley (see *The Seven Dials Mystery, #10*). Christie traveled to the city across the desert from Damascus in a six-wheeler bus, a trip she described as "fascinating and rather sinister."

She and her unknown traveling companions, including Arabs, a Frenchwoman, a German general, and a fellow Britisher known as "The Duchess of Alwiyah," made the two-day journey across the trackless desert with only one stop, the mud fort of Rutbah, manned by "wild, dark" guards of the Camel Corps who inspected the bus passengers before letting them enter the fort, to make sure they were not bandits masquerading as tourists. Christie also noted that the dangers on the desert at that time were real enough for their drivers to carry rifles under a pile of rugs on the bus.

The party crossed the Euphrates the next day, journeyed across another stretch of desert, crossed the Tigris, then went into Baghdad itself. The city, dominated by its turquoise-domed mosque, was full of rickety buildings and the sounds of vendors hawking their wares and the pungent smells of exotic spices and donkey excreta. Its crowded streets included Rashid Street, the city's main thoroughfare (down which Captain Crosbie walks at the opening of the book), as well as the dark, narrow alleyways off to the sides, lined with open-fronted shops and stalls.

By the time Christie wrote *They Came to Baghdad* over two decades later, the city had become something of a second home for her and her husband. Until the outbreak of World War II, and for a number of years after the war, the Mallowans spent part of every year in the Middle East on archaeological expeditions, and for many years they maintained a house in Baghdad. It was an old Turkish-style house, with a courtyard filled with palm trees, and a balcony overlooking the Tigris where Agatha could sit, have morning tea, and watch the women from the nearby squatters' shacks wash their pots and pans in the river, into which Baghdad's woefully inadequate plumbing discharged its wastes.

When Victoria Jones arrives in Baghdad on her adventure, the city has changed from the days when Victoria's creator first saw it. "How enormously it has grown," Christie wrote of Baghdad in the 1950s. "Most of the modern architecture is very ugly, wholly unsuitable for the climate." Even Baghdad was victimized by suburban sprawl: the quaint herders' villages (which Agatha adored) that surrounded the city in 1928, once linked to the city by palm-lined open roads, were engulfed by haphazard shanty towns and modern development.

Victoria Jones, the adventuress with a sense of humor and a talent for mimicry, has "a tendency to tell lies at both opportune and inopportune moments. . . . She lied with fluency, ease and artistic fervor." On the other hand, Victoria possesses some sterling virtues—generosity, kindness and, most important to an adventuress, courage. Victoria is one of those people with a "natural leaning towards adventure."

Victoria Jones is a pleasant diversion as a Christie character. Her madcap antics are fun to follow, since the reader knows that any scrapes she gets herself into, she will always manage to escape in the nick of time (reminiscent of the early cinema's *The Perils of Pauline* series).

Jones follows in the tradition of Christie's first heroine-adventuress, Anne Beddingfeld, in *The Man in the Brown Suit* (#5, 1924). Both Victoria and Anne become involved in adventures while away from London—Victoria in Baghdad and Anne in South Africa. And, as any good adventuress should have romance, Christie does not let us down with Victoria and Anne. Both fall in love and manage to mix romance with high adventure and intrigue.

They Came to Baghdad stands above the general run of Christie's thriller books,* thanks to the stronger-than-usual characterization, and to the exotic setting, which seems to be fairly conducive to world-domination shenanigans. In fact, Christie had a brush with just that kind of deviousness in the 1930s, in the per-

* Christie's most recent thriller was the Tommy and Tuppence novel *N or M?* (#39, 1941).

son of Dr. Jordan, the director of antiquities at the museum in Baghdad (see *Cards on the Table,* #27, 1936).

In chapter 1 in a dialogue between the banker Otto Morgenthal and Anna Scheele, Morgenthal mentions the possibility of the U.S. president (then Truman, though not mentioned by name) being assassinated while at a secret conference in Baghdad. He considers the Middle East a dangerous place for high government officials, and says, "They got the Shah of Persia last year, didn't they? They got Bernadotte in Palestine."

Morgenthal is referring to the unsuccessful assassination attempt made in 1949 on the life of Muhammed Reza Shah Pahlevi (1919–1981) by members of the Iranian leftist Tudeh party. Count Folke Bernadotte (b. 1895) was the Swedish internationalist and United Nations mediator in Palestine who was assassinated by Jewish extremists in 1948.

In chapter 3, there is an inside joke about thrillers and thriller writers. An unnamed spy slips into a phone booth at High Street Kensington Station and calls his "contact" with information on whom he has been tailing. When the contact answers, the spy identifies himself as Sanders. The contact asks the code question, "Sanders of the River?" to which the spy replies, "River Tigris." *Sanders of the River* is the 1911 thriller by Edgar Wallace (1875–1932). Christie's reference is an appropriate little nod in the direction of the best-known thriller writer of them all.

Reviews of *They Came to Baghdad* were unexpectedly good for a book in which Christie strays from classic detection. Anthony Boucher in the *New York Times* thought it was "All in all, the most satisfactory novel in some years from one of the most satisfying of novelists" (6/3/51).

"The action is rapid and profuse" wrote the *New Yorker;* "the characters are astonishingly real, considering the preposterous nature of their activities; and the author's style remains far more lucid and persuasive than that employed by the vast majority of her colleagues. Altogether one of the year's most agreeable contributions to the spy-and-counterspy diversion" (4/14/51).

The *Times Literary Supplement* (London) said, "There are several satisfactory suspects, an excellent intelligence chief, done in the modern manner; a delightful *hotelier,* and a very human heroine, whose powers of invention, like those of her creator, never fail her" (4/20/51).

Christie dedicated the book "To all my friends in Baghdad."

PLOT:

Bluff, cheerful Captain Crosbie, typical of the British military type that is found in colonial outposts, leaves his bank and walks through Rashid Street and off into a side court where he enters the dark, cool office of Mr. Dakin, a shabby, stooped businessman. Once alone, the men's personalities change: Crosbie is deferential to his authoritative superior, who has just been decoding a message. The paper reveals that Baghdad has been chosen as the location for a secret meeting between leaders of the communist and capitalist powers—even "Uncle Joe" Stalin may come—with the goal of bringing about an end to the Cold War and the struggle between the superpowers. But there is word of a secret organization, with labyrinthine connections in the Middle East, that is hell-bent on sabotaging the meeting and bringing about war between Russia and the United States, possibly by assassination of one of the leaders.

In New York, Anna Scheele, the trusted private secretary to international banker Otto Morgenthal, unexpectedly asks for a three-week leave of absence so that she can visit her sister in London—a sister her boss didn't know she had. Curiously, the name Anna Scheele had been written on a map in Dakin's office after his meeting with Crosbie.

Meanwhile, in London, bright, flighty Victoria Jones has just been sacked from her latest office job. While pondering her future in FitzJames Gardens, Victoria meets a handsome, friendly young blond named Edward. The two are immediately attracted to each other, but further developments are stymied because Edward is leaving the next day for Baghdad, where he's taken a job with Dr. Rathbone, a man who spreads culture far and wide by opening bookshops in remote places.

After their Romeo-and-Juliet-like parting, Victoria realizes that she's in love with Edward, and that she must follow him to Baghdad, even though she has no money and doesn't even know Edward's last name. Victoria manages to get to Baghdad by hiring on with a wealthy American woman as traveling companion. Though

Edward isn't in Baghdad when she arrives, Victoria finds herself thrust into adventure when a wounded secret agent dies in her hotel room.

Principal Characters: Richard Baker, Mr. Bolford, Dr. Alan Breck, Mrs. Cardew Trench, Henry Carmichael, Sir Rupert Crofton Lee, Captain Crosbie, Mr. Dakin, Edward Goring, Mrs. Hamilton Clipp, George Hamilton Clipp, Victoria Jones, Dr. John Pauncefoot Jones, Otto Morgenthal, Dr. Rathbone, Anna Scheele, Catherine Serakis, Lionel Shrivenham, Marcus Tio, Sheik Hussein El Ziyara.

First Editions: **British**: Collins, London, March 1951. 256 pp., 8s. 6d. **American**: Dodd, Mead & Co., New York, 1951. 218 pp., $2.50.

Adaptation: None.

54

THE UNDER DOG AND OTHER STORIES (1951)

This American collection of Poirot short stories contains works from the early days of Christie's career; all were published in British magazines between 1923 and 1926. Like many of the Christie short stories that gained a second life in the anthologies published during the last twenty-five years of her career, these stories appeared in more than one collection. The title story appeared in book form in England for the first time in the 1960 collection, *The Adventure of the Christmas Pudding* (#65). The other stories were to appear again in 1974 in the British and American collections, *Poirot's Early Cases* (#81).

Fans of comparative reading should note that several of these stories contain material or ideas that were expanded in later and longer works. "The Plymouth Express," for example, was enlarged into *The Mystery of the Blue Train* (#9, 1928). "The Submarine Plans" was reworked considerably in the 1930s to become "The Incredible Theft" in *Murder in the Mews* (#28, 1937). And Christie's interest in the figures of the commedia dell'arte and the harlequinade is evidenced for the first time in "The Affair at the Victory Ball." In this story, Poirot investigates the murder of Lord Cronshaw after a masked ball, which Cronshaw had attended dressed as Harlequin, along with friends dressed as Columbine, Punchinello, Punchinella, Pierrot and Pierrette. Christie was later to use the Harlequin figure in a much different role—as Mr. Harley Quin, the mysterious, enigmatic, almost supernatural resolver of problems, in her collection *The Mysterious Mr. Quin* (#12, 1930).

Anthony Boucher in the *New York Times:* "The stories' interest is, it must be admitted, more historical than intrinsic. All feature Hercule Poirot (on his own in the novelette, Boswelled by the faithful Captain Hastings in the eight short stories), and all are routine puzzles strongly influenced by the form, if not the spirit, of the Sherlock Holmes stories and evincing nothing of the novelistic skill or technical mystery brilliance which Christie was later to display. Their chief fascination, indeed, is as evidence of how far Christie has come from these beginnings" (10/14/51).

"The title novelette," wrote the *New Yorker,* "is fully up to the author's present standard (it would take a remarkably alert reader to single out the murderer before the last page in each story), the style is brisk and ladylike, and nearly all the people involved, with the exception of M. Poirot, and a few servants, and two or three persons connected with the police, are prominent members of a vanished society. Reading Miss Christie is likely to remind you of the hammocks of long-ago summers, but that may not be so bad, all things considered" (9/8/51).

PLOTS:
"The Under Dog"

Young Lily Margrave, paid companion to Lady Astwell, comes to Poirot to ask his help in the "gruesome" murder case of her employer's husband, Sir Reuben Astwell, who was bludgeoned to death in the tower retreat of his estate. Charles Leverson, a surly nephew who had argued with his uncle, is heavily incriminated, though Lady Astwell is of firm mind that someone else did in her husband.

"The Plymouth Express"

While traveling on the Plymouth Express, Naval Lieutenant Alec Simpson finds the body of a well-dressed young woman stuffed under the seat of his carriage. Poirot gets involved when the victim turns out to be the daughter of an old American millionaire friend of his.

"The Affair at the Victory Ball"

Hastings arouses Poirot's interest in a much-publicized society murder, the recent death of playboy Lord Cronshaw, the night of a costume ball. The same night that the aristocrat was found stabbed through the heart, his actress fiancée Coco Courtenay was found dead of an overdose of cocaine.

"The Market Basing Mystery"

Inspector Japp suggests that Poirot and Hastings join him for a relaxing weekend in the quiet village of Market Basing, where Japp hopes to indulge in his hobby of botany. Their plans are changed when Walter Protheroe, a local recluse, is found shot through the head, and the village doctor claims the wound was not self-inflicted.

"The Lemesurier Inheritance"

While dining at the Carlton, Hastings and Poirot run into Captain Vincent Lemesurier, of an old Northumberland family, an acquaintance of Hastings's from his days in France during the war. While chatting with Vincent and an uncle who is with him, they are interrupted by the news that Vincent's father has been seriously injured in a riding accident and not expected to live. Vincent is "bowled over" by the news, not because of any great love for his father, but because the accident fulfills an old family curse, that no firstborn son of a Lemesurier will ever inherit the family estate. Vincent dies shortly thereafter.

"The Cornish Mystery"

Plain, shy Mrs. Pengelley comes to Poirot for help when she notices that her severe "gastritis" bothers her only after meals she eats with her husband, and not at times when he is away. She has noticed a jar of weed killer, half empty, that the gardener has never used, and suspects Mr. Pengelley is poisoning her.

"The King of Clubs"

Prince Paul of Maurania comes to Poirot for advice about his fiancée, the beautiful and famous dancer Valerie Saintclair, who has been in the papers because of her involvement with impresario Henry Reedburn, recently murdered at his villa.

"The Submarine Plans"

Lord Alloway, the minister of defense, summons Poirot and Hastings to his country house, Sharples, when top-secret submarine plans are stolen from his desk during a weekend house party.

"The Adventure of the Clapham Cook"

Mrs. Todd, an irate housewife whose domestic regularity has

been impaired by the disappearance of her cook, asks Poirot to help her find the missing girl.

First Editions: British: None. **American**: Dodd, Mead & Co., New York, 1951. 248 pp., $2.50.

Adaptation: None.

55

MRS. MCGINTY'S DEAD (1952)

Poirot had been absent from a Christie novel for almost four years, since the 1948 *Taken at the Flood* (#48). For the rest of Christie's career, Poirot's appearances were to become less frequent, a reflection of Christie's boredom with his character, and of her increased interest in Jane Marple. Agatha Christie also took Ariadne Oliver out of retirement for this novel. Her previous appearance had been in 1936, as one of the four sleuths in *Cards on the Table* (#27). Mrs. Oliver's appearance had not changed in the years between novels; the feminist author still had "untidy billows of grey hair" and bags of apples. However, she must have put on weight, as she was now described as "a large woman."

In *Cards on the Table,* Mrs. Oliver discussed how difficult it was to write. She was reflecting her creator's own views on the subject. Now, in *Mrs. McGinty's Dead,* Mrs. Oliver again complains, this time about the "pure *agony*" of having one of her books adapted for the stage by someone else.

"You've no idea of the agony of having your characters taken and made to say things that they never would have said, and do things that they never would have done. And if you protest, all they say is that it's 'good theatre,' " Mrs. Oliver says to Poirot.* This little speech was aimed at all the theatre people who'd caused Christie aggravation over the years. In her autobiography she wrote that she went "into an entirely different department of writing [theatre]" because of her "annoyance over people adapting my books for the stage in a way I disliked."

---

* After their long separation between *Cards on the Table* and *Mrs. McGinty's Dead,* Ariadne and Hercule would become more frequent companions. Their later books are *Dead Man's Folly* (#61, 1956), *Third Girl* (#72, 1966), *Hallowe'en Party* (#75, 1969), and *Elephants Can Remember* (#79, 1972). Mrs. Oliver had only one solo appearance, in *Pale Horse* (#67, 1961).

With this complaint off her chest* Christie was able to dedicate *Mrs. McGinty's Dead* to her producer, Peter Saunders, "in gratitude for his kindness to authors."

Saunders produced his first Christie play, *The Hollow,* in 1951, and from that modest beginning (376 performances in the West End) moved the following year to the astonishing phenomenon of *The Mousetrap* (which as of November 1983 is in its thirty-first year in the West End, the longest running play in theatre history). This dedication is especially timely since the book appeared the same year as *The Mousetrap*'s preview production at Nottingham, October 6, 1952 (then titled *Three Blind Mice*) and the now legendary opening at the Ambassadors Theatre in the West End, November 25, 1952. (See Part Two.) Peter Saunders was also the producer of one of Christie's most acclaimed theatre pieces on both sides of the Atlantic, *Witness for the Prosecution,* which was named the best foreign play of the 1954–55 New York season.

Mrs. Oliver continues her professional complaints when she says to Poirot, "My books bring me in quite enough money—that is to say the bloodsuckers take most of it, and if I made more, they'd take more, so I don't overstrain myself." In Christie's autobiography, she expresses the same sentiment but in a more restrained manner. "Seeing the point to which taxation has now risen, I was pleased to think it was no longer really worthwhile for me to work so hard: one book a year was ample. If I wrote two books a year I should make hardly more than by writing one, and only give myself a great deal of extra work."

Christie introduced in this book the "large, earnest" Superintendent Bert Spence of the Kilchester police. Spence, an honest policeman from the "old school," teamed with Poirot, in addition to this case, in *Hallowe'en Party* (#75, 1969) and *Elephants Can Remember* (#79, 1972).

Also on hand is an amusing disorganized character that Christie uses as a foil to Poirot's orderly one: Mrs. Maureen Summerhayes.

---

* The film version of *Mrs. McGinty's Dead,* titled *Murder Most Foul* (1964), replaced Hercule Poirot with Miss Marple. Mrs. Oliver's remarks on adaptations were written before this film version. One can imagine what Mrs. Oliver would have said about the audacity of the film's producers in replacing the original detective with another. For more on this, see Part Two.

With "red hair and an attractively freckled face," [Maureen] "was usually in a distracted state of putting things down, or else looking for them. She should be doing anything but what she does, which is managing the most disorganized guest house in all of England. Poirot stays with Mrs. Summerhayes when he goes to Broadhinny to help Superintendent Spence investigate Mrs. McGinty's murder. Said Poirot to himself after seeing the chaos and disarray of the guest house, "Yes, I suffer." One of the best moments in the book comes when Poirot teaches Maureen to make an omelet.

This book received praise from the critics, which indicates that despite occasional lapses Christie was still at the top of her form in 1952. L. G. Offord in the *San Francisco Chronicle* said, "The plot may not scintillate like some other Christies, but it's perfect and the characters are wonderful" (2/17/52). Anthony Boucher wrote in his review for the *New York Times,* "This first Poirot novel in almost four years is the best Poirot since such prewar classics as *Cards on the Table*" (2/10/52). The *New Yorker* said, "The author's formula hasn't changed perceptibly since she wrote *The Mysterious Affair at Styles,* in which Poirot made his memorable first appearance, but it is still as sound and expert as any that has been invented subsequently" (2/9/52). One dissenting opinion from Sergeant Cuff in the *Saturday Review:* "Not among her best" (2/16/52).

PLOT:

There's been a murder in Broadhinny. On November 22, Mrs. McGinty, a widow of sixty-four who worked in various village houses as a daily domestic, is found murdered, knocked in the back of the head, in her cottage parlor. Her bedroom has been ransacked, the floorboards pried up. Police find her savings, thirty pounds' worth, hidden under a stone behind the house. Suspicion falls immediately on her boarder, the "sometimes cringing and sometimes truculent" James Bentley. When blood and hair that match Mrs. McGinty's group and type are found on Bentley's coat sleeve, his conviction is a foregone conclusion.

On his way home from a most satisfying meal of escargots at the Vieille Grand'mere restaurant in Soho, Poirot observes the small notice in the newspaper about Bentley's conviction. "It had not been an interesting murder," the Belgian thinks to himself.

Not interesting, that is, until Poirot reaches his flat, where his old friend Superintendent Spence of the Kilchester police is waiting for him. Spence is on the Bentley case and "went into the whole business very carefully." Spence admits that the facts all point to Bentley's guilt, but to the policeman's experienced eye Bentley just didn't look like a murderer, "and I know a lot more about murderers than they [the jury] do."

Admitting, "I have leisure . . . too much leisure. And you have intrigued me," Poirot agrees to dig deeper into the McGinty murder. Poirot sets himself up in Broadhinny at the slovenly, madcap boardinghouse run by Mr. and Mrs. Summerhayes, where he finds a serious threat to his gastronomic well-being in Maureen Summerhayes's total lack of cooking ability. Worse, as he looks into the McGinty murder, he finds a threat to his life as well.

Principal Characters: Bessie Burch, Joe Burch, Eve Carpenter, Deirdre Henderson, Evelyn Hope, Pamela Horsefall, Mrs. Kiddle, Mrs. McGinty, Michael, Mrs. Ariadne Oliver, Hercule Poirot, Dr. Rendell, Shelagh Rendell, Superintendent Bert Spence, Major John Summerhayes, Maureen Summerhayes, Mrs. Sweetman, Laura Upward, Robin Upward, Mr. Wetherby, Mrs. Wetherby, Maude Williams.

First Editions: **British**: Collins, London, March 1952. 187 pp., 9s. 6d. **American**: Dodd, Mead & Co., New York, 1952. 243 pp., $2.50.

Adaptation: The 1964 film based on *Mrs. McGinty's Dead* was titled *Murder Most Foul*, and starred Margaret Rutherford as Miss Marple. This is a Poirot novel, but the film's producers substituted Miss Marple as the detective.

56

THEY DO IT WITH MIRRORS / MURDER
WITH MIRRORS (1952)

We know from her autobiography that Christie often wrote while on expedition (though she is maddeningly quiet as to which books), and *They Do It with Mirrors* may have been written at Nimrud, Iraq. The book, however, has nothing to do with the discovery and excavation of ancient cities. Instead, it takes place in one of Christie's favorite settings, a large Victorian house in a small English village. The village is Market Kindle in the south of England and the house is called Stonygates, a Gothic monstrosity of the "Best Victorian Lavatory period." The world of Christie has changed very rapidly since the end of World War II. The Gothic monstrosity has now become a school for delinquent boys. The school's staff consists of psychiatrists, psychologists, therapists, teachers, and reform enthusiasts. When Ruth Van Rydock refers to them as "Cranks—all the lot of them," we can assume these were Christie's own sentiments. Christie's England was changing, the old mainstream values and ideas that had once been the backbone of her generation were fading rapidly. While Christie made a great effort to incorporate modern trends and problems in her postwar books, her own attitude, as reflected in her characters, remained conservative. This was especially true in her handling of youthful characters, as in this book, where giving juvenile delinquents a second chance in life is seen as a waste of time and money. "Juvenile delinquency—that's what is the rage nowadays." "What about the decent boys from decent homes? Why isn't something done for them?" Dear old Miss Marple has her say, too. She speaks out as a champion for decency and the old values so cherished by Christie and her society: "The young people with a good heredity, and brought up wisely in a good home and with grit and pluck and the ability to get on in life—well, they are really, when one comes down to it, the sort of people a country *needs.*"

In the 1930s, as discussed in the chapter on *Cards on the Table*

(#27, 1936), Christie eliminated all anti-Semitic references in her books after she met the Nazi, Dr. Jordan, in Baghdad and he startled her with his hatred of Jews. The Jewish slurs might have ceased, but Christie found other races to berate. In *They Do It with Mirrors,* she had a field day aiming her darts at the Italians. In Victorian England, one came to expect the attitude of the English middle and upper classes toward all foreigners to be less than favorable. But in 1952, when *They Do It with Mirrors* was published, was Agatha Christie still representing these dated opinions? Did middle-class England still harbor such cliché sentiments? Here are just a few of the lines Christie has her characters fire out: 1) "You know what Italians are—nothing matters to them but money"; 2) "She's half Italian, you know, and the Italians have that unconscious vein of cruelty. They've no compassion for anyone who's old or ugly, or peculiar in any way. They point with their fingers and jeer"; 3) "The Italians are never truthful. And she's a Roman Catholic of course."*

Interestingly, in this book Christie reveals that Jane Marple, as a young girl, spent some time in Italy, a rare glimpse into the spinster's early years. We're told that nearly fifty years earlier (the early 1900s) Miss Marple lived in a *"pensionnat* in Florence," and it was there that she met two American sisters, Carrie Louise and Ruth Martin who now appear as major characters in *They Do It with Mirrors.* Why the young Marple was in Italy, who her companions were, and what she saw and did remain a secret.

In *They Do It with Mirrors,* the final solution of the crimes is solved, of course, by the observing, innocent "China-blue-eyed"

---

* In the Italian edition, the insulting lines were rewritten, and the following substitutes appeared: A) "Never thought about anything but the money. He married Pippa only for that"; B) "Gina? You mean Mrs. Hudd? Why? Because she's a woman, a beautiful woman and makes a fool of Edgar. Has a vein of cruelty, even if she does not realize it. She has no understanding for anyone who's old or ill, or anyone who has some handicap"; and C) "You will not believe Gina, I hope! She is a natural liar." (Translated from the Italian edition, *Miss Marple: Giochi di Prestigio,* Oscar Mondadori, 1980.) The American editions did leave in the Italian references, however, though American publishers frequently deleted the anti-Semitic remarks from Christie's works.

Miss Marple. Her solution depends on conjuring—what the eyes of the "audience" see is only illusion; they see what they are allowed to see. Christie has mixed the art of detection with the art of theatre: Stonygates is both stage and auditorium; the characters are both actors and audience.

As the 1950s progressed, Christie's books often received less than glowing reviews from the critics. Her work was starting to decline in originality, although her books were as popular as ever with the public. A Christie for Christmas was a major literary event for her many fans. Drexel Drake in the *Chicago Sunday Tribune* said, "Stilted characters in listless tale strikingly inferior to Agatha Christie's long established level" (9/14/52). The *New Yorker:* "The author's style is as brisk and persuasive as ever, but the plot this time may be a bit too intricate for all but the most confirmed addicts" (9/13/52). In his review in the *New York Times,* Anthony Boucher wrote, "Slight disappointment, on the one hand, because it is more conventional than Mrs. Christie's fine last two novels; high gratification, on the other, because so few writers are producing the pure puzzle-novel, and no one on either side of the Atlantic does it better" (9/28/52).

PLOT:

As a young girl staying at a *pensionnat* in Florence, Jane Marple met two American sisters, Ruth and Carrie Louise Martin. Over the intervening decades, both sisters have married often, and well. One sister, Ruth, lives in America, while Carrie Louise has adopted British homes and husbands. Oddly, Miss Marple has lost touch with Carrie Louise, though she sees Ruth Van Rydock on the woman's yearly visits to England.

Carrie Louise's first husband was the millionaire philanthropist Eric Gulbrandsen, with whom she shared a passion for "causes," and who left her a wealthy widow. Her second mate was the "lazy hound" Johnny Restarick, who clearly married Carrie for her money. After his departure for the arms of another woman—ending in death in an auto smashup—Carrie Louise got back on the track by marrying Lewis Serrocold, another man with a passion for causes. Serrocold, however, is a *poor* saver-of-mankind, unlike Gulbrandsen. The Serrocolds have taken up the cause of reforming juvenile delinquents, even to the point of converting their, that is to say *her,* estate, Stonygates, into a home for wayward boys.

Mrs. Van Rydock persuades Jane to pay a visit to Stonygates, just to see what's going on. She senses *something* isn't right, but doesn't know just what, and after all, Jane has "such a nose for that sort of thing."

At Stonygates Miss Marple finds juvenile "thugs" and "queers" and "psychiatrists everywhere underfoot." But the wards of Stonygates are not the only troubled ones. Carrie Louise and Lewis Serrocold are surrounded by an odd assortment of servants, children, adopted grandchildren, and stepchildren, all with mixed feelings about the Serrocolds' reform school—and how much of Mrs. Serrocold's fortune is being spent on it.

But the murder of an unexpected visitor reveals that there is more going on at Stonygates than a conflict between family and philanthropy.

Principal Characters: Juliet Bellever, Inspector Curry, Ernie Gregg, Christian Gulbrandsen, Gina Hudd, Walter Hudd, Edgar Lawson, Jane Marple, Dr. Maverick, Alex Restarick, Stephen Restarick, Carrie Louise Serrocold, Lewis Serrocold, Mildred Strete, Ruth Van Rydock.

First Editions: **British**: Collins, London, November 1952. 192 pp., 10s. 6d. **American**: with U.S. title *Murder with Mirrors*: Dodd, Mead & Co., New York, 1952. 182 pp., $2.50.

Adaptation: None.

57

AFTER THE FUNERAL / FUNERALS ARE FATAL
(1953)

After the Funeral contains all the ingredients that made Christie novels of the 1930s and 1940s such successes: the "vast Victorian house, built in the Gothic 'style,' the large well-to-do, obnoxious family, gathered together for the reading of a will, an old butler who had been with the family for generations, and a wide variety of the typical Christie English servants." To this setting add Hercule Poirot and, *voilà,* an old-fashioned Christie yarn to please the fans.

Enderby Hall, the setting of the book, is patterned after Abney Hall, a house that was well known to Christie since her childhood. Christie's older sister, Madge, married James Watts sometime prior to the death of their father in 1901. Abney was the Watts family home, and Madge and James lived there for some time after their marriage.

In her autobiography Christie tells of spending lavish Victorian-style Christmases at Abney as a girl of twelve or thirteen with her recently widowed mother and various members of the Watts family (see *The Adventure of the Christmas Pudding,* #65, 1960). "It was a wonderful house to have Christmas in if you were a child . . . [it was] enormous Victorian Gothic, with quantities of rooms, passages, unexpected steps, back staircases, front staircases, alcoves, niches—everything in the world that a child could want."

Abney remained an important house in Agatha's life; years later, after the place had become the permanent home of her sister and brother-in-law, Agatha went into seclusion there following her disappearance in December 1926 (see *The Mystery of the Blue Train,* #9, 1928).

In later years Agatha and her daughter Rosalind were frequent visitors, especially during World War II, a period when Abney was already falling victim to the changes wrought by the war. During the visits of Agatha's youth, there had been sixteen indoor servants at Abney. Christie recalled in her autobiography that by the

1940s, Madge Watts, "the most indefatigable woman I have ever known," maintained the "enormous house, with fourteen bedrooms [and] masses of sitting rooms" with only the help of a part-time cook. According to Agatha, the house was kept spotless, and "a weed never dared lift its head in [the] kitchen garden."

When Agatha recreated Abney in 1953 as Enderby Hall, it was a nostalgic recreation—not a picture of a lone woman spending long days polishing brasses and feather-dusting cornices, but a picture of "the good old days" when there were the servants, gardeners, plenty of money (a motive for murder, of course), and scads of leisure time to plot someone's demise.

In this nostalgic vein, Christie dedicated the book "For James— In memory of happy days at Abney." James Watts, Jr. (III), Christie's nephew, only a few years younger than Agatha, was one of her favorite playmates from her fondly remembered Christmases at Abney. Christie's love of Abney is reconfirmed in the title story of *The Adventure of the Christmas Pudding* (#65, 1960), which also uses the house as its setting and which mentions the house in its dedication.

L. G. Offord in the *San Francisco Chronicle* said, "This new Christie is rich in characters . . . especially the English servants and companions . . . and has all the usual mystery of plot twisting" (3/29/53). The *New Yorker* wrote, "Miss Christie's works have a tendency to resemble one another in tone, quality, and method, and this one is probably as good as most, and maybe even a little better" (4/4/53). However, the review from Anthony Boucher in the *New York Times* perhaps sums up best the appeal of *After the Funeral*. He writes, "Agatha Christie's *Funerals Are Fatal* [American title] is much more conventional than her recent successes—so much so that only topical references keep you from thinking that this is a revival of one of her novels of the mid-thirties. But no one can write the conventional novel, complete with genealogical tree, a dubious will, and a family, full of potential murderers, so well as Christie, nor can anyone so consistently devise plot tricks to delight without reservation the heart of the connoisseur-technician" (3/15/53).

PLOT:

Old Cornelius Abernethie, dead for many years now, made a

proper Victorian fortune with Coral Cornplasters, and built a proper Victorian pile of a mansion, Enderby Hall, where he raised his seven heirs. Though still wealthy, the Abernethie family in recent years is much diminished by accident and illness. Old Abernethie's eldest son, Richard, master of Enderby Hall, is "taken very sudden" (but then, he'd never been quite the same since his only son and heir, Mortimer, died unexpectedly of polio). The remaining members of the Abernethie family gather after the funeral for the reading of Richard's will by the family attorney, Mr. Entwhistle. The will contains no surprises—the fortune is divided among the heirs. However, at the reading, Cora Abernethie Lansquenet, the late Richard's youngest sister, who's always been something of an embarrassment to the family, brightly blurts out, "it's been hushed up very nicely, hasn't it. . . . But he *was* murdered, wasn't he?"

The family is aghast at what is to all appearances Cora's unfounded remark. However, Mr. Entwhistle later decides to go to Lytchett-St. Mary to see the "rather unbalanced and excessively stupid woman," to ask why she said such a thing. Before he can, though, the Lytchett police ring him up: someone has broken into Cora Lansquenet's house and done her in with seven or eight blows of a hatchet.

Entwhistle decides it's time for professional help and pays a call on Mr. Poirot, who soon takes on the Abernethie case.

Principal Characters: Helen Abernethie, Maude Abernethie, Timothy Abernethie, Gregory Banks, Susan Abernethie Banks, George Crossfield, Miss Entwhistle, Mr. Entwhistle, Miss Gilchrist, Mr. Goby, Alexander Guthrie, Janet Lanscombe, Cora Abernethie Lansquenet, Inspector Morton, Hercule Poirot, Michael Shane, Rosamund Abernethie Shane.

First Editions: **British**: Collins, London, May 1953. 191 pp., 10s. 6d. **American**: with U.S. title *Funerals Are Fatal:* Dodd, Mead & Co., New York, 1953. 244 pp., $2.50.

Adaptation: In 1963, a film titled *Murder at the Gallop* was made, based loosely on this novel, with Miss Marple substituting for Hercule Poirot. Margaret Rutherford starred.

58

A POCKET FULL OF RYE (1953)

Sing a song of sixpence, a pocketful of rye,
Four and twenty blackbirds baked in a pie.
When the pie was opened the birds began to sing.
Wasn't that a dainty dish to set before the king?

The king was in his counting house, counting out his money,
The queen was in the parlour, eating bread and honey,
The maid was in the garden, hanging out the clothes,
When there came a little dickey bird and nipped off her nose.

This Marple novel is a typical Christie family-murder puzzle, concerned with discovering which of many likely candidates knocked off nasty businessman Rex Fortescue. The second verse of the nursery rhyme is used very loosely to structure the murders: Rex Fortescue ("the king") is in his London office ("his counting house") when he is found dead with a pocket full of rye oats. The second victim is killed "eating bread and honey" at breakfast; the third ("the maid . . . in her garden") is the parlourmaid, found in the yard near the laundry line, with a clothespin on her nose, symbolic of the dickey bird's tweak.

It is at this point that Miss Marple, angered by the death of the innocent maid, and sensing that the murderer has chosen the nursery rhyme as a theme, utters the unforgettable line, "But what I mean to say is: have you gone into the question of blackbirds?"

From this point the nursery rhyme has nothing much to do with the book, as far as clues and structure go, and unfortunately the early clues of the rye and the clothespin turn out to be little more than details that Christie uses to fit the rhyme.

The reviews for *A Pocket Full of Rye* were generally favorable. Anthony Boucher in the *New York Times* wrote, "This is the best of the novels starring Christie's spinster-detective, Miss Marple" (4/18/54). The *Times Literary Supplement* (London) wrote,

"Miss Christie has a reputation for playing fair with the reader who likes to assume detective responsibility, and also for being one too many for him. In the present case it may be felt that though the hidden mechanism of the plot is ingenious at the expense of probability (like murder itself, in this pastoral atmosphere), it does not matter very much" (12/4/53). The *New Yorker* wrote, "This is not one of the author's best books, but it is still a model of complex skulduggery in genteel surroundings" (3/27/54). And finally, Raymond Postgate from the *Spectator* wrote that *A Pocket Full of Rye* was "improbable, but so competently written that it is much above the standard" (12/25/53).

Christie dedicated *A Pocket Full of Rye* to Bruce Ingram, "who liked and published my first short stories." Ingram was the editor of the *Sketch,* in which Agatha's first short stories appeared in 1923. (See *Poirot Investigates,* #4, 1924.) This dedication does not appear in many editions of the book.

PLOT:

Rex Fortescue, "a large flabby man . . . less impressive than he should have been," is at the offices of Consolidated Investments Trust, his financial empire. Miss Grosvenor, Mr. Fortescue's "incredibly glamorous blonde" of a secretary, serves him his own special blend of tea. Moments later, he is in "painful, spasmodic movement," gasping out, "Tea—what the hell—you put in the tea. . . ."

The pathologist's verdict: poison by taxine, the alkaloid of a substance found naturally in the leaves and berries of the yew tree. Just one hitch, though. Taxine takes one to three hours to take effect. The stuff definitely wasn't in his tea.

Inspector Neele, who's on the case, is startled to find that Fortescue and his family live at Yewtree Lodge. Stranger still, Fortescue, at the time of death, is found to have in the pocket of his jacket a quantity of rye grain.

There is a second murder, with the unlikely victim done in while eating "bread and honey" with her tea. But it's the third murder, of a dumb, adenoidal "maid in her garden" that brings Jane Marple to Yewtree Lodge. Jane is soon on the trail of the murderer, who is dispatching his victims "thematically" to follow the nursery rhyme.

Principal Characters: Crump, Mrs. Crump, Mary Dove, Vivian Dubois, Ellen, Albert Evans, Adele Fortescue, Elaine Fortescue, Jennifer Fortescue, Lancelot Fortescue, Patricia Fortescue, Percival Fortescue, Rex Fortescue, Sergeant Hay, Helen MacKenzie, Jane Marple, Gladys Martin, Inspector Neele, Effie Ramsbottom, Gerald Wright.

First Editions: **British**: Collins, London, November 1953. 191 pp., 10s. 6d. **American**: Dodd, Mead & Co., New York, 1954. 211 pp., $2.75.

Adaptation: None.

59

DESTINATION UNKNOWN / SO MANY
STEPS TO DEATH (1954)

With this book Christie returned again to the "light-hearted thriller" genre which she had last tackled in 1951 with *They Came to Baghdad* (#53). Like all of Christie's thrillers written after World War II,* *Destination Unknown* suffers in comparison to the great fantasy thrillers of Ian Fleming, who published his first James Bond novel, *Casino Royale,* in 1953. Though Christie and Fleming both crammed their thrillers chock-full of secret agents, secret formulas, defecting scientists, and farfetched schemes of world domination, Christie approached her books with the same frothy, slapdash, but genteel formula she had used in her thrillers of the 1920s. Fleming's books, on the other hand, though even more fantastic than Christie's thrillers, were meatier, and filled with a ruthless and cynical evil and sexuality, an atmosphere on which post-Hiroshima Cold War readers thrived.

While Christie's pure detective books (at least the good ones from these years) remained the classy Rolls-Royces they had always been, Christie's late thrillers were little more than quaint Model-T Fords, left behind in a cloud of dust by the sleek Aston-Martins of the James Bond books.

Christie did admit to reading some James Bond. She said in an interview in the *New York Times,* "They're fun. And they have that gadget appeal to youngsters like Max's two nephews" (10/27/66).

Destination Unknown was based partly on the activities of two famous turncoat physicists of the early 1950s: Bruno Pontecorvo, who defected to Russia, and Emil Fuchs, who spied for the Russians.

Nuclear physicist Pontecorvo, born in Italy in 1913, did re-

---

* *They Came to Baghdad* (#53, 1951), *Destination Unknown, Cat Among the Pigeons* (#64, 1959), *Passenger to Frankfurt* (#76, 1970), and *Postern of Fate* (#80, 1973).

search on cosmic rays and tritium (a substance important for the making of the hydrogen bomb). Pontecorvo worked for the governments of Canada, the United States, and England. In 1950, after vacationing in Italy, Pontecorvo and his family traveled to Helsinki, Finland, where they disappeared. Five years later, Pontecorvo reappeared as a citizen of the Soviet Union, where he was engaged in atomic energy research.

Klaus Emil Fuchs was born in Germany in 1911. Fuchs left Germany in 1933 and went to England, where he completed his education. In 1943, while in the United States working on the development of the atomic bomb, Fuchs began sending secret information to the Soviet Union. After the war Fuchs became head of the theoretical physics division of the Atomic Research Center at Harwell, England (Harwell figures in Christie's book). Eventually his communist espionage activities were found out by the FBI. Fuchs was arrested in 1950, pleaded guilty, and spent the next nine years in prison. After his release in 1959 he moved to East Germany and became director of the Institute for Nuclear Physics.

Agatha Christie dedicated this foreign adventure book "To Anthony—Who likes foreign travel as much as I do." Anthony is Anthony Hicks, who married Christie's widowed daughter, Rosalind Christie Prichard in 1949. In her autobiography, Christie described Anthony as "one of the kindest people I know—he is a most remarkable and interesting character. . . . If he has a fault, it is that he discusses wine at too great a length, but then I am prejudiced because I don't like the stuff." Hicks was trained as a barrister, but studied Tibetan and Sanskrit at the School of Oriental and African Studies. In *Mallowan's Memoirs,* Max reports that Anthony had a "deep interest in Oriental religion, stimulated by a sojourn in India during the war." Her son-in-law's interest in foreign travel and culture prompted this dedication for a book set in Casablanca.

The reviews were less than favorable. Ralph Partridge in the *New Statesman and Nation* wrote, "It is a rare event for Mrs. Christie to come at the bottom of the list, but *Destination Unknown,* if written by anyone else, would not even rank for mention. (Her devotees had better not open the book, unless prepared for a shock.)" (12/25/54). Penelope Houston in the *Spectator* said, "With Mrs. Christie, of course, nothing should be taken for granted; but her brilliant strategy of deception and misdirection is not really suited to this thriller world of secret service agents and power hungry scientists" (11/19/54). The *Times Literary Supplement* (London) was more tolerant: "Readers may regret the absence of the tonic logicalities of crime's unravelling—though 'clues' are not altogether missing—for the secret service story belongs largely to adventure, but in their place is the author's obvious pleasure in the wider horizons of the more romantic genre" (11/19/54). But the review which perhaps sums up Christie's adventure foray and does it with only three words is by Sergeant Cuff in the *Saturday Review*: "Come back Poirot" (4/9/55).

If *Destination Unknown* failed to put feathers in Christie's creative cap, there were other achievements during this period to compensate. In December 1954, *Spider's Web* opened in London, while Christie's two earlier stage hits, *The Mousetrap* (1952) and *Witness for the Prosecution* (1953) were still running—a rare achievement in English theatre. (See Part Two.)

PLOT:

Thomas Betterton, the young American scientist who discovered ZE Fission, has disappeared from a scientific conference in Paris, after working at Harwell in England for eighteen months. British Intelligence is worried. He's only the latest in a series of notable scientists to have vanished into thin air, and security agent Jessop is digging into the case.

Betterton hasn't left him much to go on. There have been the usual unreliable sightings of the scientist in odd places. The missing scientist's wife, Olive, who sports a stunning head of auburn hair, is understandably upset, since she's a bride of only six months. But she doesn't give Jessop any leads, either. Jessop finds it odd, however, that the distraught wife hurries off to Morocco to get away from the emotional strain of her husband's disappearance.

She's not under strain for long; the plane bound for Casablanca crashes and Olive is killed. Jessop, on her trail, finds himself in Casablanca with no one to follow. By chance he notices another remarkably auburn young woman in Morocco, and she seems to be making the rounds of chemists, buying sleeping pills. A would-be suicide, Jessop quickly surmises. The agent approaches the depressed woman, Hilary Craven, and makes a novel proposal: instead of taking pills, would she consider suicide by going on a dangerous mission? The rather startled Hilary agrees to impersonate the late Mrs. Betterton, and she is soon off on an international escapade that includes millionaire world-manipulators, American tourists, and missing scientists.

Principal Characters: Mr. Aristides, Mrs. Calvin Baker, Dr. Louis Barron, Olive Betterton, Thomas Charles Betterton, Hilary Craven, Herr Director, Torguil Ericsson, Major Boris Andrei Pavlov Glyor, Janet Hetherington, Miss Jennson, Mr. Jessop, Mademoiselle LaRoche, Henri Laurier, Monsieur Leblanc, Mohammed, Bianca Murchison, Dr. Simon Murchison, Helga Needheim, Dr. Rubec, Paul Van Heidem, Colonel Wharton.

First Editions: **British**: Collins, London, November 1954. 191 pp., 10s. 6d. **American**: with U.S. title *So Many Steps to Death*: Dodd, Mead & Co., New York, 1955, 212 pp., $2.75.

Adaptation: None.

60

HICKORY DICKORY DOCK / HICKORY DICKORY DEATH (1955)

The title was taken from the nursery rhyme "Hickory, dickory, dock, the mouse ran up the clock . . ." but the rhyme has nothing to do with the story, other than that the street of the youth hostel where several murders are committed is located on Hickory Road. This novel is Christie's sixth book to have a nursery rhyme title. Realizing the importance of book titles, Christie managed over her long career to hit upon some that would remain fixed in the reader's mind. Some titles indicate an exotic setting, such as *Death on the Nile* (#30, 1937), or that mayhem will take place in a specified place, such as *Murder on the Orient Express* (#19, 1934). However, when we get to Christie's "nursery rhyme" novels, the title device doesn't always work with the plot structure. Her most famous and certainly her best nursery rhyme novel was *Ten Little Niggers* (#35, 1939). Here the plot structure blended in perfectly with the rhyme. With *Hickory Dickory Dock,* the title might be memorable, but the rhyme doesn't have any structural or thematic relation to the plot.

This book is one of a group of Agatha Christie's books in the 1950s that can best be labeled *Insignificant Christie*. The group includes *After the Funeral* (#57) and *A Pocket Full of Rye* (#58) in 1953, the thriller *Destination Unknown* (#59) in 1954, and the Poirot-Mrs. Oliver 1956 collaboration, *Dead Man's Folly* (#61).

Robert Barnard, the crime novelist, in his book *A Talent to Deceive* (1980), quotes the acerbic Evelyn Waugh, author of *Brideshead Revisited*. In his diary, Waugh said of *Hickory Dickory Dock* that it "began well," but deteriorated "a third of the way through into twaddle." Barnard adds, "A judgment which, unusually for him, erred on the side of charity."

However, the critics were once again generous to Christie. The *Times Literary Supplement* (London) wrote, "Poirot's return to the happy hunting grounds of detective fiction is something of an event. . . . He smokes his little cigarettes and consumes square crumpets and, indeed, does everything that is expected of him, even solving the problem, though not before an excessive amount of damage has been done. Mrs. Christie has certainly made things difficult for him. The amount of mischief going on in the hostel imposes some strain on the reader's patience as well as on Poirot's ingenuity; the author has been a little too liberal with the red herrings. Yet the thumb-nail sketches of the characters are as good as ever and in spite of the over-elaborate nature of the puzzle there is plenty of entertainment" (12/23/55). Anthony Boucher, in the *New York Times,* wrote, "The Christie fan of longest standing, who thinks he knows every one of her tricks, will still be surprised by some of the twists here, including (if this isn't saying too much in a review) a murderer interestingly patterned after a recent factual original" (11/20/55).

PLOT:

Hercule Poirot is startled when Miss Lemon, his "perfect machine" of a secretary, makes three mistakes in typing a simple letter. Clearly, something is amiss. Miss Lemon, on questioning, reveals that she is worried about her sister, Mrs. Hubbard. After spending her married life in Singapore, Mrs. Hubbard has returned to England a widow, where she is living as matron of a youth hostel in Hickory Road, an establishment that caters to an international group of students.

It seems that things, "odd things," have been disappearing from the hostel, "And all in rather an unnatural way." Miss Lemon suspects it's something more than petty thievery or kleptomania, and Poirot agrees to meet with Felicity Lemon's distressed sibling.

Mrs. Hubbard presents the Belgian with a list of stolen or vandalized items, including a diamond ring found in a plate of soup, a lipstick stolen, a rucksack slashed, and a stethoscope and a cookbook missing. "Quite fascinating," Poirot remarks. When Mrs. Hubbard returns to the hostel she finds that one student's notes, representing months of work, have had green ink poured on them. Mrs. Hubbard asks Poirot to help and he agrees.

The students are startled when Poirot proposes that the police be called in at once. It seems a drastic measure for such petty goings on, but his proposal soon elicits a confession and reveals that there is something sinister, even deadly, going on at Hickory Road.

Principal Characters: Mr. Akibombo, Achmed Ali, Celia Austin, Leonard Bateson, Sergeant Bell, Nigel Chapman, Mr. Endicott, Sally Finch, Valerie Hobhouse, Mrs. Hubbard, Elizabeth Johnson, Chandra Lal, Patricia Lane, Felicity Lemon, Colin McNabb, Mrs. Nicoletis, Hercule Poirot, Inspector Sharpe, Nigel Stanley, Jean Tomlinson.

First Editions: British: Collins, London, October 1955. 191 pp., 10s. 6d. **American:** with U.S. title *Hickory Dickory Death:* Dodd, Mead & Co., New York, 1955. 241 pp., $3.00.

Adaptation: None.

61

DEAD MAN'S FOLLY (1956)

Max Mallowan wrote in his memoirs that Nasse House, the principal setting in *Dead Man's Folly,* is modeled on Greenway House,* the Devonshire home he and Christie shared during most of their married life.

Christie first saw Greenway as a child, when she visited there with her mother from their home Ashfield in nearby Torquay. In 1939, Christie made the decision to sell Ashfield, mainly due to the growth and changes that had come to Torquay. At about the same time, Agatha heard that Greenway was for sale. She had always admired Greenway and described it as "the ideal house, a dream house." Part of Greenway's appeal was its superb white Georgian design, dating from 1780–1790. Located on a large secluded tract of woods and gardens, it overlooked the river Dart and the Devonshire countryside Christie so loved.

When Agatha and Max viewed the estate and heard the price, Christie exclaimed, "Six thousand [pounds]? It's incredibly cheap . . . it's got thirty-three acres."

Max suggested, "Why don't you buy it?" and so she did.

Greenway became Christie's favorite home, and she spent time there every year until her death, with the exception of the World War II years, when the house was requisitioned by the British Admiralty. The gardens at Greenway, which like the house itself had been somewhat run down when she bought the property, became a hobby of the Mallowans. They spent years restoring and improving the grounds; in particular they planted a number of rare trees and shrubs.

In *Dead Man's Folly,* Hercule Poirot is once again teamed up with Mrs. Ariadne Oliver, a collaboration that was to become

* For other real houses used as models for fictional ones, see *The Hollow* (#46), *After the Funeral* (#57), *The Adventure of the Christmas Pudding* (#65), and *Postern of Fate* (#80).

more frequent in the last years of Christie's career. Since Mrs. Oliver is a parody of her creator, Christie no doubt had fun placing Mrs. Oliver in a parody of Greenway, having Ariadne involved in a murder hunt in the house and gardens Christie knew so well. The first murder, in fact, takes place in the little boathouse on the river at Nasse House, obviously patterned after the boathouse at Greenway.

Unfortunately, Christie's delight in setting a murder mystery in her own home was lost on most readers of the day; Greenway was and still is a very private residence for the Christie-Mallowan family. Only Max Mallowan's comments, and Christie's autobiography, which discusses Greenway in some detail, have provided the clues.

Dead Man's Folly is also of interest because it contains a rare instance of an adolescent murder victim—the 14-year-old Marlene Tucker. The only other novel with youthful victims is *Hallowe'en Party* (#75, 1969).

When Dame Agatha died in 1976, she was buried in St. Mary's Churchyard, Cholsey, Berkshire, a site she chose herself ten years before she died, according to her biographer, Gwen Robyns. She wanted the headstone on her grave to be simple and in keeping with her style in life. On the stone is her name and age, and underneath the simple phrase *Agatha Christie the writer*. Also on the tombstone is a favorite verse of Christie's, from Edmund Spenser's *The Faerie Queene:*

> Sleepe after toyle,
> Port after stormie seas,
> Ease after warre,
> Death after life,
> Does greatly please.

Christie quotes those lines in *Dead Man's Folly,* at the end of chapter 4. Mrs. Folliat, the former mistress of Nasse House (Greenway) who had to sell the house and now lives in the small lodge on the grounds, is talking to Poirot during a walk. She bemoans the loss of the big house, but rather stoically points out that she "was always very fond" of the lodge. Poirot remarks that he is glad she has found a haven, to which she replies with the Spenser quote.

In celebration of the author's seventy-fifth birthday in 1965, Christie's longtime publisher, Collins, began a collected edition of her works, titled The Greenway Edition, after Greenway House. The first four titles issued were *The Murder of Roger Ackroyd* (#7, 1926), *The Labours of Hercules* (#47, 1947), *Crooked House* (#50, 1949), and *A Murder Is Announced* (#52, 1950). Christie celebrated a personal triumph in 1956, when she was made Commander of the British Empire (CBE).

The dedication for this book was "To Humphrey and Peggie Trevelyan."

Max Mallowan attended Lancing, a public school (that is to say, a British private school) from 1917 to 1921. One of his contemporaries (along with Evelyn Waugh, the author of *Brideshead Revisited*) was Humphrey Trevelyan. Many years after their public school days, Lord Trevelyan became chairman of the British Museum. Max served as a trustee of the Museum during this period. The Mallowans and the Trevelyans, then, had a friendship of long standing, and the two men a close professional association during the later years of Sir Max's long and distinguished archaeological career.

The reviews of *Dead Man's Folly* were mixed. Anthony Boucher wrote in the *New York Times:* "The infallibly original Agatha Christie has come up, once again, with a new and highly ingenious puzzle-construction" (11/4/56). James Sandoe wrote in *Books* (*New York Herald Tribune*): "The new Poirot and welcome enough for all that it exhibits Agatha Christie in a relatively lethargic mood, depending upon a very showy set of explanations" (11/18/56).

The *Times Literary Supplement* (London): "The solution is of the colossal ingenuity we have been conditioned to expect but a number of the necessary red herrings are either unexplained or a little too grossly *ad hoc.* . . . What should be the real appeal of *Dead Man's Folly,* however, is not much better than its logic. The scene is really excessively commonplace, there are too many characters and they are very, very flat" (12/21/56). The reviewer for the *Manchester Guardian* was less loquacious. Francis Iles wrote, "A minor Christie" (12/7/56).

PLOT:

While dictating to his secretary, Miss Lemon, Hercule Poirot receives a telephone call from his old acquaintance Ariadne Oliver. In her "booming contralto," Mrs. Oliver, of the "windswept gray hair . . . and eagle profile," demands that the eminent solver of mysteries take the next train to Nasse House, Nassecombe, Devon, where she is a houseguest.

Instead of finding Ariadne Oliver embroiled in a sordid murder, Poirot finds her organizing a murder hunt—rather like a treasure hunt—as part of a charity fete being held on the grounds at Nasse House. Along with the gypsy fortune tellers, the food and game stalls, the celebrity appearances, there is to be a mock mystery, complete with clues hidden about the grounds, all leading the successful amateur detective to a "victim" hidden in the boathouse. The "victim" chosen by Mrs. Oliver is a sniffling but well-developed teenager named Marlene Tucker. Marlene's job will be to loll about the boathouse, scene of the "crime," and read comic books until someone successfully traces the clues to her.

Poirot finds all this amusing, if silly, until Mrs. Oliver confesses that she hasn't sent for him foolishly. She suspects, if only intuitively, that something is wrong about the whole affair. It seems that she is not totally in charge of how the murder hunt is being run—there is a hint here, a suggestion there, all from various parties involved in organizing the bazaar, that make her think she is being used as a "front" for something much more serious than a game.

Mrs. Oliver's worst fears are realized, for on the day of the fete, hosted by the wealthy Sir George Stubbs and his not-too-bright but very ambitious wife, Hattie, there is a murder amidst all the festivities: Marlene Tucker, who is to be the mock victim in the murder game, becomes a real victim.

Poirot, with Mrs. Oliver in tow, is thrown into the investigation full-force—it is they who discover the body, and they set about unraveling just how much the murder hunt had to do with the real thing.

Principal Characters: Superintendent Baldwin, Amanda Brewis, Etienne De Sousa, Elsa, Amy Folliat, James Folliat, Alec Legge, Peggy Legge, Felicity Lemon, Connie Masterton, Mrs. Merdell,

Mrs. Ariadne Oliver, Hercule Poirot, Sir George Stubbs, Lady Hattie Stubbs, Marlene Tucker, Captain Jim Warburton, Michael Weyman.

First Editions: British: Collins, London, November 1956. 256 pp., 12s. 6d. **American:** Dodd, Mead & Co., New York, 1956. 216 pp., $2.95.

Adaptation: None.

62

4.50 FROM PADDINGTON / WHAT MRS. McGILLICUDDY SAW! (1957)

In *4.50 from Paddington,* Christie returned to one of her more successful and popular themes—a murder that involves a large family. Christie used this type of story in her first book, *The Mysterious Affair at Styles* (#1, 1920), and continued with it (with varying degrees of success) in such books as *Hercule Poirot's Christmas* (#32, 1938), *Crooked House* (#50, 1949), and *A Pocket Full of Rye* (#58, 1953).

One of the best of the late Christies, the *4.50 from Paddington* features Miss Marple, frail but alert as ever, at the point in her detective career when she needed someone younger to do legwork and to help her with her snooping (the dear old spinster must have been between 95 and 100 years old). So Christie created one of the most independent women in all her novels, the marvelous, Oxford-educated, thirty-two-year-old Lucy Eyelesbarrow.

Lucy loves money, and earned quite a bit of it "to the amazement of her friends and fellow scholars" when she "entered the field of domestic labour." Lucy, who was brilliant, "had taken a First in Mathematics at Oxford," and everyone thought she would pursue a distinguished academic career. But Lucy had other plans; she knew efficient domestic service was at an ebb, and with her qualifications and intelligence she would be able to earn a bundle of money in the domestic field. She was proved correct. Her services were in demand, and she could afford to pick and choose any situation that suited her. She first met Miss Marple when she was engaged by Raymond West, Miss Marple's novelist nephew, to take care of his dear Aunt Jane who was recovering from a bout of pneumonia. They liked each other immediately, each recognizing the other's deep intelligence. So when Miss Marple decided she needed help to search for a body thrown from a train, Lucy came to mind. Intrigued by the situation, Lucy was only too glad to assist.

These two worked so well together in this novel that they

should have been utilized by Christie in future books. Anthony Boucher agreed, as is evident from his review in the *New York Times:* "But the diminution of physical strength and energy obliges [Miss Marple] to rely on an efficient young legwoman, Lucy Eyelesbarrow—and I see no reason why this newly inaugurated team of Marple and Eyelesbarrow should not flourish as long as that of Wolfe and Goodwin [Nero Wolfe and his secretary Archie Goodwin]" (11/24/57).

With Lucy being so well received by the critics and fans, one has to wonder why Christie didn't continue to use her. One reason could be that at this point in Christie's career she just didn't want to bother with the development of another character. Besides, Lucy had competition from Inspector Craddock, who was first on hand in *A Murder Is Announced* (#52, 1950) to assist Miss Marple, and who makes an appearance in this book.

In future adventures, as Marple advanced still further in age, Christie usually confined her activities to limited areas and places so as not to overtax her, and in these books she usually had a co-detective or ally who could assist her with the physical detective work. Lucy is among the best of these.

An adaptation of this book was made into the 1962 MGM film titled *Murder She Said,* with the delightful English character actress Dame Margaret Rutherford portraying Miss Marple. Christie was not pleased with the choice of Miss Rutherford.*

There's an interesting point concerning the time of departure of Mrs. McGillicuddy's train at Paddington Station. In all the American editions of this book (American title: *What Mrs. McGillicuddy Saw!*), the train is listed as the 4.54 for Brackhampton, Milchester, etc. (see first page of the novel). However, in all the British editions of this book, the same train is leaving Paddington Station at 4.50 (as indicated in the title and on the first page of the British edition).

To find out why the departure time was different in these editions, we contacted Christie's American publishers, Dodd, Mead. According to them, on the original manuscript that Dodd, Mead

---

* For Christie's opinions on the film and Rutherford portraying Miss Marple refer to *The Mirror Crack'd from Side to Side* (#68, 1962) and also Part Two of this book.

received, the time was 4.54, and the original title was to be *4.54 from Paddington*. However, at the last minute Collins, Christie's English publisher, decided to change the title to *4.50 from Paddington*. When Collins notified Dodd, Mead of this last-minute change, it was too late for Dodd, Mead to make any corrections, since the manuscript had already gone to press. It's been the 4.54 ever since in all the American editions.*

The reviews were very favorable. The *Times Literary Supplement* (London) wrote, "Without the female of the species, indeed, detective fiction would be in a bad way, for the classical puzzle of crime rarely poses itself without being entangled with the romantic puzzle of love. The latter, however, is not allowed to interfere with the intellectual processes of the redoubtable Miss Marple. In *4.50 from Paddington* that admirable woman investigates the story told her by Mrs. McGillicuddy, witness of the strangling of one passenger by another in a train running momentarily parallel with her own. The necessary field work being beyond Miss Marple's powers, she seeks the assistance of a young prodigy called Lucy Eyelesbarrow [who] proves herself an able observer on the best Marplesian lines . . . Miss Christie never harrows her readers, being content to intrigue and amuse them" (11/29/57).

Christopher Pym in the *Spectator* said, "Miss Christie is always readable—even in this story of a murder in one train seen from another, and solved by a dear old drinker of cowslip wine" (11/22/57). And James Sandoe, writing in the *New York Herald Tribune:* "Agatha Christie's latest is precisely what one expects: the most delicious bamboozling possible in a babble of bright talk and a comprehensive bristle of suspicion all adeptly managed to keep you much too alert elsewhere to see the neat succession of clues that catch a murderer we never so much as thought of" (11/24/57).

PLOT:

Short, stout, matronly Elspeth McGillicuddy—down from Scotland for a holiday—is at Paddington Station, London, preparing to board the 4.50 train for Brackhampton, then by connecting

---

*This difference in the time of the train has no bearing on the plot structure.

train and car to St. Mary Mead, where she is staying with her old friend Jane Marple. Breathless and burdened with Christmas parcels, Elspeth settles into an empty first-class compartment on the lightly traveled 4.50. Not long after leaving a station, the 4.50 comes parallel to another train moving in the same direction on the adjoining track.

As the trains move into parallel motion, "giving the illusion of being stationary," the blind in one of the first-class compartments of the opposite carriage flies up. Mrs. McGillicuddy is startled to see a man with his back to the window, with his hands around the neck of a woman facing him. He is "slowly, remorselessly, strangling her." The body goes limp as Elspeth watches.

Elspeth, sensible woman that she is, collects her wits in the moments from the murder to the ticket taker's appearance at the door of her compartment. She informs him of what she has seen—he looks "extremely doubtful"—and gives him her address in Scotland, in order that she can be contacted by the authorities when the crime is discovered. At Brackhampton Station, where she is to change for the connection to Market Basing, she writes a note to the stationmaster, reporting the incident.

Elspeth arrives in St. Mary Mead and at the door of Jane Marple's house. On seeing her old friend, she can only wail, "Oh, Jane . . . I've just seen a murder!"

Jane, who believes "a true lady can neither be shocked nor surprised," merely replies, "Most distressing for you, Elspeth . . . you had better tell me about it at once."

After hearing Mrs. McGillicuddy's story, Jane suggests they wait to read the morning papers. But there is no word of the crime in the news. Even when Jane enlists the aid of Inspector Cornish, he is unable to discover any hint of a murder on any train in the area. Elspeth's story is suspect—except to Jane Marple. However, Jane decides the best thing for Elspeth to do is go on to Ceylon to spend the holidays with her son. In the meantime, she will do a bit of poking about herself, with the help of her clever young friend Lucy Eyelesbarrow, to try and discover just exactly what Mrs. McGillicuddy saw.

Principal Characters: Alfred Crackenthorpe, Lady Alice Crackenthorpe, Cedric Crackenthorpe, Emma Crackenthorpe, Harold

Crackenthorpe, Luther Crackenthorpe, Martin Crackenthorpe, Chief Inspector Dermit Craddock, Alexander Eastley, Bryan Eastley, Lucy Eyelesbarrow, Florence Hill, Madame Joliet, Mrs. Kidder, Jane Marple, Elspeth McGillicuddy, Dr. Quimper, James Stoddart-West, Anna Stravinska, David West.

First Editions: British: Collins, London, November 1957. 256 pp., 12s. 6d. **American:** with U.S. title *What Mrs. McGillicuddy Saw!:* Dodd, Mead & Co., New York, 1957. 192 pp., $2.95.

Adaptation: The film based on this novel titled *Murder She Said* was released in 1962. This was the first of the four Miss Marple movies to star Dame Margaret Rutherford.

63

ORDEAL BY INNOCENCE (1958)

This is among the handful of books that Christie mentioned as her personal favorites, though, as is usual, she gives no reasons why. It seems an unlikely choice, since *Ordeal by Innocence* has no particular features that leap out at the reader. Neither Poirot nor Marple is on hand, and there is no brilliant, unconventional device in the solution such as is found in *The Murder of Roger Ackroyd* (#7, 1926), *Ten Little Niggers* (#35, 1939), or *Curtain* (#82, 1975). What *Ordeal by Innocence* does have is a fairly conventional murder-in-retrospect plot with better than usual depiction of family tensions. The book is also notable for the use of amnesia as a crucial plot device—a weak device at that, but one which may account for Christie's fondness for the book, since she used amnesia to account for her own disappearance from her home in December 1926.

The detective in the book is Dr. Arthur Calgary, a physician who recovers from a period of amnesia to find that young Jacko Argyle has been unjustly convicted of murder because Calgary, who could have given Jacko an alibi, had lost his memory the night of the murder. Calgary is typical of the detectives Christie creates for one-time use in the non-Poirot, non-Marple books. He is not a professional detective, or a law officer, but an ordinary man who by chance is brought in contact with murder and who, by dint of a previously unknown aptitude for detection, manages to unravel the case. Calgary as a detective character is similar in these respects to Haywood in *Crooked House* (#50, 1949). Since the two are not professionals, it is interesting that Christie allows them a personal involvement in the case: Calgary feels guilty because his alibi might have saved Jacko Argyle; Haywood is in love with Sophia Leonides.

The book is set in fictional Drymouth, seven miles along the coastal road from Redquay. This location is actually the Devon coast, near Torquay, where Agatha was born. The Rubicon, which the characters in the book cross by ferry to reach the Argyle home, Sunny Point, is probably modeled on the river Dart, which empties into the Channel west of Torquay. During the last decades of her life, when *Ordeal by Innocence* was written, Christie's principal home was Greenway, a Georgian house overlooking the Dart near the coast. Like Sunny Point, Greenway House was used as a refuge for children evacuated from London during the blitz.

Christie usually wrote in the spring or summer, completing a manuscript in six to eight weeks. If *Ordeal* was written in the summer of 1958, it was probably written at Greenway House. However, we know from Christie's autobiography that she often wrote in the Middle East while on archaeological expeditions, and it is possible that *Ordeal* was written while Christie was in Nimrud and Baghdad, Iraq, during the digging season of October 1957–April 1958. If so, this would make *Ordeal* Christie's last book written in the Middle East, since 1958 was the year Max Mallowan completed his excavations at Nimrud and he and his wife discontinued their annual journeys there.

Critical opinion varied. James Sandoe in the *New York Herald Tribune Book Review* said, "We are so certain of her that it would probably be enough merely to mention that there is a new Agatha Christie. But *Ordeal by Innocence,* as sure and adroit as we knew it would be, as skillful in deploying suspicion, as surprising after all, has the particular distinction of presenting a new if presumably temporary detective in place of Poirot or Miss Marple" (3/29/59).

"Once more Mrs. Christie's skill in puzzle-making and story-telling is so consummate that we never think of missing the little Belgian octogenarian," wrote Anthony Boucher in the *New York Times*. "And yet it would be so nice to have a new Poirot novel . . . The book is unusually long for a Christie and may sag a bit in the middle, but family tensions and suspicions are adroitly handled, and the solution is characteristically surprising, trickily constructed and yet firmly based in character" (3/15/59). "The suspects . . . are not a very gripping bunch," wrote the *New Yorker,* "but Miss Christie, as tricky and inventive as ever, keeps us with them to the end" (4/11/59).

The *Times Literary Supplement* (London): "The solution of

Ordeal by Innocence is certainly not below the level of Mrs. Christie's customary ingenuity, but the book lacks other qualities which her readers have come to expect. What has become of the blitheness, the invigorating good spirits with which the game of detection is played in so many of her stories? *Ordeal by Innocence* slips out of that cheerful arena into something much too like an attempt at psychological fiction. It is too much of a conversation piece and too many people are talking—people in whom it is hard to take the necessary amount of interest because there is not space enough to establish them. The kind of workmanship that has been lavished on this tale is not a kind in which the author excels and the reader feels that Miss Marple and Poirot would thoroughly disapprove of the whole business" (12/12/58).

Christie dedicated the book "To Billy Collins with Affection and Gratitude." William Collins, Jr. was for many years head of William Collins Sons & Co., Ltd., the publishing firm founded in Glasgow in 1814 by his grandfather. It was Billy Collins who offered Agatha the contract that lured her from John Lane/The Bodley Head, which published Christie's first six books. Her relationship with Collins began in 1926 with *The Murder of Roger Ackroyd* (#7, 1926) and continued until her death in 1976. William Collins Sons & Co., Ltd. is to this day Christie's publisher.

PLOT:

When Rachel Konstam and Leo Argyle were married, they decided to devote their time, and her large fortune, to helping the less fortunate in the world, especially children. To this end during World War II their home, Sunny Point, became a refuge for children from London endangered by the blitz. The Argyles themselves were childless, and they compassionately adopted five of the Sunny Point refugees—abandoned, emotionally disturbed, half-caste—and devoted their lives to giving their children the best that money could buy.

Jacko Argyle especially was a problem—a classic delinquent. One November night Jacko asked his mother for money, which she refused, and he was heard arguing with her and threatening her. Shortly afterward, Mrs. Argyle was killed by a blow from a poker, and Jacko was arrested for the murder. Jacko's feeble alibi was that he had hitchhiked from Sunny Point to Drymouth after leaving his mother, but as he was unable to produce the driver who had given him a lift, Jacko was sentenced to life. He died in prison a few months later of pneumonia.

The Rachel Argyle tragedy is a year and a half old when Dr. Arthur Calgary, a geophysicist, returns to England from an expedition to Antarctica. Dr. Calgary actually *did* pick up Jacko the night of the murder, at the time the youth claimed. Unfortunately for Jacko, that same night Dr. Calgary was hit by a lorry, and suffered a concussion which brought on partial amnesia—he could remember nothing of that evening. Physically recovered, Calgary went to the Antarctic, and never heard a word of the Argyle case. Back in England months later, he happens on Jacko's picture in some old newspapers, along with the boy's story, and realizes that he was the man in the youth's hitchhiking story. Calgary goes to the police, who investigate the doctor's amnesia story and pronounce it valid. Though it's too late for Jacko, Calgary goes to reassure the family that the boy was innocent of his mother's murder. What Calgary doesn't take into account is that Jacko's innocence means someone else in the household killed Rachel Argyle.

Principal Characters: Christina Argyle, Hester Argyle, Jack "Jacko" Argyle, Leo Argyle, Michael Argyle, Rachel Argyle, Dr. Arthur Calgary, Joe Clegg, Maureen Clegg, Dr. Donal Craig, Mary Durrant, Philip Durrant, Major Finney, Superintendent Huish, Kirsten Lindstrom, Andrew Marshall.

First Editions: **British**: Collins, London, November 1958. 256 pp., 12s. 6d. **American**: Dodd, Mead & Co., New York, 1959. 247 pp., $2.95.

Adaptation: None.

64

CAT AMONG THE PIGEONS (1959)

Cat Among the Pigeons, written when Christie was almost seventy, is a successful combination of an above-average thriller with a conventional detective story. The skillful plotting and strong characterization set this book apart from most of Christie's thrillers and make it one of the best of her later books.

The story begins in Ramat, a small, rich Arab country, as events there set the stage for murder at Meadowbank, an exclusive girls' school in England. The international-intrigue element of *Cat Among the Pigeons* is strongly influenced by the atmosphere of world unrest and cold war in the 1950s, and lands Poirot in his first thriller since *The Big Four* (#8, 1927), thirty-two years before.

Cat Among the Pigeons has an array of memorable characters. Eileen Rich stands out as the eccentric English teacher. Likewise Miss Chadwick, the faithful "Chaddy," who helped start Meadowbank, who was so much a part of the school that Meadowbank without her would be hard to imagine. Then there's Honoria Bulstrode, the "tall, and rather noble looking" Headmistress, who was the intellectual and spiritual force behind the successful school.

Mrs. Upjohn is the most memorable of all. A parent of one of the students, she did intelligence work during the war—and loved it. Postwar excitement for Mrs. Upjohn is traveling by bus to exotic places. At the time of the murders at Meadowbank, Mrs. Upjohn is on a bus trip through Anatolia. Interestingly, Mrs. Upjohn is a good friend of Maureen Summerhayes of *Mrs. McGinty's Dead,* and a passing reference is made about Maureen to Poirot, who certainly remembered her (see #55, 1952).

Christie introduced a more serious character in this novel—the mysterious Mr. Robinson. He didn't look English, "He was not definitely Jewish, nor definitely Greek nor Portuguese nor Spanish, nor South American." Mr. Robinson, who spoke with no accent ". . . was fat and well dressed, with a yellow face, melancholy dark eyes, a broad forehead, and a generous mouth that displayed rather over-large very white teeth."

Mr. Robinson says of himself, "I'm just a man who knows about money . . . and the things that branch off from money, you know . . ." Mr. Robinson, a member of a financial syndicate called the Arrangers, also plays a role in a Marple novel, *At Bertram's Hotel* (#71, 1965), a Tommy and Tuppence novel, *Postern of Fate* (#80, 1973), and the thriller *Passenger to Frankfurt* (#76, 1970). He is notable as the only character who appears with all of Christie's major detectives.

In her autobiography Christie made no reference to this character or the reasons she created him and used him in four novels. In any case, Mr. Robinson was honest, as he tells Poirot: "We are, how shall I put it, the Arrangers behind the scenes. For kings, for presidents, for politicians . . . We work in with one another and remember this: we keep faith. Our profits are large but we are honest . . ."

Robinson was a convenient link for those in search of information, and his appearances in this and the other novels could be explained as one who tied certain facts together to help in the solving of the crimes. In three of the Robinson books, *Cat Among the Pigeons, Passenger to Frankfurt,* and *Postern of Fate,* another minor character appears who has a link with Robinson; he is Colonel Ephraim Pikeaway, the head of the Special Branch in England, and he has the utmost respect for the talents and tactics of Mr. Robinson.

A note of interest concerning Poirot and his apartment:

Did Christie goof? Or did Poirot move? Poirot for years lived in an apartment in Whitehaven Mansions, London. In this book he's residing at 228 Whitehouse Mansions. Years later, in *Elephants Can Remember* (#79, 1972), he's a tenant at Whitefriars Mansions.

Anthony Boucher in his review in the *New York Times:* "To read Agatha Christie at her best is to experience the rarefied pleasure of watching a faultless technician at work, and she is in top form in *Cat Among the Pigeons* . . ." (3/27/60). The *Times Literary Supplement* (London) wrote: "Mrs. Christie comes out strong again with *Cat Among the Pigeons,* another of her blithe detective stories . . ." (12/18/59). Ralph Partridge complained in the *New Statesman* "There is no plum, worse luck, this year in the Christie pudding, although it contains almost every stock ingredient from the thriller cupboard . . ." (11/28/59). Christopher Pym in his review in the *Spectator* had some very sharp comments: "If Miss Christie believes that the press would play that murder down, she will believe anything. But it is nothing to what she asks us to believe . . . How did we ever come to take Miss Christie seriously?" (11/6/59).

Christie's dedication for this book was "For Stella and Larry Kirwan."

PLOT:

It's the opening of the summer session at Meadowbank, an exclusive school for girls, presided over regally by Miss Bulstrode and her vicereines, the Misses Vansittart and Chadwick. Along with the predictable complement of upper-middle-class and upper-class girls, there are a few more exotic and glamorous students: a Swedish princess, and Princess Shaista, daughter of a Middle East emir.

Two months prior to the first day of the summer term, the Middle East nation of Ramat is shaken by a revolution, and the progressive, Western-educated Prince Ali is overthrown by extremists. Just as the government is about to collapse, Prince Ali meets with his private pilot Bob Rawlinson, a Britisher. To Rawlinson he entrusts the task of smuggling a valuable cache of jewels out of Ramat and to Europe, where Ali has "a man who deals with such matters for me. That is, in case I should not survive."

Rawlinson, rather overwhelmed by the trust and the burden, returns to his hotel and calls the embassy, where he leaves a cryptic message for one of the undersecretaries. He then scrawls a harmless note to his sister, Joan Sutcliffe, who is visiting Ramat with her daughter, Jennifer. When Joan and Jennifer return to the hotel, however, they find that the British Embassy has ordered them to leave Ramat at once for England . . . without even a chance to say good-bye to brother Bob.

Weeks later, after traveling by slow boat, Joan and Jennifer are back in England and Jennifer is enrolled at Meadowbank School. But it's hardly a calm term. First, there is the news that the government of Ramat, one of the "richest states in the Middle East," has fallen, and that her uncle Bob and Prince Ali, ruler of Ramat, whom her classmate Shaista was the cousin of, have been killed in a plane crash in the Arolez Mountains, trying to escape from the revolution. Then there is the messy business of Miss Springer, the unpopular games mistress, being shot dead one night in the sports pavilion, and Miss Chadwick being coshed as well, and some of the lockers being rifled. There is a dangerous cat among the studious young pigeons of Meadowbank, but only when Julia Upjohn, a friend and classmate of Jennifer, calls in Poirot does the cat lose its claws.

Principal Characters: Prince Ali Yusuf, Angèle Blanche, Honoria Bulstrode, Alice Calder, Miss Chadwick, John Edmundson, Adam Goodman, Detective Inspector Kelsey, Colonel Ephraim Pikeaway, Dennis Rathbone, Squadron Leader Bob Rawlinson, Eileen Rich, Mr. Robinson, Miss Rowan, Princess Shaista, Anne Shapland, Grace Springer, Jennifer Sutcliffe, Joan Sutcliffe, Mrs. Upjohn, Julia Upjohn, Eleanor Vansittart.

First Editions: **British**: Collins, London, November 1959. 255 pp., 12s. 6d. **American**: Dodd, Mead & Co., New York, 1960. 224 pp., $2.95.

Adaptation: None.

65

THE ADVENTURE OF THE CHRISTMAS PUDDING AND A SELECTION OF ENTREES (1960)

By 1960, the annual "Christie for Christmas" had become an inviolable tradition for the reading public. However, for reasons that are not known, in 1960 the author broke her stride: there was no new Christie novel between *Cat Among the Pigeons* (#64), the Christmas Christie for 1959, and *The Pale Horse* (#67), in November 1961.

Instead, Collins, Christie's publisher, took one longish new Poirot tale, which they used for the title story, and published it with a grab bag of five older stories. The single Marple story in the collection, "Greenshaw's Folly," made its first appearance since its magazine publication in 1957. "Four and Twenty Blackbirds" and "The Under Dog" had been reprinted in the American collections *Three Blind Mice and Other Stories* (#51, 1950) and *The Under Dog and Other Stories* (#54, 1951), respectively.

"The Dream," a supernatural tale, had appeared in 1939 in *The Regatta Mystery* (#34), as had "The Mystery of the Spanish Chest." The latter, in this collection, appears in a longer and presumably later version; in the older version the chest was made in Baghdad and not on the Iberian peninsula.

As if to make up to her readers that they weren't getting a brand-new, full-length book in their Christmas stockings, Christie went to the unusual length of writing a foreword to the collection.* In its page and a quarter the author enthusiastically (there are *ten* exclamation points) emphasizes the holiday setting of the title story; she likens the selection of tales to a sequence of courses in a Christmas dinner. She then goes on to reminisce a bit about her youthful holidays, spent at Abney, the Victorian estate belonging to the family of her brother-in-law James Watts, where Agatha

* Christie wrote a foreword to *Cards on the Table* (#27, 1936) to explain the unusual restrictions imposed on the mystery by the bridge game. She also included an Author's Note to *Death Comes as the End* (#44, 1945) to explain the historical setting.

and her mother spent Christmases after the death of Agatha's father.

She closes by saying, "So let me dedicate this book to the memory of Abney Hall—its kindness and its hospitality. And a happy Christmas to all who read this book."

Abney had earlier been used as the setting for murder in *After the Funeral* (#57, 1953). When Christie used the house again for the setting of the title story of this collection, she recreated the traditional Victorian-Edwardian holiday she had enjoyed at Abney as a girl. In *An Autobiography,* Christie gives a description of Christmas at Abney, circa 1912, and reveals that it was the model for the feast in her story.

> Christmas was the Supreme Festival, something never to be forgotten. Christmas stockings in bed. Breakfast when everyone had a separate chair heaped with presents. Then a rush to Church and back to continue present opening. At two o'clock Christmas dinner, the blinds drawn down and glittering ornaments and lights. First, oyster soup . . . turbot, then boiled turkey, roast turkey and a large roast sirloin of beef. This was followed by plum pudding, mince pies and a trifle full of sixpences . . . After that, again, innumerable kinds of dessert . . . It is one of those things that I am sure will never be seen again in this generation; indeed, I doubt nowadays if anyone's digestion would stand it. However, *our* digestions stood it quite well.

The *Times Literary Supplement* (London) was less than enthusiastic about the collection. "Miss Agatha Christie has given us so much pleasure over the years that she deserves our indulgence; and it would be idle to deny that some indulgence is needed. The short story length never did suit her well. The six stories which comprise *The Adventure of the Christmas Pudding* . . . are none of them very distinguished; their solutions are inclined to be either guessable or incredible, if not both. Miss Christie's charm lies, not in concise plotting, but in a familiar chintz-and-coziness; and short stories are too constricting. Only the title story itself comes close to being an exception. Into this story, as she tells us herself in a foreword, Miss Christie has poured nostalgic memories of her own

Childhood Christmasses [sic]. Poirot's little grey cells may not be unduly exercised but there is irresistible simplicity and buoyancy of a Christmas treat about it all. To attack Miss Christie would be like blocking the chimney against Santa Claus" (11/18/60).

PLOTS:
"The Adventure of the Christmas Pudding"

Mr. Jesmond, a member of a "very discreet" branch of the police, asks Poirot to spend the Christmas holiday at Kings Lacey, the country house of the Lacey family. Poirot is supposed to be a mere houseguest, though his real purpose, as outlined by Mr. Jesmond, is to investigate the theft of a valuable ruby belonging to the heir to the throne of "a rich and important native State." This prince has lost his heirloom to a young woman, one of his romantic dalliances, who has allowed herself to be wined and dined by the foreign prince for the sole purpose of absconding with the jewel. Mr. Jesmond's "very discreet" branch of the law know that the theft is somehow bound up with Kings Lacey, but it is to be Poirot's job to solve the case—without causing any international political scandal.

Poirot goes to the Laceys', where he experiences a traditional English country Christmas, centering on the gargantuan Christmas Day meal. In the meantime, he is challenged with solving two problems: the theft of the ruby, and the courtship of Edwina Morecombe, the Laceys' granddaughter, by the charming but thoroughly unsuitable Desmond Lee-Wortley. A practical joke in the form of a mock murder only complicates the situation.

"The Mystery of the Spanish Chest"

A longer version of "The Mystery of the Baghdad Chest" published in *The Regatta Mystery and Other Stories* (#34, 1939).

"The Under Dog"

Published in *The Under Dog and Other Stories* (#54, 1951).

"Four and Twenty Blackbirds"

Published in *Three Blind Mice and Other Stories* (#51, 1950).

"The Dream"

Published in *The Regatta Mystery and Other Stories* (#34, 1939).

"Greenshaw's Folly"

Raymond West, the novelist nephew of Jane Marple, is visiting the countryside with literary critic Horace Binder, whose hobby is collecting architectural and artistic monstrosities on film. West takes Binder to Greenshaw's Folly, a hideously eclectic mid-Victorian mansion still occupied by the last of the Greenshaws, a spinster. While on the grounds the two men encounter Miss Greenshaw, who asks them to witness her new will, which leaves everything to her housekeeper.

The spinster mentions that she would like someone to edit her grandfather's diaries for publication; West later suggests to his wife's niece Louisa that she apply for the job, which she does. Shortly after Louisa begins work at the mansion, she is witness to the brutal murder-by-arrow of Miss Greenshaw. Alfred, the lazy gardening boy, who is an archery buff, is accused, though it takes Jane Marple's acute perceptions to discover the truth about Miss Greenshaw's murder.

First Editions: British: Collins, London, October 1960. 255 pp., 12s. 6d. **American:** None.

Adaptation: None.

66

DOUBLE SIN AND OTHER STORIES (1961)

An American collection of eight stories, *Double Sin* includes four stories from the 1920s, and the rest from the mid-to-late fifties. The collection includes four Poirot, two Marple, and two supernatural stories.

"The Dressmaker's Doll" (a 1958 magazine story) and "The Last Séance," resurrected from *The Hound of Death* (#18, 1933), both deal with the supernatural.

"The Theft of the Royal Ruby" is none other than the title story of the British collection *The Adventure of the Christmas Pudding* (#65, 1960)—another of those inexplicable title changes that occur too often when Christie's works cross the Atlantic.

"Sanctuary" (reprinted here in book form after a 1954 magazine publication) marks one of Marple's appearances in this collection. It is of special interest to fans of *A Murder Is Announced* (#52, 1950), for it features some of the same inhabitants of Chipping Cleghorn, including the Rev. Julian Harmon, his wife Bunch, and Tiglash Pileser, their cat.

American critics, like their English counterparts, generally thought that these collections were not the best Christie, while adopting the attitude that "any Christie is better than none at all." They seem to long for the days when a major Christie could be counted on to show up at the booksellers every year or so, with only slightly-less-than-major mysteries in her "off" years.

Anthony Boucher in the *New York Times* pronounced *Double Sin* "Grade-B Christie, or possibly B-plus" (9/24/61), while James Sandoe in *Books* (*New York Herald Tribune*) lamented, "The short story is not really Agatha Christie's forte. . . . In lieu of a new novel and as the only 'new' Christie, this odd sorting is pleasant for all of its unevenness" (7/30/61).

Always able to find at least one enthusiastic critic treading water in a sea of lukewarm reviews, Christie was praised by L. G. Offord in the *San Francisco Chronicle:* "Eight beautiful specimens of Christie art, dated from 1925 on. Poirot is still in most of them, but there are two expert little horror stories to lend variety. 'The Theft of the Royal Ruby' . . . has the agreeably light touch that Christie can employ so well" (8/27/61).

PLOTS:

"Double Sin"

Poirot and Hastings are asked by theatrical agent Joseph Aarons, an old friend of Poirot's, to visit him at the resort of Charlock Bay. On the train, they meet young Mary Durrant, who is carrying a case of valuable miniatures to show to a prospective buyer. When the miniatures are stolen from the case, Mary asks for Poirot's help.

"Wasps' Nest"

Poirot pays a surprise visit to old acquaintance John Harrison at the latter's home, only to inform his surprised host that he is there to investigate a murder—a murder that has not yet taken place, and that may involve Harrison himself.

"The Theft of the Royal Ruby"

A slightly altered version of "The Adventure of the Christmas Pudding," published in the British collection of the same name (#65, 1960).

"The Dressmaker's Doll"

Dressmakers Sybil Fox and Alicia Coombe have a limp velvet-suited decorative doll in their shop. It's a toy which seems to have some rather sinister traits and abilities.

"Greenshaw's Folly"

Published in *The Adventure of the Christmas Pudding* (#65, 1960).

"The Double Clue"

Effete, cultured collector Marcus Hardman calls Poirot in great distress when his prized cache of medieval jewels is stolen from his wall safe.

"The Last Séance"

Published in *The Hound of Death* (#18, 1933).

"Sanctuary"

In Chipping Cleghorn, the vicar's wife, Bunch Harmon, finds a dying man in the church when she goes in to arrange flowers for the week's services. The bloody man weakly murmurs a cryptic, "sanctuary," before being taken to the doctor's house, where he dies. The evidence at first points to suicide, but Bunch's friend Jane Marple rightly deduces that the facts add up to foul play.

First Editions: British: None. **American:** Dodd, Mead & Co., New York, 1961. 247 pp., $3.50.

Adaptation: None.

67

THE PALE HORSE (1961)

The Pale Horse is generally mentioned by Christie as one of her favorite books. The title refers to the Revelation of St. John the Divine, chapter 6, verse 8.

> "And I looked, and behold a pale horse: and his name that sat on him was Death, and Hell followed with him . . ."

The forces of the Divine must have blessed this book because there are three known cases in which the symptoms of thallium poisoning (which is the murder method used in this book) were recognized, and lives saved, because of the quick thinking of individuals who just happened to have read *The Pale Horse*. Thallium is "a sparsely but widely distributed poisonous metallic element that resembles lead in physical properties and is used chiefly in the form of compounds in photoelectric cells or as a pesticide" (*Webster's New Collegiate Dictionary,* 1980). This particular poison, which Christie uses so effectively in this book, was suggested to her by a doctor in the United States. Christie's knowledge of poisons and their deadly results was always scientifically accurate.

One case which Max Mallowan relates in his memoirs concerns a woman in a Latin American country. Agatha Christie received a letter dated June 15, 1975, from a woman who recognized the attempted murder of a man whose wife was administering poison in small doses over a long period of time. The letter in part said, "But of this I am quite, quite certain—had I not read *The Pale Horse* and thus learned of the effects of thallium poisoning, X would not have survived; it was only the prompt medication which saved him; and the doctors, even if he had gone to the hospital, would not have known in time what his trouble was. With my sincere regards and admiration . . ."

Another incident concerned a nineteen-month-old baby girl who was dying of a disease that had London doctors completely baffled. The story was related in a *New York Times* article dated June 24, 1977. This real-life drama concerning an Arab baby began in Qatar on the Persian Gulf. The baby was flown in a semiconscious state to Hammersmith Hospital in London. The baby was not responding to treatment, and death seemed imminent until Marsha Maitland, a nurse, "suggested that the infant might have been poisoned by a compound of thallium, a bluish-white metal that has poisonous salts." She said she was reading *The Pale Horse* and the symptoms of the baby "were remarkably similar to those of a thallium case in the book." Tests confirmed Nurse Maitland's diagnosis. The baby received proper treatment, and owes her life to Nurse Maitland and Agatha Christie.

But the most interesting real-life drama, and one that Christie would have done great justice to if she had written the plot for it, concerned the death of six workers at Hadlands Photographic Equipment Works in the town of Bovingdon, Hartfordshire, England. All six men died from what was known as the "Bovingdon bug" for lack of knowledge of what the real causes of death were. The symptoms were vomiting, weakness, paralysis, hallucinations, and finally death.

These "strange deaths" occurred in 1971, ten years after *The Pale Horse* was published. In Bovingdon a Scotland Yard detective lunched with Dr. Hugh Johnson, an authoritative forensic specialist. The topics discussed were "the Bovingdon bug," and the extraordinary knowledge that a twenty-four-year-old man, Frederick Graham Young, seemed to possess about the symptoms of this unusual "bug." Young was working at the plant only eleven weeks when the first death occurred, that of Robert Egle, whose assistant he was.

Dr. Johnson remembered certain passages from Christie's novel *The Pale Horse* and mentioned to the Scotland Yard detective that the symptoms of the victims might be traced to a poison called thallium. This poison had not been known in Britain before. Since they were suspicious of Young's knowledge, the police searched his flat in a Hemel Hampstead boardinghouse, where they found large quantities of thallium. Young confessed to the six murders.

When Dame Agatha was informed of the Bovingdon murders she said that she hoped "this felon hadn't read her book and learned from it." However, it's a good thing that Dr. Johnson did!

In England's West Country in the 1950s, occult societies which dealt with spiritualism, witchcraft, and other forms of black magic were a popular pastime. Christie had written occult-theme short stories very early in her career, many of which appeared in *The Hound of Death* (#18, 1933), and the popularity of occult parlor societies in the 1950s no doubt prompted her to make occultism a major part of a novel for the first time in *The Pale Horse*.

Mrs. Ariadne Oliver, who usually teams up with Hercule Poirot to solve crimes, goes solo this time around (the only time she would not be with Poirot in a novel). However, Christie does resurrect (which is unusual for her) some minor characters. Colonel John Hugh Despard and his wife, Rhoda Dawes Despard, both last appearing in *Cards on the Table* (#27, 1936), return in this book. Rhoda is a cousin to the central character of *The Pale Horse,* Mark Easterbrook. Colonel Despard has the distinction of being the only character that Christie reused in one of her books who had previously been a murder suspect. And from *The Moving Finger* (#42, 1943) comes the vicar from Much Deeping, the Reverend Caleb Dane Calthrop and his wife, Maud Dane Calthrop.

Once again Mrs. Oliver offers new insights into Agatha Christie. Although Mrs. Oliver does reflect the real Agatha Christie by her sentiments, prejudices, and likes and dislikes, she certainly does not resemble Christie in physical appearance. One cannot imagine the real Agatha Christie with disheveled gray hair carrying bags of apples and being very disorganized and dithery. Christie probably created this image of Mrs. Oliver because she imagined her fans thought of her that way, and that it would disappoint them to read about an orderly, well-kept, dignified woman like Christie. Christie herself was too quiet and shy to make a good fictional character. The colorful Mrs. Oliver is certainly more interesting.

Mrs. Oliver makes it quite clear in *The Pale Horse* that she doesn't smoke or drink (as Christie did not), but she does say, "I wish I did. Like those American detectives that always have pints of rye conveniently in their desk drawers." Mrs. Oliver, at this point in her career, had fifty-five successful murder mysteries published. Only ten or twelve behind Dame Agatha.

Christie said in her autobiography that the idea for writing *The Pale Horse* came to her about fifty years before she actually wrote it. During World War I, Christie took a pharmaceutical course on Sunday afternoons. She used to worry when making up preparations that she would have to deal with both the ordinary and the metric systems of measurement. If you made a mistake with the metric system, Christie said, the danger would be "that if you go wrong you go ten times wrong." As a young student, Christie noticed one afternoon that the pharmacist, a Mr. P., made a mistake in his instructions to Christie in the making of suppositories. His calculations were wrong and Christie was afraid to tell this well-known pharmacist about it. She said, "Mr. P. the pharmacist was the sort of person who does *not* make a mistake, especially in front of a student." To get out of the dilemma, Christie "tripped, lost my footing, upset the board on which they [the suppositories] were reposing, and *trod on them firmly*."

Mr. P. was strange indeed. He would carry a dark-colored lump of curare in his pocket. "Interesting stuff," he said, "very interesting. Taken by the mouth it does you no harm at all. Enter the bloodstream, it paralyzes and kills you." He asked Christie if she could guess the reason he carried it in his pocket. Christie, of course, had not the slightest idea. He said, "Well, you know . . . it makes me feel powerful."

After Christie finished her pharmaceutical course she wondered about Mr. P. "He struck me, in spite of his cherubic appearance, as possibly rather a dangerous man. His memory remained with me so long that it was still there waiting when I first conceived the idea of writing my book *The Pale Horse*—and that must have been, I suppose, nearly fifty years later."

Another point of interest in this book is the main character, Mark Easterbrook. He is an archaeologist trying to finish writing a book on Mongol architecture. It was during this period that Christie's husband, archaeologist Max Mallowan, was completing the writing of his book *Nimrud and Its Remains,* which was published in 1966.

The major reviews for *The Pale Horse* from both sides of the Atlantic were favorable. From Anthony Boucher in the *New York Times:* "Both the smooth, deft story-telling that the public loves and the faultless intricacy of plotting that makes her the marvel of her colleagues are splendidly evident in Mrs. Christie's *The Pale Horse*. Here she deals with an eerie, supernatural theme, such as she has employed in some fine short stories but never before in a novel . . . This is the formal detective story in all its glory—and for added pleasure, we have the company of Mrs. Ariadne Oliver, surely the most amusing self-mockery in mystery fiction" (9/30/62). The *Times Literary Supplement* (London) said, "It is not for feats of detection that we turn to [Christie], nor even, since her early *tours de force,* for the criminological ingenuity of her plots, workmanlike though they are. Her cardinal virtue is simpler and more subtle. It is sheer readability; her books can be gulped down like cream or invalid jelly. This is not a matter of good writing. Miss Christie can write abominably . . . [she] has a surprise or two in hand, of course, and a relatively convincing solution to her rather implausible mystery; but the point is that the story holds unflaggingly, and holds with a grip which is gentle as well as firm" (11/24/61).

Agatha Christie dedicated this book "To John and Helen Mildmay White—with many thanks for the opportunity given me to see justice done."

PLOT:

Scholarly Mark Easterbrook, who has taken a furnished flat in Chelsea while writing his book on "certain aspects of Mogul architecture," finds himself out of sorts with his manuscript one night, and goes out for a late-night meal. The solitary scholar wanders into Luigi's, one of Chelsea's more bohemian hangouts, complete with smoky atmosphere, a wheezing espresso machine, banana-and-bacon sandwiches, poetry readings, and unwashed patrons.

While Easterbrook is taking in this foreign atmosphere, two of the female patrons get into a hair-pulling row, one calling the other "nothing but a man stealing bitch." The brawl is broken up, but not before the victor has emerged with handfuls of the loser's red hair.

After things have quieted down, Easterbrook learns that the redheaded brawler is the heiress Thomasina Tuckerton, a dropout from wealth and society to the beat life. A week later, the incident all but forgotten, Easterbrook is saddened to read in the *Times* of Miss Tuckerton's death in a nursing home, her offbeat life-style suddenly cut short.

Feeling a bit down about the news of Miss Tuckerton's early demise, Easterbrook takes a break from work to visit his friend Ariadne Oliver, who is "in a state apparently bordering on insanity" because of plotting problems in her latest murder mystery. During their brief, distracted conversation, Mrs. Oliver happens to mention how difficult it is to pull out hair.

Meanwhile, in a seedy part of London, a priest, Father Gorman, is called to a dingy rooming house to see a dying woman. Before she expires, the woman gasps out, "Wickedness . . . it must be stopped," and then tells a bizarre story to her confessor. The poor woman dies, but Gorman remembers her strange, almost delirious tale, and stops in a cafe to jot down what she told him. But the priest has been followed, and as he leaves the cafe, an unseen figure comes up behind him in the fog and deals him a fatal blow.

Detective Inspector Lejeune and police surgeon Corrigan are puzzled by the apparent lack of motive in Father Gorman's death. The only unusual item is a piece of paper, containing nine names, folded in the father's shoe. The list is a puzzler, until it's discovered that some of the names on the list belong to those recently deceased, including Miss Tuckerton. The clues lead to an unexpected place—a charming former country inn, the Pale Horse, now home to three unusual ladies—a psychic, a medium, and a witch.

Principal Characters: David Ardingly, Bella, C. R. Bradley, Eileen Brandon, Dr. Jim Corrigan, Ginger Corrigan, Reverend Caleb Dane Calthrop, Maud Dane Calthrop, Jesse Davis, Colonel John Hugh Despard, Rhoda Dawes Despard, Mark Easterbrook, Father Gorman, Thyrza Grey, Detective Inspector Lejeune, Milly, Mrs. Ariadne Oliver, Zachariah Osborne, Hermia Redcliff, Sybil Stamfordis, Poppy Stirling, Mr. Venables, Bella Webb.

First Editions: **British**: Collins, London, November 1961. 256 pp., 15s. **American**: Dodd, Mead & Co., New York, 1962. 242 pp., $3.75.

Adaptation: None.

68

THE MIRROR CRACK'D FROM SIDE TO SIDE /
THE MIRROR CRACK'D (1962)

A tragic incident in the life of actress Gene Tierney provided the
inspiration for the plot of *The Mirror Crack'd*. During World
War II, while at the peak of her stardom, Tierney and husband
Oleg Cassini had a daughter, Daria, who soon after birth showed
signs of deafness and severely impaired eyesight. Tierney happened
to read an article reporting that an epidemic of German measles in
Australia had produced a number of birth-defect babies whose
mothers had caught the disease while pregnant, especially during
the first month of pregnancy. Alarmed because she had had the
disease during early pregnancy, the actress consulted specialists
who examined her fair-haired, normal-appearing little girl. Their
shattering conclusion was that Daria was not only deaf and nearly
blind, but retarded as well. She would grow to adulthood, but with
the mind of a nineteen-month-old child.

"I felt guilt I could not explain, and self-pity that I could not
throw off," Tierney wrote of this time in her life.* Already battered
by the pressures of her career, the actress felt that "Daria's condition exacted a greater cost," and became "the breeding ground
for the emotional problems soon to come."

One of the worst blows came when the actress found what
"vagary of fate" had caused her daughter's retardation. One afternoon at a Los Angeles tennis party, Miss Tierney was approached
by a young woman, a fan, who was in the women's marines. The
woman asked if she remembered her from a previous meeting
they'd had when Tierney was making a celebrity appearance at the
Hollywood Canteen. Tierney had forgotten the girl. Then the fan
asked a startling question: "Did you happen to catch the German
measles after that night?"

Before Tierney could reply, the young woman rattled on, telling
her that when Tierney was appearing at the canteen, the women's
marine camp was quarantined with the German measles, but she,

* Gene Tierney and Mickey Hershowitz, *Self-Portrait,* Wyden Books, 1979.

being such a fan, had broken quarantine to go to the canteen to see the star.

Christie made no reference to the Tierney tragedy in her autobiography, but the similarities are so strong there can be little question she knew of the story.

Christie takes this situation and transplants it in England. The Tierney role is taken by Marina Gregg (who has nothing in common with Tierney other than being a glamorous movie star), and California has been replaced by St. Mary Mead, where the reclusive Miss Gregg and her producer-husband Jason Rudd have bought Gossington Hall, the former home of Colonel Arthur Bantry (now deceased) and his wife Dolly. Christie makes a good deal of the changes in St. Mary Mead. Though a lot of the old villagers are on hand (including, of course, Aunt Jane), by the 1950s and 1960s "new" people were moving into the village. With servants not affordable, and the upkeep on larger homes impossible, old-timers like Dolly Bantry sold the big places to new money like Marina Gregg and Jason Rudd, and then sat on the sidelines with some apprehension and watched while these glamorous folks tore down walls, put in picture windows, and dug out swimming pools.

Miss Marple, who last appeared in *4.50 from Paddington* (#62, 1957), is back on the job snooping and solving murders. Poor Miss Marple has had a fall and is taking things easy for a while. Dr. Haydock, Miss Marple's physician and friend, pays her a visit and, seeing her in low spirits, prescribes just the thing that will surely revive his favorite patient. Haydock tells Marple that what she needs "is a nice juicy murder." Of course, the doctor is always right—a murder comes Miss Marple's way not long afterward.

Inspector Dermot Craddock, who here makes his last appearance, is on hand to team up with Miss Marple, and to do the legwork. Craddock, who was skeptical of Marple's abilities as a detective in their first meeting in *A Murder Is Announced* (#52, 1950), by this point has grown to admire and trust Miss Marple and her usual acute judgment.

There is a wonderful and nostalgic scene at the beginning of the book which has Miss Marple reminiscing about the good old days in St. Mary Mead when her eyesight was good, and "From the vantage-point of her garden, so admirably placed" Miss Marple could see "all that was going on in St. Mary Mead."

This was Christie's last murder mystery to take place in the milieu of the English village. We will occasionally get a glimpse of St. Mary Mead in Marple's future books, but the plots for the stories take Marple elsewhere. Christie was generous with her observations of the English village and gave to the reader an accurate historical account of the changing social structures in this type of setting from the 1920s through the early 1960s (see *A Murder Is Announced*, #52, 1950).

The title of this book comes from a line from the Alfred Lord Tennyson poem, *The Lady of Shallot*:

> Out flew the web and floated wide;
> The mirror crack'd from side to side;
> "The curse is come upon me," cried
> The Lady of Shallot.

Christie dedicated the book "To Margaret Rutherford, in admiration." Dame Margaret Rutherford (1891–1972), the much-loved British character actress, portrayed Jane Marple in four films made between 1962 and 1964. Though the films are a grave injustice to Christie's work, Rutherford's irresistible presence has made her the definitive Jane Marple actress for millions of Christie fans—in spite of the fact that she is physically a far cry from Christie's "tall, thin, acidulated spinster."

Dame Margaret was in her late sixties when she was reluctantly persuaded to portray Jane Marple, and she admitted that she agreed partly out of financial considerations. The actress and Christie did not meet until 1962, when Christie came to the set of one of the Marple films, *Murder at the Gallop*. Rutherford related that "this delightful woman came down to me on the set and when we met face to face we instantly clicked."

In spite of their hitting it off, the two women apparently met only once. And while Christie may have liked Rutherford personally, and as an actress in *other* roles, she made no secret of her intense dislike of Rutherford's being cast as Miss Marple, and of the silly cinematic travesties she was cast in.

Gwen Robyns, who authored a biography of Rutherford as well

as of Christie, wrote to Christie asking her opinion of Rutherford as Marple. She received a reply from Christie's secretary that read, "Mrs. Christie . . . has asked me to tell you that while she thinks Mrs. Rutherford is a fine actress, she bears no resemblance to her own idea of Miss Marple."

"Entertaining and enlightening comment on the changes in English rural life decorates a faultless puzzle plot," wrote Anthony Boucher in the *New York Times* (10/6/63), while the *Times Literary Supplement* (London) said, "The pieces finally drop into place with a satisfying click; motive (a highly original one) and murderer are revealed. Agatha Christie deserves her fame. Her writing is abominably careless, her formula hopelessly out of date; but, forty-two years after her criminal debut, she still offers an incomparably readable, skillful, and amusing detective story" (12/14/62).

PLOT:

Jane Marple, now too elderly to do much in her beloved garden besides "a little light pruning," spends most of her days indoors, knitting, having tea with visitors, and keeping up on the latest in St. Mary Mead. She fondly remembers her village *before* the fishmonger had refrigeration, before the basket shop became a supermarket, and before the nearby pastures and meadows became "The Development," the newest intrusion of suburban tract homes into the countryside.

One afternoon, tiring of the saccharine, patronizing attentions of her live-in companion, Miss Knight, Jane decides to enjoy "the delicious pleasure of having escaped for an outing completely on her own" and goes for a stroll to explore the terra incognita of the Development.

While exploring the spanking-new peas-in-a-pod cottages, Jane slips on some loose stones and takes a tumble. No great harm done, but Heather Badcock, one of the residents, takes Miss Marple in for a rest and tea. And, of course, gossip—in this case, about the new residents of Gossington Hall. Jane knows the Hall well— her old friends Dolly and Colonel Bantry lived there, though Dolly sold the big house after her husband's death. But Mrs. Badcock informs her visitor that the Hall has been bought by none other than former film queen Marina Gregg—an actress Mrs. Badcock has idolized since she was a teen—and her latest husband, director Jason Rudd. "Such a lot of husbands they all have," comments Jane.

The Gregg-Rudds have apparently chosen St. Mary Mead for home because it's convenient to the studios where Miss Gregg is making her comeback film.

Not long after Miss Marple's visit with Mrs. Badcock, the owners of Gossington Hall host a benefit for a local hospital, and of course all the curious villagers turn up to meet their famous neighbors and to inspect the lavish renovation of the house, including picture windows and swimming pool. The benefit is going well, until one of the guests, the same Heather Badcock who gave Jane tea, is taken ill—terminally ill.

Miss Marple, who wasn't up to attending, hears the sad news the next day, including the interesting tidbit that Mrs. Badcock's body is being held by the authorities for a postmortem.

The inquest leaves no doubt that poor Mrs. Badcock got a dose of poison intended for *someone* at the benefit—but it takes the combined efforts of Chief Inspector Dermot Craddock and his old partner-in-detection Jane Marple to discover who was trying to do in whom.

Principal Characters: Arthur Badcock, Heather Badcock, Mary Bain, Cherry Baker, Jim Baker, Dolly Bantry, Margot Bence, Lola Brewster, Chief Inspector Dermot Eric Craddock, Gladys Dixon, Ardwyck Fenn, Dr. Maurice Gilchrist, Giuseppe, Hailey Preston, Marina Gregg, Dr. Haydock, Miss Knight, Jane Marple, Jason Rudd, Dr. Sanford, Detective Sergeant William Tiddler, Ella Zielinsky.

First Editions: **British**: Collins, London, November 1962. 255 pp., 15s. **American**: with U.S. title *The Mirror Crack'd:* Dodd, Mead & Co., New York, 1963. 246 pp., $3.75.

Adaptation: *The Mirror Crack'd,* the film version of the book, was released at the end of 1980. The film was not as successful as the previous Christie star-studded films, *Murder on the Orient Express* and *Death on the Nile*. The cast included Elizabeth Taylor, Kim Novak, Rock Hudson, and Angela Lansbury as Miss Marple.

69

THE CLOCKS (1963)

This Poirot mystery is unique in Christie work because of its two interlocking but almost totally unrelated plots, both centering on goings-on at Wilbraham Crescent, a Victorian housing block in London. *The Clocks* is also another of Christie's attempts (usually less than a complete success) to integrate espionage with pure detection, and in this regard is a cousin to Poirot's *The Big Four* (#8, 1927) and *Cat Among the Pigeons* (#64, 1959).

The clocks of the title are a vivid clue in the opening chapter, where five clocks, each set to a different time, are found in a room with a body. The identity of the victim is unknown, and the reason for the clocks being there is unknown—a good example of Christie's ability to intrigue the reader with a puzzling opening chapter. Unfortunately, as happens often with later Christies, the clock theme is a tacked-on gimmick, poorly integrated into the clueing of the story, and explained flatly in a late-chapter cop-out.

Hercule Poirot shares the spotlight in this book with Colin Lamb, a British Intelligence agent whose father is an old friend and colleague of Poirot's. Lamb felt in his particular line of work that to use his own name would be a mistake, since "it might be connected too much with my old man." Who is Colin Lamb's old man? Christie suggests between the lines that Lamb is the son of Superintendent Battle.

An interesting insight occurs in *The Clocks:* Hercule Poirot expresses to Colin Lamb his opinions about fictional detectives and their creators. Poirot thinks *The Leavenworth Case* by Anna Katharine Green, published in 1878, is admirable: "One savours its period atmosphere, its studied and deliberate melodrama." He thinks *The Adventures of Arsène Lupin* written by Maurice LeBlanc, 1907, is "fantastic" and "unreal." He calls *The Mystery of the Yellow Room* by Gaston Le Roux, 1908, "really a classic!" —a book Poirot approves of "from start to finish." Poirot continues with his opinions on the writing of his friend Mrs. Ariadne Oliver: "I do not wholly approve of her works, mind you. The happenings in them are highly improbable. The long arm of coincidence is far too freely employed. And, being young at the time, she was foolish enough to make her detective a Finn, and it is clear that she knows nothing about Finns or Finland except possibly the works of Sibelius" (Christie is talking about herself here, and her youthful foolishness in making Poirot an old Belgian at the start of his career; Christie was thirty when she created Poirot). However Poirot does think Mrs. Oliver "makes an occasional shrewd deduction." On Mr. Cyril Quain: "He is a master, Mr. Quain, of the alibi." Mr. Garry Gregson, the writer of thrillers: "He is almost the exact opposite of Mr. Quain. In Mr. Quain's books nothing much happens; in Garry Gregson's far too many things happen."

Poirot's opinions on the American school of detective fiction: "Florence Elks now. There is order and method there, colourful happenings, yes, but plenty of point in them." He continues that Elks, like many American writers, is "a little too obsessed with drink." Poirot feels that the amount of rye or bourbon consumed by the American detectives is not interesting at all. Colin Lamb asks Poirot, "What about the tough school?" Poirot says, "Violence for violence' sake? Since when has that been interesting?" However, surprisingly enough, Poirot rates American crime fiction pretty high. "I think it is more ingenious, more imaginative than English writing."

But Poirot still loves the old favorite, *The Adventures of Sherlock Holmes*. *"Maître"* is what he says of Sir Arthur Conan Doyle, lovingly and with reverence. "These tales of Sherlock Holmes are in reality far-fetched, full of fallacies and most artificially contrived. But the art of the writing—ah, that is entirely different. The pleasure of the language, the creation above all of that magnificent character, Dr. Watson. Ah, that was indeed a triumph." Such a triumph in fact, that Christie never tried to develop Poirot's friend Hastings, whom she banished to South America, into a Dr. Watson character. She knew she could never give him the necessary depth.

All the writers Poirot mentions are either dead or "made up"— Christie wasn't letting Hercule express his opinion on living writers, though he can freely speak about real writers who are deceased.

Christie didn't speak only through Poirot. In her autobiography, she expresses her opinions directly. She begins by saying her love for detective stories began early. Her sister, Madge, and she "were connoisseurs of the detective story: Madge had initiated me young on Sherlock Holmes, and I had followed hot-foot on her trail, starting with *The Leavenworth Case,* which had fascinated me when recounted to me by Madge at the age of eight. Then there was *Arsène Lupin*—but I never quite considered that a proper detective story, though the stories were exciting and great fun. There were also the Paul Beck stories, highly approved, *The Chronicles of Mark Hewitt*—and now *The Mystery of the Yellow Room.* Fired with all this, I said I should like to try *my* hand at a detective story." Madge replied, "Well, I'll bet you couldn't." No terms were ever laid on the bet, but it was at this point that the "seed had been sown" that resulted some years later in Christie's first detective book, *The Mysterious Affair at Styles* (#1, 1920).

In a *Life* magazine article, "Genteel Queen of Crime; Agatha Christie Puts Her Zest for Life into Murder" (5/14/56), by Nigel Dennis, Christie said that she enjoyed crime novels that were not written by her. She liked Margery Allingham, and also Ellery Queen, "very maddening but quite nice." She also liked Frances and Richard Lockridge's characters Mr. and Mrs. North, and of the newcomers Christie rated Michael Gilbert, author of *Small Bones Deceased* (1950), the best. Of the Dashiell Hammett, Raymond Chandler, and Mickey Spillane school of writers, Christie said: "I don't find it very interesting. All that seems to happen is, first one side bashes the other side, and then the other side bashes the first one."

The reviews of *The Clocks* were favorable. Anthony Boucher in the *New York Times Book Review:* "*The Clocks* is delightful enough for its depiction of a retired and very elderly Hercule Poirot, impatient with inactivity and eager to act as even an armchair detective; but it is also remarkable for intricacies and niceties of construction that should dazzle any younger competitors. The plot, from its opening chapter, is too carefully startling for even a line of plot synopsis; let me simply say that here is the grand-manner detective story in all its glory" (10/4/64). The *Times Literary Supplement* (London) said, "*The Clocks* is a decent little Poirot Christie, up to snuff but not outstanding . . . The unimportant crime in the Crescent is deliberately fantastic and the trails are thoroughly muddied, so muddied, in fact, that only by guesswork can Poirot arrive at the solution and we readers couldn't possibly do so" (11/21/63). Sergeant Cuff wrote in the *Saturday Review,* "Heavily overpopulated, but a sure-fire attention-gripper, naturally" (9/26/64).

The Clocks was dedicated "To my old friend Mario with happy memories of delicious food at the Caprice."

PLOT:

Sheila Webb, typist-for-hire at the Cavendish Secretarial and Typewriting Bureau, returns from her lunch break to find that she has been called by a Miss Pebmarsh of 19 Wilbraham Crescent for a job that afternoon. Sheila arrives at Number 19 and when there is no answer at the door, she follows the instructions left with the Bureau, to simply let herself in and wait in the sitting room. "The only remarkable thing about it was the profusion of clocks."

While puzzling over why Miss Pebmarsh would have so many clocks, from a grandfather to Dresden china, Sheila finds a dead man in a gray suit on the floor behind the sofa.

There are more surprises in store. Millicent Pebmarsh, who happens to walk in just as the horrified Sheila Webb finds the body, is blind. And when Inspector Hardcastle questions her, she assures him that she did *not* call the Cavendish Bureau requesting Miss Webb's services. But most curious of all, when the inspector asks Miss Pebmarsh about the quantity of clocks, all but one set almost an hour ahead, she replies, "I don't understand what you mean by the 'other clocks.'" There is a grandfather clock, she says, and "no other clocks in the sitting room."

The authorities are stumped. Fortunately Hercule Poirot, put off by the disruptions of remodeling his flat, agrees to look into this "pretty problem in murder."

Principal Characters: Colonel Beck, Josiah Bland, Valerie Bland, Edna Brent, Mr. R. H. Curry, Detective Inspector Dick Hardcastle, Mrs. Hemming, Colin Lamb, Miss Martindale, Mrs. McNaughton, Angus McNaughton, Millicent Pebmarsh, Hercule Poirot, Professor Purdy, Mrs. Ramsey, Ted Ramsey, Edith Waterhouse, James Waterhouse, Sheila Webb.

First Editions: British: Collins, London, November 1963. 256 pp., 16s. **American:** Dodd, Mead & Co., New York, 1964. 276 pp., $4.50.

Adaptation: None.

70

A CARIBBEAN MYSTERY (1964)

Hercule Poirot is a traveler. Though for his entire literary life he *says* he is going to settle down in the country to cultivate vegetable marrows, murder always beckons. He goes to Syria, to Jordan, to Egypt, and to Turkey; he takes boats, trains, and planes on long journeys—always surrounded by murder.

Jane Marple, on the other hand, is thoroughly provincial. Her idea of getting away from St. Mary Mead is going to London for the day for some bargain hunting, or taking a bus tour of famous English houses and gardens. She occasionally gets down to the shore for a few days; sometimes "getting away" is no more than walking to the outskirts of St. Mary Mead to poke around in the new housing developments that have gone up in recent years.

Her one major exception is the Caribbean vacation sponsored by her ever-generous nephew Raymond, which provides the setting for Marple's ninth appearance in a novel.

Christie visited the Caribbean in the late 1950s or early 1960s, in part to visit John Cruikshank Rose, to whom she dedicated the book with the inscription "To my old friend [JCR] . . . with happy memories of my visit to the West Indies."

John Rose's friendship with Agatha Christie and Max Mallowan was one of long standing. He had worked at Ur, the archaeological site excavated by Leonard Woolley, as an architectural draftsman. Christie met him there on her first visit in 1928, and then again on her second visit in 1930 when she also met (for the first time) her future husband, Max Mallowan. In 1932–33, when Max—accompanied by Agatha, then his wife of two years—was in charge of his first important dig at Arpachiyah, Syria, he persuaded Rose, "a Scot with a quiet sense of humour," to hire on as a draftsman. Agatha described Rose as "a beautiful draughtsman, with a quiet way of talking, and a gentle humour that I found irresistible."

Rose moved to the British island of St. Lucia when he was

hired as the planner/architect for the capital town of Castries. Though the setting of *A Caribbean Mystery* is generalized, St. Lucia is probably the model for the fictional St. Honoré in the book.

Jane Marple is somewhat more active physically in this mystery than she is in most of her late books; she trots around the bungalows and bodies at the hotel, and even resorts to sneaking through flowerbeds to spy on suspects. Like many elderly, Jane has good days and bad days; the change of scenery and Caribbean climate seem to have given her a stretch of good days.

When not sleuthing, Marple has time to bask in the sun and reflect on modern living. "Sex" was a word not mentioned in Miss Marple's younger days, "but there had been plenty of it—not talked about so much—but enjoyed far more than nowadays, or so it seemed to her." Miss Marple, living her rural existence, had gained quite a bit of knowledge "of the facts of rural life." There was "Plenty of sex, natural and unnatural. Rape, incest, perversion of all kinds. (Some kinds, indeed, that even the clever young men from Oxford who wrote books didn't seem to have heard about.)"

Along the same lines, Marple's nephew Raymond characteristically underestimates his aunt's knowledge of the "real" world. A friend of his is "house sitting" for Jane while she is away, and Raymond patronizingly remarks, "He'll look after the house all right. He's very house proud. He's a queer. I mean—" Raymond was embarrassed, "but surely even dear old Aunt Jane must have heard of queers."

While on St. Honoré Jane meets the irascible crippled millionaire Jason Rafiel, who was posthumously to get Miss Marple involved in a later case, *Nemesis* (#78, 1971).

The *Times Literary Supplement* (London) wrote, "Poor old Miss Marples [sic] (just how old *is* she, by the way?), not so nippy on her pins now, but still indefatigably unmasking murderers and now exercising her talents in a Caribbean hotel. The story is simply but fairly clued and the solution not too easily guessable" (11/19/64). Anthony Boucher in the *New York Times* said, "The plot is conventional (who erased the garrulous major who thought he recognized an unpunished murderer), but the details are handled with that exquisitely smooth technique that is uniquely Mrs. Christie's" (10/17/65). The *New Yorker* wrote, "Miss Marple, almost as spry as in former days, is on holiday from her home parish of St. Mary Mead, and she has brought her knitting with her. The murderer continues with his maneuvers, but of course he hasn't a chance. And as always when we read a book by Agatha Christie, we think, What on earth would we do without this talented, vigorous lady?" (9/25/65).

PLOT:

Jane Marple's successful novelist nephew, Raymond West, "in lordly fashion . . . suggested a trip to the West Indies" for his elderly Aunt Jane after her bout with pneumonia the winter before. The spinster is appreciative of her nephew's generosity with money, though much less so of his generosity with reading material—modern novels he tries to persuade her to read. "So difficult—all about such unpleasant people, doing such very odd things and not, apparently, even enjoying them." She agrees to the trip, and finds herself at the Golden Palm Hotel on the island of St. Honoré, watching the deep blue of the Caribbean and listening to dull retired Major Palgrave, "purple of face, with a glass eye," regaling her with "the somewhat uninteresting recollections" of a lifetime of service in Kenya.

The garrulous major barely holds Jane's attention until he starts talking about murders and suddenly asks, "Like to see the picture of a murderer?"

The major is about to show her the curious photo, pulled from his wallet, when he fixes his gaze at something or someone over Jane's right shoulder—then hurriedly stuffs the photo back in the wallet and changes the subject.

The elderly conversationalists are interrupted by other guests, and Jane doesn't have a chance to broach the subject again, especially as she is told, the next morning, that the major has expired during the night—apparently owing to complications with his blood pressure medication.

Her nose for murder itching, Aunt Jane indulges in a rare white lie: she tells the local doctor, who attended Palgrave, that the late major had a photo of hers in his wallet—and could he possibly return it to her? The day of the funeral, Dr. Graham informs Jane that "we haven't found that precious snapshot of yours—it wasn't in the major's wallet, or anywhere else among his belongings."

Marple suspects foul play—further confirmed when a question is raised as to whether or not the major really had a blood pressure problem. The big question: why was the major killed, and by whom among the assortment of guests and locals at the hotel: the Kendals, who run the hotel (she's high-strung and given to nightmares); the Dysons and Hillingdons, two attractive, friendly couples whose lives are intertwined by more than their mutual interest in botany and lepidopterology; the jocular canon and his too observant sister; the crabby, reclusive old millionaire, Mr. Rafiel; his handsome but ungentlemanly valet; or his efficient, ugly duckling secretary?

Principal Characters: Señora de Caspearo, Greg Dyson, Lucky Dyson, Dr. Graham, Colonel Edward Hillingdon, Evelyn Hillingdon, Arthur Jackson, Victoria Johnson, Molly Kendal, Tim Kendal, Jane Marple, Major Palgrave, Canon Jeremy Prescott, Joan Prescott, Jason Rafiel, Esther Walters.

First Editions: British: Collins, London, November 1964. 256 pp., 16s. **American**: Dodd, Mead & Co., New York, 1965. 245 pp., $4.50.

Adaptation: A television adaptation of this novel, starring Helen Hayes as Miss Marple, is to be aired by CBS Television in the fall/winter season of 1983–1984.

71

AT BERTRAM'S HOTEL (1965)

The fictional hotel that Christie created for Jane Marple's London murder mystery is a thinly disguised version of the well-known London hotel, Brown's. Brown's, though not as glamorous or as large as Claridge's or the Berkeley or the Savoy, is in its own way as famous; during the near century and a half that it has been in operation at the corner of Dover and Albemarle streets "in the heart of the West End," Brown's has established a reputation as one of the most charming, conservative, discreet, and traditional hotels in the world. If the finest hotels can be compared to royalty, Brown's would certainly be the Queen Mother.

Brown's began in 1837 (the year Victoria came to the throne) when James Brown, a former butler to Lord Byron, and his wife Sarah Willis Brown bought a late-seventeenth-century town house at No. 23 Dover Street and opened it as a guest house catering to the nobility and gentry. The following year Brown acquired the house next door, No. 22; two more adjoining houses were bought in the next seven years. The four floors of the houses were divided into sixteen suites, which included separate quarters for guests' servants. Brown's became a success, especially as train travel became more popular; the hotel's location near the Great Exhibition of 1851 established Brown's even more as *the* place to stay in London.

Because of deteriorating health, James Brown sold the establishment in 1859 to James John Ford, owner of Ford's Hotel in Manchester Square. The management of the hotel passed on to Ford's son Henry in 1882. Henry Ford (no relation to the model-T Henry) set out immediately to modernize and improve Brown's. He installed one of the first elevators in London, improved the baths, put in electricity, and added telephones.

In 1889, Ford purchased the adjoining St. George's Hotel in Albemarle Street, and work began at once to connect the two hotels. In 1906, three more houses were bought and added to Brown's, bringing the total number of houses to eleven.

With the purchase of the eleventh house by Henry Ford, Brown's reached its present size; under Ford's direction, which lasted forty-six years, until 1928, Brown's also acquired its comfortable, solid tea-and-chintz reputation. Though in recent years the realities of modern hotel management have brought more and more corporate businessmen to Brown's, for most years of this century it was the urban refuge of the visiting clergymen, spinsters, country doctors, and old colonels which Christie depicted in her book.

Although Brown's is a bastion of upper-middle-class respectability, an array of notables has lodged within its walls through the years. Among the Americans, J. P. Morgan was a guest during the 1870s, and Alexander Graham Bell, at the suggestion of Morgan, stayed there in 1876, when he went to England to try to interest the British government in his invention, the telephone.

In 1886, Theodore Roosevelt stayed at Brown's and it was from the hotel that he walked to St. George's Church, Hanover Square, on December 2, to marry his second wife, Edith Kermit Carow. According to Edmund Morris's *The Rise of Theodore Roosevelt* (1979), Theodore and Edith sat together in his rooms at Brown's before their marriage and discovered "how cosy and comfortable one could be, with a small economical handful of coal in the grate and heavy fog outside."

In 1905, Franklin and Eleanor Roosevelt stayed at Brown's Hotel while on their honeymoon.

Brown's was noted as a refuge for royalty. King Carlos of Spain used Brown's as a hiding place in the 1880s. It's been said that Napoleon III and the Empress Eugénie stayed at Brown's incognito following the Franco-Prussian War. The pretender to the French throne, the Comte de Paris, had a suite at the hotel between 1886 and 1894, where he regularly held court. Queen Emma, Regent of the Netherlands, and fourteen-year-old Queen Wilhelmina once stayed at Brown's. During World War I, Queen Elizabeth of the Belgians, along with her children, lived in the hotel. King Albert visited her from time to time when on leave from his command. King George II of Greece also stayed at the hotel in 1924 when he fled his homeland. Other royalty-on-the-run who stayed at Brown's include the Emperor Haile Selassie of Ethiopia and King Zog of Albania.

Rudyard Kipling is closely linked to the hotel. It's rumored (though not certain) that he wrote *The Jungle Books* and the *Just So Stories* at Brown's, and there's a Kipling Room, which has been turned into a private dining room. On the walls of the Kipling Room hang framed illustrations from his books; the green leather-topped writing desk on which he wrote stands by the window.

There is no record if Agatha Christie was among the writers who checked into Brown's. According to Bruce P. Bannister, present manager of the hotel, there is no recollection among the older members of the staff (some of whom have tenure dating back to the 1920s) of Christie having been an overnight guest. However, she did visit the hotel on occasion and have afternoon tea in the same lounge where Jane Marple has tea at the beginning of this novel. Mr. Bannister also confirmed that the "first ten pages" of *At Bertram's Hotel* "as you will see is very much in the Brown's image."

It is possible, however, that Christie stayed in the hotel in her younger years, if there is any clue in Miss Marple's remark that "I stayed there once—when I was fourteen. With my uncle and aunt. Uncle Thomas, that was, he was Canon of Ely."

In *At Bertram's Hotel* Christie contrasts the traditional, conservative world of Jane Marple and Brown's Hotel with the modern world of rebellion and changing values. The spinsters, colonels, and vicars taking tea in the lounge are swept by a breath of rather unwholesome modern air as the doors of Bertram's are blown open by the likes of race-car drivers, fast socialites, and rebellious teenagers. Something has gone wrong with the safe, predictable world of Bertram's—so Christie seems to be saying—and as if to prove her point, Christie ends the book with an uncharacteristic burst of violence.

The reviews for *At Bertram's Hotel* were mixed. Brigid Brophy wrote in the *New Statesman,* "So long as it poses a puzzle, a detective story has an excuse (and if it takes a flight of fancy, of course, a positive right) to be implausible. But Miss Agatha Christie's new novel takes no flights and, so far as I can see, offers nothing like enough signposts to give the reader a fair chance of beating the narrative, Miss Marple and the police to the solution; the excuse is removed and we are left with the bare implausibility on our hands" (11/19/65). Sergeant Cuff in the *Saturday Review of Literature* felt the book was "one of the author's very best productions, with splendid pace, bright lines" (9/24/66). The *New Yorker* wrote, "Miss Christie's pearly talent for dealing with all the words and pomps that go with murder, English style, shimmers steadily in this tale of the noisy woe that shatters the extremely expensive peace of Bertram's famously old-fashioned hotel" (10/8/66). Anthony Boucher in the *New York Times* noted that, among the book's other qualities, it demonstrated Christie's skill in contrasting generations. "I strongly suspect that future scholars of the simon-pure detective novel will hold that its greatest practitioner, out-ranking even Ellery Queen and John Dickson Carr in their best periods, has been Agatha Christie—not only for her incomparable plot construction, but for her extraordinary ability to limn character and era with so few (and such skilled) strokes. Christie, at seventy-six, is virtually as good as ever—as she roundly demonstrates in *At Bertram's Hotel*. The book is a joy to read from beginning to end, especially in its acute sensitivity to the contrasts between this era and that of Miss Marple's youth" (9/25/66).

The dedication was "For Harry Smith because I appreciate the scientific way he reads my books."

PLOT:

Raymond West's latest novel "was doing very well indeed, and he felt in a generous mood," so he and his painter wife Joan decide to treat Raymond's old Aunt Jane Marple to a holiday. The Wests had sent the spinster detective to the West Indies the year before. "She enjoyed the trip," Joan remarks, "though it was a pity she had to get mixed up in a murder case."

"That sort of thing seems to happen to her," Raymond replies.

When Joan and Raymond offer Aunt Jane a week at Bournemouth or Eastbourne or Torquay, the elderly woman admits that what she would really like is a week in London in that eminently traditional, eminently expensive bastion of Edwardian hostelry, Bertram's Hotel.

So Jane Marple leaves St. Mary Mead for Bertram's, tucked

away in chintzy rectitude on a quiet West End street. She recalls her visit of many years ago, "Jane Marple, that pink and white eager young girl . . . Such a silly girl in many ways . . . now, who was that very unsuitable young man . . . ?" Miss Marple, in her old age, finds what she wants: the impeccable service, the cushy armchairs, the excellent tea and muffins, the dowagers up from the country, the quiet old money and quieter old blood.

However, under the venerable veneer of Bertram's, not all is as . . . it once was: not only is there central heating ("Americans require at least ten degrees Fahrenheit higher than English people do") and a television room, "tucked down a passage, in a secretive way," there is an undercurrent of crime, danger, and excitement, revolving around a slick, sophisticated gang of criminals, who wouldn't blink at using as reputable an establishment as Bertram's for their disreputable doings, or hesitate to get rid of any guest, no matter how innocent or well meaning, who gets in their way.

Principal Characters: Elvira Blake, Bridget, Mrs. Carpenter, Chief Inspector Fred Davy, Michael Gorman, Miss Gorringe, Sir Ronald Graves, Lady Selina Hazy, Robert Hoffman, Mr. Humfries, Colonel Derek Luscombe, Ladislaus Malinowski, Jane Marple, Contessa Martinelli, Mildred Melford, Canon Pennyfather, Mr. Robinson, Lady Bess Sedgwick, Emma Wheeling.

First Editions: **British**: Collins, London, September 1965. 256 pp., 16s. **American**: Dodd, Mead & Co., New York, 1966. 272 pp., $4.50.

Adaptation: None.

72

THIRD GIRL (1966)

With *Third Girl*, the seventy-five-year-old Christie plunged head-long into the world of modern youth; though a number of Christie's post-World War II novels reveal the author's attempts to integrate new attitudes, mores, and life-styles into the fabric of her books, nowhere is this so evident as in *Third Girl*.

Unfortunately, the Christie who during the 1920s and 1930s had written with such enthusiasm about air-headed flappers and fast-living young aristocrats, shows her thorough disapproval of 1960s youth throughout *Third Girl*. Though the septuagenarian author easily integrates such contemporary realities as "sniffing snow," "swallowing L.S.D.," or "using hemp" into her book, it is accompanied by an almost palpable distaste for the life-style of youth, as evidenced by continual references to greasy, unwashed hair, dirty fingernails, and baggy ragtag clothing.

Into this world of hippies and druggies, Christie plunges Poirot and Mrs. Oliver; the tone of this, their fourth novel collaboration, is set in the opening scene when the young (and of course unwashed) Norma Restarick comes to Poirot for help, only to pronounce straightaway that he is "too old."

Christie may have had her own reasons for having Miss Restarick say this. She had—since the 1930s—been saying that she was tired of Poirot but "stuck with him." Now, in his thirtieth novel, Hercule may have seemed "too old" to both the teenaged characters and their seventy-five-year-old creator.

Along the same line, Ariadne Oliver comments on her own foreign, fictional detective. Since Oliver is a spokeswoman for Christie's views on writing, her comments on the subject always bear listening to.

"And they say how much they love my awful detective Sven Hjerson. If they knew how *I* hated him! But my publisher always says I'm not to say so."

The "third girl" of the title refers to a third roommate in a London flat shared by single girls; the first two girls would rent an apartment, but if they should have trouble meeting expenses they might advertise in the paper for "third girl for comfortable second floor flat, own room, central heating, Earl's Court." Christie's idea for the title may well have come from seeing such an ad in the *Times*.

The critics liked *Third Girl*. The *Times Literary Supplement* (London) wrote, "Hercule Poirot is sadly worried about getting old, and no wonder, when a disturbed young girl, the 'third girl' in a shared flat, blurts it out to him. But his excellent brain cells can still discover whether she has, as she suspects, done a murder and just who is doing down whom and for why. We readers aren't too bad at it either, but it's still a pleasure to watch cher maitre at work" (12/8/66). Anthony Boucher in the *New York Times* wrote, "Poirot returns . . . that should be enough to send you scurrying to the bookstore. The plot is only moderately good Christie (though there is one beautifully set trap for the reader, into which I plunged headlong), and for once I feel that the mistress of mystery might have cut her manuscript to advantage. But Poirot is as absurd and as able as ever; mystery writer Ariadne Oliver (one of fiction's most endearing self-caricatures) is around to help and hamper him; and Mrs. Christie displays her usual acute sense of the immediate contemporary scene—in this case the young of 'swinging' London" (10/10/67). The reviewer from *Critic* was also pleased with *Third Girl:* "Old or young, Hercule Poirot is still in top form and so is his creator, Agatha Christie. The plot is super-Christie" (10/67).

Agatha Christie dedicated this book to Nora Blackborow.

PLOT:

Hercule Poirot, having only recently completed "his *magnum opus,* an analysis of great writers of detective fiction," is sitting in his flat one morning, feeling a bit bored and restless now that a major project is completed. George, his manservant, interrupts Poirot to say that there is a young woman at the door asking to see him. Poirot is about to say no when George mentions that the girl wants "to consult you about a murder she might have committed."

Intrigued by the "might have," Poirot asks her in, and finds a rather unimpressive lass of twenty or so, with "long straggly hair" and eyes which "bore a vacant expression." He's not impressed, either, by her slovenly clothes, or her air of "Mild perplexity" (hardly an air for someone who thinks she's done murder!).

The girl tells Poirot she thinks she's killed someone, but before Poirot can ask the still-nameless girl *why* she thinks so, she says she's changed her mind and must leave, adding, "You're too old. Nobody told me you were so old . . . I'm really very sorry."

Before Poirot can think too much about this blow to his ego, he's interrupted by a call from Ariadne Oliver. She knows right away something is amiss with her friend, and insists that he come that afternoon to have tea—or rather, hot chocolate—with her. While at Mrs. Oliver's, Poirot discovers that it is his authoress friend who is responsible for the young girl's visit: Mrs. Oliver had met the girl—Norma Restarick—at a party, and mentioned Poirot to her.

Poirot is still intrigued by the girl, and enlists Mrs. Oliver's help in investigating Miss Restarick. The detective duo soon discover that not only is the girl nowhere to be found, but that no one seems to care, or *want* anyone to care, that she is missing.

Principal Characters: David Baker, Miss Battersby, Louise Birell, Frances Cary, Mr. Goby, Sir Roderick Horsefield, Felicity Lemon, Chief Inspector Neele, Mrs. Ariadne Oliver, Robert Orwell, Hercule Poirot, Claudia Reece-Holland, Andrew Restarick, Mary Restarick, Norma Restarick, Sonia, Dr. John Stillingfleet.

First Editions: **British**: Collins, London, November 1966. 256 pp., 18s. **American**: Dodd, Mead & Co., New York, 1967. 248 pp., $4.50.

Adaptation: None.

73

ENDLESS NIGHT (1967)

In *Mallowan's Memoirs,* Christie's husband writes that "fans often write to Agatha and, after revealing their own preferences, ask which stories are her favorites. Her reply is that her opinions change from time to time, but as a rule she mentions *The Murder of Roger Ackroyd* (1926), *The Pale Horse* (1961), *Moving Finger* (1943) and *Endless Night* (1967)." Max went on to say that *Endless Night* is also one of his favorites, "partly because of its construction; the penetrating understanding of a twisted character who had a chance of turning to the good and chose the course of evil."

The setting of *Endless Night* is a field called Gipsy's Acre, located on a Welsh moorland. Christie first heard of Gipsy's Acre from Nora Prichard, which led her to dedicate this book to her. The dedication reads: "To Nora Prichard from whom I first heard the legend of Gipsy's Acre." Nora Prichard is the paternal grandmother of Mathew, Agatha Christie's only grandson.

For most of its length, *Endless Night* is almost a straight novel, and the murder occurs very late. The book deals with the swinging youth of London, as did Christie's previous two novels, and Christie carries off the youthful characters in this book quite well, making *Endless Night* one of the better of Dame Agatha's late books. Crime novelist Robert Barnard in his book *A Talent to Deceive* (1980) even went so far as to say *Endless Night* was "the best of the late Christies." The *Times Literary Supplement* (London) wrote, "It is really bold of Agatha Christie to write in the persona of a working class boy who marries a poor little rich girl, but in a pleasantly gothical story of gypsy warnings she brings it all off, together with a nicely melodramatic final twist" (11/16/67). The review by P. G. Neimark in the *New York Times Book Review* was also favorable: "[Mrs. Christie has] produced a surpassing mystery that is almost as fine a novel . . . The ingenious plot manages to avoid death itself for no less than the first three-quarters of the book. Only near the denouement does *Endless Night* become a detective story . . . Not that the familiar Christie touches are lacking . . . Use of the two-way clue is dazzling. And, more than ever the rigorous Christie epistemology-psychology invades every page of the book; her characters are normal people whose own free will essentially decides their courses" (3/17/68).

PLOT:

Michael Rogers admits that "a lot of people disapproved of my way of life." A restless, drifting sort, from humble beginnings, Rogers has managed in his easygoing life to pick up a bit of French, a bit of German, a flashy if cheap way of dressing, and an interest in some of the finer things in life—beautiful homes and good modern art, both out of reach for him on his current wages as a chauffeur.

While knocking about in Kingston Bishop, "a place of no importance whatever," Rogers discovers "the Towers," a decrepit Victorian house up for auction. The house doesn't catch his fancy, but he falls in love with the beautiful property it's situated on—a tract of land known as Gipsy's Acre. The daydreaming chauffeur wonders, "how it would be if Gipsy's Acre was my acre?"

In poking around the property, Rogers hears the local tale of Gipsy's Acre—it's a "cursed" place where accidents happen, often with fatal results. Old Mrs. Lee, reputed to be a gypsy herself, warns Rogers off the place.

One afternoon the young knockabout is admiring the site when he meets a young woman who is equally enchanted with the property, and they become acquainted while eagerly talking about its potential. She is Ellie Goodman, and she is an heiress.

Before long, they are Mr. and Mrs. Rogers, Gipsy's Acre is theirs, and an architect friend of Michael's is at work on the house of their dreams. But it soon seems that there may be a real curse. Accidents occur, and ultimately, deaths.

The question: Is the curse real, or just a screen to hide the true cause of the troubles at Gipsy's Acre?

Principal Characters: Greta Andersen, Dimitri Constantine, Claudia Hardcastle, Sergeant Keen, Esther Lee, Andrew P. Lippincott,

Stanford Lloyd, Major Phillpot, Gervase Phillpot, Mrs. Rogers, Ellie Rogers, Michael Rogers, Rudolf Santonix, Dr. Shaw, Cora Van Stuyvesant.

First Editions: British: Collins, London, October 1967. 224 pp., 18s. **American:** Dodd, Mead & Co., New York, 1968. 248 pp., $4.95.

Adaptation: *Endless Night* was made into a film in 1972, which starred Hayley Mills.

74

By the Pricking of My Thumbs (1968)

Christie opens this book with a dedication "to the many readers in this and other countries who write to me asking: 'What has happened to Tommy and Tuppence? What are they doing now?'" and then cheerfully continues, "My best wishes to you all, and I hope that you will enjoy meeting Tommy and Tuppence again, years older, but with spirit unquenched!"

The Beresfords' spirit may not have been quenched, but it had at least been quietly smoldering since 1941, when the gung-ho couple tackled Nazi saboteurs in *N or M?* (#39). While many, if not most, critics would happily have let Mr. and Mrs. B vent their excess enthusiasm on their grandchildren, without benefit of Christie's chronicling their lives, Christie thought enough of the two to trot them out for a last couple of geriatric adventures.

With *By the Pricking of My Thumbs* Christie's work slips into a disappointing decline. The sure hand that guided her through the vast bulk of her work now falters; the clever mind is a bit foggy. There are glimpses of the old Christie—good ideas, some memorable character sketches, flashes of wit—but these elements from the old Christie are often no more than a mishmash of loose ends and incomplete ideas and abandoned subplots, all glued together by meandering ruminations on growing old and the state of the world.

The character of Mrs. Lancaster, a fellow patient at Sunny Ridge with Tommy's senile Aunt Ada, is of special interest since she appears in two other Christie books. In *Sleeping Murder* (#83, 1976), a Jane Marple mystery written during World War II but not published until 1976, Gwenda and Giles Reed are at a sanatorium looking for clues in a case when they meet a "charming-looking old lady with white hair." This unnamed patient at the home wanders up to the Reeds holding a glass of milk, and says three very curious things: "Is it your poor child, my dear?" Then, "Half past ten—that's the time. It's always at half past ten. Most remarkable." And finally, "Behind the fireplace . . . But don't say I told you."

The woman in *Sleeping Murder* is merely a cameo character, and has no real part in the mystery. The same is true of the scene in *Pale Horse* (#67, 1961) in which David Ardingly tells of once being in the lounge of a mental home when "a nice elderly lady there, sipping a glass of milk" made some conventional conversation and then said, "Is it your poor child who's buried there behind the fireplace? . . . Twenty-ten exactly. It's always the same time every day. Pretend you don't notice the blood."

Finally, in *By the Pricking of My Thumbs* Tuppence meets old Mrs. Lancaster in the sitting room at Sunny Ridge. Again, the character is white-haired and holding a glass of milk, and strikes up a casual conversation with Tuppence. Then, out of the blue, she says, "I see you're looking at the fireplace . . . excuse me, was it your poor child? . . . That's where it is, you know. Behind the fireplace." Then Mrs. Lancaster meanders on, "Always the same time . . . Ten past eleven. Yes, it's always the same time every morning."

While the old woman with the glass of milk is used purely for effect in her two earlier appearances, in this last instance she goes on to be a character involved in the plot. In any case, Christie must have found the white-haired old lady, the glass of milk, and her senile prattle about stopped time and a child buried behind a fireplace particularly evocative of madness.

In *An Autobiography* Christie tells of her decision to sell her family home, Ashfield, in Torquay, before World War II. One of the reasons was that the adjoining house had been turned into a home for the mentally disturbed. On more than a few occasions the "guests" at the home had wandered onto the grounds of Ashfield, and there were "some unpleasant incidents."

It is possible that the lady with the glass of milk was one of these wanderers, and that her babbling about children and fireplaces made an impression on her mystery-writer neighbor.

The year that *By the Pricking of My Thumbs* was published also marked an important personal event in the lives of Agatha and her husband: Max Mallowan was knighted by Queen Elizabeth for his services to the British Empire. At this point in his life, Mallowan was one of the most eminent archaeologists and Middle-

Eastern scholars in England. His knighthood was the culmination
of a forty-year career which began with his days as Leonard
Woolley's assistant at the excavation at Ur—where he met Agatha.
In *Mallowan's Memoirs* he described the title as "most welcome
because it also conferred a title on my beloved Agatha." Though
Agatha was by far the most famous member of the couple, she
was not to receive her Dame title until 1971.

The reviews were mixed. *Best Sellers* said, "A new Agatha
Christie is always an event and her newest is just that, an event. It
is all beautifully plotted in the way that Mrs. Christie is famous
for. The title is from *Macbeth,* 'By the pricking of my thumbs,
something wicked this way comes.' Wicked, indeed!" (12/15/68).
And the *New York Times Book Review* wrote, "A pleasant, unre-
markable couple now, the Beresfords are wonderfully revived.
Smooth, beautifully paced, and effortlessly convincing"
(12/22/68). The *Times Literary Supplement* (London) complained that "Miss Christie makes the most of it—of being a
woman, of being a country woman, an archaeologist's wife, and
now, of being old. Her hero and heroine Miss Christie has resusci-
tated from the 1920s, her even then tiresome Tommy and Tuppence, now sprightly oldsters. The general theme is senility"
(12/12/68).

PLOT:

Tommy and Tuppence Beresford, "an ordinary couple . . .
Hundreds of elderly couples just like them . . . all over England,"
visit Tommy's feeble old Aunt Ada at Sunny Ridge rest home. Old
Ada, though getting senile, is still quite a terror, and makes it clear
that she doesn't like the sight of Tuppence. "Shouldn't bring that
type of woman in here. No good her pretending she's your wife."

Mrs. Beresford decides it's best to leave Aunt Ada to her senile
fantasies, and leaves Tommy alone with his aunt. While strolling
about Sunny Ridge, Tuppence encounters an assortment of elderly
folks, all a bit dotty: the woman who swallows her thimble for fun
and attention; the old dear who is convinced there was a poison
mushroom in her stew. In the sitting room, Tuppence encounters a
solitary old woman drinking a glass of milk because "It's not
poisoned today." The woman chats about life at Sunny Ridge,
then remarks, "I see you're looking at the fireplace—was it your

poor child? That's where it is, you know. Behind the fireplace."
The woman continues, "I told them what I knew . . . but they
wouldn't believe me."

The woman's prattling is cut short by Tommy's return from
Aunt Ada's room, and he and Tuppence leave Sunny Ridge.
Three weeks later, Aunt Ada dies, and the Beresfords return to
the home to dispose of Ada's effects.

While sorting things out, Tuppence is struck by a painting in
Ada's room—of a pale pink house next to a canal and a small
bridge. She experiences a strong feeling of déjà vu—she knows that
she has seen, not the painting, but the house itself before. Tuppence
would like the painting, and learns that it was a recent gift to Aunt
Ada, from none other than the old lady with the glass of milk and
the fireplace story. Tuppence thinks it's only right that she ask the
woman—Mrs. Lancaster—if she would like the canvas back. But it
seems that Mrs. Lancaster has suddenly been taken from Sunny
Ridge by her relatives.

The Beresfords reluctantly claim the painting, and Tuppence
tries to locate the former owner. To her surprise, she seems to
have disappeared into thin air, along with her relatives. In the
meantime, Tuppence remembers that she passed the house once
on a train, hence the déjà vu, and she sets out to scour the countryside until she finds the spot again.

What she finds is a house that is much less tranquil than it
looks in the painting, and an old woman whose stories are much
less senile than they had seemed at first.

Principal Characters: Albert Batt, Tommy Beresford, Tuppence
Beresford, Nellie Bligh, Emma Boscowan, Liz Copleigh, Mr.
Eccles, Ada Fanshaw, Julia Lancaster, Elizabeth Moody, Dr.
Murray, Miss Packard, Major General Sir Josiah Penn, Alice
Perry, Amos Perry, Ivor Smith, Sir Philip Starke.

First Editions: **British**: Collins, London, November 1968. 255
pp., 21s. **American**: Dodd, Mead & Co., New York, 1968. 275
pp., $4.95.

Adaptation: None.

HALLOWE'EN PARTY (1969)

This is the fifth pairing of Poirot and Christie's delightful parody of herself—the publicity-shy, apple-craving, nondrinking Ariadne Oliver, whose "original if untidy mind," as Poirot describes it, is the perfect foil for the orderly gray cells of the famous Belgian. Though they didn't often work together, their partnership was one of long standing, beginning with *Cards on the Table* (#27) in 1936, resuming in 1952 with *Mrs. McGinty's Dead* (#55), followed by *Dead Man's Folly* (#61, 1956) and *Third Girl* (#72, 1966). This is their penultimate adventure, and incidentally, one of two Christie novels in which an adolescent is a murder victim.*

Hallowe'en Party is Poirot's fortieth book, and his thirty-first full-length mystery. Since Hercule had already retired from the Belgian police when he made his first appearance in *The Mysterious Affair at Styles* in 1920 (he had retired in 1904, at perhaps 60 years of age), he would have been a remarkably spry 125 or so when he appeared in Woodleigh Common with Ariadne in tow, wearing his unsuitable and too-tight patent leather shoes. Poirot admits to his friend Superintendent Spence that he has not one gray hair because "I attend to that with a bottle." Perhaps there was some elixir in that bottle of hair dye that we know not of.

Mrs. Oliver tells Poirot that Woodleigh Common, where the fatal party is held, is about "thirty to forty miles" outside London, "one of those places where there are a few nice houses, but where a certain amount of new building has been done."

Woodleigh Common and neighboring Medchester are fictional names, but from internal evidence it's not difficult to discover the

---

* Besides this book, where Christie disposes of two adolescents—Joyce Reynolds, who is thirteen years old, and her brother Leopold, who's eleven—she has a fourteen-year-old girl, Marlene Tucker, murdered in *Dead Man's Folly* (#61, 1956).

area the author had in mind. Southwest of London in Surrey and Sussex is an area known as the "stockbroker belt"—an affluent suburban area with large houses and old-money people mixed with newer, upper-middle-class residential developments. Its accessibility to London via the fast rail line that runs from Brighton to Victoria Station has made the area popular with business executives (hence the nickname); the area underwent a surge of growth and building in the 1960s in particular. Placing Woodleigh Common in this area is supported as well by "Kilterbury Ring," which appears late in the book. Again, the name is fictional, but there are several megalithic ruins and sites in Sussex (similar to Stonehenge in Salisbury), which are described as "rings," the most famous being Avebury.

Hallowe'en Party, with its late sixties setting, is full of references to long hair, colorful clothes, sex, and drugs used for purposes other than committing murder. Judith Butler thinks "Hemp has a nasty smell," and Mrs. Oliver remarks on the habit of newly arrived foreign maids who "go straight into hospital because they're pregnant and have a baby, and call it Auguste, or Hans or Boris or some name like that."

There is also a very contemporary reference to a Greek "shipping millionaire who had created an island garden for the woman he loved." Aristotle Onassis and Jacqueline Kennedy were married in 1968.

Readers of Christie's autobiography will note the similarity in the location of the lavatory in Apple Trees (Mrs. Drake's home) with the same chamber in Ashfield, Christie's girlhood home. In both houses, the room's location "halfway up the stairs and in full view of the hall" leads to an amusing if embarrassing anecdote.

Hallowe'en Party contains the first, and only, appearance of the word "lesbian" in Agatha Christie's work. Remarkably, it is used by an eighteen-year-old boy!

Hallowe'en Party is dedicated "To P. G. Wodehouse—whose books and stories have brightened my life for many years. Also, to show my pleasure in his having been kind enough to tell me he enjoyed books."

Christie has often been compared to P. G. Wodehouse (1881–1975), peerless chronicler of the comic foibles of the Edwardian world, and creator of Jeeves the butler. Wodehouse's

repertoire of stuffy businessmen, fluffy aunts, empty-headed in-
genues, and eccentric old maids is closely akin to Christie's. The
two obviously read and enjoyed one another.

The *Times Literary Supplement* (London) wrote, "Clever old
Agatha Christie is still plodding along her well-trodden but engaging track, this time in company with Poirot and Ariadne Oliver.
Unusually with Mrs. Christie, you can guess who did it, but the
detail of the water is a good clue" (12/11/69).

In the *New Statesman,* James Fenton gave Christie a rare socio-
political assessment. "The fate of [the author's] writing is inex-
tricably linked with the fate of the upper middle class, whose loving chronicler she is: this is why the whole corpus of her work will
provide an excellent source-book for social historians. Poirot and
the comparatively recent Christie persona, Mrs. Ariadne Oliver,
are the star performers in an investigation which touches regularly
on problems of sex murders and criminal pathology. For the first
time I guessed the villain correctly, but this may have just been
luck. At all events, the Agatha Christie message—that the middle
class is the real murdering class—remains as acceptable as always"
(12/14/69).

Late Agatha Christie draws wildly mixed reactions. In the late
books much of the clarity and tightness is missing—there's a kind
of cobwebby feeling to them. But these late mysteries are full of
marvelous observations of life and people, with expansive dis-
courses (expansive for Christie, that is) on writing, old age, time,
change, and human nature.

As is well known, Christie was very shy of interviews and personal revelations. But it is in the later books, especially, that she
shares her thoughts and feelings with her readers. In *Hallowe'en
Party* there is an excellent example when the talented, idealistic
landscape designer Michael Garfield remarks, "For success in life
one has to pursue the career one wants, one has to satisfy such artistic leanings as one has got, but one has as well to be a trades-
man. You have to sell your wares."

Agatha Christie couldn't have said it better herself.

PLOT:

Mrs. Ariadne Oliver, best-selling author of detective novels, is
visiting her friend Judith Butler, a widow and mother of twelve-

year-old Miranda, in the town of Woodleigh Common, near Medchester, about forty miles outside London.

When the book begins, Mrs. Oliver has gone with Judith and Miranda to the home of Mrs. Rowena Drake, a "handsome, middle-aged" widow, who is sponsoring a Hallowe'en party that evening for a group of local adolescents. Games and recreations are planned, including an old-fashioned bob for apples. Mrs. Oliver, noted for her "sinful" love of apples, naturally takes an interest in setting up this particular game in the library, helping herself to a few of the props along the way.

When the kids learn that the famous Mrs. Oliver is presently at Mrs. Drake's, they ply her with questions about murder and her books. Miranda's best friend, Joyce, an aggressively insecure thirteen-year-old, complains that Mrs. Oliver's last book did not have "enough blood in it," and then goes on to boast that she saw a murder once, though she didn't tell anyone about it because she didn't realize until recently that it was a murder she had seen.

No one pays much attention to Joyce's story, and party preparations continue. That night, while the guests are playing "snapdragon" in the drawing room, Joyce is murdered in the library—drowned in the tub of bobbing apples.

The murder is blamed on an unknown maniac. But Mrs. Oliver, remembering Joyce's boast about witnessing a murder, suspects something more. Distraught (so much so that for the time being she gives up apples for dates), Ariadne enlists the aid of her old friend and partner in crime solving, Hercule Poirot.

Because Joyce had a reputation for telling tall tales, folks in Woodleigh Common put no stock in her murder being connected with an earlier crime. They think Joyce's being the victim is not an important aspect of the crime. But, as Poirot points out, "The victim is always important . . . the victim, you see, is so often the cause of the crime."

Principal Characters: Judith Butler, Miranda Butler, Rowena Arabella Drake, Miss Emlyn, Lesley Ferrier, Jeremy Fullerton, Michael Garfield, Mrs. Goodbody, Mrs. Hargreaves, Desmond Holland, Harriet Leaman, Mrs. Llewellyn-Smythe, Elspeth McKay, Mrs. Ariadne Oliver, Hercule Poirot, Inspector Henry Timothy Raglan, Nicholas Ransome, Mrs. Reynolds, Ann Reynolds, Joyce Reynolds, Leopold Reynolds, Olga Seminoff, Superintendent Bert Spence, Elizabeth Whittaker.

First Editions: British: Collins, London, 1969. 255 pp., 25s. **American:** Dodd, Mead & Co., New York, 1969. 248 pp., $5.95.

Adaptation: None.

76

PASSENGER TO FRANKFURT: AN EXTRAVAGANZA (1970)

Christie wrote that *The Mystery of the Blue Train* (#9, 1928) was her worst book—in her opinion. Critics and students of Christie would be more likely to cast their votes for *Postern of Fate* (#80, 1973) or *Passenger to Frankfurt*. *Postern of Fate,* with its echoes of Christie's childhood, has at least a certain nostalgia; *Passenger to Frankfurt* has nothing to recommend it, except for the study it provides of an author in declining years tackling a subject that was never the most congenial for her.

Published to coincide with her eightieth birthday, *Passenger to Frankfurt* had 58,000 copies in print at the end of its first year of publication. The Christie touch was missing in this mishmash, but her loyal fans nonetheless bought the book. After fifty years and seventy-five or so books, it seemed anything Christie wrote would immediately head for the best-seller lists. In fact it stayed on the *New York Times* list for twenty-seven weeks.

The *Times Literary Supplement* (London) published a tribute on September 18, 1970, in celebration of Agatha Christie's eightieth birthday. The praise and appreciation for the author was flowing like wine, until the subject of her thrillers was approached. "Nor has Mrs. Christie been convincing with the thriller form, whether in her early days with, say, *The Mystery of the Blue Train,* or, alas, *Passenger to Frankfurt,* her new 'birthday book.'" The review by A. J. Hubin in the *New York Times* summed up the general critical response toward the book: "[This] book doesn't really come off; in fact it doesn't come off at all. This is doubly sad because I suspect Miss Christie has thrown more of herself . . . into this book than any other. She has looked upon the current revolt of youth, the preoccupation with violence for its own sake, the pleasure seemingly derived from wholesale destruction. She conjures up a hidden master cause, projects us a few years hence and creates a band of elderly men to deal with what is by then an international menace. Unfortunately the whole novel stays one pace removed from real, and the efforts of the benign dodderers verge on the silly" (12/13/70).

Robert Barnard, in his book *A Talent to Deceive* (1980), said of *Passenger to Frankfurt:* "The last of the thrillers, and one that slides from the unlikely to the inconceivable and finally lands up an incomprehensible muddle. Prizes should be offered to readers who can explain the ending. . . . Collins insisted she subtitle the book 'An Extravaganza.' One can think of other descriptions."

Passenger to Frankfurt was dedicated to Margaret Guillaume.

PLOT:

Sir Stafford Nye is waiting at the Frankfurt terminal for a connecting plane to London. He is returning from one of the typically humdrum missions of his undistinguished diplomatic career. Something of a maverick and given to flamboyant dress (part of the reason for his lack of diplomatic success), Nye is approached at the terminal by a young woman with "a very faint foreign accent" and an extraordinary proposition: she needs his help to get to London without being killed. She wants him intentionally to take a drugged drink, then let her steal his cloak and passport, which she will use to get back into England—in drag as Sir Stafford. Nye, with "something about him of the eighteenth-century buck," agrees. After he awakes from the Mickey and finds the woman, the cloak, and the passport gone, he reports the "theft" and returns to London.

Once back home, Nye finds himself the target of two attempted hit-and-run "accidents"—and he suspects a connection between the woman in Frankfurt and the attempts on his life. An item he places in the "personals" of the newspaper puts him in touch with her again—at the opera and at the American Embassy. Each time she has a different name—and reveals a strong connection with those high-ups in government who keep an eye on the darker side of international politics.

These high-ups soon have Nye and his mysterious acquaintance back in Germany, on the trail of a group bent on world domination —a group that includes such characters as a rumored bastard son of Hitler, and Countess von Waldsausen, a woman gluttonous for both food and power. Along the way they encounter well-organized, armed youth gangs, secret meetings of world leaders, and a professor with a formula for saving the world.

Principal Characters: Lord Edward Altamount, Karl Arguilerus, Clifford Bent, Admiral Philip Blunt, Lady Mathilda Checkheaton, Mildred Jean Cortman, Sam Cortman, Dr. Donaldson, Professor Eckstein, Monsieur le President Grosjean, Henry Horsham, Sir James Kleek, Cedric Lazenby, Amy Leatheran, Lisa Neumann, Sir Stafford Nye, Colonel Ephraim Pikeaway, Eric Pugh, Dr. Reichardt, Mr. Robinson, Robert Shoreham, Herr Heinrich Spiess, Signor Vitelli, the Grafin Charlotte von Waldsausen, Countess Renata Zerkowski.

First Editions: **British**: Collins, London, 1970. 256 pp., 25s. **American**: Dodd, Mead & Co., New York, 1970. 272 pp., $5.95.

Adaptation: None.

77

THE GOLDEN BALL AND OTHER STORIES
(1971)

There are only two stories in this collection, "Magnolia Blossom," and "Next to a Dog," that had not been published in earlier collections. Both are romances in the vein of Christie's Mary Westmacott novels, and probably date from the 1920s. The reprinted stories are from *The Hound of Death* (#18, 1933) and *The Listerdale Mystery* (#20, 1934). Neither of the early collections was published in America. The five stories from *The Hound of Death* are supernatural tales, and they show that Christie had considerable skill with this type of story on those rare occasions when she chose to exercise it. The eight stories from *The Listerdale Mystery* are mysteries in a lighthearted vein.

Readers shouldn't be confused by the title of "The Strange Case of Sir Arthur Carmichael." The poor character's name really is Arthur, and appears as such in *The Hound of Death*. However, in *The Golden Ball* collection, his name somehow got to be Andrew in the table of contents and the title of the story, while remaining good old Arthur in the text! This editorial oversight still persists in the American paperback edition, as of the third printing, 1979.

Publishers Weekly wrote, "At this time, when Agatha Christie has reached a new peak in popularity with her recent best-sellers, it seems unfortunate to present her readers with this collection of stories. Though there are no copyright dates in the galleys, it is clear, from the internal evidence, that they date back to her earliest work, in the 1920s and 1930s. They are slight in plot, sentimentally romantic, and could only appeal to readers of their own vintage" (6/14/71).

"The Listerdale Mystery"
"The Girl in the Train"
"The Manhood of Edward Robinson"
"A Fruitful Sunday"

"The Golden Ball"
"The Rajah's Emerald"
"Swan Song"
  Published in *The Listerdale Mystery* (#20, 1934)
"The Hound of Death"
"The Gipsy"
"The Lamp"
"The Strange Case of Sir Arthur Carmichael"
"The Call of Wings"
  Published in *The Hound of Death* (#18, 1933)

"Magnolia Blossom"

Beautiful Theodora Darrell has just left her wealthy husband, Richard, to run away to South Africa with her lover, Vincent Easton. While secretly ensconced in a Dover hotel, on their way to the Continent, Theo and Vincent hear the news of the collapse of her cuckolded husband's financial empire—news which stirs old loyalties in the unfaithful wife.

"Next to a Dog"

Young widow Joyce Lambert is out of a job, destitute, and desperate. The only joy in her drab, penniless existence is Terry, her half-blind, aging terrier, a gift from her husband, Michael, not long before his death. Joyce's concern about keeping and feeding her four-legged companion leads her to consider marriage to a wealthy man she despises.

First Editions: British: None. **American**: Dodd, Mead & Co., New York, 1971. 280 pp., $5.95.

Adaptation: The story "Magnolia Blossom" was adapted for television as part of the Thames Television series, *The Agatha Christie Hour*.

78

NEMESIS (1971)

In 1964, in *A Caribbean Mystery* (#70), Jane Marple met up with an eccentric millionaire named Rafiel. In the meantime Rafiel has died and left Marple an unexpected legacy: twenty thousand pounds *if* she can discover and solve a mystery with only a shred of a clue to go on, a challenge that Jane readily takes up. Marple acquired the nickname Nemesis, after the Greek goddess of retribution, during her Caribbean vacation when she had appeared one night, "her head encased in a fluffy scarf of pale pink wool," hot on the trail of a murderer, awakened Mr. Rafiel, and declared that she was Nemesis. Rafiel, in his will, set things up so Jane could play the role of Nemesis once again—this time on a bus tour.

Nemesis, in which Marple fans have the pleasure of seeing their champion snooper collect twenty thousand pounds to supplement her meager pension, was the last Marple book that Christie wrote.* Like all of Christie's last books, it was dictated into a machine and then transcribed by a secretary, rather than handwritten or typed. (The first book Christie dictated into a machine is not known; certainly *Passenger to Frankfurt,* #76, 1970, is dictated; possibly earlier books as well.)

On June 16, 1971, the eighty-year-old Christie broke her leg in a fall at her home at Wallingford, Berkshire; the fall led to a serious decline in her health.

However, a brighter note was struck the same year when Christie was made a Dame of the British Empire. It was a final tribute to the woman who had given England and the world over half a century of the art of Agatha Christie.

Nemesis was received with tolerance by most critics, who realized that Christie was by now an institution—a solid English in-

* *Sleeping Murder* (#83, 1976) and *Miss Marple's Final Cases* (#84, 1979) are posthumously published early works.

vestment—and one just didn't outright pan the work of this institution. *Best Sellers* wrote that "[*Nemesis*] may be slow-paced, but the old charm is still there and a good deal of the old magic in plotting, too" (12/15/71). The *Times Literary Supplement* (London) said it was "pleasant to meet Miss Marple again, an old, old lady now, of course, and a rather garrulous old, old lady, apt to repeat herself, but still capable, at a dead man's behest, of taking what looks like a cultural but turns out to be a mystery coach tour, and on it to discover what the dead benefactor hoped she would, knowing that a scent for evil was still, in the evening of her days, her peculiar gift" (11/12/71).

The *Saturday Review of Literature* had trouble staying awake for *Nemesis* and said so: "Miss Christie's idea is intriguing but the plot ambles so slowly and all involved are so talky that the book can safely be recommended to insomniacs" (12/25/71).

Christie's dedication was to Daphne Honeybone, who for many years was her private secretary. After Christie's death, Mrs. Honeybone continued in this capacity for Sir Max Mallowan. Mrs. Honeybone received the modest sum of £250 (about $500) under the terms of her employer's will.

PLOT:

"In the afternoon it was the custom of Miss Jane Marple to unfold her second newspaper," whereupon she would peruse the notices of births, marriages, and (especially) deaths. This afternoon, among the names of several old acquaintances who have "passed over," Jane is struck by the familiarity of the name Rafiel. "It will come to me."

Finally she remembers: the very rich and difficult Jason Rafiel, who had pooled his wits with hers in that murder business some years back, on her Caribbean holiday on St. Honoré.

About a week later, Miss Marple receives an unexpected letter from Mr. Rafiel's solicitors, asking her to call at their offices. When she arrives, the solicitors present her with a sealed letter containing an extraordinary legacy: twenty thousand pounds, *if* she will utilize her "natural flair for justice," which has led to her "natural flair for crime." The late Mr. Rafiel wants Miss Marple to solve a crime, but he doesn't give any clues as to when it happened, where, or to whom. "Our code word, my dear lady, is Nemesis."

Miss Marple takes on the challenge. She receives a note informing her that Mr. Rafiel, before his death, had paid for her journey on "Tour No. 37 of the Famous Houses and Gardens of Great Britain." Jane takes the bus tour, watching every passenger and every place visited for possible clues to an unknown crime. The observant Jane soon finds that Tour 37 does lead her to a crime in Mr. Rafiel's past.

Principal Characters: Miss Barrow, Archdeacon Brabazon, Anthea Bradbury-Scott, Clotilde Bradbury-Scott, Nora Broad, James Broadribb, Mr. Casper, Miss Cooke, Joanna Crawford, Lavinia Bradbury-Scott Glynne, Verity Hunt, Richard Jameson, Sir Andrew McNeil, Jane Marple, Emlyn Price, Jason Rafiel, Michael Rafiel, Mrs. Risely-Porter, Mrs. Sandbourne, Mr. Schuster, Elizabeth Temple, Mrs. Vinegar, Esther Walters, Professor Wanstead.

First Editions: British: Collins, London, 1971. 256 pp., £1.40. **American**: Dodd, Mead & Co., New York, 1971. 271 pp., $6.95.

Adaptation: None.

79

ELEPHANTS CAN REMEMBER (1972)

In her next to last work of detection, Dame Agatha shows signs of age—understandable since she was eighty-two years old and in failing health. At this late stage in her career a novel with a "murder in retrospect" theme posed insurmountable problems for the author's declining powers. The characters all have such vague memories, including Hercule Poirot, whose little gray cells are just not up to par. He can't seem to remember how long he's known Mrs. Ariadne Oliver. He says twenty years, but they first met in 1936 when they had dinner together at the sinister Mr. Shaitana's, which led to murder in *Cards on the Table* (#27, 1936). Mrs. Oliver, usually very reliable, even if disorganized, cannot remember if her goddaughter Celia Ravenscroft had a brother or not. And what about the suicide/murder of General Ravenscroft and his wife, Molly? It seems the event took place anywhere from ten to twenty years ago. It's understandable with murder in the past themes, as in this book, that characters would have difficulty remembering exact dates, places, etc. However, there are difficulties within the plot structure of this novel, and even with events that should easily be remembered. One example of Christie's faulty memory is her Poirot's flat in Whitefriars Mansions, when he had previously lived in Whitehouse or Whitehaven Mansions. (See *Cat Among the Pigeons,* #64, 1959.)

Mrs. Oliver, making her eighth and last appearance in this novel, had a career which lasted thirty-eight years, from 1934, when she made a minor appearance in two short stories in *Parker Pyne Investigates* (#22, 1934), to this 1972 novel. Mrs. Oliver had developed into a Christie character of importance—sharing equal billing with Poirot in her last two appearances. Through Mrs. Oliver we had a chance to glimpse a part of the personality of the real Agatha Christie, or as much as the shy Christie was willing to reveal through this fictitious character. The beginning of *Elephants Can Remember* finds Oliver attending a literary luncheon, as rare an event in her life, as it was in Agatha Christie's. Mrs. Oliver, like Christie, hates publicity and mingling with large groups of strangers. When asked if she will make a speech at the luncheon, Mrs. Oliver replies, "I can't make speeches. I get all worried and nervy and I should probably stammer or say the same thing twice. I should not only feel silly, I should probably look silly. Now it's all right with words. You can write words down or speak them into a machine or dictate them. I can do things with words so long as I know it's not a speech I'm making."

Christie says in her autobiography that "[I] can't say what I mean easily—I can write it better." She continues that she doesn't "like crowds . . . parties, and especially cocktail parties." In 1962, there was a party at the Savoy Hotel, London, to celebrate the tenth anniversary of her play *The Mousetrap*. There was no way out for Christie this time. "There was a party for it—there had to be a party for it, and what is more *I* had to go to the party." It was a grand affair, the place swelled with people, and worse than that, there were reporters and photographers for Christie to deal with. But more dreaded than the big party was the fact that she would have to speak in front of the crowd. "I *cannot* make speeches, I *never* make speeches, and I *won't* make speeches, and it is a very good thing that I *don't* make speeches because I should be so bad at them."

Christie recalled trying to enter the private room where the Savoy party was being held. She was turned back at the door. "No admission yet, madam. Another twenty minutes before anyone is allowed to go in." Christie retreated! "Why I couldn't say outright, 'I am Mrs. Christie and have been told to go in,' I don't know. It was because of my miserable, horrible, inevitable shyness."

Because of her shyness, Christie sometimes didn't return friendly greetings upon meeting, or remained quiet and alone at those dreaded parties or other public functions—and this caused many people to think that she was being rude.

Through Mrs. Oliver, Christie commented on her own writing career: "She thought the detective stories she wrote were quite good of their kind. Some were not so good and some were much better than others." Mrs. Oliver thought "she was a lucky woman who had established a happy knack of writing what quite a lot of people wanted to read. Wonderful luck that was." Christie most certainly was being unduly modest about herself and her career. But then, Christie was a modest person who liked her privacy almost to the point of obsession.

There's a bit of tenderness when Mrs. Oliver pays a visit to her old nanny, Mrs. Matcham, in chapter 7. Reading through these pages, one can feel Agatha Christie's turning back the hands of time and remembering with pleasant memories her own early childhood and the time she spent with her own nannies.

Christie also mentions in *Elephants Can Remember* three previous cases of Poirot's: *Five Little Pigs* (#41, 1943) *Hallowe'en Party* (#75, 1969) (with Mrs. Oliver), and *Mrs. McGinty's Dead* (#55, 1952). Christie had subtle ways of reminding us of some of her previous books.

In March 1972, the management of Madame Tussaud's Wax Museum in London approached Dame Agatha Christie to see if she would be willing to be measured for a portrait in wax. Christie felt honored with the request and submitted to the measurements. Her life-size wax figure was placed in the Grand Hall of the museum.

H. C. Veit in *Library Journal* said of *Elephants Can Remember:* "Agatha Christie is at her most endearingly English self in her new mystery. . . . She is cozier, chattier and more motherly than ever, in a lethal way, of course. Christie has resurrected Hercule Poirot, and all's well with the world if he is still around; she also features what must be a self-portrait, Ariadne Oliver as the slightly scatty lady novelist. The plot is total confusion. . . . It is less a mystery than a lovely gossip, ratiocination being substituted for detecting, atmosphere for action. Nevertheless, Christie has kept her sterling ear for dialogue" (1/1/73). Newgate Callendar was kind in the *New York Times Book Review.* "Criticize *Elephants Can Remember?* As well criticize the Brooklyn Bridge or the Tower of London. . . . Suffice it to say that sometimes [Hercule Poirot] talks with a French accent and sometimes without. He still takes cases for the love of the game. At least in this book he expends considerable time and money, and never is there a question of payment. Suffice it also to say that the experienced reader will figure out the solution to this not too mysterious mystery halfway through the book. This is vintage Christie. But it is, alas, not very good" (11/26/72).

PLOT:

Celebrated mystery writer Ariadne Oliver is off to one of those literary luncheons she so dreads, thankful that at this luncheon at least she won't be asked to make a speech. Unfortunately, as coffee is being served after the meal, "the moment of danger" comes, when fellow lunchers are most apt to corner her with the predictable "I *must* tell you how very fond I am of reading your books and how wonderful I think they are."

At this affair, Mrs. Oliver is cornered by Mrs. Burton-Cox, a woman of the "supremely bossy" type. However, instead of the usual aggressive fan chatter, Mrs. Burton-Cox asks the author about her goddaughter Celia Ravenscroft—a goddaughter (one of many) that Mrs. Oliver can scarcely remember beyond the fact that she gave her a Queen Anne silver strainer as a christening gift years before.

While surprised to hear Mrs. Burton-Cox mention one of her half-forgotten godchildren, she is even more surprised to hear the point of the woman's inquiry: Who killed whom, Celia's father or mother?

"I'm sure . . . you *must* remember. . . . In one of those houses by the sea . . . both found on the cliff, and they'd been shot, you know . . . whether the wife shot the husband and then shot herself, or whether the husband shot the wife and then shot himself."

Ariadne scarcely remembers the tragedy, let alone the details. Yet Mrs. Burton-Cox pushes her. "But you could ask your goddaughter . . . Children always know everything . . . it's important, you see, because of . . . my dear boy wanting to marry Celia."

Mrs. Oliver manages to extricate herself from the probing woman, but she finds herself becoming interested in what really *did* happen, years ago, to her now-grown goddaughter's mother and father.

Not knowing where to start, the author pays a visit to Whitefriars Mansions and her old friend Poirot. After hearing her rather dizzy account of the luncheon conversation, he persuades her to delve (with his guidance, of course) into the past, to find the persons who are like elephants, the persons who will still remember the important details about this all-but-forgotten tragedy.

Principal Characters: Mrs. Buckle, Mrs. Burton-Cox, Desmond Burton-Cox, Julia Carstairs, Kathleen Fenn, Chief Inspector Garroway, Mr. Goby, Dorothea Jarrow, Felicity Lemon, Mrs. Matcham, Mademoiselle Zélie Meadhouray, Mrs. Ariadne Oliver, Hercule Poirot, General Alistair Ravenscroft, Lady Margaret Ravenscroft, Celia Ravenscroft, Madame Rostentelle, Superintendent Bert Spence, Dr. Willoughby.

First Editions: British: Collins, London, 1972. 256 pp., £1.60. **American**: Dodd, Mead & Co., New York, 1972. 243 pp., $6.95.

Adaptation: None.

POSTERN OF FATE (1973)

This, the last book that Christie wrote, is a nostalgic swan song, chock-full of bric-a-brac from her Victorian childhood, and set in a thinly disguised version of Ashfield, the home where she grew up. Unfortunately, *Postern of Fate* is one of, if not *the,* very worst books Christie wrote, and as such is a sad barometer of the decline she underwent in her last years of writing.

Once again she unpacks Tommy and Tuppence Beresford from mothballs and plunges them not only into espionage and murder, but this time espionage-and-murder-in-retrospect. (It seems the Laurels, which they have purchased to "fix up" as a retirement home, was the scene of some spy-type hanky-panky "sixty or seventy years ago.") It is the first and last time Christie tries to combine these elements.

Christie's basic device in *Postern of Fate* is actually rather poetic, and had great possibilities which could have been developed had she been more in possession of her faculties when the book was written. An author at the end of a fifty-year career takes a character who has been with her since the beginning, who has in fact aged along with the author, and puts her in the author's now-derelict childhood home, full of dusty, decaying toys that the author played with as a girl. In another writer's hands this might have become a charming, magical conceit . . .

In chapter 10, the old gardener Isaac Bodlicott takes Tuppence to a small greenhouse-like structure attached to one wall of the house near the dining room. (The fact that the Beresfords, who are already living in the house, haven't previously looked into a conspicuous glass structure attached to the house is typical of the oversights in the novel.) Isaac, who has been a handyman-gardener around the place for years, knows that the little greenhouse was called K.K. or "Kai-Kai" by previous occupants of the house; he is also familiar with the enclosure's contents: an old rocking horse called Mathilde, a child's cart named Truelove, and other odds and ends long abandoned.

In chapter 5 of *An Autobiography,* Christie writes about her childhood pleasures, many of which revolved around "a small subsidiary greenhouse which adjoined the house on one side. This small greenhouse [was] called, I don't know why, K.K. (or possibly Kai-Kai?)."

Among the croquet mallets, old iron tables, and ratty tennis nets that were left in K.K. were "Mathilde . . . a large American rocking horse . . . now, a battered wreck of its former self, sans mane, sans paint, sans tail . . . [and] Truelove . . . a small painted horse and cart with pedals."

Christie tells of one of her favorite afternoon pastimes, which consisted of getting on Truelove at the top of the slope in the spacious garden of Ashfield, and "pushing off" for a bumpy ride down to the bottom of the garden where, as often as not, she would land in the branches of the monkey puzzle.*

When Tuppence takes Truelove out of the greenhouse and dusts him off a bit, she does the same thing, and winds up in the monkey puzzle—a bit undignified for a grandmother.

In *An Autobiography* Christie published several photographs from her early years at Ashfield. Two show the garden side of the house, with a structure that clearly is Kai-Kai; a third shows Agatha's older brother Monty—a grown man—hamming it up in his little sister's cart Truelove.

Even though *Postern of Fate* (like all of Christie's books in her later years) made the best-seller lists, reviewers knew all too well the reason why. Harry C. Veit in *Library Journal* said, "The tone is comfy, domestic, and sedate, just the way [Christie's] fans like it. The plot is total chaos and the clues total confusion, but I don't think it will matter a bit" (1/1/74).

In the *New York Times Book Review* Newgate Callendar lamented, "It is sad to see a veteran author working under nothing but momentum . . . [*Postern of Fate*] is a contrived affair that

---

* Monkey puzzle, or *Araucaria araucana,* is an evergreen tree native to Chile; it has thickly intertwined branches covered with prickly leaves. The tree was popular in English gardens, and derived its name from the difficulty a monkey would have in climbing it.

creeps from dullness to boredom. The writing is cutesy and labored, the ending flat. Sorry" (12/16/73).

The poem that Christie uses for the book's epigram, and from which she takes the title, is "Gates of Damascus" by English poet and playwright James Elroy Flecker (1884–1915), who is best known for his verse collection *The Golden Road to Samarkand* (1913) and his play *Hassan* (1922). Christie also quotes the poem in "The Gate of Baghdad" from her 1934 short story collection *Parker Pyne Investigates* (#22).

The dedication for this book reads: "For Hannibal and his master." Hannibal, the Beresfords' dog in *Postern,* is described as "a small black dog, very glossy, with interesting tan patches on his behind and each side of his cheeks. He was a Manchester terrier of very pure pedigree, and considered himself to be on a much higher level of sophistication and aristocracy than any other dog he met."

Hannibal is the literary pseudonym of Treacle, the Manchester terrier that was with Dame Agatha and Sir Max Mallowan during the last years of her life. His master is of course Max Mallowan. A fitting dedication for the last book Christie was to write, to two who were with her to the end.

PLOT:

Tommy and Tuppence Beresford are settling in their new home, the Laurels, in the resort town of Hollowquay, where they have chosen to retire. In the course of unpacking, Tuppence begins leafing through a collection of old children's books left in the house, many of which she can remember from her own childhood. While glancing through Robert Louis Stevenson's *The Black Arrow,* she notices that someone has underlined parts of the text, in a random, apparently meaningless manner, unless . . . She copies out the sentences and gets no meaning at all. Then she notices that it's really only letters underlined. "They've just been picked out . . . because they wanted the right letters." With this decoding method, Tuppence gets an extraordinary message from the old book: *Mary Jordan did not die naturally. It was one of us. I think I know which one.*

Tuppence, as enthusiastic as ever for adventure and intrigue, launches an investigation, sure that the message is more than a child's prank.

It seems that there was a Mary Jordan at the Laurels many years ago, and that she died by "accident" when the cook mistakenly picked poisonous foxglove leaves and put them in the salad. Thanks to the long memory of Hollowquay gossips, Tuppence learns there was more of interest to Miss Jordan than her untimely death: she was rumored to have been mixed up in "something to do with secrets—about a new submarine. Afterward they suspected that it wasn't her real name."

Mrs. Beresford's probing into the past seems harmless enough until old Isaac Bodlicott, their talkative handyman-gardener, who remembers a great deal about the secretive goings-on at the Laurels years before, is knocked dead in the garden. It seems that someone in Hollowquay *still* doesn't want anyone to know who killed Mary Jordan.

Principal Characters: Colonel Atkinson, Albert Batt, Andrew Beresford, Tommy Beresford, Tuppence Beresford, Henry Bodlicott, Isaac Bodlicott, Miss Collodon, Angus Crispen, Mary Jordan, Iris Mullins, Inspector Norris, Colonel Ephraim Pikeaway, Mr. Robinson.

First Editions: British: Collins, London, 1973. 254 pp., £2.00. **American**: Dodd, Mead & Co., New York, 1973. 310 pp., $6.95.

Adaptation: None.

81

POIROT'S EARLY CASES / HERCULE POIROT'S EARLY CASES (1974)

From the title, the reader might think that this collection contains only Poirot stories from the first decade or so of Christie's career. Not so. Among the eighteen stories, all of which appeared in earlier collections, there are cases ranging from the first collection of Poirot stories, *Poirot Investigates* (#4, 1924) to *Double Sin and Other Stories* (#66, 1961). The three stories from *Poirot Investigates* appeared only in the American edition of 1924; the 1974 collection marks their first publication in Britain.

Publishers Weekly liked this collection of vintage Poirot short stories. "These eighteen short stories are fine wine in a new bottle for aficionados of the mistress of mystery. It's exhilarating to be back in the company of the Belgian dandy, Poirot, as his habits of orderliness and use of 'the little gray cells' land him again and again one meaningful step ahead of crook, cop and reader. As always, the author is scrupulously fair with her audience—the clues are all there—but she invariably surprises us just the same" (9/16/74).

Below are the titles in this collection, and the volumes they originally appeared in.

"The Lost Mine"
"The Chocolate Box"
"The Veiled Lady"
Published in the American edition of *Poirot Investigates* (#4, 1924)
"Problem at Sea"
"How Does Your Garden Grow"
Published in *The Regatta Mystery and Other Stories* (#34, 1939)
"The Adventure of Johnnie Waverly"
"The Third Floor Flat"
Published in *Three Blind Mice and Other Stories* (#51, 1950)

"The Affair at the Victory Ball"
"The Adventure of the Clapham Cook"
"The Cornish Mystery"
"The King of Clubs"
"The Lemesurier Inheritance"
"The Plymouth Express"
"The Submarine Plans"
"The Market Basing Mystery"
    Published in *The Under Dog and Other Stories* (#54, 1951)
"The Double Clue"
"Double Sin"
"Wasps' Nest"
    Published in *Double Sin and Other Stories* (#66, 1961)

First Editions: British: Collins, London, September 1974. 253 pp., £2.25. **American:** with U.S. title: *Hercule Poirot's Early Cases:* Dodd, Mead & Co., New York, 1974. 250 pp., $6.95.

Adaptation: None.

82

CURTAIN (1975)

It is well-known that Agatha Christie wrote her last two published books, *Curtain* and *Sleeping Murder* (#83, 1976) during the London blitz in the early years of World War II. She wrote these "extra two books" because she thought she might be killed in the bombing raids that were a daily occurrence while she was living and working in London. The books were made over by deeds as gifts: *Curtain,* in which Hercule Poirot dies, and which was written first, was for her daughter, Rosalind; the other, Miss Marple's last book, *Sleeping Murder,* was for her husband Max. The two manuscripts were put in bank vaults and were "heavily insured against destruction." As we know, Christie was not killed in the bombing raids, and the two manuscripts stayed in the bank vaults until 1975, when after much persuasion from her English publisher Sir William Collins, she finally relented and allowed *Curtain* to be published. (The first-edition dust-covers let readers know that they were getting a "vintage" Christie.)

Sir William, who was to die a few months after Dame Agatha, realized, according to Christie's biographer, Gwen Robyns, "that there would be no Christie for Christmas in 1975." According to Robyns, Sir William's "trump card" in persuading Christie to publish, was that unless Hercule Poirot "was killed off by her own hand, after her death other writers might try to keep him alive. Had not Kingsley Amis written a James Bond novel round Ian Fleming's character?" Christie finally gave in.

Christie also might have had a personal reason also for allowing *Curtain* to be published in her lifetime. She had spent decades irritated with Poirot and his little gray cells, and could have received quite a bit of satisfaction from finally being rid of him while she was still alive.

Curtain went to the top of the best-seller lists and stayed there for many weeks, in both the United States and England. Christie received a $300,000 advance for the hardbound rights in the

United States, and Pocket Books paid $925,000 for the rights to reprint in paperback. By the end of the first year in paperback, *Curtain* had 2.5 million copies in print. It is interesting to note that while *Curtain* was racking up these tremendous sales in the United States, the paperback of *Murder on the Orient Express,* riding high on the success of the film, sold about 3 million copies in the States. Sales of all Christie books were now increasing at an enormous rate all over the world. In fact, by a 1977 estimate, nearly 95 million copies of her works have been sold in the United States, and 400 million throughout the world (*New York Times,* October 2, 1977).

If Agatha had been killed during one of the raids on London in the 1940s, and her final two books had been published then, she would now probably be remembered just as a good solid mystery writer of the prewar years. Of course her books of that period would be remembered best, but one can assume that most of her less popular works would be out of print now. Poirot and especially Marple would never have achieved the worldwide fame that they did. (Miss Marple had appeared in only three full-length novels and one collection of short stories when Christie wrote her final novel, *Sleeping Murder.*)

However, Christie did survive the war and produced a book a year almost to the end of her long life. A postwar generation of mystery lovers discovered Christie as generations had before them, and her fame grew rapidly with each decade. It should be noted that every one of Christie's mystery books (novels and short story collections) have remained in print almost continuously throughout her career and even now, more than seven years after her death, her books show no sign of losing popularity.

Poirot's career spanned fifty-five years (1920–1975), and when he died in *Curtain,* newspapers on both sides of the Atlantic published obituaries. The August 6, 1975, edition of the *New York Times* gave Poirot a front-page obituary, with photo, an honor accorded very few "real" people.

When Christie wrote *Curtain,* she didn't know when it would be published. One problem this presented was that the book could seem dated when it eventually came out. Christie got around this problem in several ways. First, she made the novel devoid of contemporary references—political movements, popular novels, etc.—

to keep the action from being "pinned down" in time. She also made the most of two "modern" trends—the conversion of large country homes to banal guest houses, and the passion for installing many modern bathrooms in them. This picture of the once-glorious Styles, now reduced to taking in paid guests, has built-in nostalgia for "the good old days," which would make the book seem "late" to the reader, whether published in 1947 or 1987.

This deliberate nostalgia is played up even more in the Poirot-Hastings relationship. Hastings, who had not been in a Poirot novel since 1937, is brought back from Argentina for a reunion at Styles—again a device that would have worked whether one decade or four had elapsed since he went to South America.

Christie was also clever in her portrayal of Poirot. Since she wanted to be sure that this would be Poirot's final case, but did not know how many years Poirot would be with her before *Curtain* was finally published, she hit upon the device of the wheelchair. What could better signal that the Belgian was near his end than crippling him? To strengthen this image, she made a great point of his saying, "I am a wreck . . . I can still feed myself, but otherwise have to be attended to like a baby." The reader is also shown the now-pathetic vanity of his badly dyed hair and mustache.

By creating this Poirot—indubitably on his last leg—Christie was able to age him slowly to this point in other books written over the intervening decades from the time this book was written to the time of publication.

Incidentally, had Poirot aged on the same scale as mere mortals, he would have been somewhere between 120 and 130 years old. A 3 to 2 ratio gives a good approximation of the scale used in these books; Poirot ages about two years for every three calendar years. Hastings, who was in his mid-forties when he retired in 1937, would be in his mid-eighties in 1975. Since he displays the characteristics of a robust man in his sixties, Hastings seems to live on the same charmed time scale as Poirot.

As Hastings was with Poirot in his first case, *The Mysterious Affair at Styles* (#1, 1920), it was only fitting that he should return for Poirot's swan song. He was Poirot's closest friend and confidant, even if he did exasperate Poirot with his slowness in grasping facts.

"Good-bye, cher ami, I have moved the amyl nitrate ampules away from beside my bed. I prefer to leave myself in the hands of the *bon Dieu*. May his punishment, or his mercy, be swift!

"We shall not hunt together again, my friend. Our first hunt was here—and our last . . .

"They were good days.

"Yes, they have been good days."

So ended Poirot's manuscript to Hastings (at the end of *Curtain*), which was to be opened four months after he died.

Christie was at the end of her life at this point. After all the pleasure she had given to the world with her books, it was only fitting that she should live to see her detectives Poirot and Miss Marple reach the pinnacle of their fame in the 1970s.

The reviews for this final Poirot novel were mostly on the positive side, although they were not total raves, which were rare with her late books.

A reviewer from *Critic* was not too keen on Christie and her craft: "This is better than recent Christies—which isn't saying a hell of a lot. Ms. Christie is one of the most over-rated writers of our time and her present phenomenal popularity simply proves that most readers cannot distinguish between mediocre and good suspense novels. Her one talent is intricate plotting but plot alone does not a novel make" (Winter, 1975).

H. C. Veit wrote in the *Library Journal,* "The formula has not changed; the ratiocination is again provided by Poirot, whose little grey cells still function; the bumbling legwork is still done by Hastings; and the solution is just as farfetched as ever. Will be prized for years to come" (August 1975). P. S. Prescott from *Newsweek* wrote, "One of Christie's most ingenious stories, a tour de force in which the lady who had bent all the rules of the genre before bends them yet again. Like all her stories, it is scrupulously honest. In a detective story, as in an allegory, much that happens—the concrete details that provide an illusion of reality—actually point to something else, and in *Curtain* so many events are not quite what they seem that the reader may at the end feel as foolish as Hastings. To believe the killer's motivation requires belief in some truly hokey psychology, but never mind: the credibility of the design, not the people, is what distinguishes the best of Christie's stories" (10/6/75). Francis Wyndham wrote in the *Times Literary Sup-*

plement (London), "The solution, when it is finally sprung, turns out to be as outrageously satisfying as [Agatha Christie's best]. As she presumably intended, in this one [she] has brought off the bluff to end them all" (9/29/75).

Julian Symons, crime novelist and essayist, in his *New York Times* review wrote: "It would be nice if one could say that this final adventure of the most engagingly preposterous detective of the Golden Age were the best, but unhappily it isn't so. The very best Christies are like a magician's tricks not only in the breathtaking sleights of phrase that deceive us but also in the way that, looking back afterward, we find the tricks to have been handled so that our deceit is partly self-induced. Her most staggering deceptions, like *The ABC Murders* and *And Then There Were None*, belong to the thirties, but there are other books almost as good, and at least one of her most cunning stories, *The Murder of Roger Ackroyd*, is of twenties' vintage. *Curtain* has all of *Roger Ackroyd*'s outrageousness, but only a fraction of its cunning. In the end one has a distinct sense of contrivance. This need not much affect our appreciation of Poirot, or his creator. . . . In the best stories . . . Poirot is a more convincing reasoner than any other fictional detective of his period. His vocabulary may be odd, and some of his recent cases are peopled by decidedly out-of-date characters . . . but Poirot himself is in some strange way believable. . . . Agatha Christie was not only a lady but also ladylike. . . . Her books . . . say something about manners but nothing about life. Yet within her chosen and unstrained limits, this serpent of old Thames has given all detective story addicts immense enjoyment, and she has been the champion deceiver of all time" (10/12/75).

PLOT:

At Poirot's behest the recently widowed Captain John Hastings returns to England from Argentina for a "family reunion" at Styles Court, the site of their first detective case many years before. To encourage Hastings to make the long journey, Poirot has arranged for Hastings's daughter Judith to be at Styles along with Mr. and Mrs. Franklin, her employers in England.

Time has altered many things at Styles. The once-private estate, like so many of its breed, has been converted to a guest house, the large rooms subdivided, with cramped modern bathrooms fitted in. And Poirot and Hastings are not houseguests, as before, but paying guests.

But the saddest sight of all that greets Hastings on his return is Poirot, crippled and confined to a wheelchair, still clinging to a feeble illusion of youth by dyeing his hair and mustache. Happily, the gray cells are still intact in the decaying body.

After a nostalgic reunion, Poirot gets down to business and informs Hastings that they are "here to hunt down a murderer." Hastings finds the idea "fantastic." The half dozen guests that he doesn't know already seem a harmless enough lot. Poirot shows Hastings a list of five murders, all apparently solved, all apparently unrelated. He then reveals that all the cases have one person in common, someone who had no apparent motive for the murders.

Poirot points out that this "X" might by pure chance be casually (and innocently) connected with two or three murders, but "five is a bit too thick." The Belgian then reveals that "X" is at Styles Court, and "a murder will shortly be committed—here."

Principal Characters: Major Allerton, Sir William Boyd Carrington, Elizabeth Cole, Nurse Craven, Curtiss, Barbara Franklin, Dr. John Franklin, George, Captain Arthur Hastings, Judith Hastings, Daisy Luttrell, Colonel George Luttrell, Stephen Norton, Hercule Poirot.

First Editions: British: Collins, London, 1975. 221 pp., £2.95. **American:** Dodd, Mead & Co., New York, 1975. 238 pp., $7.95.

Adaptation: None.

83

SLEEPING MURDER (1976)

Sleeping Murder and *Curtain,* written during the exceptionally productive war years, were both withheld from publication by their author for more than three decades (see *Curtain, #82,* 1975).

Christie's health had deteriorated considerably after a broken leg she suffered in 1971, when she was eighty, and it became increasingly clear to her family and her business associates that Agatha was in her final years. The decision to publish the two long-withheld manuscripts may have been influenced by financial considerations. The vast Christie audience was conditioned to have their "Christie for Christmas," and the arrival of the annual volume generated enormous revenues for the publishers and the Christie family.

The four novels that Christie wrote between 1970 and 1974, beginning with *Passenger to Frankfurt* (#76), showed a sharp decline in quality, and *Postern of Fate* (#80, 1973), the last novel Christie was to write, was so poor as to be an embarrassment to the Christie name. Collins no doubt began to wonder if Christie would produce any more publishable novels. During these years Collins also released two short story collections, *The Golden Ball and Other Stories* (#77, 1971) and *Poirot's Early Cases* (#81, 1974), which had been compiled from decades-old stories, most of which had appeared in earlier short story collections. In 1974, *Poirot's Early Cases* was the only Christie title to be published, and given the possibility of no new Christie writings, Collins was faced with the unappealing prospect of reshuffling old short stories ad infinitum to come up with the annual Christie. Given this situation, it is easy to imagine that the eighty-five-year-old author was under considerable pressure to release her two stored manuscripts.

Bantam, for example, paid $1 million for U.S. paperback rights to *Sleeping Murder.*

Agatha's reason for holding back *Curtain* was perfectly logical;

early publication would have truncated Poirot's career by several decades. But the delayed publication of *Sleeping Murder* is not so easily explainable. There seems to be no reason at all why it should not have appeared in the 1940s along with *The Body in the Library* (#40, 1942) and *The Moving Finger* (#42, 1943). The book, unlike *Curtain,* has no gimmicks or surprises that would dictate that it *had* to be the last Marple novel. Since Christie wasn't killed in the war as she feared, why didn't she release the book afterward, when a Marple novel would have nicely filled the gap between the 1943 *The Moving Finger* and the next Marple, the 1950 *A Murder Is Announced* (#52)?

Since *Sleeping Murder* is a "murder in retrospect" mystery, it may have been withheld to avoid too many such novels within a short span of years. (*Five Little Pigs,* #41, appeared in 1943, and *Sparkling Cyanide,* #45, in 1945.)

Another possibility is that Christie didn't think the book was up to her usual standards, and rather than destroy it, she put it away for a "rainy day." Certainly *Sleeping Murder* is not on a par with the rest of her 1940s novels (though by virtue of being published among the late titles, it shines out among *them*) and it is not nearly so good as *Sparkling Cyanide* and *Five Little Pigs.*

In any case, her reasons remain a secret.

The novel itself is what critic Robert Barnard called "a slightly somniferous mystery." Readers will find a few understandable contradictions, given the manuscript's early date. Colonel Bantry, who had died by the time of *The Mirror Crack'd* (#68, 1962), appears again alive and well. And the life-style of the Reeds, the Bantrys, and other inhabitants of Dillmouth, where most people have independent incomes and large staffs of servants, definitely reflects prewar standards. And when Brenda goes house-hunting, she hires a Daimler—commonplace in the 1940s, but definitely an antique auto by 1976.

Chapter 10 of *Sleeping Murder* has a cameo appearance by Christie's "crazy-old-lady-with-a-glass-of-milk," who appears twice again, many years later, in *Pale Horse* (#67, 1961) and *By the Pricking of My Thumbs* (#74, 1968).

In chapter 4, Miss Marple says, "I've always remembered the mauve irises on my nursery walls and yet I believe it was repapered when I was only three." The remark is of interest, since Christie's autobiography records that her nursery at the family home, Ashfield, had just such wallpaper, and that its green leaves and mauve blossoms had been one of her earliest memories.

Gavin Lambert in the *New York Times* wrote, "For all her adherence to formula, Christie in one way transcends it. *Sleeping Murder* is not among her most skillful works, but it displays her personal sense of what she calls 'evil,' of murder as an affront and a violation and an act of unique cruelty. She was not an imaginative or original enough writer to explore this, but when Marple tells us here that 'It was real evil that was in the air last night,' Christie makes us feel her curious primitive shiver" (9/19/76).

T. J. Binyon in the *Times Literary Supplement* (London) said, "Written some thirty years ago, *Sleeping Murder* appears to be set in the 1930s—that golden age of the detective story . . . *Sleeping Murder* has all the virtues of Agatha Christie's work: a coherent plot, firm and purposeful narration, and a pleasant, light and agreeable style. On the other hand, the red herrings are not as convincing as they might be, and the murderer's identity is not too difficult to discover—even for a reader without Miss Marple's long experience of life" (10/15/76).

Dame Agatha Christie died on January 12, 1976. Her husband Max wrote in the brief epilogue to his book *Mallowan's Memoirs* that his "beloved Agatha died, peacefully and gently," as he was wheeling her out "in her chair after luncheon to the drawing-room." Max said that his wife had been "failing for some time and death came as a merciful release."

At the time of Christie's death, her popularity was greater than it had ever been before. *Curtain* was still on the best-seller list in the U.S., England, and many other countries. Tributes poured forth for the "Queen of Crime" from major publications all over the world, and like that of Hercule Poirot, Christie's obituary received front-page coverage in the *New York Times* (1/13/76). John Leonard, writing an appraisal of Christie in the same edition of the *New York Times,* concluded with: "She gave more pleasure than most other people who have written books." *The Times* (London) wrote that Christie "was beyond question, one of the half-dozen best detective story writers in the world."

Christie was buried on January 16, in St. Mary's Churchyard in the small village of Cholsey, Berkshire. Her service was, as she'd wished, private. In death, as in life, Christie kept with her tradition of privacy and no fanfare. Her simple tombstone had inscribed on it lines from Edmund Spenser's *The Faerie Queene.*

> Sleepe after toyle, port after stormie seas,
> Ease after warre, death after life, does greatly please.

PLOT:

Orphaned Gwenda Reed, twenty-one and married only three months to Giles Reed, arrives in England. The newlyweds have decided to move there from New Zealand, and Giles, who has business to clear up in New Zealand, has insisted that Gwenda go on ahead to find them a house.

Gwenda happens on "that still charming seaside resort" of Dillmouth, where she spots a "For Sale" sign on a small white Victorian villa.

As the owner, Mrs. Hengrave, shows Gwenda the property, called Hillside, Gwenda finds herself feeling comfortable with the house—but, as they start down the stairs, Gwenda is hit by "a wave of irrational terror . . . a sickening sensation." The terror passes quickly, and the incident doesn't deter the young woman from purchasing the property.

As Gwenda settles in—still without Giles—odd things start happening. She insists that Forster, the gardener, take out a bank of forsythia in the garden and put in steps and a path to open out the view of the sea—only to discover that there once had been a path just where she wanted one. She also finds herself unconsciously walking into the wall between the drawing room and the dining room, as if there were a door there. Deciding that a door there *would* be more convenient, she asks her workmen to knock one through, only to be informed, "Won't be no difficulty about this . . . been a door here before, there has. Somebody as didn't want it has just had it plastered over."

But strangest of all is the wallpaper in the nursery. Gwenda decides the mustardy color in the room must go, and imagines a cheery wallpaper with "little bunches of scarlet poppies alternating with bunches of blue cornflowers." When the contractors unseal the cupboard in the room, many times painted over, Gwenda is startled and shaken to open the door and find inside the original wallpaper—of cornflowers and poppies.

All these coincidences have put Gwenda on edge. Even though there is still work to be done in the house, she decides that she needs a break. She accepts an invitation to visit novelist Raymond West and his wife Joan in London. The Wests, friends of Giles, do their best to entertain the distraught young woman. Included is a night at the theatre with Raymond's "perfect Period-Piece" of an aunt, Jane Marple. The play is Webster's *The Duchess of Malfi*, "with Gielgud," at His Majesty's Theatre. Gwenda enjoys the performance—that is, until the closing scene when is heard the line "Cover her face; mine eyes dazzle: she died young."

Gwenda, no doubt to the consternation of her companions and the puzzlement of the audience, screams and runs in a panic from the theatre.

The next morning Aunt Jane persuades Gwenda to unburden herself, and Gwenda tells all the curious coincidences at Hillside, concluding with the moment at the theatre when she suddenly recalled as a child seeing through the bannisters on the stairway at Hillside, a golden-haired woman sprawled at the bottom of the stairs. Her face was blue from strangulation—and a man was standing over her saying the very lines from *The Duchess of Malfi*. All Gwenda remembers beyond that is that her name was Helen.

Principal Characters: Jackie Afflick, Colonel Arthur Bantry, Dolly Bantry, Mrs. Cocker, Eleanor Fane, Walter Fane, Mr. Galbraith, Helen Spenlove Kennedy Halliday, Major Kelvin James Halliday, Dr. Haydock, Mrs. Hengrave, Dr. James Kennedy, Lady Abbot Kimble, Manning, Jane Marple, Dr. Penrose, Detective Inspector Primer, Giles Reed, Gwenda Reed, Mr. Sims, Joan West, Raymond West.

First Editions: British: Collins, London, 1976. 224 pp., £3.50. **American:** Dodd, Mead & Co., New York, 1976. 242 pp., $7.95.

Adaptation: None.

84

MISS MARPLE'S FINAL CASES AND
TWO OTHER STORIES (1979)

This volume of short stories, some going back to the 1930s, was published only in England. It contains six stories featuring Jane Marple and two non-Marple stories. The only prior appearance of these stories in England was in magazine form. All the stories were published in collections in the U.S. The two stories in which Miss Marple does not appear are "The Dressmaker's Doll" and "In a Glass Darkly."

In its review of this collection, the London *Times* wrote, "The stories are not all perfect. A decided aroma of the confectioner's comes from some. But the best two or three, simply recounted, not in any way overloaded with significances that would be better in a novel, yet not underloaded either by having characters too sketchy or too cobbled together to satisfy, are simply what this sort of thing should be. When you finish one you feel you have come to the end, not that you have got to the end" (12/20/79).

"Miss Marple Tells a Story"
"In a Glass Darkly"
   Published in *The Regatta Mystery and Other Stories* (#34, 1939).
"Strange Jest"
"The Tape-Measure Murder"
"The Case of the Caretaker"
"The Case of the Perfect Maid"
   Published in *Three Blind Mice and Other Stories* (#51, 1950)
"Sanctuary"
"The Dressmaker's Doll"
   Published in *Double Sin and Other Stories* (#66, 1961)

First Editions: British: Collins, London, 1979. 138 pp., £4.50.
American: None.

Adaptation: See *The Regatta Mystery* (#34) for information.

MISCELLANEOUS CHRISTIE BOOKS

The eleven miscellaneous books that fall outside of the mystery and thriller mainstream of Christie's works are not well known by Christie readers, with the exception of *An Autobiography*, published in 1977. This lack of familiarity is due in part to the subject matter (poetry, children's stories, personal reminiscences of the Middle East, romantic fiction), and to the fact that six of these miscellaneous titles (the romantic novels) were published originally under the pseudonym Mary Westmacott.

Since these volumes are not the classic Christie of detection and mystery, they are unlikely ever to be among her most popular works. However, it is in her autobiography and reminiscences, in the poems and in the thinly disguised autobiography of the Westmacott novels, that the reader gets the closest personal glimpse of the elusive Christie, and for that reason above all they are of interest to the serious Christie reader.

1. GIANT'S BREAD (1930)

In her autobiography, Agatha Christie described the point in her career when writing books—detective books—became "a matter of course . . . a proper job." She confessed that the longing to write a book other than the kind she was *expected* to write began to "unsettle" her.

The author decided to write a straight romantic novel, which she set about "with a rather guilty feeling." The result, *Giant's Bread*, was published in 1930 by Collins, her regular publisher, with the author's identity carefully concealed by the pseudonym Mary Westmacott.

Giant's Bread is the story of Vernon Deyre, a genius composer who, in the words of Max Mallowan, "had to liberate himself from the love of human ties in order to achieve his end and create his masterpieces."

Vernon grows up in the very sheltered world of a Victorian household, enters World War I, and is erroneously reported killed in action. When he returns, he finds his wife, Nell, has already remarried. Vernon contemplates suicide, but while lost in despair he's hit by a truck. He suffers amnesia, and assumes a new identity. Vernon's memory eventually returns, but he decides to keep his new identity and continue his life as a musician.

Mallowan suggests that the creation of Vernon Deyre may have been influenced by Roger Coke, a musician and friend of Christie's sister, Madge Watts.

Christie herself was musically talented, and in her youth had considered a career as pianist or singer. However, her shyness kept her from pursuing a concert career, although she continued to be a serious player and music lover throughout her life. Her familiarity with music is displayed abundantly in the technical details in *Giant's Bread*.

Christie recalled that her publishers "hated Mary Westmacott writing anything." They were "suspicious and disapproving" of any project she undertook which took her away from detective fiction (see also Miscellaneous Christie Books, #8, *Come, Tell Me How You Live*).

The book is dedicated to the memory of Christie's mother, Clara Miller.

The reviews for Christie's first nondetective novel were very encouraging for the "new" writer, whose real identity wouldn't be revealed for fifteen years. The *New York Times* wrote, "Her book comes well under the classification of a 'good book.' And it is only a satisfying novel that can claim that appellation. In *Giant's Bread* there are traces of the careful, detailed writing of the English novelist, and there are hints of Mary Roberts Rinehart's methods of mentioning a finished episode and explaining later how it all happened" (8/17/30). The *New Statesman* said, "When Miss Westmacott reaches the world of music, which she really knows, her book suddenly comes alive and vivifies her characters with it. . . . The chapters in which Jane appears are worth the rest of the book put together, and make one wish to encourage Miss Westmacott to go on writing—but to prune her gift for imitating what half a hundred other authors can do" (5/10/30).

First Editions: **British**: Collins, London, 1930. 437 pp., 7s. 6d.
American: Doubleday, Doran, 1930. 358 pp., $1.00.

2. UNFINISHED PORTRAIT (1934)

Christie's second Mary Westmacott novel was described by Max
Mallowan in his memoirs as a quasi-autobiographical work in
which his wife "has been more generous than most writers in self-
revelation; for she has written extensive memoirs . . . and a novel
. . . entitled *Unfinished Portrait* (1934), where we see many intimate flashes from earliest childhood till the beginnings of middle
age . . . we have [here] more nearly than anywhere else a portrait of Agatha."

Celia in the novel is Christie's autobiographical character, and
the novel incorporates many details from the author's early life—
her imaginary playmates, her aged grandmother, music studies in
Paris, a season in Cairo, an early courtship with a soldier (named
Peter Maitland in the book), and finally, a whirlwind courtship
and marriage to a handsome charming Archie Christie-like soldier
(Dermot).

The novel chronicles the rise and fall of Celia's and Dermot's
relationship, their marriage, and finally their divorce, with Celia
left to raise a daughter alone. The failure of their marriage, at a
time when Celia is already depressed by her mother's recent death,
causes her to have a nervous breakdown, during which she imagines her husband is trying to poison her.

Celia's breakdown certainly resembles Christie's own experience in 1926, but it's difficult to judge the extent of the similarities
because, as Mallowan said, *Unfinished Portrait* is a mixture of
"autobiography" and "imagination."

The novel ends when Celia is thirty-nine, preparing to "grow
up." Christie was thirty-nine when she met Max Mallowan, whom
she married the following year.

The *New York Times* wrote, "As a study of a shy, emotional
nature, verging on the pathological, *Unfinished Portrait* is moderately well done. It is worth reading for its sympathetic—and sometimes very amusing—account of Celia's childhood. And in Celia's
Grannie it introduces a grand old lady—an indomitable Victorian

with a keen love of life, a fine hand for managing 'the men' and a gruesome interest in the final takings-off of the many friends and relatives whom she survived" (12/9/34).

First Editions: British: Collins, London, 1934. 316 pp., 7s. 6d.
American: Doubleday, New York, 1934. 323 pp., $2.00.

3. ABSENT IN THE SPRING (1944)

Christie described this book as "the one book that has satisfied me completely . . . the book that I had always wanted to write, that had been clear in my mind." She began *Absent in the Spring* shortly after completion of her mystery novel *Death Comes as the End* (#44, 1945), and wrote the book in a breakneck three days, writing the first and last chapters before the rest. On the third day, after a weekend of "white heat" work, she called in sick to her volunteer job at the dispensary. When Christie arrived at work the following day, looking ghastly from creative exhaustion, her colleagues found it easy to believe she had been sick the day before.

Absent in the Spring is the story of Joan Scudamore, who undergoes a personal crisis during a period of forced isolation at a travelers' rest house in Mesopotamia, precipitated by her realization that her husband may no longer love her and may love another woman. Christie explores the theme of middle-age identity crisis in this book, perhaps expressing through Joan her own fears and doubts.

The title was taken from the Shakespeare sonnet which begins, "From you have I been absent in the spring."

The *Times Literary Supplement* (London) wrote, "The writer has succeeded in making this novel told in retrospect with its many technical difficulties, very readable indeed" (8/19/44). Rose Feld in *Books* (*New York Herald Tribune*) wrote, "Miss Westmacott's novel is a gem of a psychological portrait, the writing sensitive and probing, the outlines intense and arresting" (10/10/44).

First Editions: British: Collins, London, 1944. 160 pp. 7s. 6d.
American: Farrar & Rinehart, New York, 1944, 250 pp., $2.50.

4. THE ROSE AND THE YEW TREE (1947)

Christie took the title for this novel from "Little Gidding," the final section of T. S. Eliot's *Four Quartets:* "the moment of the rose and the moment of the yew tree are of equal duration."

The Rose and the Yew Tree is the story of John Gabriel, a plumber's son who wants to rise above his station and become a gentleman. Gabriel is awarded the Victoria Cross while fighting in World War II, and wins a seat in Parliament after the war. He later manages to win the love of the beautiful, well-bred, and gentle Isabella. She, given the choice between a comfortable marriage to her aristocratic cousin Rupert, and Gabriel's passion, chooses to be with Gabriel. They travel to central Europe, where Isabella dies in an accident while trying to shield him. His conscience awakened by Isabella's unselfish love and sacrifice, Gabriel finds religious faith.

Christie said nothing about this book in her autobiography, except that she'd carried the vague idea for it since 1929.

Max Mallowan in his memoirs said *The Rose and the Yew Tree* was "the most powerful and dramatic of all" the Westmacott novels. He thought that this book "is in the classical vein and will not be destined for oblivion."

"Although this is an able novel, quiet and intelligent, the class distinctions which motivate its characters will seem unreal to many Americans," wrote *Books* (*New York Herald Tribune*) (4/18/48). The *Times Literary Supplement* (London) said, "Miss Westmacott writes crisply and is always lucid. The pattern of the book is too vague at one point—the later stages of the hero's career—but much material has been skillfully compressed within little more than 200 pages" (11/6/48).

First Editions: British: Heinemann, London, 1948. 221 pp., 8s. 6d. **American:** Rinehart, New York, 1948. 249 pp., $2.50.

5. A DAUGHTER'S A DAUGHTER (1952)

Max Mallowan described the theme of this novel as "the potential love-hate relationship between a mother and her only child, and, fortunately, recognition of the links which make for the final reconciliation."

Ann Prentice, the mother of a nineteen-year-old daughter, Sarah, is an attractive forty-one-year-old widow who meets Richard Cauldfield and falls in love with him. Ann must then make a decision—does she want to make a new life for herself—or continue to devote her life to her daughter Sarah? Ann's motherly instinct prevails over her own second chance at happiness, and she decides not to marry Richard. Soon, mother and daughter experience conflicts toward each other, with Sarah eventually moving to Canada; Ann is left alone to pick up the pieces of her life.

This book, published in London in 1952, wasn't published in America until 1963, and then only in paperback. A hardcover edition was eventually published in the States in 1972 by Arbor House.

First Editions: **British**: Heinemann, London, 1952. 200 pp., 15s. **American**: Dell, New York, 1963. 191 pp. (paperback), price unavailable.

6. THE BURDEN (1956)

This book, the last of the Christie/Westmacott novels, is similar in theme to *A Daughter's a Daughter* (1952). The theme is sacrificial love, which instead of drawing the women closer together, nearly destroys them. In *A Daughter's a Daughter* it's the mother's love for her daughter; in *The Burden* it's the love of one sister for another.

Laura, the older sister, "a slim, fragile creature," has, because of guilt, dedicated her life to protecting her younger sister, Shirley. The life of the pretty high-spirited Shirley suffers dramatically, owing to the well-meaning but disastrous decision-making of the older sister.

The *Times Literary Supplement* (London) wrote, "*The Burden* is by a writer who has been Mary Westmacott for six books and Agatha Christie for more than anyone can count. In spite of the smart modern trimmings, this seems very much the art of storytelling that would be at home in the most staunchly traditional woman's magazine, where all problems are resolved when the mousey heroine puts on some lipstick (called, in this case, 'Fatal Apple'), and finds the love of her life" (12/7/56).

The Burden, like *A Daughter's a Daughter,* was not available in America until 1963, and then only in paperback. In 1973, it was published in hardcover by Arbor House.

First Editions: British: Heinemann, London, 1956. 236 pp., 15s. **American:** Dell, New York, 1963. 223 pp. (paperback), $.45.

7. THE ROAD OF DREAMS (1924)

In 1924, at about the time of the publication of *The Man in the Brown Suit* (#5, 1924), Christie published a small collection of poems under the title *The Road of Dreams.* The poems had been written over a period of several years, some possibly dating back to Agatha's teen years and World War I.

The collection is divided into four groups, the most interesting of which is "A Masque from Italy," revolving around Harlequin and the other characters of the commedia dell'arte; Christie herself pointed out the connection between these poems and the later character of Mr. Harley Quin, who appeared in his own collection of short stories, *The Mysterious Mr. Quin* (#12, 1930).

In 1973 these verses were republished as Volume I of *Poems.*

First Editions: British: Geoffrey Bles, London, 1924, 110 pp., price unavailable. **American:** None.

8. COME, TELL ME HOW YOU LIVE (1946)

Among Christie's enormous wartime output was this short, charming volume of reminiscences about her travels in the Middle East during the 1930s. Readers will find another side of Christie emerging in these pages—a resilient, enthusiastic traveler whose obvious love of this ancient part of the world led her to put up with fleas, sandstorms, and Stone Age plumbing, during a decade of annual journeys to Syria and Iraq. Since these excursions were working expeditions for the Mallowans (Agatha "hired on" as a labeler and sketcher of unearthed artifacts), archaeology figures prominently in the book. The title, in fact, is a pun on "tell," the Arabic word for hill or mound, which is used in the Middle East to describe the hill-like shapes of buried archaeological sites.

Christie wrote in *An Autobiography* that her publishers did not like *Come, Tell Me How You Live*. "They were suspicious and disapproving, afraid that I was getting completely out of hand." Her publishers did not like the Westmacotts and "they were now prepared to be suspicious of *Come, Tell Me How You Live,* or anything in fact, that enticed me away from mystery stories. However, the book was a success . . ." Christie published the book under Agatha Christie Mallowan so it wouldn't be confused with her detective books.

"A witty, chuckling book," said *Books* (*New York Herald Tribune*). "Only a person with irrepressible bounce could have stood it all and turned up with such an entertaining book" (11/17/46).

Eric Forbes-Boyd in the *Christian Science Monitor* enthused that the book was "the lightest and gayest account imaginable, and yet at the same time it presents the life and the people with the greatest clarity. We chuckle incessantly at the diverting characters . . . each is richly and unmistakably alive; and when we close the book, we have laughed our way to an understanding of the East that is quite beyond what is to be gained from the ordinary travel book" (11/29/46).

Agatha Christie dedicated this affectionate account of her time spent in Syria before the war:

To my husband, Max Mallowan; to the Colonel, Bumps, Mac and Guilford, this meandering chronicle is affectionately dedicated.

The Colonel was a retired colonel from the Indian army, A. H. Burn, who joined Max as an assistant during the second season at Chagar Bazar. The Colonel, an amateur archaeologist, was very good at handling the local men who worked at the sites. He also was blessed with a sense of humor. Louis Osman, a young architect who also was Max's assistant, had the nickname of "Bumps"; the reason, according to Max in his memoirs, was that he "referred to all the hummocks, that is the ancient tells which litter the plain, as bumps . . ." Mac was Robin Macartney, a young architect fresh from the Architectural Association, who joined Max at the beginnning of the dig at Chagar Bazar. Mac was "a man endowed with a cast-iron stomach and few words, assets that I have always regarded as indispensable on a survey," said Max. And

Guilford was also a young architect assistant who joined Max toward the end of the digging expeditions at Tell Brak. He earned Christie's respect "by being able to cut a horse's toe-nails."

First Editions: British: Collins, London, 1946. 192 pp., 10s. 6d.
American: Dodd, Mead & Co., New York, 1946. 225 pp., $3.00.

9. STAR OVER BETHLEHEM AND OTHER STORIES (1965)

This, Christie's only venture into books for children, has a slightly misleading title, since it contains five poems and six short stories, all of a religious and "Christmasy" nature. Max Mallowan thought it to be his wife's "most charming and among the most original of her works," and said, "These sweet tales . . . may fairly be styled 'Holy Detective Stories.'"

Like *Come, Tell Me How You Live, Star Over Bethlehem* was published under the name Agatha Christie Mallowan.

First Editions: British: Collins, London, 1965. 79 pp., price unavailable. **American:** Dodd, Mead & Co., New York, 1965. 79 pp., price unavailable.

10. POEMS (1973)

Christie's second and last volume of poetry includes her complete early collection *The Road of Dreams* (1924)—published here as Volume I—along with twenty-seven later verses. The dating of the poems is difficult, though titles such as "In Baghdad" and "The Nile" indicate origins during the years when Christie traveled often to the Middle East. Only one of the poems, "Picnic 1960," is easily dated.

Christie's verse is short, conventional, and inclined toward the trite and sentimental. In one late poem, "Racial Musings," Christie contemplates racial intermarriage and concludes that, "Oh, coffee-coloured world/You'll be a BORE."

Suffice it to say that, were it not for the author's name, these poems probably would not have seen their way into print, at least not under the imprint of a major publisher.

First Editions: **British**: Collins, London, 1973. 124 pp., price unavailable. **American**: Dodd, Mead & Co., New York, 1973. 124 pp., price unavailable.

11. AN AUTOBIOGRAPHY (1977)

On April 2, 1950, in a small room in a mud-brick house in Nimrud, Iraq, while sitting at a wood table placed near a window with a view of the snow-capped mountains of Kurdistan, Agatha Christie began writing her memoirs. Fifteen years and many hundreds of pages later—October 11, 1965, to be exact—at her home at Winterbrook House, Wallingford, Berkshire, the manuscript was completed.

Christie made it clear from the beginning that she did not intend to write a thorough, tidy, scholarly version of her life. She planned to indulge herself, "to plunge my hand into a lucky dip and come up with a handful of assorted memories."

She was true to her intentions. Fully a third of this, her longest book, is devoted to her untroubled, idyllic childhood in the golden age of late Victorian/Edwardian England. The balance of her life is recalled in her "lucky dip" fashion—many anecdotes of World War II and of travels around the world, a good deal of circumspection about her married life, nothing about her famous disappearance in 1926, and only a smattering of notes and comments on her immensely successful career.

Still, *An Autobiography* remains the most complete and intimate portrait of Christie, and ranks among her most charming and readable works; it is an invaluable resource for the serious Christie reader.

The manuscript was withheld from publication until the year after Christie's death, and was revised and edited by her daughter, Rosalind Hicks.

Atlantic Monthly described *An Autobiography* as "a book with much leisurely charm, full of vivid characterizations, information about the construction of her mystery novels, comic anecdotes, and flashes of satirical asperity. The few dull spots hardly count" (11/26/77).

"[Christie] has woven a beguiling web of reminiscence and reflection," observed the *Economist*. "The book's prevailing tone is of a child-like gaiety and enjoyment of life." The appeal of her autobiography, even to one allergic to her fiction, is the insignificance of the remembered detail: it adds an artless charm and freshness to the picture of her life that would be lost in a more studied self-portrait" (11/26/77).

And T. J. Binyon in the *Times Literary Supplement* (London) wrote that "there is an undeniable charm in the reminiscences of a leisurely childhood and youth, and the whole is narrated with an engaging good sense and humour. Yet there is a lack of depth about the work, which remains throughout on the level of the family anecdote. One hopes it will be complemented by the work of a sympathetic and perceptive biographer, who will be able to give some explanation of the unique phenomenon that was Agatha Christie" (11/11/77).

First Editions: British: Collins, London, 1977. 542 pp., £7.95.
American: Dodd, Mead & Co., New York, 1977. 529 pp., $15.00.

PART TWO

Christie
on
Stage, Film, and Television

PLAYS

Christie's theatre career is in its own way as spectacularly success-ful as her publishing career: though she had her share of stage flops, short runs, and unproduced plays, the name Agatha Christie is theatrical gold, in spite of the fact that plays were for her a side-line, a way of passing time between novels. Many Christie plays were adapted from her works by other playwrights, though the plays on which her reputation rests were written by her. First and foremost is *The Mousetrap* (1952), the world's longest con-tinuously running play and a breaker of all theatrical records. Close on its heels is *Witness for the Prosecution* (1953), Chris-tie's best piece of stagecraft. To that, add Christie's rare achieve-ment of three plays on the boards simultaneously in London's West End, and you have a theatrical career that many a play-wright would envy.

1. ALIBI (1928)
Christie's first work to reach the stage was *The Murder of Roger Ackroyd* (#7, 1926), which was adapted by Michael Morton un-der the title *Alibi*. The play opened May 15, 1928, at Prince of Wales's Theatre, London, produced by Gerald du Maurier, with Charles Laughton as director and star.

Alibi also marked the beginning of the author's fifty-year-long battle, and disappointment, with her stage and screen adapters. Though she recognized Morton's experience at adapting plays, Christie "much disliked his first suggestion, which was to take about twenty years off Poirot's age, call him Beau Poirot and have lots of girls fall in love with him." The author won her battle to keep Poirot Poirot, but she did have to compromise by allowing the cutting out of one of the most brilliant characters in all her works, Caroline Sheppard, the doctor's sister. "I resented the re-moval of Caroline a good deal; I liked the part she played in village life; and I like the idea of village life—reflected through the life of the doctor and his masterful sister." On the stage, the demanding, "acidulous spinster," Caroline, was replaced by a young, attractive romantic ingenue.

The *Times* (London) didn't care much for *Alibi:* "The question that troubles us . . . is whether you can make a play out of a theoretical analysis. If we do not weary of Poirot shooting questions to the right and left, Poirot with uplifted finger expounding his views to a half-circle of listeners, it is because Mr. Charles Laughton, with little help from the text, makes a personality out of the fat and sentimental little ratiocinator" (5/16/28).

The play ran for 250 performances.

With adaptations for the American audience by John Anderson, the play opened under the title *The Fatal Alibi* at the Booth Theatre, February 9, 1932. Jed Harris produced and Charles Laughton was again star and director. The American run was only twenty-four performances.

Brooks Atkinson, in the *New York Times,* thought "the narrative and the characterizations are too abstract for the morbid excitements of a crime thriller, and that Laughton's "poster portraiture" of Poirot "diverts attention from the play." *The Fatal Alibi,* he concluded, "is hard to follow in the theatre. The clues, the motives, the circumstances of evidence are all pretty generally abstract" (2/10/32).

Alibi (*British production*)

Mrs. Ackroyd	Lady Tree
Flora Ackroyd	Jane Welsh
Parker	Henry Daniell
Major Blunt	Basil Loder
Ursula Bourne	Iris Noel
Geoffrey Raymond	Henry Forbes-Robertson
Caryl Sheppard	Gillian Lind
Hercule Poirot	Charles Laughton
Doctor Sheppard	J. H. Roberts
Ralph Paton	Cyril Nash
Sir Roger Ackroyd	Norman V. Norman
Inspector Davies	John Darwin
Mr. Hammond	J. Smith-Wright
Margot	Constance Anderson

The Fatal Alibi (*American production*)

Geoffrey Raymond	Edward Crandall
Mrs. Ackroyd	Effie Shannon
Major Blunt	Kenneth Hunter
Flora Ackroyd	Jane Wyatt
Parker	Donald Randolph
Caryl Sheppard	Helen Vinson
Hercule Poirot	Charles Laughton
Ursula Bourne	Jane Bramley
Sir Roger Ackroyd	Lionel Pape
Ralph Paton	Lowell Gilmore
Doctor Sheppard	Moffat Johnston
Inspector Davies	Lawrence Cecil
Mr. Hammond	Fothringham Lysons
Margot	Andree Corday

2. BLACK COFFEE (1930)

In her autobiography, Christie states that her first original play, *Black Coffee,* had been completed before the adaptation of *The Murder of Roger Ackroyd.*

"It was a conventional spy thriller," she recalled, "and although full of clichés, it was not, I think, at all bad."

The *Times* (London), reviewing the opening night performance of December 8, 1930, at the Embassy Theatre, London, wrote, "An audience confronted with a play based on a pure problem is also likely to be bored. . . . Mrs. Christie steers her play with much dexterity; yet there are times when it is perilously near the doldrums" (12/9/30).

The production was notable for the appearance of Francis Sullivan, who was to become a friend of the Mallowans, as Poirot. The *Times* (London) judged "his contribution to the evening's entertainment a considerable one." The author, as hard to please as ever, complained, "It always seems strange to me that whoever plays Poirot is always an outsized man. Charles Laughton had plenty of avoirdupois, and Francis Sullivan was broad, thick, and about 6'2" tall."

The play, which had tryouts at the Everyman Theatre, Hampstead, was produced by Andre Van Gyseghem, and ran less than 100 performances in the West End.

There was no American production.

Black Coffee

Miss Caroline Amory	Josephine Middleton
Lucia Amory	Joyce Bland
Richard Amory	Lawrence Hardman
Barbara Amory	Judith Mentrath
Edward Raynor	Andre Van Gyseghem
Sir Claud Amory	Wallace Evennett
Dr. Carelli	Donald Wolfit
Hercule Poirot	Francis L. Sullivan
Captain Arthur Hastings	John Boxer
Inspector Japp	Richard Fisher
Treadwell	Walter Tennyson
Dr. Graham	Frank Follows
Johnson	George F. Wiggins

3. LOVE FROM A STRANGER (1936)

"Philomel Cottage," from *The Listerdale Mystery* (#20, 1934), was adapted under the title *Love from a Stranger* by actor-author Frank Vosper. After tryouts at Wyndham's Theatre by the 1930 Players, the play was produced by Murray Macdonald at the New Theatre, London, March 31, 1936, for a run of 149 performances.

The *Times* (London) enthused, "The suspense is maintained; each turn of the story is clear and striking; the terror-stricken self-control of the girl and the man's gross and abominable insanity are depicted . . . with every refinement of a murderous thriller. . . . The play does not call for the high terrors of the imagination. . . . But a successful thriller it certainly is" (4/1/36).

The American production opened September 21, 1936, at the Erlanger Theatre, and moved to the Fulton Theatre, New York, on September 29. Frank Vosper was still in the lead, and the American cast was noteworthy for Jessie Royce Landis and Mildred Natwick.

The play did not go over well in America, and ran for only thirty-one performances on Broadway. The *New York Times* criticized Vosper for taking Christie's story and "spinning it out to a dangerous length. Only in the last act does it settle down to the serious business at hand. . . . But it does take unholy time to get there, and the author's occasional hints appear to be lugged in like the flowers" (9/30/36).

Curiously, Frank Vosper's life ended in a mystery worthy of Christie. In 1937, on a transatlantic crossing, he suddenly disappeared from ship. Weeks later, his bruised body—he was apparently a victim of foul play—was washed up on the shores of France.

Love from a Stranger (*British production*)

Louise Garrard	Muriel Aked
Mavis Wilson	Norait Howard
Cecily Harrington	Marie Ney
Bruce Lovell	Frank Vosper
Nigel Lawrence	Geoffrey King
Hodgson	Charles Hodges
Ethel	Esma Cannon
Dr. Gribble	S. Major Jones

Love from a Stranger (*American production*)

Louise Garrard	Minna Phillips
Mavis Wilson	Olive Reeves-Smith
Cecily Harrington	Jessie Royce Landis
Bruce Lovell	Frank Vosper
Nigel Lawrence	Leslie Austen
Hodgson	A. G. Andrews
Ethel	Mildred Natwick
Dr. Gribble	George Graham

4. AKHNATON (c. 1937, never produced)

Akhnaton is a fascinating curiosity in Christie's theatrical career, the stage counterpart to *Death Comes as the End* (#44, 1945). There is a certain irony that, in the career that produced *Witness for the Prosecution* (1953) and *The Mousetrap* (1952), the author's most ambitious and serious play has never been staged, and the script waited thirty-five years even for publication. Christie herself doubted that the play would ever be produced.

If her name did not appear on the title page, the reader would be hard pressed to guess the writer of *Akhnaton*. There is no body in the library, no chintzy drawing rooms, no vicars or retired colonels, no nosy gardeners or gossipy spinsters. Instead, there is a two-hour dramatization, setting circa 1350 B.C., of Pharaoh Akhnaton's attempt to bring his nation to the worship of a new, monotheistic deity—Aton, the Sun God—and to abandon the old "pagan" god, Amon.

Christie's interest in the ancient world was, of course, an outgrowth of her marriage to Max Mallowan, and of the Mallowans' friendship with such Egyptologists as Howard Carter, discoverer of Tutankhamen's tomb (whom Christie met in 1931 at Luxor), and Stephen Glanville. The latter encouraged Agatha to read ancient literature, such as the Amarna letters, and to set works of hers, like *Death Comes as the End,* in ancient Egypt.

Mallowan, who is understandably biased toward the work his wife did with settings and characters near and dear to his archaeologist's heart, describes *Akhnaton* (in *Mallowan's Memoirs*) as "Agatha's most beautiful and profound play . . . brilliant in its delineation of character, tense with drama. . . . The treatment comes as near to historical plausibility as any play about the past can be. . . . The Egyptian court life and the vagaries of Egyptian religion come alive. . . . It seems to me that the characters themselves are here submitted to exceptionally penetrating analytical treatment. . . . Perhaps one day this lovely play . . . will be performed on the stage."

Akhnaton was published by Collins and Dodd, Mead in 1973.

5. PERIL AT END HOUSE (1940)

Adapted by Arnold Ridley from the novel (#15, 1932), *Peril* was produced by A. R. Whitmore, and opened at the Vaudeville Theatre, London, on May 1, 1940.

The *Times* (London) commented that "Hercule Poirot is the most talkative of detectives, and the greatest part of this intricate story . . . comes to us through his perpetually ratiocinative talk. . . . There are times when we should prefer that the syllogisms were acted rather than spoken, but the talk is on the whole agreeably lucid and vivid . . . it cannot be said that the talk anywhere conspicuously hangs fire. . . . Mr. Sullivan conspicuously enjoys Poirot's eloquence and handles it skillfully" (5/2/40).

There was no American production.

Peril at End House

Stranger	Wilfred Fletcher
Henry	Donald Bisset
Terry Ord	Tully Comber
Frances Rice	Phoebe Kershaw
Hercule Poirot	Francis L. Sullivan
Captain Hastings	Ian Fleming
"Nick" Buckley	Olga Edwards
Commander Challenger	William Senior
Stanley Croft	Beckett Bould
Ellen [Wilson]	Josephine Middleton
Maggie Buckley	Isabel Dean
Charles Vyse	Brian Oulton
Mrs. Croft	May Hallat
Inspector Weston	Charles Mortimer
Dr. Helena Graham	Margery Caldicott
Janet Buckley	Nancy Poultney

6. TEN LITTLE NIGGERS/TEN LITTLE INDIANS (1943)

"I suppose it was *Ten Little Niggers* that set me on the path of being a playwright as well as a writer of books," Christie wrote in *An Autobiography*. Though she had two earlier original plays to her credit, *Black Coffee* (1930) ran less than 100 performances and *Akhnaton* (1937) has never been staged, *Ten Little Niggers* marks the beginning of Christie's success as an adapter of her books and stories, which would reach its zenith with *The Mousetrap* (1952) and *Witness for the Prosecution* (1953).

Christie originally showed her adaptation of her novel *Ten Little Niggers* (#35, 1939) to Charles Cochran, who wanted to produce it but could not find backers. Bertie Mayer, another stage producer, liked the play when he read it some time later, and convinced Irene Hentschel to produce and direct it. *Ten Little Niggers* opened at the St. James's Theatre, London, November 17, 1943, after tryouts at the Wimbledon Theatre, starting September 29. The play had 260 performances at the St. James's.

The *Times* (London) reviewer said, "This is not a play. It is a kind of theatrical game, with Miss Irene Hentschel pitting all her wits as a producer against our natural tendency to weary of flagrant absurdity prolonging itself throughout three acts. She has some admirable actors at her disposal; the stage action she invents for them is unfailingly ingenious; and she wins her game very comfortably" (11/18/43).

On June 27, 1944, the play opened at the Broadhurst Theatre in New York under the more acceptable American title of *Ten Little Indians*. Produced by the Shubert brothers and Albert de Courville, directed by de Courville, with scenery by Howard Bay, the play ran a respectable 425 performances.

Lewis Nichols, in the *New York Times* wrote, "If melodrama could be graded only qualitatively by the number of corpses, *Ten Little Indians* no doubt would run forever. . . . Like the number of corpses and potential corpses, all the ingredients were there. But as it has turned out, *Ten Little Indians* does not climb far above the potential stage. The chief troubles with the play are its talkativeness and its lack of full explanation for its grisly doings" (6/28/44).

Christie's adaptation is notable for the changed ending, which considerably alters the fate of two of the characters in the original novel. (See #35.) "I must make two of the characters innocent, to be reunited at the end and come safe out of the ordeal. This would not be contrary to the spirit of the original nursery rhyme, since there is one version . . . which ends, 'He got married and then there were none.'"

An adjunct to the stage career of *Ten Little Niggers* was *Something's Afoot,* a musical murder-mystery spoof which opened at the Lyceum Theatre, New York, on May 27, 1976. The show, which made no mention of any connection with Christie, uses the plot of ten guests marooned on an island estate, with the addition of Miss Tweed, a Christie-like character played by Tessie O'Shea. *Something's Afoot,* with music, lyrics, and book by James McDonald, David Vos, and Robert Gerlach, cannot be considered an adaptation of Christie, and is best described as "inspired by."

Ten Little Niggers (*British production*)

Mr. Rogers	William Murray
Mrs. Rogers	Hilda Bruce-Potter
Fred Narracott	Reginald Barlow
Vera Claythorne	Linden Travers
Philip Lombard	Terence de Marney
Anthony Marston	Michael Blake
William Blore	Percy Walsh
General Mackenzie	Eric Cowley
Emily Brent	Henrietta Watson
Sir Lawrence Wargrave	Allan Jeayes
Dr. Armstrong	Gwyn Nicholls

Ten Little Indians (*American production*)

Mr. Rogers	Neil Fitzgerald
Mrs. Rogers	Georgia Harvey
Fred Narracott	Patrick O'Connor
Vera Claythorne	Claudia Morgan
Philip Lombard	Michael Whalen
Anthony Marston	Anthony Kemble Cooper
William Blore	J. Pat O'Malley
General Mackenzie	Nicholas Joy
Emily Brent	Estelle Winwood
Sir Lawrence Wargrave	Halliwell Hobbes
Dr. Armstrong	Harry Worth

7. APPOINTMENT WITH DEATH (1945)

Christie's adaptation of her mystery of the same title (#31, 1938), which was set in Jerusalem and Jordan, opened at the Piccadilly Theatre, London, on March 31, 1945, produced by Terence de Marney.

The *Times* (London) wrote, "It is not until the end of the second act that Mrs. Boynton's appointment, which had always seemed imminent, is actually kept. . . . There is ingenuity here, but all the polish of the acting and the production cannot disguise the artificiality of the characters and their behavior; and what is acceptable as a kind of crossword in crime within the pages of a book becomes tedious on the stage" (4/2/45).

There have been no American productions.

Appointment with Death

Mrs. Boynton	Mary Clare
Ginevra Boynton	Deryn Kerbey
Lennox Boynton	Ian Lubbock
Nadine Boynton	Beryl Machin
Lift Boy	John Glennon
Alderman Higgs	Percy Walsh
Clerk Bedouin	Anthony Dorset
Lady Westholme	Janet Burnell
Miss Pryce	Joan Hickson
Dr. Gerard	Gerard Hinze
Sarah King	Carla Lehmann
Jefferson Cope	Alan Sedgwick
Raymond Boynton	John Wynn
Dragoman	Harold Berens
Colonel Carbury	Owen Reynolds
Lady Visitor	Cherry Herbert
Hotel Visitors	Corinne Whitehouse Joseph Blanchard

8. MURDER ON THE NILE/HIDDEN HORIZON (1946)

Christie's adaptation of one of her most famous books *Murder on the Nile* (#30, 1937) opened on March 19, 1946, at the Ambassadors Theatre, London, produced by Claude Guerney. The *Times* (London) was less than enthusiastic: "Once more the 'Who did it?' piece, and this time in almost its crudest form. Motives are distributed among the passengers in the Observation Saloon of the Nile steamer as lightly as though they were raffle tickets, and none of those who receive one has sufficient personality to make us wish that he or she will not be the winner or loser. All depends accordingly on the ingenuity of the mystery, and its solution, when at last it is revealed, can scarcely be said to throw a retrospective fascination on the details of the case; it is something which has very likely crossed our minds more than once only to be dismissed as altogether too easy" (3/20/46).

The Broadway production, with the curious title change to *Hidden Horizon,* opened at the Plymouth Theatre, New York, on September 19, 1946, produced by the Shuberts, in association with Albert de Courville, directed by de Courville, sets by Charles Elson, costumes by Everett Staples. The production, which was distinguished mainly by the appearance of Diana Barrymore and Halliwell Hobbes, limped through twelve performances before closing.

Brooks Atkinson, in his review in the *New York Times,* made clear the reasons for the play's short run.

" 'It's a very bad business,' remarked the studious skipper of a Nile river paddle-boat when he heard that his most opulent passenger had been murdered. Most students of the drama at the Plymouth last evening regarded the skipper's remark as sensible. For Agatha Christie's crime plaything, turned on there together with the air-conditioning, was the most unnecessary article of the season—dull in theme, dull in story, dull in the acting" (9/20/46).

Murder on the Nile (*British production*)

1st Beadseller	Richard Spranger
2nd Beadseller	Christmas Grose
Steward	James Roberts
Miss ffolliot-ffoulkes	Helen Haye
Christina Grant	Joanna Derrill
Smith	Ronald Millar
Louise	Jacqueline Robert
Dr. Bessner	Hugo Schuster
Simon Mostyn	Ivan Brandt
Kay Mostyn	Rosemary Scott
Father Borrondale	David Horne
Jacqueline de Severac	Vivienne Bennett
Tibbotts	Walter Lindsay

Hidden Horizon (*American production*)

1st Beadseller	Monty Banks, Jr.
2nd Beadseller	David Andrews
Steward	Charles Alexander
Miss ffolliot-ffoulkes	Eva Leonard-Boyne
Christina Grant	Joy Ann Page

Smith	David Manners
Louise	Edith Kingdon
Dr. Bessner	Peter Von Zerneck
Simon Mostyn	Blair Davies
Kay Mostyn	Barbara Joyce
Archdeacon Pennyfeather	Halliwell Hobbes
Jacqueline de Severac	Diana Barrymore
McNaught	Winston Ross
Two Egyptian Policemen	{ Leland Hamilton { Damian Nimer

9. THE MURDER AT THE VICARAGE (1949)

In 1943, when she adapted *Ten Little Niggers,* Christie resolved that, from then on, only *she* would adapt her works for the stage. Her resolve faltered, for on December 14, 1949, the first Jane Marple novel (#13, 1930) opened in a two-act stage adaptation by Moie Charles and Barbara Toy. The production, at the Playhouse, London, was produced by Reginald Tate, who also starred as Lawrence Redding. The production was a success, and ran for 1,776 performances.

The *Times* (London) observed, "Everyone has a motive for killing. Nobody, unhappily, has any good stage reason for living. It is not until the final scene—the pressure of events then forcing two of the characters into melodramatic life—that we become aware that there was, after all, an effective one-act play in Miss Christie's novel.

"Meanwhile our entertainment depends on innumerable clues turning now outwards and now away from one or other of the walking ciphers of the vicarage and on the rather thin theatrical excitement of first one, then another confession, both of which possibly cancel each other. . . . There is perhaps a certain piquancy to the fact that Hercule Poirot's place is taken by an inquisitive village spinster, but she uses the master's methods and is immensely ratiocinative" (12/15/49).

There was no American production. A successful revival of *Murder at the Vicarage* opened at the Savoy Theatre, London, July 28, 1975. Barbara Mullen portrayed Miss Marple.

The Murder at the Vicarage

The Rev. Leonard Clement	Jack Lambert
Griselda [Clement]	Genine Graham
Dennis [Clement]	Michael Newell
Mary	Betty Sinclair
The Rev. Ronald Hanes	Michael Darbyshire
Lettice Protheroe	Andrea Lea
Miss Marple	Barbara Mullen
Mrs. Price Ridley	Mildred Cottell
Anne Protheroe	Alvys Mabon
Lawrence Redding	Reginald Tate
Dr. Haydock	Francis Roberts
Inspector Slack	Stanley Van Beers

10. THE HOLLOW (1951)

Christie adapted her ambitious mystery novel *The Hollow* (#46, 1946) for the stage against the advice of her daughter, Rosalind, who warned, "It's a good book, and I like it, but you can't make it into a play."

In order to adapt it for the stage, Christie dropped Poirot entirely, with the confession that she had always thought the book ruined by Hercule's presence, and the play was her opportunity to get him out of the way. *The Hollow* was directed by Hobert Gregg, and opened at the Fortune Theatre on June 7, 1951; it had a run of 376 performances.

Christie's husband, Max, thought *The Hollow* was the best of his wife's staged works after *Witness for the Prosecution* (1953). He thought *The Hollow* "exploited the dramatic potential of the novel to the full, with the utmost economy in assembling the plot . . ."

The *Times* (London) observed, "Mrs. Christie's first act is as patient in its exposition as a Pinero first act, only a great deal duller; but once the fatal shot has been fired and the police arrive to ask questions there can be nothing but admiration for the impudent skill with which she directs suspense first this way, then that, and yet contrives to let certainty arrive in due course with an effect of genuine surprise" (6/8/51).

There was no American production.

The Hollow

Henrietta Angkatell — Beryl Baxter
Sir Henry Angkatell — George Thorpe
Lady Angkatell — Jeanne de Casalis
Midge Harvey — Jessica Spencer
Mr. Gudgeon — A. J. Brown
Edward Angkatell — Colin Douglas
Doris [Saunders] — Patricia Jones
Gerda Christow — Joan Newell
Dr. John Christow — Ernest Clark
Veronica Cray — Dianne Foster
Inspector Colquhoun — Martin Wyldeck
Detective Sergeant Penny — Shaw Taylor

11. THE MOUSETRAP (1952)

Christie's most successful play, if "successful" is an adequate word to describe the longest continuously running stage play in history, began in 1947, when Christie was asked by the BBC to write a radio play for the occasion of Queen Mary's eightieth birthday (see *Three Blind Mice,* #51).

After the radio drama *Three Blind Mice* was broadcast, Christie decided to turn it into a short story and a full-length stage play. The short story version was published in the United States in *Three Blind Mice and Other Stories,* but withheld from publication in British collections so as not to reveal the ending of the plot of the planned stage production.

Peter Saunders, who had successfully staged *The Hollow* in London in 1951 produced the new Christie play, which had regional tryouts under the original radio play title of *Three Blind Mice.* Before the London opening, the title was changed because of a conflict with an earlier play of the same name. Christie's son-in-law Anthony Hicks (daughter Rosalind's second husband) suggested the new title, *The Mousetrap,* after *Hamlet,* act III, scene 2, where Hamlet is about to stage the "play within a play," which points up his mother's treachery and infidelity to Hamlet's father.

"And what do you call the play?" King Claudius asks.

"The Mousetrap," Hamlet replies.

The Mousetrap opened at the Ambassadors Theatre, London, on November 25, 1952, with Richard Attenborough and his wife, Sheila Sim, in the lead roles. Peter Coates directed and provided the sets.

"I must say that I had no feeling whatsoever that I had a great success on my hands, or anything remotely resembling that," Christie wrote in her autobiography of the opening of *The Mousetrap*. Max Mallowan in his memoirs recalled that Agatha predicted "a three months' run" for the play. "Once the play caught on," Mallowan continues, "there was competition to see it; indeed a frenzied desire to get a seat."

It was producer Saunders who saw that his hit play had the potential for an open-ended run, if the play could be promoted as a "tradition" for London theatregoers, a must-see for visitors and for Christie fans. He wisely kept the play in a small house (the Ambassadors had 490 seats; the St. Martins, to which the play later moved, has 550 seats) to insure the play's survival during whatever slack periods might come at the box office.

"Once the play was entrenched," writes Mallowan, "it was hard to move, and seeing *The Mousetrap* became a part of The American Tour, as important as a glimpse of Buckingham Palace and a visit to the Tower of London."

The importance of the American tourist in keeping the play on the boards for three decades has been insured in part by an agreement between Christie (and later her grandson Mathew, who was given the copyright of the play as a tenth birthday present) and the British producers. They agreed *not* to allow a Broadway production or U.S. road show of the play until after the English production has closed; the same embargo is in effect in Australia.

An off-Broadway production opened November 5, 1960, at the Maidman Playhouse and ran for 192 performances, closing April 23, 1961. The play was produced by Robert D. Feldstein in association with Spice Wood Enterprises; Adrian Hall directed.

A similar performance restriction applies to the filming of the play. The film rights were sold long ago to producers Victor Saville and Eddie Small, who were aware at the time that it might be years before their investment paid off. Both have since died, and the rights are still being held by their heirs against that (probably) distant day when the London production will close.

The Mousetrap celebrated its thirtieth birthday on November 25, 1982, with its 12,483rd performance. The play has grossed over £7,000,000 (about $14,000,000), and has been seen by five million theatregoers. The eight characters have been played by 182 actors, and the play has had twelve directors.

The *Times* (London) wrote, "The piece admirably fulfils the special requirements of the theatre. . . . The people are nicely assorted. . . . These provide the colour, the mystification, the suspects, and the screams . . . [the characters] fit the play as snugly as pieces in a jigsaw puzzle. There remain the alarming silences, which are perhaps the truest test of such a piece on the stage" (11/26/52).

Lewis Funke in the *New York Times* said that the play, "though not great, as was conceded by critical colleagues in London, is as they also admitted, good enough . . . it is the Christie skill and polish in throwing you off the scent that keeps this entertainment going. . . . 'The Mousetrap' will not exactly shake you up, but neither will it let you down" (11/7/60).

The Mousetrap (*British production*)

Mollie Ralston	Sheila Sim
Giles Ralston	John Paul
Christopher Wren	Allan McClelland
Mrs. Boyle	Mignon O'Doherty
Major Metcalf	Aubrey Dexter
Miss Casewell	Jessica Spencer
Mr. Paravicini	Martin Miller
Detective Sergeant Trotter	Richard Attenborough

The Mousetrap (*American production—off-Broadway*)

Mollie Ralston	Angela Thornton
Giles Ralston	John Irving
Christopher Wren	John Wynne-Evans
Mrs. Boyle	Margaretta Warwick
Major Metcalf	John Scanlon
Miss Casewell	Barbara Stanton
Mr. Paravicini	Allen Joseph
Detective Sergeant Trotter	Barry Newman

12. WITNESS FOR THE PROSECUTION (1953)

"One night at the theatre stands out in my memory specially," Christie said in her memoirs of the opening night of *Witness for the Prosecution*. "I can safely say that that was the only first night I have enjoyed."

The author's lack of first night jitters was due in part to her own satisfaction with her stage adaptation of the short story from *The Hound of Death* (#18, 1933); in the decades since the play's premiere, critics and theatre historians have tended to agree that *Witness* is Christie's best piece of stagecraft.

The writing of the play was not without problems. Christie had to read "quantities" of trial transcripts to get a feel for the setting, and she consulted with barristers on details of law and authenticity. Most interesting, she had to fight with "everyone" to keep her new, different, and violent ending in the play—an ending which she felt worked in the context of theatre. Christie felt so strongly about the changed denouement that she refused to allow the play to be produced if the producers and advisors insisted on the same ending as the original story.

Witness for the Prosecution opened at the Winter Garden Theatre, London, for a run of 458 performances, on October 28, 1953. It was produced by Peter Saunders and directed by Wallace Douglas, with decor by Michael Weight.

The American production opened at the Henry Miller Theatre, New York, on December 16, 1954, and ran 645 performances. The play was produced by Gilbert Miller and Peter Saunders and directed by Robert Lewis; design was by Raymond Sovey and costumes were supervised by Kathryn Miller. The play won the New York Drama Critics' Circle Award for best foreign play of the New York 1954–1955 season.

"The author has two ends in view, and she attains them both," said the *Times* (London). "[Christie] leaves herself with a denouement which is at once surprising and credible. . . . Mrs. Christie . . . has got the audience in her pocket . . . the evidence brings the trial to a triumphantly satisfying conclusion. It is only then that the accomplished thriller writer shows her real hand" (10/29/53).

The *New York Times* review of the Broadway opening described the play as "skillfully written, neatly directed, and extremely well acted. . . . The solution is the management's secret. But the ingenuity of play and performance is bound to leak out somewhere" (12/17/54).

Witness for the Prosecution (*British production*)

Greta	Rosalie Westwater
Carter	Walter Horsburgh
Mr. Mayhew	Milton Rosmer
Leonard Vole	Derek Blomfield
Sir Wilfrid Robarts, Q.C.	David Horne
Inspector Hearne	David Raven
Plainclothes Detective	Kenn Kennedy
Romaine	Patricia Jessel
Clerk of the Court	Philip Holles
Mr. Justice Wainwright	Percy Marmont
Alderman	Walter Horsburgh
Mr. Myers, Q.C.	D. A. Clarke-Smith
Court Usher	Nicolas Tannar
Court Stenographer	John Bryning
Warder	Denzil Ellis
The Judge's Clerk	Muir Little
1st Barrister	George Dudley
2nd Barrister	Jack Bulloch
3rd Barrister	Lionel Gadsden
4th Barrister	John Farries Moss
5th Barrister	Richard Coke
6th Barrister	Agnes Fraser
1st Member of the Jury	Lauderdale Beckett
2nd Member of the Jury	Iris Fraser Foss
3rd Member of the Jury	Kenn Kennedy
A Policeman	David Homewood
Dr. Wyatt	Graham Stuart
Janet Mackenzie	Jean Stuart
Mr. Clegg	Peter Franklin
The Other Woman	Rosemary Wallace

Witness for the Prosecution (*American production*)

Carter	Gordon Nelson
Greta	Mary Barclay
Mr. Mayhew	Robin Craven

Leonard Vole	Gene Lyons
Sir Wilfrid Robarts, Q.C.	Francis L. Sullivan
Inspector Hearne	Claude Horton
Plainclothes Detective	Ralph Leonard
Romaine	Patricia Jessel
1st Member of the Jury	Jack Bittner
2nd Member of the Jury	Andrew George
3rd Member of the Jury	Dolores Rashid
Court Usher	Arthur Oshlag
Clerk of the Court	Ronald Dawson
Mr. Justice Wainwright	Horace Braham
Alderman	R. Cobden-Smith
Mr. Myers, Q.C.	Ernest Clark
Janet Mackenzie	Una O'Connor

13. SPIDER'S WEB (1954)

This, Christie's first original play since *Akhnaton* (circa 1937), was written especially for British actress Margaret Lockwood, who approached Peter Saunders, producer of *The Mousetrap* (1952) and *Witness for the Prosecution* (1953), to ask him to request a new, custom-tailored play from the author. Christie, who at the time was "hot property" in the West End, due to her simultaneous runs of *Mousetrap* and *Witness,* complied with Saunders's request, and *Spider's Web* became the third Christie play to run simultaneously in London when it opened December 13, 1954, at the Savoy Theatre. The production was produced and directed by Wallace Douglas, with decor by Michael Weight; Margaret Lockwood appeared as Clarissa Hailsham-Brown, the role that had been written for her. *Spider's Web* ran for 774 performances.

The *Times* (London) wrote, "Miss Agatha Christie tries this time to combine a story of murder with a comedy of character . . . the common ground on which both sections may stand is dangerously small. . . . The thriller gives all the characters a turn and yet contrives at the end to produce a twist. It is a twist which surprises rather than satisfies the logical mind" (12/15/54).

The *Daily Telegraph* (London), in a review by W. A. Darlington, complained that the characters exhibited "a gaity which, if it were plausible, would be unseemly" (12/14/54).

Alan Dent in the *News-Chronicle* (London) found the solution "far more baffling than the mystery," then added, "but it is always a pleasure to be baffled by Agatha Christie" (12/14/54).

Spider's Web was staged off-off-Broadway at Lolly's Theatre Club, New York, in 1974, in a production directed by Anthony de Vito. Howard Thompson in the *New York Times* called the modest production (the theatre only seated seventy) "smooth, typical Christie . . . the denouement is satisfactory, if not the usual Christie dazzler" (1/17/74).

The author, in her autobiography, said that she enjoyed writing the part of Clarissa in *Spider's Web,* and described Margaret Lockwood in the role as "having an enormous flair for comedy, as well as being able to be dramatic . . . she was enchanting."

Christie also recalled that she considered titling the play *Clarissa Finds a Body.*

There was no American production.

Spider's Web

Sir Rowland Delahaye	Felix Aylmer
Hugo Birch	Harold Scott
Jeremy Warrender	Myles Eason
Clarissa Hailsham-Brown	Margaret Lockwood
Pippa Hailsham-Brown	Margaret Barton
Mildred Peake	Judith Furse
Elgin	Sidney Monckton
Oliver Costello	Charles Morgan
Henry Hailsham-Brown	John Warwick
Inspector Lord	Campbell Singer
Constable Jones	Desmond Llewellyn

14. TOWARDS ZERO (1956)

Christie adapted her 1944 novel *Towards Zero* (#43) for the stage in collaboration with Gerald Verner; the play was produced by Peter Saunders and directed by Murray Macdonald, with decor by Michael Weight, and opened at the St. James's Theatre, London, on September 4, 1956 for a brief run.

The *Times* (London) observed that "the tempo imposed on her by the three-act drama is, as *Towards Zero* shows . . . just a little too swift for Miss Christie's bewildering cunning. The final revelation comes too close upon the heels of the preliminary inquiry. She cannot tease us quite enough for the full display of her skill at finessing. . . . Even so, the piece, compactly full of all the ripest ingredients, remains a fair specimen. . . . A not too strenuously diverting evening in which we do not smell a rat until it is too late" (9/15/56).

There was no American production.

Towards Zero

Thomas Royde	Cyril Raymond
Kay Strange	Mary Law
Mary Aldin	Gillian Lind
Mathey Treves	Frederick Leister
Nevile Strange	George Baker
Lady Tressilian	Janet Barrow
Audrey Strange	Gwen Cherrell
Ted Latimer	Michael Scott
Superintendent Battle	William Kendall
Inspector Leach	Max Brimmell
P. C. Benson	Michael Nightingale

15. VERDICT (1958)

Christie considered *Verdict* her best play after *Witness for the Prosecution* (1953), though in her autobiography she admitted the play was not a public success—a fact she attributed to *Verdict*'s not being a detective story or thriller.

"It *was* a play that concerned murder," she wrote, "but its real background and point were that an idealist is always dangerous, a possible destroyer of those who love him—and poses the question of how far you can sacrifice, not yourself, but those you love, to what you believe in, even though they do not."

"An Improbable Verdict—Play by Agatha Christie Booed" was the headline of the opening night review in the *Times* (London). The review went on to say, "Miss Agatha Christie has brought off some mighty stage surprises in her time. Alas, all the surprises in her latest play . . . are surprises that people should behave as she makes them behave. . . . And the gallery booed . . . but all things considered not on this occasion perhaps so surprising" (5/23/58).

Verdict was produced by Peter Saunders and directed by Charles Hickman, with decor by Joan Jefferson Farjeon. It ran for less than 250 performances.

Christie's autobiography records that her original title for the play was *No Fields of Amaranth,* from Walter Savage Landor's poem, "There are no flowers of amaranth on this side of the grave." She considered *Verdict* "a bad title."

There was no American production.

Verdict

Lester Cole	George Roubicek
Mrs. Roper	Gretchen Franklin
Lisa Koletzky	Patricia Jessel
Professor Karl Hendryk	Gerard Heinz
Dr. Stoner	Derek Oldham
Anya Hendryk	Viola Keats
Helen Rollander	Moira Redmond
Sir William Rollander	Norman Claridge
Detective Inspector Ogden	Michael Golden
Sergeant Pearce	Gerald Sim

16. THE UNEXPECTED GUEST (1958)

Written during the same period as *Verdict* (1958), *The Unexpected Guest,* an original play by Christie, reached the stage only a short time after its earlier and less successful sister-play. Peter Saunders once again produced, while Hubert Gregg directed and Michael Weight provided decor. The play opened at the Duchess Theatre, London, on August 12, 1958, and ran for 604 performances.

The *Times* (London) noted that though the play was "officially labeled a 'whodunit,' it is not until the piece is well underway that this becomes apparent. The exercise Miss Christie has set herself this time is to disguise a detective mystery as a thriller . . . the play [eventually runs] to formula, with repetitious police interviews, each one disclosing some fresh particle of evidence, none of which gives any clue to Miss Christie's closely guarded secret. . . . One's sympathy goes out to Mr. Philip Newman, as the dead man, for all the nightly vigils ahead" (8/13/58).

There was no American production.

The Unexpected Guest

Richard Warwick	Philip Newman
Laura Warwick	Renee Asherson
Michael Starkwedder	Nigel Stock
Miss Bennett	Winifred Oughton
Jan Warwick	Christopher Sandford
Mrs. Warwick	Violet Farebrother
Henry Angell	Paul Curran
Inspector Thomas	Michael Golden
Sergeant Cadwallader	Tenniel Evans
Julian Farrar	Roy Purcell

17. GO BACK FOR MURDER (1960)

Christie's adaptation of her 1946 novel *Five Little Pigs* (#41, 1943) opened at the Duchess Theatre, London, on March 23, 1960, under the title *Go Back for Murder*. The play was produced by Peter Saunders, directed by Hubert Gregg, with decor by Michael Weight and lighting by Michael Northen. The play ran for less than 250 performances.

The *Times* (London) observed, "Audiences show no obvious signs of growing tired of watching suspects in a case of murder rounded up and put through the hoops . . . by a dogged policeman. But Miss Agatha Christie evidently thinks it time that they had a change. She tries to vary the routine without altering its fundamental pattern . . . [in] *Go Back for Murder*. . . . It must be said, however, that Miss Christie has often got more excitement from the routine police investigation than she manages to get from this variation on the routine" (3/24/60).

There was no American production.

Go Back for Murder

Justin Fogg	Robert Urquhart
Turnball	Peter Hutton
Carla [Lemarchant]	Ann Firbank
Jeff Rogers	Mark Eden

Philip Blake	Anthony Marlowe
Meredith Blake	Laurence Hardy
Lady Melksham	Lisa Daniely
Miss Williams	Margot Boyd
Angela Warren	Dorothy Bromiley
Carolyn Crale	Ann Firbank
Amyas Crale	Nigel Green

18. RULE OF THREE (1962)

Christie's only venture into the one-act play form opened at the Duchess Theatre, London, on December 20, 1962. Produced by Peter Saunders and directed by Hubert Gregg, with decor by Peter Rise and lighting by Michael Northen, the three one-acters ("The Rats," "Afternoon at the Seaside," "The Patient") ran for ninety-two performances.

"Loose Ends in a Triple Bill—Naive Evening with Agatha Christie" was the headline of the *Times* (London) review. The reviewer went on to say, "As the talents of short-story writer and novelist often do not go hand in hand, so the successful writer of one-act plays quite frequently fails with a full-length play. And vice-versa, of course, as the new Agatha Christie programme demonstrates . . . it is a harmless, naive evening, full of readymade lines like, 'I'm not blind,' . . . and 'I think you must allow me to be the best judge of that.' . . . [The plays] will probably appeal to amateurs and the less demanding reps, but hardly one would have thought a probable addition to West End entertainments" (12/21/62).

There was no American production.

Rule of Three
"The Rats"

Sandra Gray	Betty McDowall
Jennifer Brice	Mercy Haystead
David Forrester	David Langton
Alec Hanbury	Raymond Bowers

"Afternoon at the Seaside"

Bob Wheeler	David Langton
Noreen Somers	Betty McDowall

Arthur Somers	Michael Beint
George Crum	Robert Raglan
Mrs. Crum	Mabelle George
A Mother	Vera Cook
A Young Man	John Quayle
Beach Attendant	John Abineri
Mrs. Gunner	Margot Boyd
Percy Gunner	Raymond Bowers
The Beauty	Mercy Haystead
Inspector Foley	Robin May

"The Patient"

Lansen	Raymond Bowers
Dr. Ginzberg	Robert Raglan
Inspector Cray	David Langton
Bryan Wingfield	Michael Beint
Emmeline Ross	Vera Cook
William Ross	Robin May
Brenda Jackson	Betty McDowall
The Patient	Rosemary Martin

19. FIDDLERS THREE (1972)

Agatha Christie wrote a play, *Fiddlers Five*, which had a brief life in the summer of 1971 when it toured in the provinces. The play closed before it reached the West End. However, after a complete rewrite by Christie, the play resurfaced the following year with a new title, *Fiddlers Three*.

This comedy-thriller was first offered to Peter Saunders, who had presented all of Christie's plays since *The Hollow* in 1951. Saunders decided against presenting this new Christie work because he felt the play was not up to Christie's usual standards.

Fiddlers Three opened in Guilford in August 1972. The play, directed by Allan Davis, once again failed to find a home in London's West End and eventually died a quiet death in the provinces.

This, Christie's last theatre piece, written when she was eighty years old, was a sad farewell to the theatre from one of the stage's most popular and successful playwrights.

20. A MURDER IS ANNOUNCED (1977)

After a hiatus of fifteen years, a new Christie work appeared on the London stage—this time, *A Murder Is Announced* (#52, 1950), adapted by Leslie Darbon from Christie's 1950 novel. It opened September 21, 1977, at the Vaudeville Theatre, for a run of 429 performances.

The posthumous adaptation (Christie died in January 1976) was produced by Peter Saunders and directed by Robert Chetwyn.

The *Times* (London) remarked, "Agatha Christie's hand has not posthumously stirred the ingredients of her story into a play. That has been left to Leslie Darbon, who has learnt something about plots and ominous curtain lines from Christie's work, although he has left out the fairly vital sense of atmosphere . . . there is no sense of village life, more of suburban dullness. . . . There are enough twists to stir the audience. . . . But the dialogue is stiff . . . and there is almost no mood of mystery" (9/22/77).

There was no American production.

A Murder Is Announced

Julia Simmons	Patricia Brake
Letitia Blacklock	Dinah Sheridan
Dora Bunner	Eleanor Summerfield
Patrick Simmons	Christopher Scoular
Mitzi	Mia Nadasi
Miss Marple	Dulcie Gray
Phillipa Haymes	Barbara Flynn
Mrs. Swettenham	Nancy Nevinson
Rudi Scherz	Michael Dyerball
Inspector Craddock	James Grout
Sergeant Mellors	Michael Fleming
Edmund Swettenham	Gareth Armstrong

21. CARDS ON THE TABLE (1981)

The stage adaptation of Christie's successful novel *Cards on the Table* (#27, 1936) was presented by Peter Saunders, and directed by Peter Davis. Leslie Darbon, who did the dramatization of *A Murder Is Announced* in 1977, was responsible for adapting this piece. *Cards on the Table* opened at the Vaudeville Theatre, London, on December 9, 1981. An interesting point is that Darbon cut out of the plot Hercule Poirot and Colonel Race. The play did keep Superintendent Battle and Mrs. Oliver. (As Christie readers are aware, the novel *Cards on the Table* is unique in that Christie sets up the book with four murder suspects and four crime experts.)

The *Times* (London) said, "Leslie Darbon's new Christie adaptation, *Cards on the Table*, . . . is a puzzle with as many wrong turnings as a Rubik cube and with a merry line in deception. . . . The puzzle is more intriguing for the performances . . . and more amusing for the good humour of Mr Darbon's dialogue. Some may hate this breed altogether, but, of its kind, *Cards on the Table* is a Champion" (12/11/81).

Cards on the Table

Mary	Lennett Edwards
Shaitana	William Eedle
Mrs. Oliver	Margaret Courtenay
Anne Meredith	Belinda Carroll
Mrs. Lorrimer	Pauline Jameson
Dr. Roberts	Derek Waring
Major Despard	Gary Raymond
Supt. Battle	Gordon Jackson
Butler	Charles Wallace
Sgt. O'Connor	James Harvey
Mrs. Burgess	Patricia Dresscoll
Rhoda Dawes	Mary Tamm
Doris	Jeanne Mockford
Stephens	Henry Knowles

FILMS

Though Christie's works have a long history of translation to the motion picture screen, from the silent era to the present, the adaptations have been notoriously unsuccessful, with a few exceptions, as Christie herself was usually the first to point out. Part of the difficulty lies in effectively translating the intricacies and timing of a Christie puzzle onto film; another problem has always been the reluctance of producers and directors to leave Christie alone—they tend to change locales, change eras, add characters, change detectives, toss in sex and violence, not to mention slapstick humor. In spite of all this, in the long list of Christie screen adaptations there are a few memorable and lasting films: Rene Clair's *And Then There Were None* (1945), Billy Wilder's *Witness for the Prosecution* (1957), and Sidney Lumet's *Murder on the Orient Express* (1974).

Given the large number of unfilmed Christie works, the opportunities they provide for all-star casts, and the Christie track record at the box office, it is unlikely that the silver screen's mixed-bag of a love affair with Christie will be over any time soon.

1. DIE ABENTEUER G.m.b.H. (ADVENTURE INC.) (1928)
The first adaptation of a Christie book for the screen was this 1928 German-made silent, based on the Tommy and Tuppence novel *The Secret Adversary* (#2, 1922), directed by Fred Sauer and starring Carlo Aldini and Eve Gray as Tommy and Tuppence.

2. THE PASSING OF MR. QUINN (1928)
The first British-made film based on a Christie story, this 1928 silent inexplicably added a second "n" to the title character's name. The film, which was adapted from the short story "The Coming of

Mr. Quin" from the collection *The Mysterious Mr. Quin* (#12, 1930), was produced and directed by Julius Hagen, scripted by Leslie Hiscott, and starred Trilby Clark as Mrs. Appleby, Ursula Jeans as the maid, and Stewart Rome as the doctor hero. (The Harley Quin stories were published in magazines prior to being collected in book form in 1930.)

3. ALIBI (1931)

Alibi, the first Christie sound film, was based on the 1928 play of the same title, which had been adapted by Michael Morton from the novel *The Murder of Roger Ackroyd* (#7, 1926). *Alibi* was filmed at Twickenham Studios in 1931, produced by Julius Hagen, and directed by Leslie Hiscott, who had written the script for *The Passing of Mr. Quinn* (1928). *Alibi* was the first of three films in which Austin Trevor played Poirot. Trevor, who is best remembered for his performances in *Goodbye, Mr. Chips* and *The Red Shoes,* was terribly miscast as the Belgian: Trevor was young, handsome, and, *sacre Dieu!*, clean shaven!

Alibi also starred Elizabeth Allen, Clare Greet, and Franklin Dyall.

4. BLACK COFFEE (1931)

In 1931 Twickenham Studios filmed Christie's original play of the same title, which had opened in London the previous year. Leslie Hiscott directed, and Austin Trevor was once again in the Poirot role. Also starring were Richard Cooper, Adrienne Allen, Melville Cooper, and C. V. France. The *Times* (London), which made no mention of Trevor's almost total dissimilarity to Poirot, said, "The film nowhere departs from the beaten track of detective stories, but it is, in its own kind, a reasonable and competent piece of work" (8/24/31).

5. LORD EDGWARE DIES (1934)

The last of the three films with Austin Trevor as Poirot, *Lord Edgware Dies,* was based on the 1933 novel of the same title

(#17). The film was made by Real Art Studios, produced by Julius Hagen, and directed by Henry Edwards. The cast also included Jane Carr, Richard Cooper, and John Turnbull.

6. LOVE FROM A STRANGER (1937)

Love from a Stranger was filmed in England in 1936–37 by Trafalgar Studios, produced by Max Schach, and released in the United States by United Artists. The screenplay was adapted by Frances Marion from Frank Vosper's 1936 stage play of the same title, which actor-author Vosper had adapted from the Christie short story "Philomel Cottage," published first in the collection *The Listerdale Mystery* (#20, 1934).

Though filmed in Britain, *Love from a Stranger* bears the strong imprint of Hollywood. The director was the American Rowland V. Lee (best known for *The Count of Monte Cristo,* 1934, *Son of Frankenstein,* 1939, and *The Bridge of San Luis Rey,* 1944), and the stars were the American Ann Harding, and British-born Basil Rathbone, both of whom had long Hollywood careers.

The *New York Times,* in a review by Frank S. Nugent, said, "*Love from a Stranger,* for all its excellence of production and performance, is a throwback to . . . melodramatic ancestors. . . . We have been immunized to its kind of theatrical harrowing and trained to defend ourselves by laughing at the wrong moments. . . . If you feel like taking it seriously it is a tense and moving melodrama; if you want to laugh at it you can. You will be right either way" (4/19/37).

Cast:

Carol Howard	Ann Harding
Gerald Lovell	Basil Rathbone
Kate Meadows	Binnie Hale
Ronald Bruce	Bruce Seton
Aunt Lou	Jean Cadell
Dr. Gribble	Brian Powley
Emmy	Joan Hickson
Hobson	Donald Calthrop
Mr. Tuttle	Eugene Leahy

7. AND THEN THERE WERE NONE/TEN LITTLE NIGGERS (1945)

The best of the early Christie film adaptations is the 1945 version of Christie's famous book *Ten Little Niggers/Ten Little Indians* (#35, 1939). It was directed by French director Rene Clair and produced by him for Twentieth Century-Fox, with a screenplay by Dudley Nichols based on Christie's book and the 1943 play.

In addition to Clair's evocative and true-to-the-original direction, *And Then There Were None* benefited from a fine cast of Hollywood actors, with appropriately stylish and moody sets by Ernst Fetge and costumes by Rene Hubert.

The screenplay used Christie's own second ending (different from that of the novel), which she had used in the stage version. The "happy" ending of the film and play were based on a version of the nursery rhyme which ended with the verse, "He got married and then there were none," instead of "He went and hanged himself and then there were none," which Christie had used in the novel.

For British release, the title was changed back to the original novel title, which was more familiar to British audiences.

Bosley Crowther in the *New York Times* enthused, "It sips with delicacy and taste. . . . Rene Clair has produced an exciting film and has directed a splendid cast in it with humor and a light macabre touch" (11/1/45).

Cast:

Judge Quincannon	Barry Fitzgerald
Doctor Armstrong	Walter Huston
Philip Lombard	Louis Hayward
Blore	Roland Young
Vera Claythorne	June Duprez
General Mandrake	C. Aubrey Smith
Emily Brent	Judith Anderson
Prince Nikki Starloff	Mischa Auer
Rogers	Richard Haydn
Mrs. Rogers	Queenie Leonard

8. LOVE FROM A STRANGER/A STRANGER PASSES (2nd Version) (1947)

Ten years after the original film version was made in England, Eagle-Lion films, an independent American film-making company, remade *Love from a Stranger* (1937). The second version, which was scripted by Philip MacDonald, was released in the United States in 1947, and in Britain the same year under the title *A Stranger Passes*. James J. Geller produced and Richard Whorf directed.

"The thrill has gone from *Love from a Stranger*," lamented the *New York Times*. "When first filmed ten years ago it was a pretty good piece of antimacassar melodrama . . . the audience knows only too well how the honeymoon will end . . . no suspense or surprise is left to stimulate the spectator . . . the average movie-goer is a pretty 'hep' customer and the chances are he will be so far ahead of the story that its climactic scene will explode with all the thunder of a cap pistol" (11/28/47).

Cast:

Manuel Cortez	John Hodiak
Cecily Harrington	Sylvia Sidney
Mavis Wilson	Ann Richards
Nigel Lawrence	John Howard
Auntie Loo-Loo	Isobel Elsom
Billings	Ernest Cossart
Ethel	Anita Sharp-Bolster
Dr. Gribble	Philip Tonge
Inspector Hobday	Fred Worlock

9. WITNESS FOR THE PROSECUTION (1957)

After a decade's hiatus, Christie's work returned to the screen with Billy Wilder's superb version of *Witness for the Prosecution,* produced for United Artists by Arthur Hornblow, Jr. The screenplay was written by Wilder and Harry Kurnitz, and was based on Christie's own successful stage version (1953) of her story (#18, 1933), the rights to which she sold to United Artists for the then considerable sum of £116,000. Wilder—who by 1957 had directed such film classics as *Double Indemnity* (a topic he tackled more than once), *Lost Weekend, Sunset Boulevard, Stalag 17, Sabrina,* and *The Seven Year Itch*—showed a masterly hand in casting his Christie film, and the performances of Charles Laughton, Elsa Lanchester, and Marlene Dietrich have remained among the best of those stars' careers.

Witness for the Prosecution received six Academy Award nominations: Best Picture; Best Actor (Laughton); Best Supporting Actress (Lanchester); Best Director (Wilder); Best Sound; and Best Film Editing. Though the film did not win an Oscar in any of the nominated categories, the success of the film is indicated by its popularity at the box office: in the first year of release, according to *Variety,* the film earned its distributors $3.75 million.

Bosley Crowther in the *New York Times* raved that "*Witness for the Prosecution* comes off extraordinarily well. This results mainly from Billy Wilder's splendid staging of some splintering courtroom scenes and a first-rate theatrical performance by Charles Laughton . . . there's never a dull or worthless moment . . . the air in the courtroom fairly crackles with emotional electricity, until that staggering surprise in the last reel. Then the whole drama explodes. . . . But it is Mr. Laughton who runs away with the show. . . . Mr. Laughton adds a wealth of comical by-play to his bag of courtroom tricks. . . . The added dimensions of Mr. Laughton bulge this black-and-white drama into a hit" (2/7/58).

Cast:

Leonard Vole	Tyrone Power
Christine Vole	Marlene Dietrich
Sir Wilfrid Robarts	Charles Laughton
Miss Plimsoll	Elsa Lanchester
Brogan-Moore	John Williams
Mayhew	Henry Daniell
Carter	Ian Wolfe
Janet Mackenzie	Una O'Connor
Mr. Myers	Torin Thatcher
Judge	Frances Compton
Mrs. French	Norma Varden
Inspector Hearne	Philip Tonge
Diana	Ruta Lee

Miss McHugh	Molly Roden
Miss Johnson	Otiola Nesmith
Miss O'Brien	Marjorie Eaton

10. THE SPIDER'S WEB (1960)

The Danzigers, a low-budget British film company, acquired the rights to the 1954 Christie play of the same name, and the film was released in 1960 by United Artists, England. The production was directed by Godfrey Grayson, a regular Danziger studio director, and starred Glynis Johns as Clarissa Hailsham-Brown and John Justin as her husband Henry. The cast included well-known British comedy stars Jack Hulbert, as Lord Roland Delahaye, and Cicely Courtneidge as Miss Peake. Even their considerable talents and popularity couldn't save *The Spider's Web* from being a mediocre effort, and the film was never released in the United States.

11. MURDER SHE SAID (1962)

In 1960 Christie sold the rights to several of her books to British MGM. It was a sale about which the author had mixed feelings.

"I kept off films for years because I thought they would give me too many heartaches," Christie is quoted as saying by biographer Gwen Robyns in *The Mystery of Agatha Christie.* "Then I sold the rights to MGM, hoping that they would use them for television. But they chose films. It was too awful . . . all the climaxes were so poor you could see them coming. I get an unregenerated pleasure when I think they're not being a success."

MGM signed Margaret Rutherford to play Jane Marple—a choice Christie was not at all happy with (see *The Mirror Crack'd from Side to Side,* #68, 1962). And *Murder She Said,* based on the novel *4.50 from Paddington* (#62, 1957), was released in 1961. The film was produced by George N. Brown and directed by George Pollock, who, according to Rutherford's autobiography, was instrumental in persuading her to appear in a film about murder (a subject she found distasteful). The script was by David Pursall and Jack Seddon, and is notable for the elimination of the character of Elspeth McGillicuddy in order to enable Miss Marple to witness the murder on the train.

A. H. Weiler in the *New York Times* found the film "typical . . . of an old-fashioned genre. But in the capable and willing hands of this British troupe . . . this modest whodunit comes off as a thoroughly satisfying and suspenseful diversion. It is . . . mainly Miss Rutherford's show . . . [she] dominates most of the scenes with a forceful characterization that enhances the humor of her lines and the suspense in the 'Murder'" (1/8/62).

Rutherford's husband, Stringer Davis, appeared in this, as well as in the next three Rutherford–Marple films.

Cast:

Miss Jane Marple	Margaret Rutherford
Dr. Quimper	Arthur Kennedy
Emma [Crackenthorpe]	Muriel Pavlow
Mr. Crackenthorpe	James Robertson Justice
Inspector Craddock	Charles Tingwell
Bryan Eastley	Ronald Howard
Cedric [Crackenthorpe]	Thorley Walters
Harold [Crackenthorpe]	Conrad Phillips
Mrs. Kidder	Joan Hickson
Alexander [Eastley]	Ronnie Raymond
Mr. Stringer	Stringer Davis
Albert	Gerald Cross
Hillman	Michael Golden

12. MURDER AT THE GALLOP (1963)

For their second film with Margaret Rutherford as Jane Marple, MGM adapted a Poirot novel, *After the Funeral* (#57, 1953), a change of detective which Christie called "too awful." The script was by David Pursall and Jack Seddon, assisted by James P. Cavanagh. The film was produced by Lawrence P. Bachmann and George N. Brown, and directed by George Pollock.

Bosley Crowther in the *New York Times* described the film as "another little fun thing. . . . *Murder at the Gallop* moves slowly and without much fuss or feathers, but it holds the pace of one of those nice mystery fictions that are so good for reading yourself to sleep" (6/18/63).

Cast:

Jane Marple	Margaret Rutherford
Hector Enderby	Robert Morley
Miss Gilchrist	Flora Robson
Inspector Craddock	Charles Tingwell
Mr. Stringer	Stringer Davis
Hillman	Duncan Lamont
Rosamund Shane	Katya Douglas
Michael Shane	James Villiers
George Crossfield	Robert Urquhart
Sergeant Bacon	Gordon Harris

13. MURDER MOST FOUL (1964)

By chance, when MGM retitled their adaptation of *Mrs. McGinty's Dead* (#55, 1952) as *Murder Most Foul,* they chose a title that Christie had given as an example of a "rotten" title for a mystery story. The producers apparently were not aware that Mr. Eastwood, in the short story "Mr. Eastwood's Adventure" from the collection *The Listerdale Mystery* (#20, 1934), had complained about publishers changing his short story titles to such as "Murder Most Foul."

This third MGM Rutherford–Marple film was released in England in 1964, and in the U.S. in 1965, after *Murder Ahoy,* the fourth in the MGM series, had already been shown here. Lawrence P. Bachmann and Ben Arbeid were the producers; George Pollock directed; the script was once again by David Pursall and Jack Seddon.

A. H. Weiler in the *New York Times* wrote, "Jane Marple appears lightly bored with an avocation she once relished . . . the freshness, fun, and games that were the cachet of her first two adventures are mainly missing from this merely mild probe into homicide. . . . While Miss Rutherford's talents are still obvious, it is clear that she is struggling mightily in an unimportant cause" (5/24/65).

Cast:

Jane Marple	Margaret Rutherford
Driffold Cosgood	Ron Moody

Inspector Craddock	Charles Tingwell
Mrs. Thomas	Megs Jenkins
Ralph Summers	Ralph Michael
Justice Crosby	Andrew Cruikshank
Bill Hanson	James Bolam
Mr. Stringer	Stringer Davis
Sheila Upward	Francesca Annis
Eva McGinigall	Allison Seebohm
Theatrical Agent	Dennis Price
Constable Wells	Terry Scott

14. MURDER AHOY! (1964)

The fourth film in the MGM series with Margaret Rutherford was not based on any Christie work, but on an original story with a nautical setting by David Pursall and Jack Seddon, who had scripted the earlier adaptations. The film was produced by Lawrence P. Bachmann and directed by George Pollock, and was released in 1964.

A. H. Weiler in the *New York Times* wrote, "This . . . film adventure involving Margaret Rutherford as . . . Miss Marple, finds her looking slightly queasy and in the doldrums most of the way. . . . It is . . . a simple matter of lots of dialogue, only a bit of which is truly funny, and a modicum of action, which is rarely exciting, intriguing, or comic. . . . Miss Rutherford . . . makes a brave attempt to make this 'murder' bright and cheerful. . . . It is a commendable try, but Miss Rutherford, poor dear, cannot do it all alone" (9/23/64).

Cast:

Miss Marple	Margaret Rutherford
Capt. deCourcy Rhumstone	Lionel Jeffries
Inspector Craddock	Charles Tingwell
Mr. Stringer	Stringer Davis
Comdr. Breeze-Connington	William Mervyn
Lieut. Compton	Francie Mathews
Sgt. Bacon	Terence Edmund
Kelly	Tony Quinn
Matron Alice Fanbraid	Joan Benham

Lieut. Comdr. Dimchurch	Gerald Cross
Sub-Lieut. Humbert	Derek Nimmo
Asst. Matron Shirley Boston	Norma Foster
Petty Officer Lamb	Roy Holder
Dusty Miller	Bernard Adams
Cecil ffolly-Hardwicke	Henry Longhurst
Lord Rudkin	Henry Oscar
Bishop Faulkner	Miles Malleson

15. TEN LITTLE INDIANS (2nd Version) (1965)

This second version of the Christie classic was produced in England by Oliver A. Unger. It was filmed in 1965 and released by Seven Arts in 1966. The screenplay by Peter Welbeck and Peter Yeldham moved the setting to the Alps, where a curious cast of American stars (Hugh O'Brian of "Wyatt Earp" fame, and pop singer Fabian) and veteran British character actors were knocked off one by one. The ninety-two-minute film was directed by George Pollock, who had also directed the MGM Margaret Rutherford–Marple films.

Bosley Crowther in the *New York Times* commented, "It would be foolish to say this remake comes within a country mile of that former movie version which was directed by Rene Clair. But it does have sufficient of the essence of Miss Christie's strange and creepy tale . . . to make it a gripping entertainment for youthful (and unfamiliar) mystery fans" (2/10/66).

Cast:

Hugh Lombard	Hugh O'Brian
Ann Clyde	Shirley Eaton
Mike Raven	Fabian
General Mandrake	Leo Genn
William Blore	Stanley Holloway
Frau Grohmann	Marianne Hoppe
Judge Cannon	Wilfrid Hyde-White
Ilona Bergen	Dahlia Lavi
Dr. Armstrong	Dennis Price
Herr Grohmann	Mario Adorf

16. THE ALPHABET MURDERS (1966)

Philip Jenkinson, a British film critic who wrote an essay, "The Agatha Christie Films," which was included in *Agatha Christie: First Lady of Crime* (1977), gives the genesis of *The Alphabet Murders*.

"It was hoped that a film would be made from *The ABC Murders*" [#25, 1936] Jenkinson writes. "Director Seth Holt and star Zero Mostel were retained and an adaptation made, which included a bedroom scene for Poirot. Dame Agatha was not amused and the production was abandoned on what was to have been the first day of shooting."

The project was revived by MGM with a different production team—and without a bedroom scene—and was released in 1966. Lawrence P. Bachmann produced. The director was Frank Tashlin, who was best known for his Bugs Bunny cartoons and his Jayne Mansfield and Jerry Lewis films. The screenplay was by David Pursall and Jack Seddon, who had scripted the Margaret Rutherford–Marple films for MGM. One of the surprises of the film was the casting of the young American Tony Randall as Poirot; with skillful makeup, Randall did manage to achieve a somewhat too youthful but nevertheless Poirot-like appearance.

A. H. Weiler in the *New York Times* commented, "Neither Mr. Randall's Poirot, nor the gags, chases, and red herrings offered, are inventive, comical, or charming enough to make this more than a routine run-through of cliches and clues. . . . What [the director] and his writers and cast have failed to do is to make Poirot and his intriguing gallery of friends and foes the classic characters that have genuinely fascinated millions of Agatha Christie readers all these years. Poirot in pictures is simply an unexciting, bizarre 'Belgian with a beak' involved in murders that are not especially exciting" (7/17/66).

The film also contained a cameo appearance by Margaret Rutherford, who said, "This is simple as A. B. C."

Cast:

Hercule Poirot	Tony Randall
Amanda Beatrice Cross	Anita Ekberg
Hastings	Robert Morley
Japp	Maurice Denham

Duncan Doncaster	Guy Rolfe
Lady Diane	Sheila Allen
Franklin	James Villiers
Don Fortune	Julian Glover
Betty Barnard	Grazina Frame
"X"	Clive Morton
Sir Carmichael Clarke	Cyril Luckham

17. ENDLESS NIGHT (1972)

In 1972 United Artists filmed an adaptation of the novel *Endless Night* (#73, 1967), one of Christie's personal favorite books. The film was written and directed by Sidney Gilliat, and starred Hayley Mills, Hywel Bennett, Britt Ekland, Per Oscarsson, and George Sanders.

Ronald Hayman, in a review in the *Times* (London), said that the filmmakers gave Christie "the treatment she deserves, and the result is a film rotten with the stink of red herrings. They even cheat over the narrator, who turns out to be leading us up an almost endless garden path. . . . And there is some unintentional comedy when Hayley Mills, playing an American millionairess, dances lissom eurythmics in the open air" (10/6/72).

Endless Night was not a success in England, and was never released in theatres in the United States, though it does occasionally appear on late-night television.

18. MURDER ON THE ORIENT EXPRESS (1974)

Because of her displeasure with British MGM's four Jane Marple films of the early sixties, Christie made it known to film producers that she was not at all inclined to sell any more film rights to her books. When Nat Cohen, chairman of EMI Films, decided that he would like his studio to produce a new Christie film, he knew getting rights would be difficult, if not impossible. To give his project the best chance, he asked John Brabourne, one of England's best-known and most respected producers, to get involved, and the men decided that *Murder on the Orient Express* (#19, 1934) was the perfect book to adapt—if they could just get the rights.

Brabourne's concept for the film was a far cry from the low-budget, farcical MGM Marple films. He envisioned a glamorous, expensive production, with an international all-star cast, a big-name director, a true-to-the-original screenplay, a top designer and music composer, and authentic location settings. Brabourne believed that, if their concept was properly presented to Christie, she could be persuaded. To break the ice with the intractable author, Brabourne asked his father-in-law, Lord Louis Mountbatten, to meet with Christie. Mountbatten, hero naval commander, former Viceroy of India, and uncle to Prince Philip, was one of the most famous and powerful men in England, and someone Christie could hardly refuse to have lunch with. And though at that time Christie and Mountbatten had not met, they had an important professional link, since, as a youth, Mountbatten had written to Christie with the idea for *The Murder of Roger Ackroyd* (see #7).

Over a period of eighteen months Christie, her family, and advisors met with Mountbatten, Brabourne, and EMI executives at the Savoy Grill, until a final agreement was reached. According to the agreement, the family-controlled corporation that held the Christie rights would receive an advance plus a percentage of the film's profits.

Brabourne and coproducer Richard Goodwin assembled an impressive crew: Sidney Lumet as director (*Twelve Angry Men, The Pawnbroker, The Anderson Tapes, Serpico, Dog Day Afternoon*). Richard Rodney Bennett provided the score, and Paul Dehn wrote the screenplay. Tony Walton was the production designer, and it was he who borrowed the real Orient Express cars from the Compagnie Internationale des Wagon-lits Museum in France that give such an impeccably authentic air to the film.

When *Murder on the Orient Express* was released by EMI in Britain (Paramount in the U.S.), it became an immediate hit with audiences. Even Agatha Christie liked it, though typically she was not one to hold back what reservations she did have. Christie biographer Gwen Robyns quotes Christie as saying, "It was well made except for one mistake. It was Albert Finney, as my detective Hercule Poirot. I wrote that he had the finest moustache in England—and he didn't in the film. I thought that a pity—why shouldn't he?" In *Mallowan's Memoirs,* Christie's husband says, "Agatha herself has always been allergic to the adaptation of her books by the cinema, but was persuaded to give a rather grudging appreciation to this one."

The gala premiere was held at the ABC cinema in Shaftesbury Avenue, London, with Queen Elizabeth in attendance. The banquet held at Claridge's afterward was the last public event the eighty-four-year-old author attended before her death.

Christie must certainly have been pleased with her profits from the film, since *Orient Express* became the biggest money-making British-financed film up to that time. The revenues from Canadian and American distribution alone exceeded $19 million by 1980.

David Robinson in the *Times* (London) said that "Sidney Lumet's adaptation of *Murder on the Orient Express* is a deliberate period pastiche. . . . It is touchingly loyal to Mrs. Christie . . . and to the period. . . . It stays precisely at the level of Agatha Christie, demands the same adjustments, the same precarious suspension of disbelief" (11/22/74).

Vincent Canby in the *New York Times* called the film a "terrifically entertaining super-valentine to a kind of whodunit that may well be one of the last fixed points in our inflationary universe. . . . [The film] is much less a literal re-creation of a type of thirties movie than an elaborate and witty tribute that never for a moment condescends to the subject. . . . [The performances are] fun to watch both for the goals achieved and the risks taken" (9/25/74).

The film won three out of seven of the British Film Awards that year—Best Picture; Best Actor (Albert Finney); and Best Actress (Wendy Hiller). In the United States, the film received six Academy Award nominations: Best Actor (Albert Finney); Best Supporting Actress (Ingrid Bergman); Best Screenplay Adapted from Other Material (Paul Dehn); Best Cinematography (Geoffrey Unsworth); Best Original Dramatic Music Score (Richard Rodney Bennett); and Best Costume Design (Tony Walton). The only winner was Ingrid Bergman—her third Oscar.

Cast:

Hercule Poirot	Albert Finney
Mrs. Hubbard	Lauren Bacall
Bianchi	Martin Balsam
Greta Ohlsson	Ingrid Bergman

Countess Andrenyi	Jacqueline Bisset
Pierre Paul Michael	Jean-Pierre Cassel
Colonel Arbuthnot	Sean Connery
Beddoes	John Gielgud
Princess Dragomiroff	Wendy Hiller
Hector MacQueen	Anthony Perkins
Mary Debenham	Vanessa Redgrave
Hildegarde Schmidt	Rachel Roberts
Ratchett	Richard Widmark
Count Andrenyi	Michael York
Hardman	Colin Blakely
Dr. Constantine	George Coulouris
Foscarelli	Denis Quilley

19. TEN LITTLE INDIANS/AND THEN THERE WERE NONE (3rd Version) (1975)

This 1975 Avco-Embassy release, which "updates" Christie's story to modern-day Iran, is an embarrassing addition to the collection of Christie films, especially coming as it does between the superb EMI versions of *Murder on the Orient Express* (1974) and *Death on the Nile* (1978). Harry Alan Towers produced, and Peter Collinson directed the Peter Welbeck screenplay (Welbeck had coscripted the 1965 version produced by Seven Arts).

Vincent Canby's scathing review in the *New York Times* described the film as "less like a movie than a movie deal, the kind that gets put together over drinks at the Carlton Hotel Bar during the Cannes Film Festival. . . . *Ten Little Indians* is an international movie mess of the sort that damages the reputations of everyone connected with it. . . . It was directed by Peter Collinson, who has made some bad movies in the past but nothing to compare with this lethargic, seemingly post-synchronized version of Miss Christie's great old story. . . . Oliver Reed . . . moves through the film like a cruise director on a sinking ship. He pretends to a cheerfulness that has absolutely nothing to do with the story or with the quality of the movie being made" (4/24/75).

Canby's review was headlined, "Christie Remake in Iran Is a Global Disaster."

The film was released in Britain under the title *And Then There Were None*.

Cast:

Hugh Lombard	Oliver Reed
Vera Clyde	Elke Sommer
Ilona	Stephane Audran
Raven	Charles Aznavour
Judge Cannon	Richard Attenborough
Blore	Gert Frobe
Dr. Armstrong	Herbert Lom
Elsa Martino	Marla Rohm
General	Adolfo Celi
Martino	Alberto De Mendoza

20. DEATH ON THE NILE (1978)

EMI–Paramount decided to follow up on their 1974 success, *Murder on the Orient Express,* and in 1978 released *Death on the Nile,* based on the 1937 novel (#30). It was another big-budget, all-star film, heavy on period glamor and exotic locations. Anthony Shaffer scripted, and John Guillermin directed. Though not as big a box-office draw as its predecessor, *Death on the Nile* still netted its U.S. and Canadian distributors $8 million (according to figures published in *Variety*), while in England the film netted almost $2 million.

Hilton Kramer in the *New York Times* described the film as "a big, expensive, star-studded bore in which a lot of famous talent is permitted—no, encouraged—to do a series of camp turns on their own worst mannerisms . . . the real heroes of this film are the costume designer, Anthony Powell, and the makeup man, Freddie Williamson. Their artful creations keep us wondering what extravagant things will turn up next, and thus provide the only suspense there is in this so-called murder mystery" (11/6/78).

Cast:

Hercule Poirot	Peter Ustinov
Jacqueline de Bellefort	Mia Farrow
Linnet Ridgeway Doyle	Lois Chiles
Simon Doyle	Simon MacCorkindale

Mrs. Van Schuyler	Bette Davis
Miss Bowers	Maggie Smith
Colonel Race	David Niven
Salome Otterbourne	Angela Lansbury
Rosalie Otterbourne	Olivia Hussey
Dr. Bessner	Jack Warden
Andrew Pennington	George Kennedy

21. THE MIRROR CRACK'D (1980)

Following their successes, *Murder on the Orient Express* (1974) and *Death on the Nile* (1978), EMI Films produced their first Jane Marple film, based on the 1962 novel (#68). *The Mirror Crack'd* may have been chosen in part because of the opportunities it provided for a high-powered all-star cast, topped by Elizabeth Taylor and Kim Novak as bitchy rival actresses.

John Brabourne and Richard Goodwin produced, and Guy Hamilton directed. The screenplay was written by Jonathan Hales and Barry Sandler.

The surprise of the film was the casting of Angela Lansbury as Jane Marple. Though Lansbury was closer in physique to Jane Marple than Dame Margaret Rutherford was, Lansbury, even with makeup, found it hard to disguise that she was thirty years too young for the role. Lansbury's job was made even more difficult by the popularity of the Rutherford characterization.

This film was only moderately successful. According to *Variety,* it netted its distribution in the U.S. and Canada $5.5 million, which with today's dollar value, and considering the cost of filming and distributing, is a very meager return.

Variety called the film "a worthy if more leisurely successor to *Murder on the Orient Express* . . . a nostalgic throwback to the genteel murder mystery pix of the '50's . . . roles . . . frequently veer from melodrama into camp. But somehow the curious concoction works" (12/11/80).

Cast:

Miss Marple	Angela Lansbury
Ella Zielinsky	Geraldine Chaplin
Marty N. Fenn	Tony Curtis

Inspector Craddock	Edward Fox
Jason Rudd	Rock Hudson
Lola Brewster	Kim Novak
Marina Rudd	Elizabeth Taylor
Margot Bence	Marella Oppenheim
Cherry	Wendy Morgan
Mrs. Bantry	Margaret Courtenay
Bates, the Butler	Charles Gray
Heather Badcock	Maureen Bennett
Miss Giles	Carolyn Pickles
The Major	Eric Dodson
Vicar	Charles Lloyd-Pack

22. EVIL UNDER THE SUN (1982)

EMI's fourth all-star Christie film adaptation, this one from the 1941 novel (#38), was released in the United States in March 1982. John Brabourne and Richard Goodwin were the producers; Guy Hamilton directed and Anthony Shaffer (author of *Sleuth*) provided the script.

The film was not as successful as *Murder on the Orient Express* (1974) or *Death on the Nile* (1978), netting only $4 million, (according to *Variety*) for its U.S. and Canadian distributors. The film nevertheless was a good atmospheric piece with plenty of style. Vincent Canby in the *New York Times* said that the film "has nothing but style, but its style goes a long way . . . the revels that must continually be interrupted to get in plot points prevent the movie from becoming the high comedy the cast could handle so effortlessly. This is not to say [the film] doesn't have memorable moments. It does" (3/5/82).

Cast:

Hercule Poirot	Peter Ustinov
Sir Horace Blatt	Colin Blakely
Christine Redfern	Jane Birkin
Patrick Redfern	Nicholas Clay
Daphne Castle	Maggie Smith
Rex Brewster	Roddy McDowall
Myra Gardener	Sylvia Miles

Odell Gardener	James Mason
Kenneth Marshall	Denis Quilley
Arlena Marshall	Diana Rigg
Linda Marshall	Emily Hone
Police Sergeant	John Alearson
Police Inspector	Paul Antrim
Police Surgeon	Cyril Conway

TELEVISION

As early as 1956, a Christie mystery was adapted as a television drama, though it was not until almost thirty years later that the possibility of Christie on television began to be explored fully in serious, true-to-the-original adaptations. At present, three novels and ten short stories have been filmed for TV in Britain and shown to British and American audiences, and additional adaptations have been completed or are in production in England and America.

1. A MURDER IS ANNOUNCED (1956)

On December 30, 1956, an adaptation of *A Murder Is Announced* (#52, 1950) was presented on NBC television as part of their *Goodyear TV Playhouse* series. This early television production of a major Christie work was directed by Paul Stanley. William Templeton adapted the book into a one-hour drama. The famous British singer, actress, and comedienne, Gracie Fields, portrayed Miss Jane Marple, the first actress to do so in any major presentation of a Christie work for the stage, screen, or television. Also in the cast was the great stage actress Jessica Tandy who created the role of Blanche Dubois in Tennessee Williams's *A Streetcar Named Desire,* and in one of his earliest acting roles, "Agent 007," Roger Moore.

The review from the *New York Times* was by no means enthusiastic. "The mystery on the *Goodyear Playhouse* over Channel 4 last night was not whodunit—but rather why. Why, for example, did Jessica Tandy and Gracie Fields ever get involved in such an inferior melodrama? . . . Miss Fields eventually deduces the criminal. It was murder from beginning to end."

Cast:

Letitia Blacklock	Jessica Tandy
Dora Bunner	Betty Sinclair

Miss Murgatroyd   Josephine Brown
Miss Hinchcliff   Pat Nye
Jane Marple   Gracie Fields
Inspector Craddock   Malcolm Kuin
Patrick Simmons   Roger Moore

2. THE SEVEN DIALS MYSTERY (1981)

On April 16, 1981, Mobil Showcase (which is syndicated nationally) aired the film adaptation of the novel *The Seven Dials Mystery* (#10, 1929). The film, the first in Mobil's series of made-for-TV films, was produced in England by London Weekend Television and had been televised in Britain March 8. The executive producer and director was Tony Wharmby, and the script was by Pat Sandys. Cheryl Campbell starred as Lady Eileen Brent, with John Gielgud in a cameo appearance as her father. The producers were able to secure permission from the Christie family to film at Greenway House, Agatha's Georgian estate in Devon.

The *New York Times* commented, "If *The Seven Dials Mystery* were only half as impressive as the ad campaign heralding its arrival, television would indeed be fortunate. However, after much huffing and puffing, the Mobil Showcase Network is left with the unseemly task of bringing forth a dud. . . . Stuffed with enough red herrings to trigger persistent visions of sour cream and onions, it succeeds only in being tiresomely silly" (4/16/80).

Cast:
Lady Eileen Brent   Cheryl Campbell
Jimmy Thesiger   James Warwick
Bill Eversleigh   Christopher Scoular
Loraine Wade   Lucy Gutteridge
Marquis of Caterham   Sir John Gielgud
Supt. Battle   Harry Andrews
Sir Oswald Coote   Leslie Sands
Lady Coote   Joyce Redman
George Lomax   Terence Alexander
Sir Stanley Digby   Noel Johnson
O'Rourke   Thom Delaney
Rupert Bateman   James Griffiths

Gerry Wade	Robert Longden
Countess Radzsky	Rula Lenska
Ronny Devereux	John Vine
Vera	Henrietta Baynes
Nancy	Lynne Ross
Helen	Sarah Crowden
Tredwell	Brian Wilde
Stevens	Roger Sloman
Dr. Cartwright	Charles Morgan
John Bauer	Douglas W. Iles

3. WHY DIDN'T THEY ASK EVANS? (1981)

This television film, based on the 1934 novel of the same title (#21), was originally filmed by London Weekend Television as a TV miniseries, but before release the producers decided to recut the series into a three-hour film.

Jack Williams was the producer; Tony Wharmby and John Davies directed, and Pat Sandys wrote the script. The film was televised in England March 30, 1981. Mobil Showcase sponsored the film in America, airing it on national TV on May 21, 1981.

John J. O'Connor in the *New York Times* wrote, "This Christie adaptation . . . is not memorable, exactly, but it provides a diverting way to pass an evening" (5/21/81).

Michael Ratcliff in the *Times* (London) described *Evans* as "thirties throughout, and nicely acted, just this side of parody . . . it might have worked, but for one thing. It was twice as long as it should have been . . . [the film] was about as crisp and riveting as an old lettuce leaf."

Cast:

Lady Frances Derwent	Francesca Annis
Bobby Jones	James Warwick
Rev. Thomas Jones	Sir John Gielgud
Badger Beadon	Robert Longden
Dr. Nicholson	Eric Porter
Moira Nicholson	Madeline Smith
Roger Bassington-ffrench	Leigh Lawson
Sylvia Bassington-ffrench	Connie Booth
Henry Bassington-ffrench	Eirik Barclay

Dr. George Arbuthnot	Rowland Davies
Dr. Thomas	Bernard Miles
Amelia Cayman	Mitzi Rogers
Mrs. Roberts	Lynda Marchal
Ross	Mischa De La Motte

4. MURDER IS EASY (1982)

An American production company, headed by David L. Wolper and Stan Margulies of *Roots* fame, filmed their adaptation of the 1939 Christie novel (#33), with an American and British cast, on location in England. The film was shown on American TV on January 2, 1982, on the CBS network. Carmen Culver wrote the script and Claude Whatham directed.

The *New York Times* said, "There are nice bits and pieces along the way—but it's easy early in the game to figure out who is the last person anyone would suspect" (12/31/81).

Cast:

Lavinia Fullerton	Helen Hayes
Honoria Waynflete	Olivia de Havilland
Luke Williams	Bill Bixby
Bridget Conway	Lesley-Anne Down
Lord Easterfield	Timothy West

5. WITNESS FOR THE PROSECUTION (1982)

This 1982 television adaptation of the 1953 play and 1957 film featured an all-star cast which included Sir Ralph Richardson, Deborah Kerr, Diana Rigg, and Beau Bridges. The film was produced by Norman Rosemont in association with United Artists and directed by Alan Gibson. John Gay adapted the teleplay from the Christie stage play and from Billy Wilder's and Harry Kurnitz's screenplay.

John J. O'Connor in the *New York Times* wrote, "Television would have to come up with a very special package to justify still another version of [*Witness for the Prosecution*]. . . . [Even] the smaller parts have been filled with . . . distinguished actors. . . . The direction, crisp and carefully focused. . . . *Witness for the Prosecution* still works wondrously well, its twists and turns devised to the point of perfection. It's still a great deal of fun" (12/3/82).

Variety complained that the "new TV-movie version comes off as a labored courtroom melodrama. It's so loaded with 'unexpected' plot twists . . . that character detail and credibility end up taking a back seat. . . . The director has filmed this TV movie in such a broad and theatrical style that one expects the characters to break out regularly into song, as in a Gilbert & Sullivan operetta. . . . There's a new mass-media vogue for Agatha Christie. And that, rather than any new vision on the part of [the producer and director], is the reason for this pointless remake" (12/8/82).

Cast:

Leonard Vole	Beau Bridges
Sir Wilfrid Robarts, Q.C.	Sir Ralph Richardson
Romaine	Diana Rigg
Nurse Plimsoll	Deborah Kerr
Janet Mackenzie	Wendy Hiller
Mr. Myers	Donald Pleasance
Mr. Mayhew	David Langton

6. THE AGATHA CHRISTIE HOUR (1982–83)

Thames Television in England produced ten one-hour dramas based on the short stories of Agatha Christie. *The Agatha Christie Hour,* presented on English television at the end of 1982, was produced by Pat Sandys, with John Frankau as the executive producer. Four of these dramatizations were shown on American television at the beginning of 1983 as part of the PBS series titled *Mystery.*

"The Case of the Middle-Aged Wife" was the first of the Christie stories to be shown. Dramatized by Freda Kelsall and directed by Michael Simpson, the drama was shown in England on September 7, 1982. The stars were Maurice Denham, Gwen Watford, and Peter Jones. This story appeared in the Christie collection *Parker Pyne Investigates* (#22, 1934).

"In a Glass Darkly" was dramatized by William Corlett, directed by Desmond Davis, and starred Nicholas Clay and Emma Piper. It was shown in England on September 14, 1982. This story was collected twice, in *The Regatta Mystery* (#34, 1939) and in *Miss Marple's Final Cases* (#84, 1979).

"The Girl in the Train" was televised in England on September 21, 1982, and in the U.S. on March 10, 1983. This story, taken from the collections *The Listerdale Mystery* (#20, 1934), and *The Golden Ball* (#77, 1971) was dramatized by William Corlett, directed by Brian Farnham, and starred Osmond Bullock and Sarah Berger.

"The Fourth Man," published in *The Hound of Death* (#18, 1933) and *Witness for the Prosecution* (#49, 1948), was televised in England on September 28, 1982. The drama starred John Nettles, Prune Clarke and Fiona Mathieson. It was dramatized by William Corlett and directed by Michael Simpson.

"The Case of the Discontented Soldier" aired in England on October 5, 1982. It was dramatized by T. R. Bowen, directed by Michael Simpson, and starred William Gaunt, Patricia Garwood, and Maurice Denham. Lally Bowers played Ariadne Oliver, Christie's own lighthearted version of herself. The story is from *Parker Pyne Investigates* (#22, 1934).

"Magnolia Blossom" was published in *The Golden Ball* (#77, 1971). The television drama was shown in England on October 12, 1982, and in the U.S. on February 24, 1983. The story was dramatized by John Bryden Rodgers, directed by John Frankau, and starred Ralph Bates, Ciaran Madden, and Jeremy Clyde.

"The Mystery of the Blue Jar" was published in *The Hound of Death* (#18, 1933) and *Witness for the Prosecution* (#49, 1948). It was shown in England on television on October 19, 1982. The story was dramatized by T. R. Bowen, directed by Cyril Coke, and starred Michael Aldridge, Robin Kermode, and Isabelle Spade.

"The Red Signal" was presented on English television on November 2, 1982, and on American television on March 3, 1983. Taken from the collections *The Hound of Death* (#18, 1933), and *Witness for the Prosecution* (#49, 1948), the story was dramatized by William Corlett, directed by John Frankau, and starred Richard Morant, Joanna David, and Christopher Cazenove.

"Jane in Search of a Job" was published in *The Listerdale Mystery* (#20, 1934) and *The Golden Ball* (#77, 1971). Shown in England on November 9, 1982, the story was dramatized by Gerald Savory, directed by Christopher Hodson and starred Elizabeth Garvie, Amanda Redman, and Andrew Bicknell.

"The Manhood of Edward Robinson" was the last in the series to be televised in England (November 16, 1982), and the first story to be televised in the U.S. (February 17, 1983). From the collections *The Listerdale Mystery* (#20, 1934) and *The Golden Ball* (#77, 1971), the story was dramatized by Gerald Savory, directed by Brian Farnham and starred Nicholas Farrell, Cherie Lunghi, and Ann Thornton.

7. A CARIBBEAN MYSTERY (1983–84)

During the 1983–84 season, CBS Television scheduled a prime-time airing of a two-hour adaptation of Miss Marple's West Indies adventure, produced by Stan Margulies in association with Warner Brothers Television, starring Helen Hayes as Jane Marple, Barnard Hughes as Mr. Rafiel, and Maurice Evans as Major Palgrave. (Exact broadcast information not available at time of publication.)

8. SPARKLING CYANIDE (1983–84)

Like *A Caribbean Mystery, Sparkling Cyanide* was produced by Stan Margulies/Warner Brothers for a CBS prime-time broadcast starring Anthony Andrews and Harry Morgan. (Exact broadcast information not available at time of publication.)

9. PARTNERS IN CRIME (1984)

This adaptation of the Tommy and Tuppence Beresford short-story series was produced by London Weekend Television, produced by Jack Williams and directed by Tony Wharmby, with Francesca Annis as Tuppence and James Warwick as Tommy. The series was scheduled for airing in the United States on PBS as part of the Mobil Showcase *Mystery* series, from November 29 to December 27, 1984. (Complete information not available at time of publication.)

The Christie Lists

THE CHRISTIE LISTS

By any standard Christie's output is large, and a reader is apt to get lost among the many titles, character names, place names, and plots—many of which are reminiscent of one another. To help Christie readers find their way through the kingdom of the Queen of Crime, as well as through *The Agatha Christie Companion,* we have included lists of various sorts to help you find what you're looking for, or what you didn't even know you were missing.

Happy hunting!

Agatha Christie Book Titles

THE ABC MURDERS—#25 (1936—Poirot, Inspector Japp, Hastings)

ABSENT IN THE SPRING—Misc. #3 (1944—Mary Westmacott, pseud.)

THE ADVENTURE OF THE CHRISTMAS PUDDING AND A SELECTION OF ENTREES—#65 (1960—Short Stories)

AFTER THE FUNERAL—#57 (1953—Poirot) (U.S.: FUNERALS ARE FATAL)

AN AUTOBIOGRAPHY—Misc. #11 (1977)

AN OVERDOSE OF DEATH—#37 (1953—Dell PB—Poirot, Inspector Japp) (English: ONE, TWO, BUCKLE MY SHOE) (Also U.S.: THE PATRIOTIC MURDERS)

AND THEN THERE WERE NONE—#35 (1939) (English: TEN LITTLE NIGGERS) (Also U.S.: TEN LITTLE INDIANS—1978 Greenway edition)

APPOINTMENT WITH DEATH—#31 (1938—Poirot)

AT BERTRAM'S HOTEL—#71 (1965—Miss Marple)

THE BIG FOUR—#8 (1927—Poirot, Hastings)

THE BODY IN THE LIBRARY—#40 (1942—Miss Marple)

THE BOOMERANG CLUE—#21 (1934) (English: WHY DIDN'T THEY ASK EVANS?)

THE BURDEN—Misc. #6 (1956—Mary Westmacott, pseud.)

BY THE PRICKING OF MY THUMBS—#74 (1968—Tommy and Tuppence)

CARDS ON THE TABLE—#27 (1936—Poirot, Mrs. Oliver, Superintendent Battle, Colonel Race)

A CARIBBEAN MYSTERY—#70 (1964—Miss Marple)

CAT AMONG THE PIGEONS—#64 (1959—Poirot)

THE CLOCKS—#69 (1963—Poirot)

COME, TELL ME HOW YOU LIVE—Misc. #8 (1946—Agatha Christie Mallowan)

CROOKED HOUSE—#50 (1949)

CURTAIN—#82 (1975—Poirot, Hastings)

HICKORY DICKORY DEATH—#60 (1955—Poirot) (English: HICKORY DICKORY DOCK)

HICKORY DICKORY DOCK—#60 (1955—Poirot) (U.S.: HICKORY DICKORY DEATH)

A HOLIDAY FOR MURDER—#32 (1947—Avon PB—Poirot) (English: HERCULE POIROT'S CHRISTMAS) (Also U.S.: MURDER FOR CHRISTMAS)

THE HOLLOW—#46 (1946—Poirot) (U.S.: MURDER AFTER HOURS)

THE HOUND OF DEATH—#18 (1933—Short Stories)

THE LABOURS OF HERCULES—#47 (1947—Poirot, Short Stories)

THE LISTERDALE MYSTERY—#20 (1934—Short Stories)

LORD EDGWARE DIES—#17 (1933—Poirot, Inspector Japp, Hastings) (U.S.: THIRTEEN AT DINNER)

THE MAN IN THE BROWN SUIT—#5 (1924—Colonel Race)

THE MIRROR CRACK'D—#68 (1962—Miss Marple) (English: THE MIRROR CRACK'D FROM SIDE TO SIDE)

THE MIRROR CRACK'D FROM SIDE TO SIDE—#68 (1962 —Miss Marple) (U.S.: THE MIRROR CRACK'D)

MISS MARPLE'S FINAL CASES AND TWO OTHER STORIES—#84 (1979—Miss Marple, Short Stories)

MRS. McGINTY'S DEAD—#55 (1952—Poirot, Mrs. Oliver)

MR. PARKER PYNE, DETECTIVE—#22 (1934—Short Stories, Parker Pyne) (English: PARKER PYNE INVESTIGATES)

THE MOUSETRAP AND OTHER STORIES—#51 (1950—Short Stories) (Also U.S.: THREE BLIND MICE AND OTHER STORIES)

THE MOVING FINGER—#42 (1943—Miss Marple)

MURDER AFTER HOURS—#46 (1946—Poirot) (English: THE HOLLOW)

MURDER AT HAZELMOOR—#14 (1931) (English: THE SITTAFORD MYSTERY)

THE MURDER AT THE VICARAGE—#13 (1930—Miss Marple)

MURDER FOR CHRISTMAS—#32 (1938—Poirot) (English: HERCULE POIROT'S CHRISTMAS) (Also U.S.: A HOLIDAY FOR MURDER—1947—Avon PB)

MURDER IN THE CALAIS COACH—#19 (1934—Poirot) (English: MURDER ON THE ORIENT EXPRESS)

THERE WERE NONE) (Also U.S.: TEN LITTLE INDI-
ANS—1978—Greenway edition)

THERE IS A TIDE—#48 (1948—Poirot) (English: TAKEN
AT THE FLOOD)

THEY CAME TO BAGHDAD—#53 (1951)

THEY DO IT WITH MIRRORS—#56 (1952—Miss Marple)
(U.S.: MURDER WITH MIRRORS)

THIRD GIRL—#72 (1966—Poirot, Mrs. Oliver)

THIRTEEN AT DINNER—#17 (1933—Poirot, Inspector Japp,
Hastings) (English: LORD EDGWARE DIES)

THE THIRTEEN PROBLEMS—#16 (1932—Miss Marple, Short
Stories) (U.S.: THE TUESDAY CLUB MURDERS)

THREE ACT TRAGEDY—#23 (1935—Poirot) (U.S.: MUR-
DER IN THREE ACTS)

THREE BLIND MICE AND OTHER STORIES—#51 (1950—
Short Stories) (U.S.: THE MOUSETRAP AND OTHER
STORIES)

TOWARDS ZERO—#43 (1944—Superintendent Battle)

THE TUESDAY CLUB MURDERS—#16 (1932—Miss Marple,
Short Stories) (English: THE THIRTEEN PROBLEMS)

THE UNDER DOG AND OTHER STORIES—#54 (1951—
Short Stories)

UNFINISHED PORTRAIT—Misc. #2 (1934—Mary Westmacott, pseud.)

WHAT MRS. McGILLICUDDY SAW!—#62 (1957—Miss Marple) (English: 4.50 FROM PADDINGTON)

WHY DIDN'T THEY ASK EVANS?—#21 (1934) (U.S.: THE
BOOMERANG CLUE)

WITNESS FOR THE PROSECUTION AND OTHER STORIES
—#49 (1948—Short Stories)

AGATHA CHRISTIE SHORT STORY TITLES

Accident
> *Published in* The Listerdale Mystery—#20 (1934) (English)
>> Witness for the Prosecution—#49 (1948) (U.S.)

The Adventure of Johnnie Waverly (Poirot, Hastings)
> *Published in* Three Blind Mice—#51 (1950) (U.S.)
>> The Mousetrap—#51 (1952) (PB) (U.S.)
>> Poirot's Early Cases—#81 (1974) (English)
>> Hercule Poirot's Early Cases—#81 (1974) (U.S.)

The Adventure of the Cheap Flat (Poirot, Inspector Japp, Hastings)
> *Published in* Poirot Investigates—#4 (1924)

The Adventure of the Christmas Pudding (slightly different version of The Theft of the Royal Ruby) (Poirot)
> *Published in* The Adventure of the Christmas Pudding—#65 (1960) (English)

The Adventure of the Clapham Cook (Poirot, Hastings)
> *Published in* The Under Dog—#54 (1951) (U.S.)
>> Poirot's Early Cases—#81 (1974) (English)
>> Hercule Poirot's Early Cases—#81 (1974) (U.S.)

The Adventure of the Egyptian Tomb (Poirot, Hastings)
> *Published in* Poirot Investigates—#4 (1924)

The Adventure of the Italian Nobleman (Poirot, Hastings)
> *Published in* Poirot Investigates—#4 (1924)

The Adventure of the Sinister Stranger (Tommy and Tuppence)
> *Published in* Partners in Crime—#11 (1929)

The Adventure of "The Western Star" (Poirot, Hastings)
> *Published in* Poirot Investigates—#4 (1924)

The Affair at the Bungalow (Miss Marple)
> *Published in* Thirteen Problems—#16 (1932) (English)
>> The Tuesday Club Murders—#16 (1933) (U.S.)

The Affair at the Victory Ball (Poirot, Inspector Japp, Hastings)
> *Published in* The Under Dog—#54 (1951) (U.S.)
>> Poirot's Early Cases—#81 (1974) (English)
>> Hercule Poirot's Early Cases—#81 (1974) (U.S.)

The Affair of the Pink Pearl (Tommy and Tuppence)
  Published in Partners in Crime—#11 (1929)
The Ambassador's Boots (Tommy and Tuppence)
  Published in Partners in Crime—#11 (1929)
The Apples of the Hesperides (Poirot)
  Published in The Labours of Hercules—#47 (1947)
The Arcadian Deer (Poirot)
  Published in The Labours of Hercules—#47 (1947)
At the Bells and Motley (Harley Quin)
  Published in The Mysterious Mr. Quin—#12 (1930)
The Augean Stables (Poirot)
  Published in The Labours of Hercules—#47 (1947)
The Bird with the Broken Wing (Harley Quin)
  Published in The Mysterious Mr. Quin—#12 (1930)
Blindman's Buff (Tommy and Tuppence)
  Published in Partners in Crime—#11 (1929)
The Bloodstained Pavement (Miss Marple)
  Published in Thirteen Problems—#16 (1932) (English)
          The Tuesday Club Murders—#16 (1933) (U.S.)
The Blue Geranium (Miss Marple)
  Published in Thirteen Problems—#16 (1932) (English)
          The Tuesday Club Murders—#16 (1933) (U.S.)
The Call of Wings
  Published in The Hound of Death—#18 (1933) (English)
          The Golden Ball—#77 (1971) (U.S.)
The Capture of Cerberus (Poirot, Inspector Japp)
  Published in The Labours of Hercules—#47 (1947)
The Case of the Caretaker (Miss Marple)
  Published in Three Blind Mice—#51 (1950) (U.S.)
          The Mousetrap—#51 (1952) (PB) (U.S.)
          Miss Marple's Final Cases—#84 (1979) (English)
The Case of the City Clerk (Parker Pyne)
  Published in Parker Pyne Investigates—#22 (1934) (English)
          Mr. Parker Pyne, Detective—#22 (1934) (U.S.)
The Case of the Discontented Husband (Parker Pyne)
  Published in Parker Pyne Investigates—#22 (1934) (English)
          Mr. Parker Pyne, Detective—#22 (1934) (U.S.)

The Case of the Discontented Soldier (Mrs. Oliver, Parker Pyne)
  Published in Parker Pyne Investigates—#22 (1934) (English)
                Mr. Parker Pyne, Detective—#22 (1934) (U.S.)
The Case of the Distressed Lady (Parker Pyne)
  Published in Parker Pyne Investigates—#22 (1934) (English)
                Mr. Parker Pyne, Detective—#22 (1934) (U.S.)
The Case of the Middle-Aged Wife (Parker Pyne)
  Published in Parker Pyne Investigates—#22 (1934) (English)
                Mr. Parker Pyne, Detective—#22 (1934) (U.S.)
The Case of the Missing Lady (Tommy and Tuppence)
  Published in Partners in Crime—#11 (1929)
The Case of the Missing Will (Poirot, Hastings)
  Published in Poirot Investigates—#4 (1924)
The Case of the Perfect Maid (Miss Marple)
  Published in Three Blind Mice—#51 (1950) (U.S.)
                The Mousetrap—#51 (1952) (PB) (U.S.)
                Miss Marple's Final Cases—#84 (1979) (English)
The Case of the Retired Jeweller (Alternate title for The Tape-Measure Murder)
The Case of the Rich Woman (Mrs. Oliver, Parker Pyne)
  Published in Parker Pyne Investigates—#22 (1934) (English)
                Mr. Parker Pyne, Detective—#22 (1934) (U.S.)
The Chess Problem (see *The Big Four,* chapter 11; published separately at times)
The Chocolate Box (Poirot, Hastings)
  Published in Poirot Investigates—#4 (1925) (U.S. edition only)
                Poirot's Early Cases—#81 (1974) (English)
                Hercule Poirot's Early Cases—#81 (1974) (U.S.)
A Christmas Tragedy (Miss Marple)
  Published in Thirteen Problems—#16 (1932) (English)
                The Tuesday Club Murders—#16 (1933) (U.S.)
The Clergyman's Daughter (Tommy and Tuppence)
  Published in Partners in Crime—#11 (1929)
The Coming of Mr. Quin (Harley Quin)
  Published in The Mysterious Mr. Quin—#12 (1930)
The Companion (Miss Marple)
  Published in Thirteen Problems—#16 (1932) (English)
                The Tuesday Club Murders—#16 (1933) (U.S.)

The Cornish Mystery (Poirot, Hastings)
>*Published in* The Under Dog—#54 (1951) (U.S.)
>>Poirot's Early Cases—#81 (1974) (English)
>>Hercule Poirot's Early Cases—#81 (1974) (U.S.)

The Crackler (Tommy and Tuppence)
>*Published in* Partners in Crime—#11 (1929)

The Cretan Bull (Poirot)
>*Published in* The Labours of Hercules—#47 (1947)

The Dead Harlequin (Harley Quin)
>*Published in* The Mysterious Mr. Quin—#12 (1930)

Dead Man's Mirror (Expanded version of The Second Gong) (Poirot)
>*Published in* Murder in the Mews—#28 (1937) (English)
>>Dead Man's Mirror—#28 (1937) (U.S.)

Death by Drowning (Miss Marple)
>*Published in* Thirteen Problems—#16 (1932) (English)
>>The Tuesday Club Murders—#16 (1933) (U.S.)

Death on the Nile (Parker Pyne)
>*Published in* Parker Pyne Investigates—#22 (1934) (English)
>>Mr. Parker Pyne, Detective—#22 (1934) (U.S.)

The Disappearance of Mrs. Leigh Gordon (Alternate title for The Case of the Missing Lady)

The Disappearance of Mr. Davenheim (Poirot, Inspector Japp, Hastings)
>*Published in* Poirot Investigates—#4 (1924)

The Double Clue (Poirot, Hastings)
>*Published in* Double Sin—#66 (1961) (U.S.)
>>Poirot's Early Cases—#81 (1974) (English)
>>Hercule Poirot's Early Cases—#81 (1974) (U.S.)

Double Sin (Poirot, Hastings)
>*Published in* Double Sin—#66 (1961) (U.S.)
>>Poirot's Early Cases—#81 (1974) (English)
>>Hercule Poirot's Early Cases—#81 (1974) (U.S.)

The Dream (Poirot)
>*Published in* The Regatta Mystery—#34 (1939) (U.S.)
>>The Adventure of the Christmas Pudding—#65 (1960) (English)

The Dressmaker's Doll
    Published in Double Sin—#66 (1961) (U.S.)
                    Miss Marple's Final Cases—#84 (1979) (English)
The Erymanthian Boar (Poirot)
    Published in The Labours of Hercules—#47 (1947)
The Face of Helen (Harley Quin)
    Published in The Mysterious Mr. Quin—#12 (1930)
A Fairy in the Flat (Tommy and Tuppence)
    Published in Partners in Crime—#11 (1929)
Finessing the King (Tommy and Tuppence)
    Published in Partners in Crime—#11 (1929)
The Flock of Geryon (Poirot, Inspector Japp)
    Published in The Labours of Hercules—#47 (1947)
Four and Twenty Blackbirds (Poirot)
    Published in Three Blind Mice—#51 (1950) (U.S.)
                    The Mousetrap—#51 (1952) (PB) (U.S.)
                    The Adventure of the Christmas Pudding—#65
                    (1960) (English)
The Four Suspects (Miss Marple)
    Published in Thirteen Problems—#16 (1932) (English)
                    The Tuesday Club Murders—#16 (1933) (U.S.)
The Fourth Man
    Published in The Hound of Death—#18 (1933) (English)
                    Witness for the Prosecution—#49 (1948) (U.S.)
A Fruitful Sunday
    Published in The Listerdale Mystery—#20 (1934) (English)
                    The Golden Ball—#77 (1971) (U.S.)
The Gate of Baghdad (Parker Pyne)
    Published in Parker Pyne Investigates—#22 (1934) (English)
                    Mr. Parker Pyne, Detective—#22 (1934) (U.S.)
The Gentleman Dressed in Newspaper (Tommy and Tuppence)
    Published in Partners in Crime—#11 (1929)
The Gipsy
    Published in The Hound of Death—#18 (1933) (English)
                    The Golden Ball—#77 (1971) (U.S.)
The Girdle of Hyppolita (Poirot, Inspector Japp)
    Published in The Labours of Hercules—#47 (1947)
The Girl in the Train
    Published in The Listerdale Mystery—#20 (1934) (English)
                    The Golden Ball—#77 (1971) (U.S.)

The Golden Ball
> *Published in* The Listerdale Mystery—#20 (1934) (English)
>> The Golden Ball—#77 (1971) (U.S.)

Greenshaw's Folly (Miss Marple)
> *Published in* The Adventure of the Christmas Pudding—#65
>> (1961) (English)
>> Double Sin—#66 (1961) (U.S.)

The Harlequin Tea Set
> *Published in* Hardinge, George, ed: *Winter's Crime 3* (London,
>> Macmillan, 1971)
>> Ellery Queen's Murdercade (London, Gollancz,
>> 1975)
>> (this story does not appear in any of the standard
>> Christie collections)

Harlequin's Lane (Harley Quin)
> *Published in* The Mysterious Mr. Quin—#12 (1930)

Have You Got Everything You Want? (Parker Pyne)
> *Published in* Parker Pyne Investigates—#22 (1934) (English)
>> Mr. Parker Pyne, Detective—#22 (1934) (U.S.)

The Herb of Death (Miss Marple)
> *Published in* Thirteen Problems—#16 (1932) (English)
>> The Tuesday Club Murders—#16 (1933) (U.S.)

The Horses of Diomedes (Poirot)
> *Published in* The Labours of Hercules—#47 (1947)

The Hound of Death
> *Published in* The Hound of Death—#18 (1933) (English)
>> The Golden Ball—#77 (1971) (U.S.)

The House at Shiraz (Parker Pyne)
> *Published in* Parker Pyne Investigates—#22 (1934) (English)
>> Mr. Parker Pyne, Detective—#22 (1934) (U.S.)

The House of Lurking Death (Tommy and Tuppence)
> *Published in* Partners in Crime—#11 (1929)

How Does Your Garden Grow? (Poirot)
> *Published in* The Regatta Mystery—#34 (1939) (U.S.)
>> Poirot's Early Cases—#81 (1974) (English)
>> Hercule Poirot's Early Cases—#81 (1974) (U.S.)

The Idol House of Astarte (Miss Marple)
> *Published in* Thirteen Problems—#16 (1932) (English)
>> The Tuesday Club Murders—#16 (1933) (U.S.)

In a Glass Darkly
    Published in The Regatta Mystery—#34 (1939) (U.S.)
                    Miss Marple's Final Cases—#84 (1979) (English)
The Incredible Theft (Expanded version of The Submarine Plans)
    (Poirot)
    Published in Murder in the Mews—#28 (1937) (English)
Ingots of Gold (Miss Marple)
    Published in Thirteen Problems—#16 (1932) (English)
                    The Tuesday Club Murders—#16 (1933) (U.S.)
Jane in Search of a Job
    Published in The Listerdale Mystery—#20 (1934) (English)
                    The Golden Ball—#77 (1971) (U.S.)
The Jewel Robbery at the Grand Metropolitan (Poirot, Hastings)
    Published in Poirot Investigates—#4 (1924)
The Kidnapped Prime Minister (Poirot, Inspector Japp, Hastings)
    Published in Poirot Investigates—#4 (1924)
The Kidnapping of Johnnie Waverly (Alternate title for The Ad-
    venture of Johnnie Waverly)
The King of Clubs (Poirot, Hastings)
    Published in The Under Dog—#54 (1951) (U.S.)
                    Poirot's Early Cases—#81 (1974) (English)
                    Hercule Poirot's Early Cases—#81 (1974) (U.S.)
The Lamp
    Published in The Hound of Death—#18 (1933) (English)
                    The Golden Ball—#77 (1971) (U.S.)
The Last Séance
    Published in The Hound of Death—#18 (1933) (English)
                    Double Sin—#66 (1961) (U.S.)
The Lemesurier Inheritance (Poirot, Hastings)
    Published in The Under Dog—#54 (1951) (U.S.)
                    Poirot's Early Cases—#81 (1974) (English)
                    Hercule Poirot's Early Cases—#81 (1974) (U.S.)
The Lernean Hydra (Poirot)
    Published in The Labours of Hercules—#47 (1947)
The Listerdale Mystery
    Published in The Listerdale Mystery—#20 (1934) (English)
                    The Golden Ball—#77 (1971) (U.S.)

The Lost Mine (Poirot, Hastings)
   Published in Poirot Investigates—#4 (1925) (U.S. edition only)
                  Poirot's Early Cases—#81 (1974) (English)
                  Hercule Poirot's Early Cases—#81 (1974) (U.S.)
The Love Detectives (Harley Quin)
   Published in Three Blind Mice—#51 (1950) (U.S.)
                  The Mousetrap—#51 (1952) (U.S.)
Magnolia Blossom
   Published in The Golden Ball—#77 (1971) (U.S.)
The Man from the Sea (Harley Quin)
   Published in The Mysterious Mr. Quin—#12 (1930)
The Man in the Mist (Tommy and Tuppence)
   Published in Partners in Crime—#11 (1929)
The Man Who Was No. 16 (Tommy and Tuppence)
   Published in Partners in Crime—#11 (1929)
The Manhood of Edward Robinson
   Published in The Listerdale Mystery—#20 (1934) (English)
                  The Golden Ball—#77 (1971) (U.S.)
The Market Basing Mystery (Poirot, Inspector Japp, Hastings)
   Published in The Under Dog—#54 (1951) (U.S.)
                  Poirot's Early Cases—#81 (1974) (English)
                  Hercule Poirot's Early Cases—#81 (1974) (U.S.)
The Million Dollar Bond Robbery (Poirot, Hastings)
   Published in Poirot Investigates—#4 (1924)
Miss Marple Tells a Story (Miss Marple)
   Published in The Regatta Mystery—#34 (1939) (U.S.)
                  Miss Marple's Final Cases—#84 (1979) (English)
Mr. Eastwood's Adventure
   Published in The Listerdale Mystery—#20 (1934) (English)
Motive vs. Opportunity (Miss Marple)
   Published in Thirteen Problems—#16 (1932) (English)
                  The Tuesday Club Murders—#16 (1933) (U.S.)
Murder in the Mews (Poirot, Inspector Japp)
   Published in Murder in the Mews—#28 (1937) (English)
                  Dead Man's Mirror—#28 (1937) (U.S.)
The Mystery of Hunter's Lodge (Poirot, Inspector Japp, Hastings)
   Published in Poirot Investigates—#4 (1924)

The Mystery of the Baghdad Chest (See also expanded version with title The Mystery of the Spanish Chest) (Poirot, Hastings)
> *Published in* The Regatta Mystery—#34 (1939) (U.S.)

The Mystery of the Blue Jar
> *Published in* The Hound of Death—#18 (1933) (English)
> > Witness for the Prosecution—#49 (1948) (U.S.)

The Mystery of the Crime in Cabin 66 (Poirot)
> *Published in* Poirot Knows the Murderer (Polybooks U.S. and English, 1946, 62 pp.)
> > (this story does not appear in any of the standard Christie collections)

The Mystery of the Spanish Chest (Slightly expanded version of The Mystery of the Baghdad Chest) (Poirot)
> *Published in* The Adventure of the Christmas Pudding—#65 (1960) (English)

The Mystery of the Spanish Shawl (Alternate title for Mr. Eastwood's Adventure)

The Nemean Lion (Poirot)
> *Published in* The Labours of Hercules—#47 (1947)

Next to a Dog
> *Published in* The Golden Ball—#77 (1971) (U.S.)

The Oracle at Delphi (Parker Pyne)
> *Published in* Parker Pyne Investigates—#22 (1934) (English)
> > Mr. Parker Pyne, Detective—#22 (1934) (U.S.)

The Pearl of Price (Parker Pyne)
> *Published in* Parker Pyne Investigates—#22 (1934) (English)
> > Mr. Parker Pyne, Detective—#22 (1934) (U.S.)

The Perfect Maid (Alternate title for The Case of the Perfect Maid)

Philomel Cottage
> *Published in* The Listerdale Mystery—#20 (1934) (English)
> > Witness for the Prosecution—#49 (1948) (U.S.)

The Plymouth Express (Poirot, Inspector Japp, Hastings)
> *Published in* The Under Dog—#54 (1951) (U.S.)
> > Poirot's Early Cases—#81 (1974) (English)
> > Hercule Poirot's Early Cases—#81 (1974) (U.S.)

A Pot of Tea (Tommy and Tuppence)
> *Published in* Partners in Crime—#11 (1929)

Problem at Pollensa Bay (Parker Pyne)
  Published in The Regatta Mystery—#34 (1939) (U.S.)
Problem at Sea (Poirot)
  Published in The Regatta Mystery—#34 (1939) (U.S.)
                Poirot's Early Cases—#81 (1974) (English)
                Hercule Poirot's Early Cases—#81 (1974) (U.S.)
The Rajah's Emerald
  Published in The Listerdale Mystery—#20 (1934) (English)
                The Golden Ball—#77 (1971) (U.S.)
The Red House (Tommy and Tuppence)
  Published in Partners in Crime—#11 (1929)
The Red Signal
  Published in The Hound of Death—#18 (1933) (English)
                Witness for the Prosecution—#49 (1948) (U.S.)
The Regatta Mystery (Parker Pyne)
  Published in The Regatta Mystery—#34 (1939) (U.S.)
Sanctuary (Miss Marple)
  Published in Double Sin—#66 (1961) (U.S.)
                Miss Marple's Final Cases—#84 (1979) (English)
The Second Gong (See also expanded version with title Dead Man's
  Mirror)
  Published in Witness for the Prosecution—#49 (1948) (U.S.)
The Shadow on the Glass (Harley Quin)
  Published in The Mysterious Mr. Quin—#12 (1930)
The Sign in the Sky (Harley Quin)
  Published in The Mysterious Mr. Quin —#12 (1930)
Sing a Song of Sixpence
  Published in The Listerdale Mystery—#20 (1934) (English)
                Witness for the Prosecution—#49 (1948) (U.S.)
SOS
  Published in The Hound of Death—#18 (1933) (English)
                Witness for the Prosecution—#49 (1948) (U.S.)
The Soul of the Croupier (Harley Quin)
  Published in The Mysterious Mr. Quin—#12 (1930)
The Strange Case of Sir Arthur Carmichael (Also called The Strange
  Case of Sir Andrew Carmichael)
  Published in The Hound of Death—#18 (1933) (English)
                The Golden Ball—#77 (1971) (U.S.)

Strange Jest (Miss Marple)
> *Published in* Three Blind Mice—#51 (1950) (U.S.)
> > The Mousetrap—#51 (1952) (PB) (U.S.)
> > Miss Marple's Final Cases—#84 (1979) (English)

The Stymphalean Birds (Poirot)
> *Published in* The Labours of Hercules—#47 (1947)

The Submarine Plans (See also expanded version with title The Incredible Theft) (Poirot, Hastings)
> *Published in* The Under Dog—#54 (1951) (U.S.)
> > Poirot's Early Cases—#81 (1974) (English)
> > Hercule Poirot's Early Cases—#81 (1974) (U.S.)

The Sunningdale Mystery (Tommy and Tuppence)
> *Published in* Partners in Crime—#11 (1929)

Swan Song
> *Published in* The Listerdale Mystery—#20 (1934) (English)
> > The Golden Ball—#77 (1971) (U.S.)

The Tape-Measure Murder (Miss Marple)
> *Published in* Three Blind Mice—#51 (1950) (U.S.)
> > The Mousetrap—#51 (1952) (PB) (U.S.)
> > Miss Marple's Final Cases—#84 (1979) (English)

The Theft of the Royal Ruby (Slightly different version of The Adventure of the Christmas Pudding) (Poirot)
> *Published in* Double Sin—#66 (1961) (U.S.)

The Third Floor Flat (Poirot)
> *Published in* Three Blind Mice—#51 (1950) (U.S.)
> > The Mousetrap—#51 (1952) (PB) (U.S.)
> > Poirot's Early Cases—#81 (1974) (English)
> > Hercule Poirot's Early Cases—#81 (1974) (U.S.)

Three Blind Mice
> *Published in* Three Blind Mice—#51 (1950) (U.S.)
> > The Mousetrap—#51 (1952) (PB) (U.S.)

The Thumb Mark of Saint Peter (Miss Marple)
> *Published in* Thirteen Problems—#16 (1932) (English)
> > The Tuesday Club Murders—#16 (1933) (U.S.)

The Tragedy of Marsdon Manor (Poirot, Hastings)
> *Published in* Poirot Investigates—#4 (1924)

Triangle at Rhodes (Poirot)
> *Published in* Murder in the Mews—#28 (1937) (English)
> > Dead Man's Mirror—#28 (1937) (U.S.)

The Tuesday Night Club (Miss Marple)
   Published in Thirteen Problems—#16 (1932) (English)
                  The Tuesday Club Murders—#16 (1933) (U.S.)
The Unbreakable Alibi (Tommy and Tuppence)
   Published in Partners in Crime—#11 (1929)
The Under Dog (Poirot)
   Published in The Under Dog—#54 (1951) (U.S.)
                  The Adventure of the Christmas Pudding—#65
                  (1960) (English)
The Veiled Lady (Poirot, Inspector Japp, Hastings)
   Published in Poirot Investigates—#4 (1924) (U.S. ed. only)
                  Poirot's Early Cases—#81 (1974) (English)
                  Hercule Poirot's Early Cases—#81 (1974) (U.S.)
A Village Murder (Alternate title for The Tape-Measure Murder)
The Voice in the Dark (Harley Quin)
   Published in The Mysterious Mr. Quin—#12 (1930)
Wasps' Nest (Poirot)
   Published in Double Sin—#66 (1961) (U.S.)
                  Poirot's Early Cases—#81 (1974) (English)
                  Hercule Poirot's Early Cases—#81 (1974) (U.S.)
Where There's a Will (Alternate title for Wireless)
   Published in Witness for the Prosecution—#49 (1948) (U.S.)
Wireless (Alternate title for Where There's a Will)
   Published in The Hound of Death—#18 (1933) (English)
Witness for the Prosecution
   Published in The Hound of Death—#18 (1933) (English)
                  Witness for the Prosecution—#49 (1948) (U.S.)
The World's End (Harley Quin)
   Published in The Mysterious Mr. Quin—#12 (1930)
Yellow Iris (Poirot)
   Published in The Regatta Mystery—#34 (1939) (U.S.)

HERCULE POIROT BOOK TITLES

THE ABC MURDERS—#25 (1936)

THE ADVENTURE OF THE CHRISTMAS PUDDING AND OTHER STORIES—#65 (1960—Some Poirot Short Stories)

AFTER THE FUNERAL—#57 (1953) (U.S.: FUNERALS ARE FATAL)

AN OVERDOSE OF DEATH—#37 (1940) (English: ONE, TWO, BUCKLE MY SHOE) (Also U.S.: THE PATRIOTIC MURDERS)

APPOINTMENT WITH DEATH—#31 (1938)

THE BIG FOUR—#8 (1927)

CARDS ON THE TABLE—#27 (1936)

CAT AMONG THE PIGEONS—#64 (1959)

THE CLOCKS—#69 (1963)

CURTAIN—#82 (1975)

DEAD MAN'S FOLLY—#61 (1956)

DEAD MAN'S MIRROR—#28 (1937—Short Stories) (English: MURDER IN THE MEWS)

DEATH IN THE AIR—#24 (1935) (English: DEATH IN THE CLOUDS)

DEATH IN THE CLOUDS—#24 (1935) (U.S.: DEATH IN THE AIR)

DEATH ON THE NILE—#30 (1937)

DOUBLE SIN AND OTHER STORIES—#66 (1961—Some Poirot Short Stories)

DUMB WITNESS—#29 (1937) (U.S.: POIROT LOSES A CLIENT)

ELEPHANTS CAN REMEMBER—#79 (1972)

EVIL UNDER THE SUN—#38 (1941)

FIVE LITTLE PIGS—#41 (1943) (U.S.: MURDER IN RETROSPECT)

FUNERALS ARE FATAL—#57 (1953) (English: AFTER THE FUNERAL)

HALLOWE'EN PARTY—#75 (1969)

HERCULE POIROT'S CHRISTMAS—#32 (1938) (U.S.: MURDER FOR CHRISTMAS) (Also U.S.: A HOLIDAY FOR MURDER)

HERCULE POIROT'S EARLY CASES—#81 (1974—Short Stories) (English: POIROT'S EARLY CASES)

HICKORY DICKORY DEATH—#60 (1955) (English: HICKORY DICKORY DOCK)

HICKORY DICKORY DOCK—#60 (1955) (U.S.: HICKORY DICKORY DEATH)

A HOLIDAY FOR MURDER—#32 (1938) (English: HERCULE POIROT'S CHRISTMAS) (Also U.S.: MURDER FOR CHRISTMAS)

THE HOLLOW—#46 (1946) (U.S.: MURDER AFTER HOURS)

THE LABOURS OF HERCULES—#47 (1947—Short Stories)

LORD EDGWARE DIES—#17 (1933) (U.S.: THIRTEEN AT DINNER)

THE MOUSETRAP AND OTHER STORIES—#51 (1950—Some Poirot Short Stories) (Also U.S.: THREE BLIND MICE AND OTHER STORIES)

MRS. McGINTY'S DEAD—#55 (1952)

MURDER AFTER HOURS—#46 (1946) (English: THE HOLLOW)

MURDER FOR CHRISTMAS—#32 (1938) (English: HERCULE POIROT'S CHRISTMAS) (Also U.S.: A HOLIDAY FOR MURDER)

MURDER IN THE CALAIS COACH—#19 (1934) (English: MURDER ON THE ORIENT EXPRESS)

MURDER IN MESOPOTAMIA—#26 (1936)

MURDER IN THE MEWS—#28 (1937—Short Stories) (U.S.: DEAD MAN'S MIRROR)

MURDER IN RETROSPECT—#41 (1943) (English: FIVE LITTLE PIGS)

MURDER IN THREE ACTS—#23 (1935) (English: THREE ACT TRAGEDY)

THE MURDER OF ROGER ACKROYD—#7 (1926)

MURDER ON THE LINKS—#3 (1923)

MURDER ON THE ORIENT EXPRESS—#19 (1934) (U.S.: MURDER IN THE CALAIS COACH)

THE MYSTERIOUS AFFAIR AT STYLES—#1 (1920)

THE MYSTERY OF THE BLUE TRAIN—#9 (1928)

ONE, TWO, BUCKLE MY SHOE—#37 (1940) (U.S.: THE PATRIOTIC MURDERS) (Also U.S.: AN OVERDOSE OF DEATH)

THE PATRIOTIC MURDERS—#37 (1940) (English: ONE, TWO, BUCKLE MY SHOE) (Also U.S.: AN OVERDOSE OF DEATH)

PERIL AT END HOUSE—#15 (1932)

POIROT INVESTIGATES—#4 (1924—Short Stories)

POIROT LOSES A CLIENT—#29 (1937) (English: DUMB WITNESS)

POIROT'S EARLY CASES—#81 (1974—Short Stories) (U.S.: HERCULE POIROT'S EARLY CASES)

THE REGATTA MYSTERY AND OTHER STORIES—#34 (1939—Some Poirot Short Stories)

SAD CYPRESS—#36 (1940)

TAKEN AT THE FLOOD—#48 (1948) (U.S.: THERE IS A TIDE)

THERE IS A TIDE—#48 (1948) (English: TAKEN AT THE FLOOD)

THIRD GIRL—#72 (1966)

THIRTEEN AT DINNER—#17 (1933) (English: LORD EDGWARE DIES)

THREE ACT TRAGEDY—#23 (1935) (U.S.: MURDER IN THREE ACTS)

THREE BLIND MICE AND OTHER STORIES—#51 (1950—Some Poirot Short Stories) (Also U.S.: THE MOUSETRAP AND OTHER STORIES)

THE UNDER DOG AND OTHER STORIES—#54 (1951—Some Poirot Short Stories)

WITNESS FOR THE PROSECUTION AND OTHER STORIES—#49 (1948—Some Poirot Short Stories)

HERCULE POIROT SHORT STORY TITLES

The Adventure of Johnnie Waverly
    Published in Three Blind Mice—#51 (1950) (U.S.)
                The Mousetrap—#51 (1952) (PB) (U.S.)
                Poirot's Early Cases—#81 (1974) (English)
                Hercule Poirot's Early Cases—#81 (1974) (U.S.)
The Adventure of the Cheap Flat
    Published in Poirot Investigates—#4 (1924)
The Adventure of the Christmas Pudding
    Published in The Adventure of the Christmas Pudding—#65
                (1960) (English)
The Adventure of the Clapham Cook
    Published in The Under Dog—#54 (1951) (U.S.)
                Poirot's Early Cases—#81 (1974) (English)
                Hercule Poirot's Early Cases—#81 (1974) (U.S.)
The Adventure of the Egyptian Tomb
    Published in Poirot Investigates—#4 (1924)
The Adventure of the Italian Nobleman
    Published in Poirot Investigates—#4 (1924)
The Adventure of "The Western Star"
    Published in Poirot Investigates—#4 (1924)
The Affair at the Victory Ball
    Published in The Under Dog—#54 (1951) (U.S.)
                Poirot's Early Cases—#81 (1974) (English)
                Hercule Poirot's Early Cases—#81 (1974) (U.S.)
The Apples of the Hesperides
    Published in The Labours of Hercules—#47 (1947)
The Arcadian Deer
    Published in The Labours of Hercules—#47 (1947)
The Augean Stables
    Published in The Labours of Hercules—#47 (1947)
The Capture of Cerberus
    Published in The Labours of Hercules—#47 (1947)

The Case of the Missing Will
       Published in Poirot Investigates—#4 (1924)
The Chocolate Box
       Published in Poirot Investigates—#4 (1925) (U.S. edition only)
                     Poirot's Early Cases—#81 (1974) (English)
                     Hercule Poirot's Early Cases—#81 (1974) (U.S.)
The Cornish Mystery
       Published in The Under Dog—#54 (1951) (U.S.)
                     Poirot's Early Cases—#81 (1974) (English)
                     Hercule Poirot's Early Cases—#81 (1974) (U.S.)
The Cretan Bull
       Published in The Labours of Hercules—#47 (1947)
Dead Man's Mirror (Expanded version of The Second Gong)
       Published in Murder in the Mews—#28 (1937) (English)
                     Dead Man's Mirror—#28 (1937) (U.S.)
The Disappearance of Mr. Davenheim
       Published in Poirot Investigates—#4 (1924)
The Double Clue
       Published in Double Sin—#66 (1961) (U.S.)
                     Poirot's Early Cases—#81 (1974) (English)
                     Hercule Poirot's Early Cases—#81 (1974) (U.S.)
Double Sin
       Published in Double Sin—#66 (1961) (U.S.)
                     Poirot's Early Cases—#81 (1974) (English)
                     Hercule Poirot's Early Cases—#81 (1974) (U.S.)
The Dream
       Published in The Regatta Mystery—#34 (1939) (U.S.)
                     The Adventure of the Christmas Pudding—#65
                     (1960) (English)
The Erymanthian Boar
       Published in The Labours of Hercules—#47 (1947)
The Flock of Geryon
       Published in The Labours of Hercules—#47 (1947)
Four and Twenty Blackbirds
       Published in Three Blind Mice—#51 (1950) (U.S.)
                     The Mousetrap—#51 (1952) (PB) (U.S.)
                     The Adventure of the Christmas Pudding—#65
                     (1960) (English)

The Girdle of Hyppolita
  Published in The Labours of Hercules—#47 (1947)
The Horses of Diomedes
  Published in The Labours of Hercules—#47 (1947)
How Does Your Garden Grow?
  Published in The Regatta Mystery—#34 (1939) (U.S.)
              Poirot's Early Cases—#81 (1974) (English)
              Hercule Poirot's Early Cases—#81 (1974) (U.S.)
The Incredible Theft (Expanded version of The Submarine Plans)
  Published in Murder in the Mews—#28 (1937) (English)
              Dead Man's Mirror—#28 (1937) (U.S.)
The Jewel Robbery at the Grand Metropolitan
  Published in Poirot Investigates—#4 (1924)
The Kidnapped Prime Minister
  Published in Poirot Investigates—#4 (1924)
The Kidnapping of Johnnie Waverly (Alternate title for The Adventure of Johnnie Waverly)
The King of Clubs
  Published in The Under Dog—#54 (1951) (U.S.)
              Poirot's Early Cases—#81 (1974) (English)
              Hercule Poirot's Early Cases—#81 (1974) (U.S.)
The Lemesurier Inheritance
  Published in The Under Dog—#54 (1951) (U.S.)
              Poirot's Early Cases—#81 (1974) (English)
              Hercule Poirot's Early Cases—#81 (1974) (U.S.)
The Lernean Hydra
  Published in The Labours of Hercules—#47 (1947)
The Lost Mine
  Published in Poirot Investigates—#4 (1925) (U.S. edition only)
              Poirot's Early Cases—#81 (1974) (English)
              Hercule Poirot's Early Cases—#81 (1974) (U.S.)
The Market Basing Mystery
  Published in The Under Dog—#54 (1951) (U.S.)
              Poirot's Early Cases—#81 (1974) (English)
              Hercule Poirot's Early Cases—#81 (1974) (U.S.)
The Million Dollar Bond Robbery
  Published in Poirot Investigates—#4 (1924)

Murder in the Mews
> *Published in* Murder in the Mews—#28 (1937) (English)
> > Dead Man's Mirror—#28 (1937) (U.S.)

The Mystery of Hunter's Lodge
> *Published in* Poirot Investigates—#4 (1924)

The Mystery of the Baghdad Chest (See also expanded version with title The Mystery of the Spanish Chest)
> *Published in* The Regatta Mystery—#34 (1939) (U.S.)

The Mystery of the Crime in Cabin 66
> *Published in* Poirot Knows the Murderer (London and New York: Polybooks, 1946, 62 pp.) (This story does not appear in any of the standard Christie collections)

The Mystery of the Spanish Chest (Expanded version of The Mystery of the Baghdad Chest)
> *Published in* The Adventure of the Christmas Pudding—#65 (1960) (English)

The Nemean Lion
> *Published in* The Labours of Hercules—#47 (1947)

The Plymouth Express
> *Published in* The Under Dog—#54 (1951) (U.S.)
> > Poirot's Early Cases—#81 (1974) (English)
> > Hercule Poirot's Early Cases—#81 (1974) (U.S.)

Problem at Sea
> *Published in* The Regatta Mystery—#34 (1939) (U.S.)
> > Poirot's Early Cases—#81 (1974) (English)
> > Hercule Poirot's Early Cases—#81 (1974) (U.S.)

The Stymphalean Birds
> *Published in* The Labours of Hercules—#47 (1947)

The Submarine Plans (See expanded version with title The Incredible Theft)
> *Published in* The Under Dog—#54 (1951) (U.S.)
> > Poirot's Early Cases—#81 (1974) (English)
> > Hercule Poirot's Early Cases—#81 (1974) (U.S.)

The Theft of the Royal Ruby (Slightly different version of The Adventure of the Christmas Pudding)
> *Published in* Double Sin—#66 (1961) (U.S.)

The Third Floor Flat

  Published in Three Blind Mice—#51 (1950) (U.S.)

       The Mousetrap—#51 (1952) (PB) (U.S.)

       Poirot's Early Cases—#81 (1974) (English)

       Hercule Poirot's Early Cases—#81 (1974) (U.S.)

The Tragedy of Marsdon Manor

  Published in Poirot Investigates—#4 (1924)

Triangle at Rhodes

  Published in Murder in the Mews—#28 (1937) (English)

       Dead Man's Mirror—#28 (1937) (U.S.)

The Under Dog

  Published in The Under Dog—#54 (1951) (U.S.)

       The Adventure of the Christmas Pudding—#65 (1960) (English)

The Veiled Lady

  Published in Poirot Investigates—#4 (1925) (U.S. edition only)

       Poirot's Early Cases—#81 (1974) (English)

       Hercule Poirot's Early Cases—#81 (1974) (U.S.)

Wasps' Nest

  Published in Double Sin—#66 (1961) (U.S.)

       Poirot's Early Cases—#81 (1974) (English)

       Hercule Poirot's Early Cases—#81 (1974) (U.S.)

Yellow Iris

  Published in The Regatta Mystery—#34 (1939) (U.S.)

Miss Jane Marple Book Titles

THE ADVENTURE OF THE CHRISTMAS PUDDING AND OTHER STORIES—#65 (1960—Some Miss Marple Short Stories)

AT BERTRAM'S HOTEL—#71 (1965)

THE BODY IN THE LIBRARY—#40 (1942)

A CARIBBEAN MYSTERY—#70 (1964)

DOUBLE SIN AND OTHER STORIES—#66 (1961—Some Miss Marple Short Stories)

4.50 FROM PADDINGTON—#62 (1957) (U.S.: WHAT MRS. McGILLICUDDY SAW!)

THE MIRROR CRACK'D—#68 (1962) (English: THE MIRROR CRACK'D FROM SIDE TO SIDE)

THE MIRROR CRACK'D FROM SIDE TO SIDE—#68 (1962) (U.S.: THE MIRROR CRACK'D)

MISS MARPLE'S FINAL CASES AND TWO OTHER STORIES—#84 (1979—Some Miss Marple Short Stories)

THE MOUSETRAP AND OTHER STORIES—#51 (1950—Some Miss Marple Short Stories) (Also U.S.: THREE BLIND MICE AND OTHER STORIES)

THE MOVING FINGER—#42 (1943)

THE MURDER AT THE VICARAGE—#13 (1930)

A MURDER IS ANNOUNCED—#52 (1950)

MURDER WITH MIRRORS—#56 (1952) (English: THEY DO IT WITH MIRRORS)

NEMESIS—#78 (1971)

A POCKET FULL OF RYE—#58 (1953)

THE REGATTA MYSTERY AND OTHER STORIES—#34 (1939—Some Miss Marple Short Stories)

SLEEPING MURDER—#83 (1976)

THEY DO IT WITH MIRRORS—#56 (1952) (U.S.: MURDER WITH MIRRORS)

THE THIRTEEN PROBLEMS—#16 (1932—Short Stories) (U.S.: THE TUESDAY CLUB MURDERS)

THREE BLIND MICE AND OTHER STORIES—#51 (1950—
 Some Miss Marple Short Stories) (Also U.S.: THE MOUSE-
 TRAP AND OTHER STORIES)
THE TUESDAY CLUB MURDERS—#16 (1932—Short Stories)
 (English: THE THIRTEEN PROBLEMS)
WHAT MRS. McGILLICUDDY SAW!—#62 (1957) (English:
 4.50 FROM PADDINGTON)

MISS JANE MARPLE SHORT STORY TITLES

The Affair at the Bungalow
    Published in The Thirteen Problems—#16 (1932) (English)
        The Tuesday Club Murders—#16 (1933) (U.S.)

The Bloodstained Pavement
    Published in The Thirteen Problems—#16 (1932) (English)
        The Tuesday Club Murders—#16 (1933) (U.S.)

The Blue Geranium
    Published in The Thirteen Problems—#16 (1932) (English)
        The Tuesday Club Murders—#16 (1933) (U.S.)

The Case of the Caretaker
    Published in Three Blind Mice—#51 (1950) (U.S.)
        The Mousetrap—#51 (1952) (PB) (U.S.)
        Miss Marple's Final Cases—#84 (1979) (English)

The Case of the Perfect Maid
    Published in Three Blind Mice—#51 (1950) (U.S.)
        The Mousetrap—#51 (1952) (PB) (U.S.)
        Miss Marple's Final Cases—#84 (1979) (English)

The Case of the Retired Jeweller (Alternate title for The Tape-Measure Murder)

A Christmas Tragedy
    Published in The Thirteen Problems—#16 (1932) (English)
        The Tuesday Club Murders—#16 (1933) (U.S.)

The Companion
    Published in The Thirteen Problems—#16 (1932) (English)
        The Tuesday Club Murders—#16 (1933) (U.S.)

Death by Drowning
    Published in The Thirteen Problems—#16 (1932) (English)
        The Tuesday Club Murders—#16 (1933) (U.S.)

The Four Suspects
    Published in The Thirteen Problems—#16 (1932) (English)
        The Tuesday Club Murders—#16 (1933) (U.S.)

Greenshaw's Folly
>*Published in* The Adventure of the Christmas Pudding—#65
>>(1960) (English)
>>Double Sin—#66 (1961) (U.S.)

The Herb of Death
>*Published in* The Thirteen Problems—#16 (1932) (English)
>>The Tuesday Club Murders—#16 (1933) (U.S.)

The Idol House of Astarte
>*Published in* The Thirteen Problems—#16 (1932) (English)
>>The Tuesday Club Murders—#16 (1933) (U.S.)

Ingots of Gold
>*Published in* The Thirteen Problems—#16 (1932) (English)
>>The Tuesday Club Murders—#16 (1933) (U.S.)

Miss Marple Tells a Story
>*Published in* The Regatta Mystery—#34 (1939) (U.S.)
>>Miss Marple's Final Cases—#84 (1979) (English)

Motive vs. Opportunity
>*Published in* The Thirteen Problems—#16 (1932) (English)
>>The Tuesday Club Murders—#16 (1933) (U.S.)

The Perfect Maid (Alternate title for The Case of the Perfect Maid)
Sanctuary
>*Published in* Double Sin—#66 (1961) (U.S.)
>>Miss Marple's Final Cases—#84 (1979) (English)

Strange Jest
>*Published in* Three Blind Mice—#51 (1950) (U.S.)
>>The Mousetrap—#51 (1952) (PB) (U.S.)
>>Miss Marple's Final Cases—#84 (1979) (English)

The Tape-Measure Murder
>*Published in* Three Blind Mice—#51 (1950) (U.S.)
>>The Mousetrap—#51 (1952) (PB) (U.S.)
>>Miss Marple's Final Cases—#84 (1979) (English)

The Thumb Mark of Saint Peter
>*Published in* The Thirteen Problems—#16 (1932) (English)
>>The Tuesday Club Murders—#16 (1933) (U.S.)

The Tuesday Night Club
>*Published in* The Thirteen Problems—#16 (1932) (English)
>>The Tuesday Club Murders—#16 (1933) (U.S.)

TOMMY AND TUPPENCE BERESFORD
BOOK TITLES

BY THE PRICKING OF MY THUMBS—#74 (1968)
N OR M?—#39 (1941)
PARTNERS IN CRIME—#11 (1929—Short Stories)
POSTERN OF FATE—#80 (1973)
THE SECRET ADVERSARY—#2 (1922)

TOMMY AND TUPPENCE BERESFORD SHORT STORY TITLES

The short stories of Tommy and Tuppence Beresford listed below were all published in *Partners in Crime*—#11 (1929)

The Adventure of the Sinister Stranger
The Affair of the Pink Pearl
The Ambassador's Boot
Blindman's Buff
The Case of the Missing Lady
The Clergyman's Daughter
The Crackler
A Fairy in the Flat
Finessing the King
The Gentleman Dressed in Newspaper
The House of Lurking Death
The Man in the Mist
The Man Who Was No. 16
A Pot of Tea
The Red House
The Sunningdale Mystery
The Unbreakable Alibi

Mrs. Ariadne Oliver Book Titles

CARDS ON THE TABLE—#27 (1936)
DEAD MAN'S FOLLY—#61 (1956)
ELEPHANTS CAN REMEMBER—#79 (1972)
HALLOWE'EN PARTY—#75 (1969)
MR. PARKER PYNE, DETECTIVE—#22 (1934—Some Mrs. Oliver Short Stories) (English: PARKER PYNE INVESTIGATES)
MRS. McGINTY'S DEAD—#55 (1952)
THE PALE HORSE—#67 (1961)
PARKER PYNE INVESTIGATES—#22 (1934—Some Mrs. Oliver Short Stories) (U.S.: MR. PARKER PYNE, DETECTIVE)
THIRD GIRL—#72 (1966)

Mrs. Ariadne Oliver Short Story Titles

The Case of the Discontented Soldier
The Case of the Rich Woman
    Both published in Parker Pyne Investigates—#22 (1934)
        (English)
           Mr. Parker Pyne, Detective—#22 (1934)
           (U.S.)

Captain Arthur Hastings Book Titles

THE ABC MURDERS—#25 (1936)

THE BIG FOUR—#8 (1927)

CURTAIN—#82 (1975)

DUMB WITNESS—#29 (1937) (U.S.: POIROT LOSES A CLIENT)

LORD EDGWARE DIES—#17 (1933) (U.S.: THIRTEEN AT DINNER)

MURDER ON THE LINKS—#3 (1923)

THE MYSTERIOUS AFFAIR AT STYLES—#1 (1920)

PERIL AT END HOUSE—#15 (1932)

POIROT INVESTIGATES—#4 (1924)

POIROT LOSES A CLIENT—#29 (1937) (English: DUMB WITNESS)

THIRTEEN AT DINNER—#17 (1933) (English: LORD EDGWARE DIES)

Captain Arthur Hastings Short Story Titles

The Adventure of Johnnie Waverly
Published in Three Blind Mice—#51 (1950) (U.S.)
The Mousetrap—#51 (1952) (PB) (U.S.)
Poirot's Early Cases—#81 (1974) (English)
Hercule Poirot's Early Cases—#81 (1974) (U.S.)

The Adventure of the Cheap Flat
Published in Poirot Investigates—#4 (1924)

The Adventure of the Clapham Cook
Published in The Under Dog—#54 (1951) (U.S.)
Poirot's Early Cases—#81 (1974) (English)
Hercule Poirot's Early Cases—#81 (1974) (U.S.)

The Adventure of the Egyptian Tomb
Published in Poirot Investigates—#4 (1924)

The Adventure of the Italian Nobleman
Published in Poirot Investigates—#4 (1924)

The Adventure of "The Western Star"
Published in Poirot Investigates—#4 (1924)

The Affair at the Victory Ball
Published in The Under Dog—#54 (1951) (U.S.)
Poirot's Early Cases—#81 (1974) (English)
Hercule Poirot's Early Cases—#81 (1974) (U.S.)

The Case of the Missing Will
Published in Poirot Investigates—#4 (1924)

The Chocolate Box
Published in Poirot Investigates—#4 (1925) (U.S. edition only)
Poirot's Early Cases—#81 (1974) (English)
Hercule Poirot's Early Cases—#81 (1974) (U.S.)

The Cornish Mystery
Published in The Under Dog—#54 (1951) (U.S.)
Poirot's Early Cases—#81 (1974) (English)
Hercule Poirot's Early Cases—#81 (1974) (U.S.)

The Disappearance of Mr. Davenheim
Published in Poirot Investigates—#4 (1924)

The Double Clue
    Published in Double Sin—#66 (1961) (U.S.)
                Poirot's Early Cases—#81 (1974) (English)
                Hercule Poirot's Early Cases—#81 (1974) (U.S.)
Double Sin
    Published in Double Sin—#66 (1961) (U.S.)
                Poirot's Early Cases—#81 (1974) (English)
                Hercule Poirot's Early Cases—#81 (1974) (U.S.)
The Jewel Robbery at the Grand Metropolitan
    Published in Poirot Investigates—#4 (1924)
The Kidnapped Prime Minister
    Published in Poirot Investigates—#4 (1924)
The King of Clubs
    Published in The Under Dog—#54 (1951) (U.S.)
                Poirot's Early Cases—#81 (1974) (English)
                Hercule Poirot's Early Cases—#81 (1974) (U.S.)
The Lemesurier Inheritance
    Published in The Under Dog—#54 (1951) (U.S.)
                Poirot's Early Cases—#81 (1974) (English)
                Hercule Poirot's Early Cases—#81 (1974) (U.S.)
The Lost Mine
    Published in Poirot Investigates—#4 (1925) (U.S. edition only)
                Poirot's Early Cases—#81 (1974) (English)
                Hercule Poirot's Early Cases—#81 (1974) (U.S.)
The Market Basing Mystery
    Published in The Under Dog—#54 (1951) (U.S.)
                Poirot's Early Cases—#81 (1974) (English)
                Hercule Poirot's Early Cases—#81 (1974) (U.S.)
The Million Dollar Bond Robbery
    Published in Poirot Investigates—#4 (1924)
The Mystery of Hunter's Lodge
    Published in Poirot Investigates—#4 (1924)
The Mystery of the Baghdad Chest
    Published in The Regatta Mystery—#34 (1939) (U.S.)
The Plymouth Express
    Published in The Under Dog—#54 (1951) (U.S.)
                Poirot's Early Cases—#81 (1974) (English)
                Hercule Poirot's Early Cases—#81 (1974) (U.S.)

The Submarine Plans
>*Published in* The Under Dog—#54 (1951) (U.S.)
>>Poirot's Early Cases—#81 (1974) (English)
>>Hercule Poirot's Early Cases—#81 (1974) (U.S.)

The Tragedy of Marsdon Manor
>*Published in* Poirot Investigates—#4 (1924)

The Veiled Lady
>*Published in* Poirot Investigates—#4 (1924)
>>Poirot's Early Cases—#81 (1974) (English)
>>Hercule Poirot's Early Cases—#81 (1974) (U.S.)

CHIEF INSPECTOR JAMES JAPP BOOK TITLES

THE ABC MURDERS—#25 (1936)

AN OVERDOSE OF DEATH—#37 (1940) (English: ONE, TWO, BUCKLE MY SHOE) (Also U.S.: THE PATRIOTIC MURDERS)

THE BIG FOUR—#8 (1927)

DEAD MAN'S MIRROR—#28 (1937—Some Inspector Japp Short Stories) (English: MURDER IN THE MEWS)

DEATH IN THE AIR—#24 (1935) (English: DEATH IN THE CLOUDS)

DEATH IN THE CLOUDS—#24 (1935) (U.S.: DEATH IN THE AIR)

THE LABOURS OF HERCULES—#47 (1947—Some Inspector Japp Short Stories)

LORD EDGWARE DIES—#17 (1933) (U.S.: THIRTEEN AT DINNER)

MURDER IN THE MEWS—#28 (1937—Some Inspector Japp Short Stories) (U.S.: DEAD MAN'S MIRROR)

THE MYSTERIOUS AFFAIR AT STYLES—#1 (1920)

ONE, TWO, BUCKLE MY SHOE—#37 (1940) (U.S.: THE PATRIOTIC MURDERS) (Also U.S.: AN OVERDOSE OF DEATH)

THE PATRIOTIC MURDERS—#37 (1940) (English: ONE, TWO, BUCKLE MY SHOE) (Also U.S.: AN OVERDOSE OF DEATH)

PERIL AT END HOUSE—#15 (1932)

POIROT INVESTIGATES—#4 (1924—Some Inspector Japp Short Stories)

THIRTEEN AT DINNER—#17 (1933) (English: LORD EDGWARE DIES)

THE UNDER DOG AND OTHER STORIES—#54 (1951—Some Inspector Japp Short Stories)

Chief Inspector James Japp
Short Story Titles

The Adventure of the Cheap Flat
  Published in Poirot Investigates—#4 (1924)
The Affair at the Victory Ball
  Published in The Under Dog—#54 (1951) (U.S.)
        Poirot's Early Cases—#81 (1974) (English)
        Hercule Poirot's Early Cases—#81 (1974) (U.S.)
The Capture of Cerberus
  Published in The Labours of Hercules—#47 (1947)
The Disappearance of Mr. Davenheim
  Published in Poirot Investigates—#4 (1924)
The Flock of Geryon
  Published in The Labours of Hercules—#47 (1947)
The Girdle of Hyppolita
  Published in The Labours of Hercules—#47 (1947)
The Kidnapped Prime Minister
  Published in Poirot Investigates—#4 (1924)
The Market Basing Mystery
  Published in The Under Dog—#54 (1951) (U.S.)
        Poirot's Early Cases—#81 (1974) (English)
        Hercule Poirot's Early Cases—#81 (1974) (U.S.)
Murder in the Mews
  Published in Murder in the Mews—#28 (1937) (English)
        Dead Man's Mirror—#28 (1937) (U.S.)
The Mystery of Hunter's Lodge
  Published in Poirot Investigates—#4 (1924)
The Plymouth Express
  Published in The Under Dog—#54 (1951) (U.S.)
        Poirot's Early Cases—#81 (1974) (English)
        Hercule Poirot's Early Cases—#81 (1974) (U.S.)
The Veiled Lady
  Published in Poirot Investigates—#4 (1924)
        Poirot's Early Cases—#81 (1974) (English)
        Hercule Poirot's Early Cases—#81 (1974) (U.S.)

Superintendent Battle Book Titles

CARDS ON THE TABLE—#27 (1936)
EASY TO KILL—#33 (1939) (English: MURDER IS EASY)
MURDER IS EASY—#33 (1939) (U.S.: EASY TO KILL)
THE SECRET OF CHIMNEYS—#6 (1925)
THE SEVEN DIALS MYSTERY—#10 (1929)
TOWARDS ZERO—#43 (1944)

Colonel Johnny Race Book Titles

CARDS ON THE TABLE—#27 (1936)
DEATH ON THE NILE—#30 (1937)
THE MAN IN THE BROWN SUIT—#5 (1924)
REMEMBERED DEATH—#45 (1945) (English: SPARKLING
    CYANIDE)
SPARKLING CYANIDE—#45 (1945) (U.S.: REMEMBERED
    DEATH)

Mr. Parker Pyne Short Story Titles

The short stories of Mr. Parker Pyne listed below were all published in *Parker Pyne Investigates*—#22 (1934) (English) and *Mr. Parker Pyne, Detective*—#22 (1934) (U.S.).

The Case of the City Clerk

The Case of the Discontented Husband

The Case of the Discontented Soldier

The Case of the Distressed Lady

The Case of the Middle-Aged Wife

The Case of the Rich Woman

Death on the Nile

The Gate of Baghdad

Have You Got Everything You Want?

The House at Shiraz

The Oracle at Delphi

The Pearl of Price

MR. HARLEY QUIN SHORT STORY TITLES

The short stories of Mr. Harley Quin listed below were all published in *The Mysterious Mr. Quin*—#12 (1930), except for "The Love Detectives," published in *Three Blind Mice*—#51 (1950) (U.S.), and *The Mousetrap*—#51 (1952) (U.S.) (PB).

At the Bells and Motley
The Bird with the Broken Wing
The Coming of Mr. Quin
The Dead Harlequin
The Face of Helen
Harlequin's Lane
The Love Detectives
The Man from the Sea
The Shadow on the Glass
The Sign in the Sky
The Soul of the Croupier
The Voice in the Dark
The World's End

Select Bibliography of Books about Agatha Christie, Her Life and Works

The publishing information listed for these books is for the American editions only.

Barnard, Robert. *A Talent to Deceive—An Appreciation of Agatha Christie.* New York: Dodd, Mead & Co., 1980.

East, Andy. *The Agatha Christie Quizbook.* New York: Drake Publishers, Inc., 1975.

Feinman, Jeffrey. *The Mysterious World of Agatha Christie.* New York: Grosset & Dunlap, 1975.

Keating, H.R.F., ed. *Agatha Christie, First Lady of Crime.* New York: Holt, Rinehart & Winston, 1977.

Mallowan, Max. *Mallowan's Memoirs.* New York: Dodd, Mead & Co., 1977.

Ramsey, G. C. *Agatha Christie, Mistress of Mystery.* New York: Dodd, Mead & Co., 1967.

Riley, Dick, and McAllister, Pam, eds. *The Bedside, Bathtub & Armchair Companion to Agatha Christie.* New York: Frederick Ungar Publishing Co., 1979.

Robyns, Gwen. *The Mystery of Agatha Christie.* Doubleday & Company, Inc., 1978.

Toye, Randall. *The Agatha Christie Who's Who.* New York: Holt, Rinehart & Winston, 1980.

—— and Gaffney, Judith Hawkins. *The Agatha Christie Crossword Puzzle Book.* New York: Holt, Rinehart & Winston, 1981.

Tynan, Kathleen. *Agatha.* New York: Random House, 1978 (Hardcover). New York: Ballantine Books, 1979 (Paperback). (A fictional account of the disappearance in 1926.)

Wynne, Nancy Blue. *An Agatha Christie Chronology.* New York: Ace Books, 1976.

Select Chronology of Agatha Christie's Life and Works

1890 Born on September 15

1901 Death of her father, Frederick Alvah Miller

1904 Max Mallowan born May 6

1906 Attends finishing school in Paris

1913 Meets Archibald Christie

1914 Marries first husband, Archie, on December 24

1919 Rosalind, Christie's only child, born

1920 *The Mysterious Affair at Styles,* Christie's first book, the first appearance of Hercule Poirot

1922 *The Secret Adversary,* Christie's first thriller novel, and the first appearance of Tommy and Tuppence Beresford

1924 Christie signs book contract with Collins

1926 Death of her mother, Clara
Christie disappears for ten days in December
Murder of Roger Ackroyd, first book published with Collins and Christie's first major success

1928 *Die Abenteuer G.m.b.H.* (Adventure Inc.) (A German-made silent film), the first adaptation of a Christie book for the screen, based on *The Secret Adversary*
The Passing of Mr. Quinn, the first British-made film based on a Christie work
Alibi, the first work to reach the stage, adapted by Michael Morton from the novel *The Murder of Roger Ackroyd*
Divorce from Archie Christie granted in April
Christie visits the Middle East for the first time

1930 Miss Jane Marple appears for the first time in a novel, *Murder at the Vicarage*
Giant's Bread, first romantic novel, published under the name Mary Westmacott
Black Coffee, Christie's first original play, opens in London
Christie meets Max Mallowan at Ur in the Middle East
Christie and Max are married in Scotland, September 11

1931   *Alibi,* the first sound film of a Christie work
1933   Christie accompanies Max to Arpachiyah, where he conducts his first dig
1934   *Murder on the Orient Express* published, one of Christie's and Poirot's most popular and successful books
1935   *The ABC Murders* published
        Cards on the Table published, introduction, in a novel, of Christie's lightly sketched portrayal of herself, Mrs. Ariadne Oliver
1937   *Death on the Nile* published, the best of the Christie foreign background books
1939   Christie buys Greenway House in Devon
        Ten Little Niggers published, one of Christie's most brilliant deceptions
1942   *The Body in the Library* published
1943   *Five Little Pigs* published, Christie's first use of the "murder in retrospect" theme
        Mathew Prichard, Christie's grandson, born
1944   *Towards Zero* published
1945   *Ten Little Niggers* (*And Then There Were None* in U.S.) film version released, based on her novel
1946   *Come, Tell Me How You Live* published under name of Agatha Christie Mallowan
1947   *The Labours of Hercules* published, one of the best Christie short story collections, features Poirot
        Christie writes a half-hour radio play, *Three Blind Mice,* for special broadcast in celebration of Queen Mary's birthday
1948   Max prepares for the most important dig in his career, at the historical site of Nimrud
1949   Christie accompanies Max to Nimrud where digging begins
        The excavations continue for ten years
1950   *A Murder Is Announced* published
        Christie begins writing her autobiography while at Nimrud
1952   *The Mousetrap* opens in London on November 25, destined to become the world's longest-running play
1953   The play *Witness for the Prosecution* opens in London, is an artistic as well as commercial success

1955 *Witness for the Prosecution* wins the New York Drama Critics' Circle Award for best foreign play of the 1954–55 New York season

1956 Christie honored as a Commander of the British Empire (CBE)

1957 *4.50 from Paddington* published
The film version of *Witness for the Prosecution* released, receives excellent reviews and is a box office success

1958 The film *Witness for the Prosecution* receives six Academy Award nominations, including best picture (receives none)

1960 Max honored as a Commander of the British Empire (CBE)

1962 Christie's first husband, Archie Christie, dies

1964 The film *Murder She Said,* based on *4.50 from Paddington,* released, the first of four Miss Marple films starring Dame Margaret Rutherford

1965 *At Bertram's Hotel* published
After fifteen years, Christie finishes the writing of her autobiography

1966 Max Mallowan's book *Nimrud and Its Remains* published

1968 Max is knighted for his work in archaeology

1971 Christie honored as a Dame of the British Empire (DBE)

1973 *Postern of Fate* published, the last book written by Christie

1974 The star-studded film *Murder on the Orient Express* released, a smashing success with critics, public, and Christie

1975 *Curtain* published, Poirot's final case

1976 Dame Agatha Christie dies, January 12

1976 *Sleeping Murder* published, Miss Marple's final case

1977 *An Autobiography* published

1978 Sir Max Mallowan dies, August 19

INDEX